Advanced Networking Technologies

Other related titles:

You may also like

- PBTE107 | Duong | Physical Layer Security For 6G Networks | 2024
- PBPC027 | Ranjan | Managing Internet of Things Applications Across Edge and Cloud Data Centres | 2024
- PBSE018 | Arslan | Physical Layer Security for Wireless Sensing and Communication | 2022
- PBPC033 | Taheri | Edge Computing: Models, technologies and applications| 2020

We also publish a wide range of books on the following topics:
Computing and Networks
Control, Robotics and Sensors
Electrical Regulations
Electromagnetics and Radar
Energy Engineering
Healthcare Technologies
History and Management of Technology
IET Codes and Guidance
Materials, Circuits and Devices
Model Forms
Nanomaterials and Nanotechnologies
Optics, Photonics and Lasers
Production, Design and Manufacturing
Security
Telecommunications
Transportation

All books are available in print via https://shop.theiet.org or as eBooks via our Digital Library https://digital-library.theiet.org.

IET COMPUTING 79

Advanced Networking Technologies

Edited by
Yue Cao, Hai Lin, Bo Zhao and Yuan Zhuang

Institution of Engineering and Technology

About the IET

This book is published by the Institution of Engineering and Technology (The IET).

We inspire, inform and influence the global engineering community to engineer a better world. As a diverse home across engineering and technology, we share knowledge that helps make better sense of the world, to accelerate innovation and solve the global challenges that matter.

The IET is a not-for-profit organisation. The surplus we make from our books is used to support activities and products for the engineering community and promote the positive role of science, engineering and technology in the world. This includes education resources and outreach, scholarships and awards, events and courses, publications, professional development and mentoring, and advocacy to governments.

To discover more about the IET please visit https://www.theiet.org/.

About IET books

The IET publishes books across many engineering and technology disciplines. Our authors and editors offer fresh perspectives from universities and industry. Within our subject areas, we have several book series steered by editorial boards made up of leading subject experts.

We peer review each book at the proposal stage to ensure the quality and relevance of our publications.

Get involved

If you are interested in becoming an author, editor, series advisor, or peer reviewer please visit https://www.theiet.org/publishing/publishing-with-iet-books/ or contact author_support@theiet.org.

Discovering our electronic content

All of our books are available online via the IET's Digital Library. Our Digital Library is the home of technical documents, eBooks, conference publications, real-life case studies and journal articles. To find out more, please visit https://digital-library.theiet.org.

In collaboration with the United Nations and the International Publishers Association, the IET is a Signatory member of the SDG Publishers Compact. The Compact aims to accelerate progress to achieve the Sustainable Development Goals (SDGs) by 2030. Signatories aspire to develop sustainable practices and act as champions of the SDGs during the Decade of Action (2020–2030), publishing books and journals that will help inform, develop, and inspire action in that direction.

In line with our sustainable goals, our UK printing partner has FSC accreditation, which is reducing our environmental impact to the planet. We use a print-on-demand model to further reduce our carbon footprint.

Published by The Institution of Engineering and Technology, London, United Kingdom

The Institution of Engineering and Technology (the "**Publisher**") is registered as a Charity in England & Wales (no. 211014) and Scotland (no. SC038698).

First published 2025

The Institution of Engineering and Technology
Futures Place
Kings Way, Stevenage,
Herts, SG1 2UA,
United Kingdom

www.theiet.org

British Library Cataloguing in Publication Data

A catalogue record for this product is available from the British Library

ISBN 978-1-83724-172-9 (hardback)
ISBN 978-1-83724-173-6 (PDF)

Typeset in India by MPS Limited

Cover image credit: lupengyu/Moment via Getty Images

Contents

About the editors xv

1 Terminologies, opportunities, and challenges **1**
Yue Cao, Hai Lin, Bo Zhao and Yuan Zhuang

1.1 Terminologies 1
1.2 Opportunities and challenges 10

2 Software-defined networking and network functions virtualization technologies **17**
Jie Huang, Yue Cao and Hai Lin

2.1 Development of the network 17
2.2 Overview of SDN 19
2.2.1 Motivation of SDN 19
2.2.2 Basic concepts and architecture of SDN 20
2.2.3 Introduction of OpenFlow 23
2.3 Overview of NFV 26
2.3.1 Concept of NFV 27
2.3.2 Advantage of NFV 28
2.3.3 NFV framework 29
2.3.4 Application of NFV 30
2.4 Security of SDN and NFV 33
2.4.1 Security of SDN 34
2.4.2 Security of NFV 38
2.5 Expansion of SDN and NFV 40
2.5.1 Introduction of SD-WAN 40
2.5.2 Advantage of SD-WAN 42
2.5.3 Introduction of IBN 42
2.5.4 Challenges of IBN 44
2.6 Conclusion 45
References 46

3 Transmission control protocol for message exchange **51**
Mansi Zhang, Yue Cao and Bo Zhao

3.1 Introduction of TCP 51
3.1.1 End-to-end communication 51

3.1.2 TCP/IP protocol stack 52
3.1.3 Transport layer 53
3.2 The structure of TCP segment 54
3.2.1 Source port and destination port fields 54
3.2.2 Sequence number and acknowledgment number fields 55
3.2.3 Data offset 55
3.2.4 Reserved field 55
3.2.5 Flag field 55
3.2.6 Window size field 56
3.2.7 Checksum field 56
3.2.8 Urgent pointer field 56
3.2.9 Options field 56
3.3 TCP functionality and implementation principles 57
3.3.1 Connection management 58
3.3.2 Reliable transmission 59
3.3.3 Flow control 60
3.3.4 Congestion control 61
3.4 TCP security problems 64
3.4.1 SYN flood attack 64
3.4.2 SYN flood attack defense 65
3.4.3 ACK flood attack 67
3.4.4 ACK flood attack defense 67
3.4.5 ISN prediction attack 69
3.4.6 ISN prediction attack defense 70
3.5 Conclusion 70
References 71

4 Dynamic routing and access control lists **75**
Zhijie Fan, Yue Cao and Hai Lin

4.1 Introduction 75
4.2 Routing algorithm 77
4.2.1 Link state routing algorithm 78
4.2.2 Distance vector routing algorithm 79
4.2.3 Hierarchical routing 81
4.3 Routing in the Internet 82
4.3.1 Routing within the autonomous system: Routing Information Protocol (RIP) 82
4.3.2 Routing within the autonomous system: OSPF 84
4.3.3 Routing between autonomous systems: BGP 87
4.4 Routing in ad hoc network 88
4.4.1 Proactive routing 89
4.4.2 Reactive routing 90
4.4.3 Hybrid routing 91
4.4.4 Geographic routing 92
4.4.5 Artificial Intelligence (AI)-based routing protocols 94

4.4.6 Secured ad hoc routing protocols 96
4.4.7 Blockchain-based routing protocols 100
4.5 Access Control Lists (ACLs) 101
4.5.1 Overview 101
4.5.2 Usage 102
4.5.3 Operating principle 103
4.5.4 Applications 104
4.6 Conclusion 104
References 104

5 Deterministic networks for real-time applications 109
Sifan Li, Yue Cao and Yuan Zhuang

5.1 The introduction of network basics 109
5.1.1 Basic concept of network 109
5.1.2 Classification of network topology 110
5.1.3 Common network protocols and communication modes 111
5.2 The introduction of deterministic network 112
5.2.1 Definition and characteristics of deterministic networks 112
5.2.2 Evolution and applications of deterministic networks 112
5.3 Equipment of deterministic network 115
5.3.1 Time synchronization hardware 115
5.3.2 Design of hard real-time system 116
5.4 The technology of flow management 120
5.4.1 Classification of flow scheduling algorithms 120
5.4.2 Bandwidth allocation and flow control method 125
5.5 Data and control 126
5.5.1 Clock synchronization management 126
5.5.2 Packet filtering and classification 127
5.5.3 Security measures 129
5.6 The technology of switch 132
5.6.1 Introduction of switch equipment 132
5.6.2 Clock synchronization technology 133
5.6.3 Time sensitive scheduling 134
5.6.4 Congestion management 135
5.7 The introduction of deterministic network frontier 137
5.7.1 Development trend of deterministic network 137
5.7.2 Related standards of deterministic network 139
5.8 Conclusion 139
References 140

6 Delay-tolerant network 145
Yujie Song, Xinyu Li and Yue Cao

6.1 Introduction 145
6.2 The presentative characteristics of DTN 146
6.2.1 Nodes 146

6.2.2 Connectivities 147
6.2.3 Networks 147
6.3 The architecture of DTN 148
6.3.1 Overall architecture 148
6.3.2 Protocol stack 148
6.4 The advantages and disadvantages in DTN 155
6.4.1 Advantages 155
6.4.2 Disadvantages 156
6.4.3 Challenges 157
6.5 Technologies in DTN 158
6.5.1 Store-carry-forward mechanism 158
6.5.2 Routing category 158
6.6 DTN security 166
6.6.1 Physical layer security 166
6.6.2 Data link layer security 168
6.6.3 Network layer security 168
6.6.4 Transport layer security 169
6.6.5 Bundle layer security 170
6.6.6 The security requirements 170
6.7 Applications in DTN 171
6.8 Conclusion 171
References 172

7 Mobile and wireless networks **177**
Shuohan Liu, Junqiao Gao, Yue Cao and Hai Lin

7.1 Mobile networks 177
7.1.1 Introduction to mobile networks 177
7.1.2 Key Performance Indicators (KPIs) 178
7.1.3 Overview of mobile network generations 179
7.2 Cellular networks 181
7.2.1 Fundamentals of cellular network 181
7.2.2 Spectrum management methodologies 182
7.2.3 Handover processes in cellular networks 184
7.2.4 Cellular network infrastructure components 185
7.2.5 First-generation mobile networks (1G) 186
7.2.6 2G network: analog-to-digital communications 187
7.2.7 3G network: voice-centric to data-centric services 188
7.2.8 4G network: evolution and architectural mastery 190
7.2.9 5G network: industrial revolution with high-speed connectivity 191
7.2.10 6G network: the next frontier of connectivity 193
7.3 Mobile IP and mobility in cellular networks 196
7.3.1 Mobile IP: concept 196
7.3.2 Mobile IP: indirect routing 197
7.3.3 Mobile IP: Agent Discovery 198

7.3.4 Mobility in cellular network 199
7.4 Security in mobile networks 199
7.4.1 Limitation of cellular networks 199
7.4.2 Security issues in 3G network 200
7.4.3 Security issues in 4G network 201
7.4.4 Security issues in 5G network 202
7.4.5 Security defense in cellular networks 202
7.4.6 Future security trends in mobile networks 204
7.5 Conclusion 205
References 205

8 Edge computing 209
Zhenning Wang, Yue Cao, Hai Lin, and Bo Zhao

8.1 Development of edge computing 209
8.1.1 The origin of edge computing 209
8.1.2 The overview of edge computing 210
8.2 Development of edge computing 210
8.2.1 Computing paradigm 211
8.2.2 Three-tier network architecture 212
8.2.3 Multi-cloud networking 214
8.3 Optimization-oriented edge computing 215
8.3.1 Basic model overview 215
8.3.2 Optimization problems in edge computing 215
8.3.3 Optimization objectives in edge computing 222
8.3.4 Optimization methods in edge computing 224
8.4 The application of edge computing 229
8.4.1 Smart IoT 230
8.4.2 Smart city 230
8.4.3 Healthcare 230
8.4.4 Intelligent transportation 231
8.4.5 Retail industry 231
8.4.6 Smart manufacturing 232
8.4.7 Digital Twins (DT) 232
8.5 The technology challenges of edge computing 233
8.5.1 Security and privacy 233
8.5.2 Model and architecture 235
8.5.3 Dynamic 236
8.5.4 Development opportunity 236
8.6 Conclusion 237
References 237

9 Internet of Things and CPS 243
Jiaxin Hou, Haotian Wang, Yu'ang Zhang and Yue Cao

9.1 The basic concept of Internet of Things (IoT) 243
9.2 The architecture of IoT 244

9.3 Enabling technologies of IoT 246
9.3.1 Perception layer technology 246
9.3.2 Network communication technology 249
9.3.3 IoT protocols 252
9.3.4 Data processing and intelligent analysis 256
9.3.5 Security issues and defense 258
9.4 Use cases of IoT and CPS 261
9.4.1 Smart agriculture 262
9.4.2 Smart city 263
9.4.3 Smart home 265
9.4.4 Intelligent manufacturing 266
9.4.5 Smart grid 267
9.5 Conclusion 269
References 269

10 Intelligent transportation system **275**
Yujie Song, Junqiao Gao, Yue Cao and Bo Zhao

10.1 Introduction 275
10.2 The presentative characteristics of ITS development stages 278
10.2.1 Electronation and informatization 279
10.2.2 Networking and cooperation 279
10.2.3 Digital intelligence and automation 280
10.3 The architecture of ITS 282
10.3.1 Overall architecture 282
10.3.2 Perceiving system 282
10.3.3 Comprehensive strategy 283
10.3.4 Networking and communication 283
10.3.5 Operation center 283
10.3.6 Command center 283
10.4 The advantages and disadvantages in ITS 283
10.4.1 Advantages 283
10.4.2 Disadvantages 284
10.4.3 Challenges 285
10.5 Technologies in ITS 287
10.5.1 Perceiving with sensors 287
10.5.2 Data processing 288
10.5.3 Networking and communication 291
10.5.4 Operation and management 293
10.6 Information security in ITS 293
10.6.1 Communication security 293
10.6.2 Terminal security 294
10.6.3 Cloud security 294
10.7 Application in ITS 295
10.7.1 Smart bus 295
10.7.2 Smart parking 295
10.7.3 Smart hub 295

10.7.4 Vehicle supervision 295
10.7.5 Road digital perceiving 295
10.7.6 Road smart maintenance 295
10.8 Conclusion 296
References 296

11 Multimedia networks **301**
Zixuan Li, Haotian Wang and Yue Cao

11.1 Multimedia networks 301
11.1.1 Multimedia networking applications 301
11.1.2 Audio and video nature 301
11.1.3 Multimedia networking application types 303
11.1.4 Problems faced in application development 305
11.2 Streaming stored video 306
11.2.1 Streaming storage video overview 306
11.2.2 The need for streaming storage video 307
11.2.3 Streaming multimedia: UDP 308
11.2.4 Streaming multimedia: HTTP 309
11.2.5 Emerging trends in streaming stored video 311
11.3 Voice-over-IP 312
11.3.1 Basic concept 312
11.3.2 VoIP principles and architecture 313
11.3.3 VoIP: fixed playback delay 313
11.3.4 VoIP evolution: WebRTC, 5G, and AI 316
11.4 Protocols for real-time conversational applications 317
11.4.1 RTP 317
11.4.2 Session Initiation Protocol (SIP) 320
11.4.3 Dynamic Adaptive Streaming over HTTP (DASH) 323
11.5 Network support for multimedia 325
11.5.1 Three network layer approaches 325
11.5.2 Three important regulatory principles 329
11.5.3 Edge computing and multimedia networks 330
11.5.4 Multi-cloud networking services and Web 3.0 331
11.6 Conclusion 332
References 332

12 Open questions and future directions **337**
Yue Cao, Hai Lin, Bo Zhao and Yuan Zhuang

Index **343**

About the editors

Yue Cao is a professor at the School of Cyber Science and Engineering, Wuhan University, China. He was previously a research fellow with the University of Surrey, Northumbria University, Lancaster University, UK, and Beihang University in Beijing, China. His multidisciplinary research interests focus on wireless networks, service optimization cyber security, and ITS. He is CEng, FIET, FBCS, FBCS, and FHEA. He received his PhD degree from the Institute for Communication Systems (ICS), formerly known as the Centre for Communication Systems Research, University of Surrey, Guildford, UK.

Hai Lin is an associate professor at the School of Cyber Science and Engineering, Wuhan University, China. He previously held a post-doctoral research position with France Telecom and was a researcher with ZTE Europe. His research interests include the Internet of Things, Edge computing, sensor networks, and future networks. He received his MS degree in computer science from the University of Pierre and Marie Curie in Paris and his PhD degree from the Institute Telecom Paris, France.

Bo Zhao is the president of the School of Cyber Science and Engineering, Wuhan University, China. He is a senior member of the Chinese Computer Federation (CFF). His research interests include information system security, trusted computing, embedded systems, cloud computing security, and network security technology. He has published 70+ academic papers. He is also the director of the Chinese Cryptology Society. He received his PhD degree in computer software and theory from Wuhan University, China.

Yuan Zhuang is a professor at the State Key Laboratory of Information Engineering in Surveying, Mapping, and Remote Sensing, Wuhan University, China. His research interests include multi-sensors integration, real-time location systems, wireless positioning, the Internet of Things (IoT), and machine learning for navigation applications. He has co-authored over 80 academic papers and holds 18 patents. He received his master's degree in microelectronics and solid-state electronics from Southeast University, Nanjing, China, and his PhD degree in geomatics engineering from the University of Calgary, Canada.

Chapter 1
Terminologies, opportunities, and challenges

Yue Cao[1], Hai Lin[1], Bo Zhao[1] and Yuan Zhuang[2]

1.1 Terminologies

The following are abbreviations of terminologies and corresponding full names used in this book.

Abbreviation	Full name
US	United States
ARPANET	Advanced Research Projects Agency Network
UCLA	University of California, Los Angeles
UCSB	University of California, Santa Barbara
NCP	Network Control Protocol
TCP/IP	Transmission Control Protocol/Internet Protocol
ISO	International Organization for Standardization
IEC	International Electrotechnical Commission
OSI	Open System Interconnection
DoD	United States Department of Defense
MILNET	Military Network
NSFNET	National Science Foundation Network
SDN	Software-Defined Networking
ONF	Open Networking Foundation
API	Application Programming Interface
ONOS	Open Network Operating System
NAT	Network Address Translation
TCAM	Ternary Content Addressable Memory
MPLS	Multiprotocol Label Switching
MAC	Media Access Control
UDP	User Datagram Protocol
TLS	Transport Layer Security

(Continued)

[1]School of Cyber Science and Engineering, Wuhan University, China
[2]The State Key Laboratory of Surveying, Mapping and Remote Sensing, Wuhan University, China

(continued)

Abbreviation	Full name
ESTI	European Telecommunications Standards Institute
NFV	Network Functions Virtualization
IT	Information Technology
VM	Virtual Machine
Cloud OS	Cloud Operating System
ETSI	European Telecommunications Standards Institute
VNF	Virtualized Network Function
NFVI	Network Function Virtualization Infrastructure
NFV M&O	Network Function Virtualization Management and Orchestration
VIM	Virtualized Infrastructure Manager
VNFM	Virtualization Network Function Manager
NFVO	Network Function Virtualization Orchestrator
CPU	Central Processing Unit
RAN	Radio Access Network
BBU	Building Baseband Unit
EPC	Evolved Packet Core
MME	Mobility Management Entity
HSS	Home Subscriber Server
PGW	Packet Gateway
PCRF	Policy and Charging Rules Function
VoLTE	Voice over LTE
IMS	IP Multimedia Subsystem
CSCF	Call Session Control Function
CPE	Customer Premise Equipment
RG	Residential Gateway
STB	Set-Top-Box
IPTV	Internet Protocol Television
DHCP	Dynamic Host Configuration Protocol
VPN Gateway	Virtual Private Network Gateway
CDN	Content Delivery Network
SSL	Secure Sockets Layer
PKI	Public Key Infrastructure
DNS	Domain Name System
APLOMEB	Access Point Location and Mobility Estimation for Broadband
DoS	Denial of Service
DDoS	Distributed Denial of Service
SFC	Service Function Chain
SGX	Software Guard eXtension
WAN	Wide Area Network
SD-WAN	Software-Defined Wide Area Network

(Continued)

(continued)

Abbreviation	Full name
IBN	Intent-Based Networking
AI	Artificial Intelligence
CC	Cloud Computing
RestAPI	Representational State Transfer Application Programming Interface
OMP	Overlay Management Protocol
DTLS	Datagram Transport Layer Security
MP-BGP	Multiprotocol Border Gateway Protocol
SLA	Service Level Agreement
IETF	Internet Engineering Task Force
ML	Machine Learning
TCP	Transmission Control Protocol
HTTP	HyperText Transfer Protocol
SMTP	Simple Mail Transfer Protocol
SNMP	Simple Network Management Protocol
FTP	File Transfer Protocol
Telnet	Telecommunication Network protocol
ECN	Explicit Congestion Notification
MSS	Maximum Segment Size
RTT	Round Trip Time
PAWS	Protection Against Wrapped Sequence numbers
SACK	Selective ACKnowledgements
RTO	Retransmission Time Out
SRTT	Smoothed Round Trip Time
RTTVAR	Round Trip Time VARiation
AIMD	Additive Increase/Multiplicative Decrease
CWND	Congestion Window
RWND	Receive Window
SYN	Synchronize flag
FIN	FINish flag
ACK	ACKnowledgment flag
PSH	PuSH flag
RST	ReSeT flag
URG	URGent flag
ECE	Explicit Congestion notification flag Echo
CWR	Congestion Window Reduced flag
IPS	Intrusion Prevention Systems
ISN	Initial Sequence Number
PRNG	Pseudo Random Number Generator
RAM	Random Access Memory

(Continued)

(continued)

Abbreviation	Full name
ISP	Internet Service Provider
AS	Autonomous System
IGP	Interior Gateway Protocol
EGP	External Gateway Protocol
RIP	Routing Information Protocol
OSPF	Open Shortest Path First
XNS	Xerox Network System
BSD	Berkeley Software Distribution
BGP	Border Gateway Protocol
RFC	Request for Comment
LSDB	Link State Database
TTL	Time-To-Live
MANET	Mobile Ad hoc Network
DSDV	Destination Sequenced Distance Vector
OLSR	Optimized Link State Routing
MPR	Multipoint Relay
AODV	Ad hoc On-demand Distance Vector
RREQ	Route Request
RREP	Route Reply
RERR	Route Error
DSR	Dynamic Source Routing
ZRP	Zone Routing Protocol
ZHLS	Zone-Based Hierarchical Link State
GPSR	Greedy Perimeter Stateless Routing
GPS	Global Positioning System
CGR	Contention-based Geographic Routing
DFD	Dynamic Forwarding Delay
NIQ	Neighbor Information Query
RTQ	Reply To Query
ACO	Ant Colony Optimization
ACECR	Ant Colony-based Energy Control Routing
FHACO	Fuzzy Hierarchy Ant Colony Optimization
PSO	Particle Swarm Optimization
CSA	Cuckoo Search-based routing Algorithm
RL	Reinforcement Learning
QoS	Quality of Service
RLRP	Reinforcement Learning Routing Packet Protocol
PLR	Packet Loss Rate
LA	Learning Automata
LAFTRA	Learning Automata-based Fault-Tolerant Routing Algorithm

(Continued)

(continued)

Abbreviation	Full name
ACL	Access Control List
IoT	Internet of Things
IP	Internet Protocol
DetNet	Deterministic Networking
TSN	Time-Sensitive Networking
LANs	Local Area Networks
WANs	Wide Area Networks
CAVs	Connected and Autonomous Vehicles
V2V	Vehicle-to-Vehicle
V2I	Vehicle-to-Infrastructure
UAVs	Unmanned Aerial Vehicles
IIoT	Industrial IoT
PTP	Precision Time Protocol
FPGA	Field-Programmable Gate Array
RTOS	Real-Time Operating System
TDMA	Time Division Multiple Access
NTP	Network Time Protocol
MMU	Memory Management Unit
HAL	Hardware Abstraction Layer
FCFS	First Come, First Served
RR	Round Robin
WRR	Weighted Round Robin
WFQ	Weighted Fair Queuing
CBWFQ	Class-Based Weighted Fair Queuing
DRR	Deficit Round Robin
SRPT	Shortest Remaining Processing Time
TAS	Time-Aware Scheduler
WLAN	Wireless Local Area Networks
CN	Cellular Networks
ADOV	Ad hoc On-Demand Distance Vector
IPNs	Interplanetary Networks
MANETs	Mobile Ad-hoc Networks
VANETs	Vehicular Ad-hoc Networks
WMN	Wireless Mesh Networks
SCF	Store-Carry-Forward
E2E	End-to-End
IoVs	Internet of Vehicles
WSNs	Wireless Sensor Networks
PSNs	Pocket Switched Networks
MACPs	Media Access Control Protocols

(Continued)

(continued)

Abbreviation	Full name
RSUs	Roadside Units
QoE	Quality of Experience
LTP	Licklider Transmission Protocol
ARQ	Automatic RepeatreQuest
CASE	Common Application Service Element
SASE	Special Application Service Element
OBUs	On-board Units
SaW	Spray and Wait
BSaW	Binary Spray and Wait
FIFO	First-in-First-Out
SCR	Single-Copy Replication
DBR	Domain-Based single copy Routing
SaF	Spray and Focus
RET	Random and Encounter Time
RF	Radio Frequency
KPI	Key Performance Indicator
MTBF	Mean Time Between Failures
AMPS	Advanced Mobile Phone System
GSM	Global System for Mobile Communications
SMS	Short Message Service
GPRS	General Packet Radio Service
EDGE	Enhanced Data rates for GSM Evolution
UMTS	Universal Mobile Telecommunications System
HSPA	High-Speed Packet Access
LTE	Long-Term Evolution
FDD	Frequency Division Duplex
TDD	Time Division Duplex
MIMO	Multiple Input Multiple Output
mMTC	massive Machine Type Communications
URLLC	Ultra-Reliable Low-Latency Communication
CDMA	Code Division Multiple Access
TD-LTE	Time-Division Long-Term Evolution
BS	Base Station
MSC	Mobile Switching Center
BSC	Base Station Controller
PTSN	Public Switched Telephone Network
NMT	Nordic Mobile Telephone
FDMA	Frequency Division Multiple Access
SIM	Subscriber Identity Module
W-CDMA	Wideband Code Division Multiple Access

(Continued)

(continued)

Abbreviation	Full name
UTRAN	UMTS Terrestrial Radio Access Network
PDSN	Packet Data Serving Node
MRF	Media Resource Function
NR	New Radio
OFDM	Orthogonal Frequency-Division Multiplexing
VLC	Visible-Light Communications
FA	Foreign Agent
HA	Home Agent
CoA	Care-of Address
GRE	Generic Routing Encapsulation
TMSI	Temporary Mobile Subscriber Identity
SN	Service Network
VLR	Visitor Location Register
IMSI	International Mobile Subscribers Identity
NDS	Network Domain Security
WGN	White Gaussian Noise
PLS	Physical Layer Security
MTS	Mobile Telephone System
TD-SCDMA	Time Division-Synchronous Code Division Multiple Access
OFDMA	Orthogonal Frequency-Division Multiple Access
VPN	Virtual Private Network
SGW/MGCF	Signaling Gateway/Media Gateway Control Function
V2X	Vehicle-to-Everything
WEP	Wired Equivalent Privacy
MEC	Mobile Edge Computing
CSC	Cloud Service Centers
MCNS	Multi-Cloud Network Services
D2D	Device-to-Device
SBS	Small Base Stations
MBS	Marco Base Stations
SCA	Successive Convex Approximation
ADMM	Alternating Direction Method of Multipliers
DNN	Deep Neural Networks
RNN	Recurrent Neural Networks
DQN	Deep Q-Network
NE	Nash Equilibrium
DT	Digital Twins
EICU	Emergency Intensive Care Unit
AR	Augmented Reality
VR	Virtual Reality

(Continued)

(continued)

Abbreviation	Full name
CPS	Cyber-Physical Systems
RFID	Radio-Frequency Identification
GNSS	Global Navigation Satellite System
LoRa	Long Range
NB-IoT	Narrowband Internet of Things
LoRaWAN	Long Range Wide Area Network
XMPP	Extensible Messaging and Presence Protocol
MQTT	Message Queuing Telemetry Transport
LwM2M	Lightweight Machine-to-Machine
AMQP	Advanced Message Queuing Protocol
CoAP	Constrained Application Protocol
DDS	Data Distribution Service
AIoT	Artificial Intelligence Internet of Things
CNNs	Convolutional Neural Networks
RNNs	Recurrent Neural Networks
CORS	Cross-Origin Resource Sharing
IaaS	Infrastructure as a Service
PaaS	Platform as a Service
SaaS	Software as a Service
FaaS	Function as a Service
ERP	Enterprise Resource Planning
CRM	Customer Relationship Management
SCADA	Supervisory Control and Data Acquisition
RTD	Real Time Differential
RTK	Real Time Kinematic
MMS	Multimedia Message Service
HD	High Definition
GEO	Geostationary Earth Orbit
LEO	Low Earth Orbit
MEO	Middle Earth Orbit
URI	Uniform Resource Identifier
SNPL	Securing Nodes in Perception Layer
MITM	Man-in-the-Middle
KNN	K-Nearest Neighbor
IDS	Intrusion Detection System
CAA	Context Aware Authentication
2FA	Two Factor Authentication
6LoWPAN	IPv6 over Low-Power Wireless Personal Area Networks
RPL	Routing Protocol for Low-Power and Lossy Networks
GIS	Geographic Information System

(Continued)

(continued)

Abbreviation	Full name
LLM	Large Language Model
ITS	Intelligent Transportation System
5G	5 Generation
ISTEA	Intermodal Surface Transportation Efficiency Act
USDT	United States Department of Transportation
DRIVE	Dedicated Road Infrastructure for Vehicle Safety in Europe
PROMOTE	Program for Mobility in Transportation in Europe
VICS	Vehicle Information and Communication System
ETC	Electronic Toll Collection
DSRC	dedicated Short Range Communication
VII	Vehicle-Infrastructure Integration
VDMS	Vehicle Data Management System
TDMS	Traffic Data Management System
EDMS	Energy Data Management System
MaaS	Mobility as a Service
TF	Time-Frequency
SNR	Signal-to-Noise
5G NGC	5G Next Generation Core
NSA	Non-stand Alone
SA	Stand Alone
APIs	Application Programming Interfaces
PCM	Pulse Code Modulation
MP3	MPEG-1 Audio Layer 3
AAC	Advanced Audio Coding
VoIP	Voice-over-Internet Protocol
P2P	Peer-to-Peer
RTP	Real-Time Protocol
SIP	Session Initiation Protocol
RTSP	Real-Time Streaming Protocol
HEVC	High Efficiency Video Coding
AV1	AOMedia Video 1
HTTP/2	Hypertext Transfer Protocol Version 2
QUIC	Quick UDP Internet Connections
ITU-T	International Telecommunication Union Telecommunication Standardization Sector
G.711	A Specific ITU-T Standard for Audio Compression
SS7	Signaling System No. 7
ISDN	Integrated Services Digital Network
H.323	A Standard for Multimedia Communication Over Networks
ICE	Interactive Connectivity Establishment

(Continued)

(continued)

Abbreviation	Full name
5G	Fifth Generation Mobile Network
NLP	Natural Language Processing
ASR	Automatic Speech Recognition
SRTP	Secure Real-time Transport Protocol
AES	Advanced Encryption Standard
MIKEY	Multimedia Internet KEYing
DTLS-SRTP	Datagram Transport Layer Security for SRTP
RED	Redundancy Encoding
WebRTC	Web Real-Time Communication
ASCII	American Standard Code for Information Interchange
DASH	Dynamic Adaptive Streaming over HTTP
MPEG	Moving Picture Experts Group
HLS	HTTP Live Streaming
HDS	HTTP Dynamic Streaming
MPD	Media Presentation Description
TS	Transport Stream
SAP	Stream Access Point
IDR	Intra-coded Picture, Decoded Reference
DS	Distinguished Service
PHB	Per-Hop Behavior
DSCP	Differentiated Services Code Point
RSVP	Resource Reservation Protocol
AWS	Amazon Web Services
DID	Decentralized Identity
IPFS	InterPlanetary File System
CSP	Cloud Service Provider

1.2 Opportunities and challenges

Advanced networking methods and technologies are emerging as critical components to enable novel applications. They are supported by recent technological advances in wireless communications along with the integration of various functionalities such as sensing, communication, and artificial intelligence. The main goal of advanced networking is to achieve more efficient, stable, and secure networks in Internet, and mobile communication systems. To fulfil the increasing network demand from applications, advanced networking technologies such as load balancing, fault-tolerance technology, encryption technology, virtualization technology, and cloud computing are used to improve network speed, optimize network performance, enhance network security, and provide a better user experience. The aim of this book is to introduce innovative advances in networking technologies. The book is written in a tutorial way to benefit a broad audience in computer science, communication, and networking. It also puts a particular focus on cyber security for all advanced network concepts and technologies.

The chapter related to Software-Defined Networking (SDN) and Network Functions Virtualization (NFV) technologies brings revolutionary changes to network management through virtualization and centralized control, including cost reduction, rapid deployment, increased flexibility and openness, and simplified network configuration and management. Software-Defined Wide Area Network (SD-WAN) simplifies WAN management by integrating SDN and NFV technologies, optimizing traffic allocation and cost-effectiveness. Here, Intent-Based Networking (IBN) further enhances the efficiency and accuracy of network management through automation and intelligence, enabling the network to better adapt to changes in business needs. While improving the robustness of the network through closed-loop management and continuous learning, IBN also reduces operation and maintenance costs. The development of these technologies has opened up the possibility of innovation and improvement in the network field, particularly in terms of increasing efficiency, reducing costs, enhancing security, and meeting emerging business needs. Despite the above opportunities, the combination of SDN and NFV significantly enhances network flexibility and programmability, but it also brings many challenges. On the one hand, as independent systems, the integration process of SDN and NFV faces problems of interface standardization, coordination mechanism design, and architectural complexity. On the other hand, in terms of quotas and traffic scheduling, meeting real-time and quality of service while avoiding resource competition becomes difficult. In addition, large-scale deployment may lead to reduced system scalability and stability. Centralized control and virtualization capabilities also expand the security attack surface, such as data isolation and privacy protection in multi-tenant environments. As an extension of SDN and NFV technologies, SD-WAN and IBN face technical integration and compatibility issues, security risks, performance and reliability guarantees, and management and orchestration complexities. For IBN, there are particular issues to address, such as the lack of intent definition, the accuracy of intent translation, thc impact of intent dependence on performance, and limited dataset limitations. Addressing these issues is key to the development of future communication networks.

In the chapter related to Transmission Control Protocol (TCP), opportunities in the field of modern networking are numerous, with the TCP enabling reliable and efficient data transmission across diverse networks. The TCP, serving as a fundamental component of TCP/IP protocol stack, supports critical functionalities (e.g., end-to-end communication, reliable data transfer, and congestion control). These features are essential for the seamless operation of modern applications, ranging from email and web browsing to file transfer. As network demands grow, advancements in congestion control algorithms and innovative security measures create avenues to enhance network performance, improve resource utilization, as well as expand the scope of network-dependent applications. However, challenges still remain in the evolution of TCP. The protocol must address vulnerabilities (e.g., SYN flood and ACK flood attacks) which threaten the integrity as well as availability of network services. Additionally, TCP faces increasing strain from exponential traffic growth and the rising complexity of network environments. These issues demand continuous refinement of congestion control mechanisms, enhanced security frameworks, and innovative approaches to protocol resilience. Addressing these challenges is critical to maintaining the reliability, security, and adaptability of TCP in a rapidly evolving digital landscape.

In the chapter on Dynamic Routing and Access Control Lists (ACL), AI and machine learning offer powerful tools to enhance routing efficiency and adaptability by predicting network behavior and optimizing routes dynamically. Similarly, blockchain technology provides a promising solution for securing routing processes, ensuring data integrity, and mitigating attacks through decentralized trust mechanisms. In the context of ACLs, context-aware and dynamic rule-setting mechanisms can further enhance security by adapting to real-time network conditions. Moreover, hybrid approaches that combine proactive, reactive, and secure-aware routing protocols can offer better resilience and performance in diverse scenarios. These advancements pave the way for more intelligent, secure, and scalable networking systems. However, dynamic routing and ACL face several challenges in adapting to modern networking needs. Scalability is a primary concern as network size and complexity grow, often exceeding the capabilities of traditional routing protocols like RIP and OSPF. Maintaining efficient route computation, fast convergence, and minimal overhead becomes increasingly difficult in large-scale and highly dynamic environments. Additionally, ad hoc and mobile networks introduce unique challenges, such as frequent topology changes and unpredictable link failures, which require routing protocols to adapt in real time. Security is another pressing issue, as routing protocols and ACLs are vulnerable to attacks such as spoofing, black hole, and wormhole attacks. Protecting these systems from both external threats and insider misuse remains a persistent challenge, particularly in decentralized or resource-constrained environments.

The chapter related to Deterministic Networks for Real Time Applications presents numerous opportunities to revolutionize critical industries. Enhanced time synchronization and real-time capabilities can unlock innovations in autonomous driving, industrial automation, and IoT systems, enabling unprecedented levels of safety and efficiency. Advanced flow management strategies, combined with machine learning, provide opportunities for dynamic optimization of network resources, allowing for more adaptive and intelligent operations. Furthermore, the development of time-sensitive switches and congestion management technologies can significantly enhance reliability and resilience in high-demand applications like industrial control and smart grids. As ongoing research expands the boundaries of deterministic networking, there is immense potential to create ultra-reliable, low-latency networks critical for next-generation technologies like 6G and digital twins. Deterministic networking faces critical challenges that demand urgent solutions to enable its transformative potential. Establishing a robust foundational infrastructure, including time synchronization hardware and hard real-time systems, is essential for ensuring deterministic performance. Achieving efficient and predictable network behavior requires advanced flow scheduling algorithms, bandwidth allocation, and flow control strategies. Enhancing adaptability and intelligence in data and control mechanisms calls for the integration of machine learning for packet filtering and classification. Furthermore, improving network reliability and responsiveness necessitates innovations in switch technology, such as time-sensitive scheduling and congestion management. Addressing these challenges is crucial for advancing deterministic networks and their applications.

In the chapter related to Delay-Tolerant Network (DTN), with the development of communication technologies, the characteristics of high-speed data transmission and Store-Carry-Forward (SCF) mechanism of DTN can be integrated, to support various applications, e.g., emergency communications and disaster rescue. For example, at a disaster rescue site, mobile devices carried by rescue personnel can be used to cache data collected at the site. Then, those devices transmit the data quickly to the command center after entering the 5G/6G coverage area to achieve efficient information sharing. Furthermore, numerous devices are connected by heterogeneous networks, and the high-level requirements of DTN have emerged, such as high robustness, high security, and high adaption in a dynamic environment. Especially, in the Internet of Things (IoTs) environment, there exists a large number of low-power, intermittently connected devices such as sensor nodes. The characteristics of DTNs make them well adapted to the communication requirements of these devices, providing an effective communication solution for IoTs devices. Moreover, opportunities arise from data value mining. DTN can be utilized as an important means of big data collection, aggregating massive data distributed in different geographic locations and under different network environments to the data center. Therefore, DTN has a wide range of applications and development prospects in the future. Due to the components and characteristics of DTN (e.g., the high mobility of nodes, unstable connectivity, and dynamical topology change), several challenges have emerged, such as energy constraint, limited bandwidth, buffer management, data organization, and dynamical routing. First, the energy constraint will affect the reliability and efficiency of communication; thus, how to optimize the utilization of energy in a dynamic environment has become an important challenge for improving the quality of service and experience. Second, limited bandwidth is caused by low power on-board units of mobile nodes with energy constraints, thus how to improve the efficiency of data transmission within the constraint of limited bandwidths is focused on in recent years. Third, due to the limited storage space in mobile nodes, how to effectively manage buffers has become a crucial problem. Fourth, data organization focuses on how to generate the data allocation strategy and allocate data to output queues based on link status, bandwidth, spare buffer, etc. Fifth, dynamical routing is a high-level challenge in DTN, i.e., mobile nodes perceive the dynamic status of networks and the physical world, utilizing that information to construct a reliable path for routing.

In the chapter related to Mobile and Wireless Networks, mobile and wireless networks present significant opportunities. The transition from 4G to 5G, along with the development of 6G, leads to substantial improvements in bandwidth, latency, and connectivity, enabling applications such as autonomous driving, smart cities, and industrial automation. Additionally, the integration of IoT devices across sectors like healthcare and agriculture enhances real-time monitoring and boosts efficiency. Innovations in energy efficiency, combined with the integration of AI and blockchain, optimize networks, strengthen security, and improve maintenance. Moreover, network slicing and edge computing allow the creation of customized virtual networks, as well as support for low-latency applications. Finally, satellite network integration extends connectivity to remote areas, fostering global digital inclusion. Here, mobile and wireless networks face several significant challenges due to the open nature of wireless medium, which makes them vulnerable to unauthorized access, signal jamming, and eavesdropping. The competition for bandwidth in shared frequency bands leads to performance issues, especially as the number of connected devices, such as smartphones, IoT sensors, and vehicles, continues to grow. Additionally, the complexity of integrating mobility management, resource allocation, and diverse devices increases design and maintenance challenges, creating potential security vulnerabilities. Power constraints are another concern, as most wireless devices rely on battery power, limiting their capacity to handle resource-intensive tasks. Environmental factors, such as interference and signal attenuation, further contribute to unstable connections and service disruptions. Security risks, including identity theft, spoofing, and denial-of-service attacks, are prevalent, particularly in systems with weak encryption. Moreover, the rapid growth of connected devices exacerbates challenges related to scalability and real-time communication.

In the chapter related to edge computing, with the development of emerging technologies such as artificial intelligence, opportunities have been brought to the development of edge computing. First, the continuous advancement of artificial intelligence and machine learning technologies has further developed edge intelligence. The intelligence of edge devices can achieve a higher level of autonomous decision-making and behavior. Meanwhile, the deep integration of edge computing with 5G/6G can promote the development of more application scenarios, such as augmented reality, virtual reality, and cloud games. In addition, a variety of incentive mechanisms derived from economic theory have gradually been applied to edge computing scenarios. This has brought new vitality to the development of edge computing. Finally, edge intelligent devices may integrate more sensors and multimodal sensing technologies in the future. Then, by combining multimodal sensing with edge computing, edge devices can sense, understand, and respond to the real world more intelligently. However, with the advancement of various computing technologies, edge computing still faces many challenges. Firstly, the increased complexity of the scene brings new challenges to problem optimization. Traditional optimization methods are difficult to achieve efficient decision-making in dynamic and complex environments. Secondly, the allocation of computing resources in dynamic scenes is also a challenge. Meanwhile, resource management and scheduling in multidimensional networks or more complex heterogeneous networks also face important challenges. Finally, the characteristics of individual selfishness and rationality are foreseeable. It is difficult for various edge nodes to actively participate in the task process without compensation, which brings challenges to edge computing. This makes it urgent to introduce multiple incentive methods in edge computing scenarios.

In the chapter related to IoT and Cyber-Physical Systems (CPS), the convergence of IoT with advanced technologies such as 5G, AI, and machine learning opens up new possibilities for creating smart solutions across industries. For instance, smart cities can leverage IoT and CPS to improve urban planning, optimize resource allocation, and enhance the quality of life for residents. In healthcare, IoT devices can enable remote patient monitoring, leading to better patient outcomes and reduced healthcare costs. The industrial sector can benefit from IoT and CPS through predictive maintenance, which reduces downtime and improves the lifespan of equipment. Additionally, the rise of edge computing provides opportunities for processing data closer to the source, reducing latency and enabling real-time decision-making. The IoT and CPS are changing traditional industries and creating new business models. This provides significant opportunities for economic growth and social progress. Regarding challenges, one of the primary concerns is the security and privacy of data, as the increase in connected devices amplifies the attack surface for potential cyber threats. Ensuring data integrity and confidentiality while maintaining system resilience against sophisticated attacks is crucial. Besides, the heterogeneity of IoT devices and the lack of standardized protocols can lead to interoperability issues, complicating the integration of different devices and systems. Scalability is another significant challenge, as the IoT ecosystem must accommodate the growing number of devices without compromising performance. Furthermore, the management of massive amounts of data generated by IoT devices requires advanced data processing and intelligent analysis capabilities, which in turn demand more sophisticated algorithms and increased computational power. Addressing these challenges is essential for the sustainable growth and adoption of IoT and CPS technologies.

Following the above effort on IoT and CPS, the development of underpinned technologies for ITS (e.g., communication, scheduling, and security), several opportunities are shed light on by facilitating the travel mode of people, including policy support, investment increase, market demand growth, technological innovation, and new application scenarios expansion. First, governments have introduced a series of policies and plans to support the development of ITS as an important means to solve transportation problems, promoting the construction of smart cities. For example, the Chinese government has issued documents such as the outline for the construction of a powerful country in transportation. The introduction of these policies provides a clear direction and strong support for the development of ITS. Second, with the acceleration of urbanization, the problem of traffic congestion in cities is becoming increasingly serious. Fortunately, ITS is able to effectively alleviate traffic congestion by optimizing traffic signal control and providing real-time traffic information. Third, ITS is an important part of the smart city and can be deeply integrated with energy management, environmental protection, and public safety to realize the sustainable development of cities. Although the data filtering and processing technologies can be utilized to address the problem of efficient data transmission, decision-making, and data flow management in ITS, various challenges still exist, including untimely data sharing, non-uniform industry standards, inadequate infrastructures, poor data quality, privacy leakage risk, and cross-domain cooperation. First, the lack of effective data communication and sharing among departments and platforms is one of the challenges, i.e., the existence of serious data transmission barriers leads to the fragmented distribution of traffic data, low data utilization, and difficulty in data synchronization. Second, non-uniform industry standards will cause mismatched control strategies, interfaces, and policies, reducing the robustness and adaptability of ITS. Third, ITS requires the data support of numerous infrastructures in the real world, such as roadside units, routers, and base stations. Fourth, poor data quality affects the efficiency of data processing and information aggregation, causing traffic congestion, traffic accidents, and property damage. Fifth, privacy data leakage will result in threats to travel security, traffic disruption, and information leakage in sensitive areas. Sixth, cross-domain cooperation requires various technology support in multiple fields to underpin the operation of a holistic system in ITS.

The chapter related to Multimedia Networking introduces the potential of advanced protocols and encoding standards like H.265/HEVC and AV1, which enable seamless HD and 4K video streaming even in bandwidth-limited environments. Additionally, edge computing, CDNs, and adaptive streaming protocols such as DASH improve user experience by optimizing latency and bandwidth usage. These innovations open new possibilities for immersive and interactive experiences, allowing for better multimedia applications in entertainment, education, and remote collaboration. Despite these opportunities, several challenges persist. Issues such as bandwidth constraints, latency, jitter control, and maintaining stable transmission in dynamic network environments persist. Real-time communication and efficient data handling in decentralized systems also present significant hurdles. Furthermore, ensuring secure and fair content distribution through new technologies like blockchain and decentralized networks requires overcoming technical and operational barriers.

Chapter 2

Software-defined networking and network functions virtualization technologies

Jie Huang[1], *Yue Cao*[1] *and Hai Lin*[1]

The chapter presents an overview of Software-Defined Networking (SDN), an overview of Network Functions Virtualization (NFV), security of SDN, security of NFV, and other related technologies.

2.1 Development of the network

The Cuban Missile Crisis in 1962 brought an unprecedented crisis to mankind. In 1969, the US Defense Advanced Research Projects Agency began to study ARPANET (Advanced Research Projects Agency Network) [1], with the goal of applying science and technology to the military domain. ARPANET was initially interconnected with only four nodes (the four nodes were mainly research institutions that studied ARPANET): University of California, Los Angeles (UCLA), University of California, Santa Barbara (UCSB), Stanford University, and the University of Utah. Network communication at that time was based on the Network Control Protocol (NCP), developed by Robert Kahn. However, the NCP had certain limitations, so scientists began to develop the next-generation network communication protocol.

In 1973, the Transmission Control Protocol/Internet Protocol (TCP/IP) [2] was proposed, which has become the core of Internet architecture since then, creating a new era of network communication. In 1974, the International Organization for Standardization (ISO) released the famous ISO/IEC (International Electrotechnical Commission) 7498 standard, which first defined the Layered Network Model, namely what was usually called the seven-layer reference model of Open System Interconnection (OSI) [3]. On New Year's Day in 1983, the TCP/IP protocol officially replaced the NCP protocol in ARPANET. The same year, the DoD (United States Department of Defense) split ARPANET into two parts, one for scientific and

[1] School of Cyber Science and Engineering, Wuhan University, China

technological research, still called ARPANET, and the other for military communications, known as MILNET (Military Network).

In 1984, the DoD adopted the TCP/IP protocol as the standard for computer network communication. Until then, the TCP/IP protocol became popular across the United States. In 1986, the National Science Foundation built the NSFNET (National Science Foundation Network) Wide Area Network, which laid the foundation for the birth of Internet. Based on NSFnet, the network continued to develop after ARPANET was officially closed and withdrew from the stage of history in 1990. In 1996, with the wide spread of World Wide Web, the term Internet had become popular. In the following ten years, Internet has successfully accommodated various underlying network technologies and abundant upper-level applications, bringing changes to the world [4].

In the early days of Internet, an enterprise, a university, or a research institution could organize its computer resources through the network, providing a small-scale experimental environment and auxiliary services for internal personnel. Therefore, the initial scale of internet services, number of devices, and maintenance costs were all small. The cost of network operation and management was acceptable. However, with the expansion of the scale of network services and the increase of external services (e.g., enterprises need to expand), the challenges for large-scale operation and maintenance have increased with high cost, resulting in the birth of traditional data centers. Traditional data centers can help enterprises host part of their business, reducing IT operation and maintenance costs.

With the increase in business, expansion of data centers, and improvement of hardware performance, the servers' computing resources were underutilized, so virtualization technology has emerged. The core idea of virtualization technology is that there are multiple virtual logical hosts on one host, and these logical hosts share the underlying physical resources. Each logical host is independent of others and does not interfere with each other while running different operating systems. The virtualization technology has flexibility, while managers can reasonably allocate and manage resources according to users' access needs, traffic load, etc. The flexibility of virtualization technology also promoted the birth of cloud computing [5].

With the continuous development of network, users perceive more requests, which has also brought many challenges to the network operation. The most intuitive is the rapid expansion of network scale. The expansion of network scale refers to the increase in network connections and the surge in network traffic, mainly due to the application of technologies such as the Internet of Things [6], virtual reality [7], and 4K/8K video [8]. However, the existing Internet architecture builds on TCP/IP, and each access device must have an IP address to communicate with other devices. The increase in the number of connections means an increase in the IP addresses. In addition, since the number of IP addresses is limited, the address space may be exhausted, while the sharp increase in traffic also increases the pressure on network bandwidth. Some new services, such as 4K/8K video, virtual reality games, etc., have posed critical requirements such as ultra high network throughput, ultra low packet loss rate, delay, etc.

To solve aforementioned problems that continue to emerge in the development of Internet, the traditional method was to embed various protocols into existing networks continuously. However, while solving the problem, these methods further aggravated the complexity of Internet architecture and the difficulty of network management. Meanwhile, due to the closure of manufacturer's equipment, the lifetime for design, implementation, and promotion of new protocols is very long [9]. In addition, the closed network architecture does nothing to the opening of industrial chain and the innovation of technical services. Later, some researchers realized that the root cause of these problems lies in the current architecture of Internet itself, and therefore, they turned to investigate new network architectures, aiming to solve the problems existing in the current network.

2.2 Overview of SDN

SDN is a new technology that makes computer networks further programmable [10], which decouples the traditional closed network system into a data plane, a control plane, and an application plane [11], logically realizing the management of network in a centralized control way. The network architecture based on the OpenFlow protocol initially implements the prototype design of SDN. The concept of SDN was first proposed by Professor Nick Mckeown of Stanford University in 2009, as a new type of network architecture discussed in academia. However, in recent years, SDN has developed rapidly and has been adopted by many companies. The most successful case is the data center networking B4 established by Google from 2010 to 2012.

SDN has become a research hotspot in recent years, regarded as the core technology of the next-generation Internet. The outstanding feature of SDN is its openness and programmability, and it has been applied in the domain of network virtualization, data center networking, wireless local area networks, and cloud computing. The basic ideas of SDN architecture are logically centralized control and data forwarding separation. The SDN separates the control plane of network from embedded nodes. Moreover, SDN utilizes a software-driven central controller to control the entire network, replacing the traditional control plane based on system embeddings with an open and programmable soft control plane. This architecture effectively simplifies the management of network, providing users with good network programmability.

2.2.1 Motivation of SDN

Under the influence of Moore's Law, network hardware has made great progress in the past few decades. In contrast, the development of network management and control functions has been quite slow due to the closed architecture of traditional networks. Traditional networks are based on distributed control architectures. The control and forwarding of traffic in traditional networks rely on network devices. These devices communicate with each other by running the TCP/IP protocol, which integrates control and forwarding. They all contain independent control planes and data planes, all preset by the manufacturers. In addition, traditional network devices mostly operate in a black-box manner. If the user wants to add new functions, the device manufacturer needs to re-develop, which will require a long period. If the user wants to change the configuration according to individual needs, user must log in to each device using the interface provided by the manufacturer to operate. What's more, the changes that the user can achieve are limited.

The development of big data and cloud computing has realized the virtualization deployment of a mass of servers. The virtualized servers can take full advantage of the original resources through resource abstraction and integration. Traditional networks have many limitations in dealing with server virtualization deployment. Although the virtualized servers could deploy in legacy networks with a certain resource configuration, it is quite time-consuming. Studies have shown that if a large-scale data center has network equipment and comes from different manufacturers, it takes hours or days to deploy a new virtual machine. With the popularity of cloud computing in the future, more data centers will appear and replace existing network services. In this case, researchers have proposed an SDN open network architecture with the idea of transfer and control separation, and this is convenient for the cloud service providers to fast complete network deployment. The application of SDN technology could update and save human resources to a greater extent, realizing the automation of services.

2.2.2 Basic concepts and architecture of SDN

The generally recognized definition of SDN nowadays is the OpenFlow-based SDN definition, which is given by the Open Networking Foundation (ONF) in the white paper "Software-Defined Networking: The New Norm for Networks." According to the definition of ONF, SDN is an emerging network architecture, which separates network control functions from forwarding functions and implements control programmability. Here, SDN is composed of the infrastructure layer (also called the forwarding layer), the control layer, and the application layer (Figure 2.1) [12].

- The infrastructure layer is composed of network devices and is responsible for data forwarding according to the policies issued by the control layer.
- The control layer is based on software implementation and has a global network view. Through standard interfaces, the control layer can open up the abstracted network functions and services to the application layer. Also, the control layer is able to control and coordinate the forwarding behavior of underlying network devices downward.
- The application layer is composed of various network application services. Here, users can develop various network applications through the open interfaces of control layer and modify the network forwarding behavior according to business requirements.

The various layers of SDN realize quotas and network services through standard open interfaces. The communication interface between the control layer and the infrastructure layer is called the southbound interface. Similarly, the communication interface between the control layer and the application layer is called the northbound interface. OpenFlow, which will be introduced in the next subsection, is a kind of

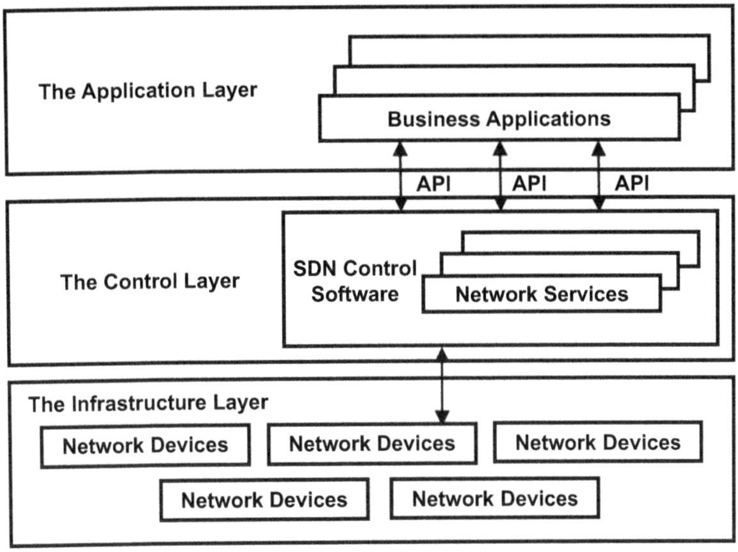

Figure 2.1 Structure of SDN

southbound interface protocol and also the first standard protocol in the SDN architecture given by ONF [13]. It is used to define the communication interface between the controller and forwarding device, which supports direct access and configuration of the forwarding plane of network devices (including physical/virtual switches and routers).

The architecture of SDN has the following four key characteristics:

- **Flow-based forwarding.** The packet switches controlled by the SDN control plane are distributed in the data plane. The forwarding of packets in SDN can be based on the values of header fields of protocol data units in the data link layer, network layer, and transport layer. This is different from traditional routers that only forward IP data packets according to the destination IP address. The entries in the flow table of each packet switch are calculated, managed, and installed by the SDN control plane, so that the forwarding rules of SDN are specified in detail in the flow table of each packet switch.
- **The forwarding plane is separated from the control plane.** To distinguish the forwarding plane and forwarding device, the forwarding plane is replaced by the data plane in subsequent content. In the traditional forwarding device router, the data plane and control plane are located in the same device. However, in SDN, the data plane is decoupled from the control plane and is no longer uniformly integrated into the network device. The data plane has many relatively simple and fast packet switches that perform match + action rules based on their respective flow tables in SDN [14]. The control plane consists of several servers and corresponding software. These servers compute and manage the flow tables in these packet switches along with software.

- **Centralized network control function.** The control plane in SDN is realized by various software, which can be on different machines or away from packet switches located in the data plane. The software implementation of the SDN control plane consists of two components, one of which is the SDN controller [15], regarded as the network operating system. The other component is several network control applications. The SDN controller maintains accurate network state information, such as the status of remote links, packet switches, and hosts, providing network state information to various control applications running on the control plane. In addition, the SDN controller will also enable these control plane applications to monitor, program, and control the packet switches in the data plane. The software-based controller can logically and centrally control the network with a global network view, which could contribute to simplifying network design and operation, optimizing network resources, responding quickly in real-time, and realizing rapid business deployment.
- **Programmable network.** The entire SDN network can be programmable with various network applications in the SDN control plane, enabling network services and customized services [12]. The SDN controller can use these network control applications to control each packet switch in the data plane. The network control application can also decide which packets must be blocked when entering a packet switch called access control. In addition, the network control application can also configure the packet switch to perform load-balancing measures when forwarding packets.

It is easy to see that under the SDN architecture, the routing software in traditional routers does not exist, so routing information is no longer exchanged between routers. In the control plane, there is a logically centralized remote controller called the SDN controller. The SDN controller is the most complex in the SDN architecture. The remote controller can be physically composed of multiple servers in different locations and can be divided into three layers, the communication layer, the network-wide state management layer, and the interface to the network control application layer.

The communication layer is the bottom layer in the SDN controller, whose task is to complete the communication between the SDN controller and controlled network devices, which is located at the data level, through the southbound Application Programming Interface (API). The network-wide state management layer is the middle layer of the SDN controller. If the SDN control layer wants to make any final control decisions, for example, configure the flow table in all packet switches for end-to-end forwarding, implement load balancing, or implement some special firewall capability, it is necessary for the controller to master the host information, link information, packet switch information, and information of other equipment controlled by the SDN controller.

The interface to the network control application layer is the top layer of the SDN controller. The interaction between the SDN controller and network control application needs to be done through the northbound API. This API allows network control applications to read or write network state and flow tables in the network-wide state management layer.

There have been some open-source SDN controllers [16], the most representative of which are Open Daylight [17] and Open Network Operating System (ONOS) [18]. The SDN controller maintains the status information of each host and the entire network, which can calculate the best route for each packet and generate its correct forwarding table for each router. In this way, in SDN, the work of routers becomes very simple, by just looking up and forwarding the received packets. It is known that the network equipment is produced by different manufacturers and can be used in different networks. However, with SDN remote controllers, the network equipment has a unified logical switching function.

2.2.3 Introduction of OpenFlow

SDN extends the execution method of traditional data plane match + action, adds new content, and becomes a generalized forwarding, which can be divided into the following two steps:

Step 1 *Matching*: The difference from the traditional method is that SDN could match with the fields in the headers of each layer (data link layer, network layer, and transport layer) in the network architecture.
Step 2 Perform *actions*: SDN not only forwards packets but also performs load balancing, rewriting IP headers [similar to address translation in Network Address Translation (NAT) routers [19]], and artificially blocking or dropping some packets, like the functions of a firewall [20].

In the generalized forwarding of SDN, the device that completes the match + action is not limited to the network layer, so it is no longer called a router, but an OpenFlow switch, packet switch, or more simply a switch. Correspondingly, in SDN, the Flow Table [21] replaces the forwarding table in traditional routers. In this process, the OpenFlow protocol plays an important role [22]. Before introducing the OpenFlow protocol, it is necessary to know about the OpenFlow network, which consists of OpenFlow switches, controllers, and applications on the controller, as shown in Figures 2.2 and 2.3.

The OpenFlow network follows the design principle of separate control and forwarding. The network intelligence is realized by the controller software, which runs at the far end and application program on the controller. The network device forwards high-speed data according to the forwarding decision issued by the controller. The OpenFlow protocol defines the standard interface for communication between the controller and forwarding device in the OpenFlow network (the southbound interface).

Under the OpenFlow network architecture, the controller becomes the core of network processing and faces enormous pressure. In order to meet the function of controller to handle network events and calculate forwarding decisions frequently, OpenFlow defines network forwarding rules in the form of flow matching and adopts the same processing method for a group of data packets with the same characteristics. On the one hand, the controller can achieve a good compromise between scalability and flexibility, realizing variable-granularity network control. On the other hand,

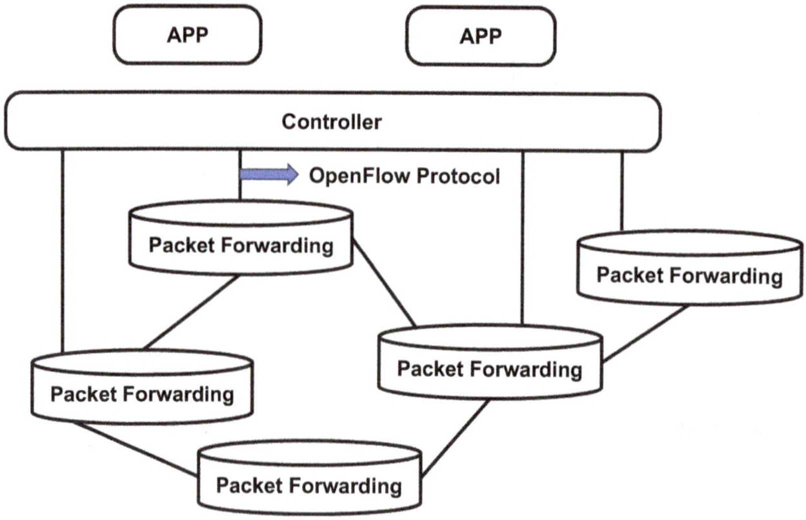

Figure 2.2 Network architecture of OpenFlow

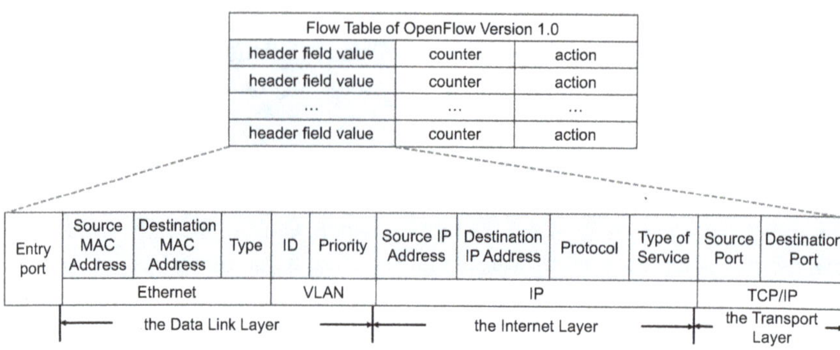

Figure 2.3 OpenFlow table diagram

existing network equipment can be fully utilized to achieve wire-speed forwarding of flow meters [via Ternary Content Addressable Memory (TCAM) [23]].

The flow switching method also enables the OpenFlow network to be backward compatible with IPv4 [24], VLAN [25], Ethernet [26], Multi-Protocol Label Switching (MPLS) [27], and other protocols, supporting semantically independent data packet forwarding. That is, there is no need to distinguish between IP, Media Access Control (MAC) [28], and other forwarding technologies. Therefore, the OpenFlow no longer makes a distinction between switch and router, but uniformly defines the network forwarding device as an OpenFlow switch, whose core components include one or more flow tables, group tables, OpenFlow channels that communicate with external controllers, and the OpenFlow protocol (switch architecture of OpenFlow version 1.4.0).

The OpenFlow protocol is a highly recognized standard. It is the earliest southbound interface protocol of SDN, which defines the communication interface for the controller to manage the OpenFlow switch remotely. Most SDN products use OpenFlow as the communication interface between their control and data planes, although it is not mandatory for SDN. Since its initial release in late 2009, OpenFlow has undergone updates every year. Version 1.5.1 was released in March 2015, following 12 updates, and version 1.3 is considered more mature.

- OpenFlow supports three message types: controller-to-switch, asynchronous, and symmetric. The controller-to-switch message is initiated by the controller to manage and view the network status of the OpenFlow switch.
- The asynchronous message is initiated by the switch to update information, such as network events and switch status changes to the controller.
- The symmetric message is used for connection establishment and heartbeat detection, which can be initiated by the switch or controller.

The OpenFlow provides reliable transmission and processing of the message, which does not provide message acknowledgment automatically, nor does it ensure that messages are processed in sequence. Barrier messages [21] are utilized to process messages in a specified order, instructing the switch to finish processing previous messages before starting to process messages after the barrier. The flow tables in the OpenFlow switch are managed by the SDN remote controller, which uses OpenFlow to manage flow tables in the OpenFlow switch through a secure channel. Each OpenFlow switch must have one or more flow tables, where each flow table contains multiple flow table entries, each of which includes three fields: header field value (or matching field), counter, and action.

- The header field value contains a set of fields used to match the corresponding header of incoming packet, and it is also called a match field [29]. Packets that do not match are discarded or sent to the SDN remote controller for more processing.
- The counter field [30] is a set of counters, one that records the number of packets that have been matched with the flow entry, and the other that records the time elapsed since the last update of flow entry.
- The action field [31] refers to a set of actions. When a packet matches with a flow entry, the OpenFlow switch executes one or more of the following actions indicated by the action field in the flow entry, such as forwarding the packet to the specified port, discarding the packet, and forwarding the packet from multiple ports after replication, then rewriting the header fields of packet (including the headers of the data link layer, the Internet layer, and the transport layer).

To sum up, matching in OpenFlow differs from the layered processing principles of computer network architectures. An OpenFlow switch can process frames of the data link layer, IP datagrams of the Internet layer, and TCP or User Datagram Protocol (UDP) packets of the transport layer [32]. In an SDN network based on the OpenFlow

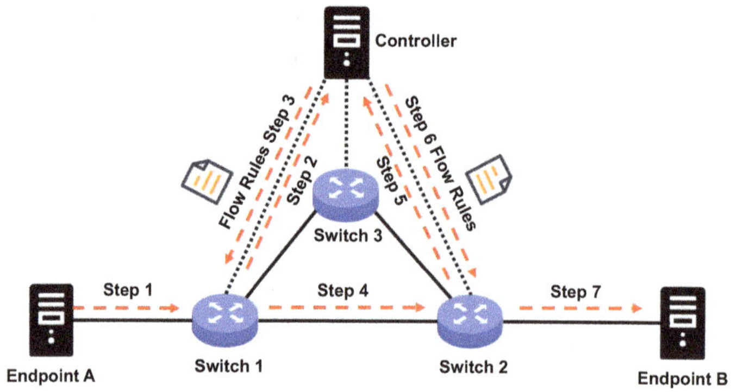

Figure 2.4 OpenFlow-based workflow for SDN

protocol, when endpoint A communicates with endpoint B for the first time, its basic communication flow roughly includes seven steps as shown in Figure 2.4.

Step 1: Endpoint A joins the network and sends data packets to switch 1.
Step 2: Switch 1 checks its own flow table. If there is no entry in the flow table matching the data packet, switch 1 forwards the data packet to the controller through the Packet-In event. Switch 1 can directly send the data packet to the controller through the TCP protocol or use Transport Layer Security (TLS) to encrypt the data packet when sending a message to the controller.
Step 3: After the controller receives the request information of switch 1, it generates the corresponding reply policy and sends the policy to the specified port of switch 1 through the Packet-Out event.
Step 4: Switch 1 executes the response policy issued by the controller and forwards the data packet to switch 2.
Step 5: If there is no match for the data packet in the flow table of switch 2, similar to the processing method of Step 2, switch 2 will forward the received data packet information to the controller through the Packet-In event. If the flow table of switch 2 contains a match, then jump to Step 7, that is, switch 2 forwards the data packet to endpoint B according to the corresponding forwarding rule in the flow table.
Step 6: Similar to Step 3, the controller issues the corresponding response policy to the specified port of switch 2, according to the request information of switch 2.
Step 7: Switch 2 executes the response policy issued by the controller and forwards the data packet to endpoint B.

2.3 Overview of NFV

With the continuous promotion of concept of SDN, different research institutions and standardization organizations have proposed other reference architectures of SDN, which account for the user and industry needs. For example, the European Telecommunications Standards Institute (ESTI) has proposed the Network Functions Virtualization (NFV) architecture from the perspective of network operators [33].

While SDN makes networks programmable by separating the control and data planes, NFV aims to virtualize network functions and deploy them on general-purpose hardware [34]. NFV builds and deploys network functions by developing standard virtualization technologies on industry-standard high-performance servers, switches, and storage devices. Moreover, NFV is proposed to implement network functions in software that can run on industry-standard servers. The functions can be dynamically deployed on demand in different locations in the network without reinstalling new dedicated hardware equipment.

The essence behind NFV technology is that what hardware can do, the software can also achieve. The core idea of NFV is that software decouples with dedicated hardware, and its core technology is virtualization. In addition, in the specific use process, NFV is used in the software platform to support SDN technology as it can exist in physical and virtual servers, which is only necessary to rectify the overall architecture in the specific practice process. In addition, there is a dedicated management system inside NFV, so it can meet the needs of cloud computing and be well connected when applying in the 5G communication system. It is promising that the application of NFV will bring about a network revolution, realizing the transformation of dedicated hardware to general-purpose hardware and on-demand business.

2.3.1 Concept of NFV

NFV is one of the network architectures, which virtualizes network node functions into software modules through Information Technology (IT) virtualization technology. These software modules can be connected according to business flows, providing communication services for enterprises jointly. Technically, NFV provides network services in Virtual Machines (VMs) working in cloud infrastructures, where each VM performs different network operations (e.g., firewall, intrusion detection, deep packet inspection, load balancing, etc.) [35].

Before the emergence of NFV, traditional network equipment was integrated with software and hardware. The equipment was very professional, and specific equipment had its own function realization. The control plane was separated from the device after the introduction of NFV. The control plane was based on VMs, and the VMs were based on Cloud Operating System (Cloud OS). A unified virtualization platform is in the data center, and network devices can be virtualized through the Cloud OS [36]. In this way, when enterprises need to deploy new services, they only need to create corresponding virtual machines on the open virtual machine platform. After that, they can install software packages for corresponding functions. This method is called network function virtualization.

The application of NFV will redefine the network device architecture. In the NFV architecture [37], the bottom layer is specific physical devices, such as servers, storage, and network devices, used to realize computational virtualization, storage virtualization, and network virtualization (that is, the control plane of network device is separated from the underlying hardware, and the control plane of device is installed on the server virtual machine). The computational virtualization refers to creating multiple virtual systems on one server. The storage virtualization refers to multiple storage devices being virtualized into one logical storage device. The third concept, network virtualization, means that the underlying hardware is separated from the control plane of a network device, which is installed on the server virtual machine. More surprisingly, diverse service software can be installed on the virtualized device.

2.3.2 Advantage of NFV

NFV is a virtualization technology, which deploys software network functions on a stable commercial computing resource platform. Accordingly, NFV avoids the complex connection configuration in the traditional heterogeneous network function deployment process. Combined with flexible load balancing and other management mechanisms, it effectively solves the problems in traditional network functional hardware devices, which are caused by connection configuration and network traffic overload, including high equipment price, management difficulties, and high failure rate. Generally speaking, NFV has the following advantages [38]:

- **Low cost.** Traditional special equipment is expensive and has low substitutability. Whenever there is a problem with the basic dedicated equipment, the machine with trouble must be replaced by the same type of machine to make the communication system run. However, after adopting NFV technology, dedicated servers can replace special-purpose servers and reduce the demand for special-purpose equipment. In addition to this, NFV helps to reduce equipment costs, effectively control the construction cost of communication network systems, and reduce energy overhead.
- **Fast deployment.** NFV can use the decoupling of software and hardware to improve network elasticity, thereby shortening the deployment cycle of equipment and business innovation cycle of network operation. It also increases the speed of market launch and enables operators to reduce the network maturity cycle to a considerable degree.
- **High flexibility.** NFV can introduce precise services based on geographic location and user group, expanding/contracting services as needed in a short period. Additionally, during the system migration process, using NFV increases flexibility and improves the fault tolerance rate. The debugger can delete according to the actual needs, and the work efficiency is greatly improved.
- **High openness.** The mobility of functions increases when network functions are virtualized, and as a result, it can be more convenient to carry out new businesses. NFV improves business innovation and shortens the development of new business cycles. Based on the security of information transmission, the quality of business is fundamentally guaranteed, thus enabling a broader and more diverse ecosystem while promoting openness at the same time. The utilization of NFV also encourages more innovation and introduces new business, using lower risk to bring new revenue growth.
- **Easy to configure.** The network can be configured on demand in near real-time based on requirements, while network resources are dynamically optimized using general-purpose hardware and software to implement functions. Network devices can coexist in multiple versions and tenants. A single platform can provide services for different applications, users, and tenants, allowing operators to

share resources across services and various customer groups. The devices also support multi-user sharing and are likely to tailor network functions.

2.3.3 NFV framework

Implementing NFV technology in different ways results in diverse NFV architecture frameworks, while a chaotic NFV architecture framework can hinder the development and popularization of NFV technology. Therefore, ETSI standardizes the NFV structure framework, which aims to form a unified NFV standard structure, simplify the development of Virtualized Network Function (VNF), and promote the deployment of NFV. The overall architecture of NFV is as follows, which can be divided into three parts, mainly including VNF, Network Function Virtualization Infrastructure (NFVI), and Network Function Virtualization Management and Orchestration (NFV M&O) [39].

The first part (blue part in Figure 2.5) is the VNF module, which is the same in terms of functional performance as the network function implemented by dedicated hardware. Network functions are feature modules in traditional network infrastructure, with fixed internal functions and well-defined external interfaces. A network function can consist of multiple components and can be deployed on various virtual machines. Each virtual machine implements one of the components, and different virtual machines manage different VNF components. EM infers to the network element management function.

The second part (orange part in Figure 2.5) is the NFVI module. NFVI is a general term for the software and hardware structure that provides the environment

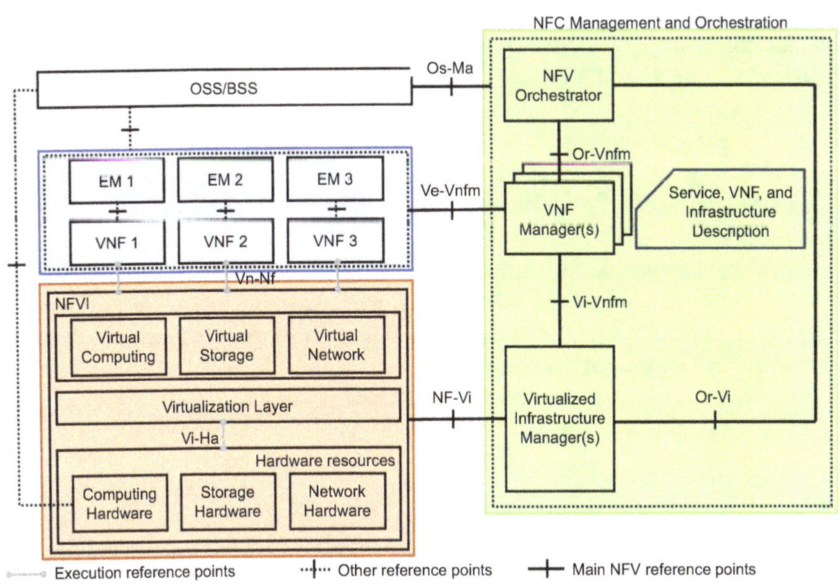

Figure 2.5 Architecture of NFV

required for NFV deployment, management, and operation. NFVI includes hardware resources, a virtualization layer, and virtualized resources. Among them, hardware resources mainly include computing resources (composed of computing hardware devices), storage resources (composed of storage devices), and network resources (composed of nodes and connection links). These hardware resources provide computing power, storage power, and network connectivity to the VNF through a virtualization layer (e.g., VM, virtual machine manager, etc.), which is mainly responsible for abstracting hardware resources and decoupling VNF with underlying hardware resources. VNF can run on logically independent physical hardware resources by using physical resources abstracted and logically segmented by the virtualization layer. Virtualized resources [40] are abstractions of computing resources, network resources, and storage resources. Similar to hardware resources, virtualized resources include virtualized computing resources, virtualized storage resources, and virtualized network resources. Virtualized computing resources and virtualized storage resources, in a data center environment, usually provide computing resources and storage resources to the upper VNF in the form of VMs. Virtualized network resources usually refer to virtual nodes and virtual network links, where virtual nodes are software with hosting or routing functions (e.g., operating systems in VMs). Virtual links provide mutual connectivity between virtual nodes, which makes virtual nodes have physical link properties that can change dynamically.

The third part (green part in Figure 2.5) is the NFV M&O, from bottom to top are Virtualized Infrastructure Manager(s) (VIM), Virtualization Network Function Managers (VNFM), and Network Function Virtualization Orchestrator (NFVO). The VIM [41] is mainly responsible for monitoring resource usage in NFVI. Beyond that, the VIM will perform lifecycle management and allocation scheduling of software/hardware resources in NFVI, such as allocation of Central Processing Unit (CPU) resources, network link bandwidth, etc. The VNF managers are mainly responsible for the management of VNF life cycle, such as the initialization, update, extension, termination of VNF, etc. The NFV orchestrator [42] is mainly responsible for coordinating the VNF manager and virtualization facility manager, realizing the deployment and implementation of network function service chain on the virtualization facility. In addition, the NFV M&O sets a database and provides a series of standard interfaces. The database stores the information provided by the network administrator, such as VNF deployment rules and VNF life cycle attributes. Standard interfaces are responsible for the communication between different components in NFV M&O and cooperation of NFV M&O, with traditional network management systems (e.g., operation support systems and business support systems). NFV M&O can realize the coordinated management of VNFs and traditional equipment, through the combined use of databases and these interfaces.

2.3.4 Application of NFV

NFV is used in various network scenarios widely due to the advantages of cost-saving, simple operation management, and flexible deployment. NFV has related applications in both data layer processing and control layer management. Below are five examples of NFV industrial applications to illustrate.

2.3.4.1 Cloud data center network function virtualization

Due to the fixedness, traditional hardware network functions cannot provide users with isolated and flexibly scalable network function services, which support multi-tenancy in cloud data centers [43]. With the rise of NFV technology, cloud data centers can provide themselves and users with isolated, efficient, and flexible network function services by deploying VNF. By using NFV, cloud data centers can provide flexible and reliable network functions for their own data center network to handle all network traffic passing through. Also, the utilization of NFV enables independent configurable network services by running VNF on VMs of different tenants, achieving multi-tenant support for network functions.

2.3.4.2 Cellular base station virtualization

The Radio Access Network (RAN) [44,45] of traditional cellular networks usually consists of independent base stations. These base stations process and transmit wireless signals for the mobile phone, forwarding its data to the core network [46] through the backhaul link [47]. However, the processing power of traditional RAN base stations is usually not fully used, and there will be excess processing power most of the time. Moreover, base stations with excess processing power cannot share idle processing power. In addition, the planning and optimization of traditional RAN base station deployment are complex and difficult to accomplish. The deployment of entire base station system facilities also requires a lot of space.

Over time, the RAN network architecture has evolved from an integrated base station to a distributed base station. To realize flexible virtualized cellular network base stations, the operators have also been able to use the network structure of distributed base stations by virtualizing Building Baseband Unit (BBU, the digital functional unit) pool resources in the data center in the form of cloud RAN. The Cloud RAN [48] reduces the deployment of hardware base stations by using the NFV architecture (centralization and virtualization of BBUs), significantly reducing operators' operating, energy, and housing rental costs. In addition, taking advantage of the dynamic expansion and resource sharing of NFV technology, cloud RAN saves a lot of computing resource deployment overhead. According to statistics, cloud RAN can reduce computing resource deployment by 22% for base station traffic [48] through dynamic sharing processing.

2.3.4.3 Mobile core network virtualization

Cloud Evolved Packet Core (EPC) [49,50] solves the problems in traditional mobile core networks by applying NFV technology. The VNF goals implemented by cloud EPC include Mobility Management Entities (MME), Home Subscriber Server (HSS), Packet Data Network Gateway, can also be written as PDN Gateway (PGW), and Policy and Charging Rules Function (PCRF). In addition, cellular network operators can achieve better Voice over LTE (VoLTE), which is supported by virtualizing some components in the IP Multimedia Subsystem (IMS), such as Call Session Control Functions (CSCF), etc.

By implementing the mentioned VNF above, cloud EPC eliminates the geographical limitation of distributed network resources, building a more intelligent, flexible, and scalable network architecture. When encountering resources or performance bottlenecks, the cloud EPC can share and allocate hardware resources by utilizing NFV dynamic expansion and resource sharing. At the same time, cloud EPC can also reduce equipment deployment overhead. The cloud EPC can also provide reliable and stable network services when local resources fail. Through NFV technology, cloud EPC can realize flexible deployment of PGW. For example, deploying PGW and base station (eNodeB) together can avoid long-distance tunnels.

2.3.4.4 Home network virtualization

Network service providers typically provide home services to users through Customer Premise Equipment (CPE) [51]. Traditional CPE includes Residential Gateways (RGs) for Internet connectivity and Set-Top-Boxes (STBs) for multimedia services. Due to the interactive network flow control capabilities, the transmission of Internet Protocol Television (IPTV) [52] service becomes complicated, such as fast-forward and rewind. By deploying virtualized STBs and related virtualization components of residential gateways such as firewalls, Dynamic Host Configuration Protocol (DHCP), Virtual Private Network Gateway (VPN Gateway), NAT, etc., in the data center to ensure the physical connectivity from users to the Internet, network service operators only need to provide inexpensive and low-maintenance network connection equipment.

This virtualized network architecture brings many benefits to network operators and users. First, operators reduce the burden of operator product maintenance by avoiding frequent maintenance and updating for CPE equipment. Second, the NFV architecture can provide extensive storage capacity and realize the sharing of multiple devices in different locations through resource sharing, helping service providers improve the quality of user experience. Furthermore, the NFV architecture can achieve the controllable content supply capability of content providers to users through the dynamic quality of service management and controlled sharing between application traffic. Finally, the NFV architecture can minimize the dependence of different services on CPE and realize the smooth introduction of new services.

2.3.4.5 Virtualization of Content Delivery Network

The number of netizens has surged with the development of Internet. The network access path is long when users use the network, so the quality of users' access has been seriously affected [53]. The problem of poor access quality is particularly prominent in areas where remote Internet users are rapidly increasing, especially when the link between users and websites is congested by sudden large-traffic data. To solve this problem, researchers proposed the Content Delivery Network (CDN). CDN services are usually deployed at the edge of network, as shown in Figure 2.6. With the help of CDN services, the network distance between users and content has been greatly shortened, providing users with a better network experience.

However, CDN providers and operators use dedicated hardware to provide CDN services to users currently. Due to the design of hardware resources that are to be fully loaded at peak times, these dedicated cache resources are not fully utilized at most times except peak periods. In addition, the ability of dedicated equipment to

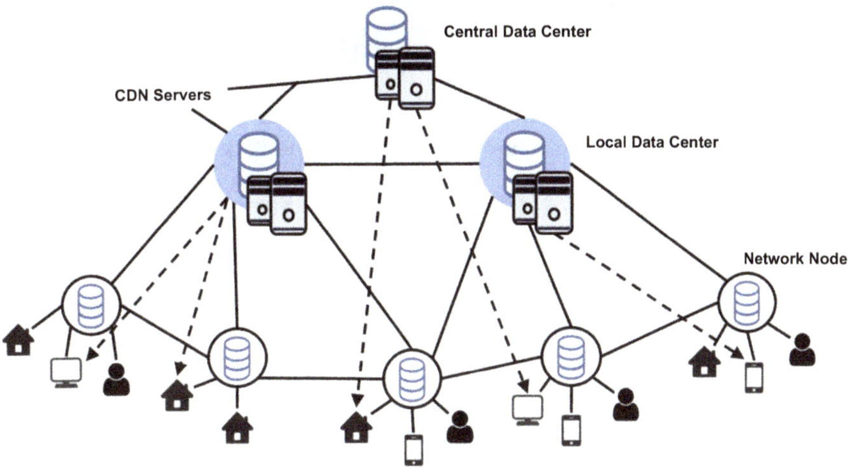

Figure 2.6 Traditional deployment of CDN

deal with burst traffic is limited, and the CDN nodes deployed by different service providers are currently independent of each other, so the utilization efficiency of the overall capacity of the CDN is not high enough.

The emergence of the idea of decoupling software and hardware of NFV technology is able to solve the existing problems of CDN. Using NFV, CDN nodes can be deployed in the standard environment as virtual applications. As there is less demand for resources in the CDN, the resources can be allocated to other types of VNF dynamically, realizing the dynamic invocation of CDN resources. In addition, since VNF exists in the form of software, if new requirements arise during the information delivery process, they can also be responded to through flexible deployment of software.

2.4 Security of SDN and NFV

Note that SDN and NFV are often mentioned together in 5G technology [54,55]. SDN and NFV optimize modern networks from different perspectives, which are independent of each other and form their own systems, making the entire network programmable and flexible. However, NFV and SDN must complement and integrate each other in the future. For example, using NFV technology in SDN can provide SDN with more flexible network services. Using SDN with NFV M&O can control network traffic forwarding efficiently. What's more, the combination of SDN and NFV provides programmable network connections between VNFs to the NFV platform, achieving efficient and flexible traffic scheduling. The combined use of SDN and NFV will have a significant impact on the development of future communication networks, but it will also bring new problems and challenges.

2.4.1 Security of SDN

2.4.1.1 Comparison of SDN safety models and traditional cyber security models

The centralized control of SDN enables the controller to have great control capability over network traffic. Also, the controller has unique advantages in the fine grain and real-time push of various configuration strategies under the centralized control of SDN. However, this working mode also brings a larger impact on the safety model of network, mainly reflected in two aspects.

On the one hand, SDN is different from traditional networks in how to control information flows. As shown in Figure 2.7(a), security devices such as firewalls are deployed at key positions in the traditional network, and information flows forcibly flowed through these security devices so that security devices can monitor and detect them in real time. Compared with traditional networks, SDN is a flow rule-driven network. The flow rules are issued by the controller. Whether and when the information flow in the SDN flows through a certain security device is determined by the flow rules, and thus, the physical security device itself does not have the right to decide. As shown in Figure 2.7(b), if the flow rules, which are issued by the controller, specify the forwarding method of data packets to execute according to path 1 (red path), since the data packets in path 1 flow through the SDN security device, the security device can check the data packet according to the relevant security policy. Conversely, if the forwarding method of data packets is performed according to path 2 (green path), then the packets can bypass the security device in the SDN, failing pre-deployed security measures.

On the other hand, SDN is different from traditional networks in obtaining cyber security situation information. In the traditional network, as shown in Figure 2.7(a), when the administrator needs to obtain the security situation information of current network, due to the lack of a unified control center in the network, the administrator needs to send a status request information to multiple devices at the same time. After the administrator evaluates the received status information comprehensively, the current security situation information of network can be obtained. In SDN, as shown in

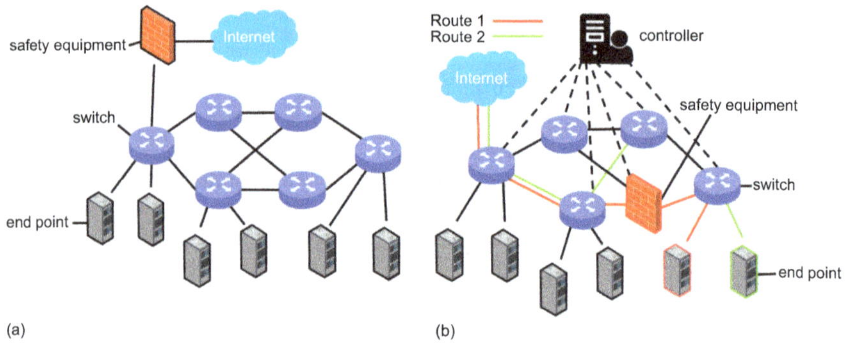

Figure 2.7 Security model of traditional network and security model of SDN (a) Security model of traditional network (b) Security model of SDN

Figure 2.7(b), the controller, as the command and control center of entire network, has established a global view of the network, and can obtain various state information of the entire network in real time. Therefore, the security situation information of network can be easily obtained directly from the controller. However, this convenient way, which is to obtain network situation information in SDN, is also easily exploited by attackers, enabling them to obtain the security situation information of network, without difficulty and wait for an opportunity to launch a large-scale attack.

2.4.1.2 Security issues of OpenFlow

According to OpenFlow, the controller and switch are connected through a secure channel, which uses TLS to encrypt and authenticate messages [56]. Since the authentication process of TLS involves multiple handshakes and information confirmation steps, the operation is relatively cumbersome. Therefore, after OpenFlow version 1.3.0, the new version of OpenFlow sets the TLS protocol as an optional option, allowing the control channel not to take TLS encryption. Although security solutions related to SDN have been proposed continuously, OpenFlow still faces some significant security issues in recent years.

- **Secure channel optional.** Since protocols after OpenFlow version 1.3.0 make TLS optional, SDN networks that lack TLS protocol protection are vulnerable to eavesdropping, controller impersonation, or other attacks on OpenFlow channels.
- **The vulnerability of TLS.** Versions of the OpenFlow before 1.5.1 did not specify the reference specification and protocol version number, which are used for TLS encryption. Inconsistencies or errors in the version number may also cause interoperability failures, bringing some security issues to SDN. At the same time, the vulnerability of TLS protocol itself also makes the OpenFlow protocol face security risks, such as man-in-the-middle attacks. In addition, although the TLS can improve the security of channel between the switch and controller, it cannot prevent the switch from modifying the flow rules.
- **Lack of security specifications for communication between multiple controllers.** The existing OpenFlow protocol only gives the communication specifications between controllers and switches. However, it does not specify security protocols and standards for communication between multiple controllers, which results in communication between controllers still facing security issues such as authentication and data synchronization.

2.4.1.3 Typical security problems in SDN

There are eight typical security threats in SDN as follows:

- **Legitimacy and consistency issues of flow rules (SDN-specific).** Multiple custom or third-party-provided applications are running on the controller at the same time, and the flow rules generated by these applications may compete with, conflict with, or override each other. Due to time delay or malicious tampering by attackers, the flow rules sent down to the controller and switch are inconsistent.

Additionally, there is currently no efficient and secure synchronization scheme for flow rules between different controllers.

- **Vulnerability of the controller (SDN-specific).** It means the most serious threats, failures, or malicious controllers in SDN can put the entire SDN network at risk. Moreover, conventional IDS technology makes it difficult to discover the originator of a specific attack in SDN and is not yet sufficient to ensure the security of SDN.
- **Lack of trust mechanism between controller and application (SDN-specific).** Between controllers and applications, there is a lack of effective trust assessment and management mechanisms. What's more, the technique for verifying that network devices are secure is not the same as that for applications. In addition, malicious applications can be easily developed, then authorized legitimate applications can be tampered with and applied to the controller.
- **Threats between control layer and infrastructure layer (e.g., OpenFlow protocol security) (SDN-specific).** This mainly guides to the security threats faced by the Interface Protocol, such as Denial of Service (DoS)/Distributed Denial of Service (DDoS) attacks or data theft. In addition, TLS/Secure Sockets Layer (SSL) encryption is based on Public Key Infrastructure (PKI), which is insufficient to guarantee secure communication between the switch and controller. What's more, some of the existing literature has analyzed the security issues of TLS/SSL protocol.
- **Vulnerability of the management station (non-SDN-specific).** An attacker can exploit the vulnerability of management station to access the controller of SDN. The vulnerability of management stations also exists in traditional networks, but the centralized control of SDN results in the vulnerability, which can quickly scale to the entire network.
- **Vulnerability of the switch (non-SDN-specific).** An attack on a switch can cause packets in the network to appear partially abnormal. If an attacker sends false requests through the attacked switch to the controller or other switches, the threat can spread rapidly throughout the network.
- **Lack of effective trusted resources for forensics, remediation, etc. (non-SDN-specific).** Secure and reliable forensic mechanisms are required with trusted resources for SDN to repair faults, which ensures rapid network recovery.
- **Fake/False network data (non-SDN-specific).** This is mainly generated by illegal users or devices, such as forged stream rules, etc.

According to the logical architecture of separation of control and forwarding, the security problems faced by SDN can be divided into five aspects, as shown in Figure 2.8 [57].

- **Security of the application layer.** The application layer mainly includes various applications. In SDN, in addition to the flow rules formulated by the administrator, some flow rules will also be formulated by OpenFlow applications, security service applications, and other third-party applications. The flow rules will be sent to the relevant switches and network devices through the controller. Nowadays, the security protection mechanism for the application is not perfect.

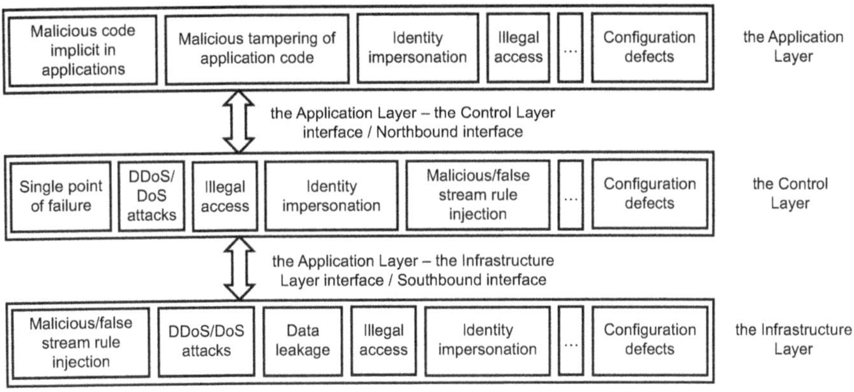

Figure 2.8 Main threats in each layer of SDN

Various switches and network devices in the infrastructure layer fully trust the flow rules issued by the controller, executing them without thinking. Once these applications participating in the formulation of flow rules are tampered with and attacked, it will bring unpredictable harm to SDN. Therefore, the security threats that the application layer will have mainly include malicious code implicit in the application, malicious tampering of the application code, identity counterfeiting, illegal access, and configuration defects of the application itself.

- **Security of the control layer.** The controller is the core of SDN and the weakest link in the security chain. SDN conducts centralized control of the network through the controller. Attackers connected to the controller will have the ability to control the entire network, which will bring unpredictable harm to SDN. The typical security problem of the control layer is the single point of failure of the controller caused by centralized control, which is mainly reflected in two aspects:
  1) **DoS/DDoS attack:** The attacker creates a series of illegal accesses that cause the controller to overload, resulting in the controller system resources being unavailable to legitimate users. Since the new flow request arrives at the switch, if there is no matching flow rule on the switch, the data packet or the header of data packet will be forwarded to the controller, while the controller will formulate the corresponding reply flow rules. Therefore, attackers will use switches in the SDN to initiate a large number of false request messages to the controller, causing the controller to overload and interrupt the requested service of a legitimate switch.
  2) **The controller is logically or physically compromised:** This mainly refers to the physical or logical destruction of critical controllers in the SDN, resulting in the denial of user's reasonable request for service. In addition, the security threats faced by the control layer mainly include illegal access, identity counterfeiting, malicious/fake flow rule injection, and configuration defects of the controller.

- **Security of the infrastructure layer.** The infrastructure layer is composed of essential equipment such as a switch, which is mainly responsible for data processing, forwarding, and state collection, having absolute trust in the flow rules issued by the controller. Therefore, the main security threats faced by this layer include malicious/fake flow rule injection, DDoS/DoS attacks, data leakage, illegal access, identity counterfeiting, and configuration defects of the switch. In addition, the infrastructure layer may also face threats, such as switch flow table confusion caused by disordered control instructions from fake controllers.
- **Security of southbound interface.** It mainly refers to the security threats caused by the vulnerability of OpenFlow [58]. The OpenFlow security channel uses SSL/TLS to encrypt data. However, the SSL/TLS protocol itself is insecure, and the specifications after OpenFlow version 1.3.0 make TLS an optional option, allowing the control channel to take no security measures. Therefore, the southbound interface faces security threats such as eavesdropping and controller counterfeiting.
- **Security of northbound interface.** The standardization of northbound API has become a hot topic in SDN [59]. Due to the wide variety and continuous updating of applications, there is currently no unified regulation, which is about the authentication method and authentication granularity of the northbound interface, for the application. In addition, relative to the southbound interface between the control layer and the infrastructure layer, the trust relationship established by the northbound interface between the controller and application is more fragile. Thus, attackers can take advantage of the openness and programmability of northbound interface to access some important resources in the controller. As a result, the threshold for attacking northbound interfaces is lower for attackers. Currently, the security problems faced by northbound interfaces mainly include illegal access, data leakage, message tampering, identity counterfeiting, vulnerabilities in the application itself, and new vulnerabilities introduced by different applications when cooperating.

So far, with the continuous emergence of various security solutions, though the security problems faced by SDN have been alleviated to a certain extent, some critical security problems still exist. The future security research of SDN will also focus on the following aspects, including the design and development of a new controller/network operating system for security, cross-domain collaborative security communication of controllers, standardization of northbound interface security protocols, DoS/DDoS attack detection and prevention technology for the controller.

2.4.2 Security of NFV

With the maturity of NFV, the industry has gradually adopted NFV in engineering. However, the security problems existing in NFV still cannot be ignored. Starting from the implementation of NFV, the security problems can be divided into two categories, one of which is in traditional NFV architecture, and the other is in NFV outsourcing scenarios.

2.4.2.1 Security issues in traditional NFV architecture

The security problems in NFV architecture mainly include concerns about the issues in NFVI and VNF. Among them, the security problems in NFVI are divided into NFVI external management security problems and NFVI's own security problems.

- NFVI external management threats are mainly due to the improper operation of NFV platform facility managers, and such security problems can usually be avoided by formulating strict facility operating procedures.
- NFVI's own threats usually come from design and implementation flaws, which are in the hardware and software of itself. Therefore, devices in NFVI should reduce their threats through a secure authentication process.

Security threats in VNFs mainly come from defects in VNF management and implementation. Therefore, VNFs should adopt standard security mechanisms to authenticate, authorize, encrypt, and verify to enhance security for the management and operation of VNFs. For example, VNFs can use standard authentication and authorization mechanisms to perform access control of virtual machines, encrypt sensitive data using standard encryption algorithms, and use secure network protocols such as TLS or IPSec to enhance the security of network communications.

2.4.2.2 Security issues in NFV outsourcing scenario

Sherry *et al.* [60] proposed the concept of enterprise network function outsourcing, that is, using a Domain Name System-based approach to redirect enterprise network traffic to the cloud platform with minimal delay. It realizes Access Point Location and Mobility Estimation for Broadband (APLOMEB), an NFV platform with simple expansion functions and configuring network function topology on the cloud platform. This solution can utilize economies of scale of cloud computing platforms to reduce the overhead of deploying network functions within the enterprise network. Since the NFV platform is outsourced to a third-party cloud service platform, the operation of VNF is completely dependent on the physical resources and personnel management, which are provided by an untrusted third party. Therefore, deploying VNF on a third-party cloud platform has the following problems:

- Cloud service providers may replace user-desired VNF with cheap VNF in order to save costs and interfere with the normal operation of VNF maliciously.
- There may be policy configuration errors in VNF deployment in the cloud platform.
- The privacy of enterprise network traffic flowing through the cloud platform cannot be guaranteed.

Therefore, in the NFV outsourcing scenario, how to verify whether the execution of network functions and network Service Function Chain (SFC) is consistent with user expectations has become a challenge. Another challenge is the privacy protection of outsourced traffic. Nowadays, the academic community mainly realizes the verification of NF and SFC by designing verification protocols, which are based on cryptography and statistical theory.

However, using cryptography and statistical theory to solve problems, such as traffic privacy problems in the NFV platform outsourcing scenario and VNF execution correctness verification problems, is usually limited, less practical, and difficult to design. With the development of trusted computing, the rise of trusted hardware provides new solutions to security problems in the NFV platform outsourcing scenario. Here, in an untrusted high-level operating system, Software Guard eXtension (SGX) technology of Intel, as the latest trusted computing technology, can provide an isolated runtime environment and remote authentication functions for the program, so as to ensure that the deployment of program is correct in the untrusted third-party cloud service platform, as well as operational integrity and privacy of the program.

In general, to solve the traffic privacy and verification of correctness of function execution problems of NFV technology in outsourcing scenarios, the current cryptographic search and the use of trusted hardware can be used, despite each having its own merits. The encryption search method does not need additional hardware support, but the implementation is complex (supports fewer NF operations), inefficient, and consumes a large number of resources. The trusted hardware method is simple and efficient, supporting arbitrary NF operations. However, it requires special hardware support with additional hardware overhead.

2.5 Expansion of SDN and NFV

SDN and NFV revolutionize traditional network management through network virtualization and centralized control, providing greater flexibility and scalability. This revolution lays the foundation for the development of technologies in WAN, SD-WAN, and Intent-Based Networking (IBN). SD-WAN simplifies WAN management by leveraging SDN and NFV technologies, enabling intelligent traffic allocation and cost optimization. IBN further enhances the efficiency and security of network management through automation and Artificial Intelligence (AI), based on SDN technology, enabling the network to better adapt to changing business needs and technical environments.

2.5.1 Introduction of SD-WAN

In the existing literature, SD-WAN is referred to as a combination of SDN and NFV approaches, connecting SDN, NFV, Cloud Computing (CC), and comprehensive area network services (e.g., broadband internet services) [61,62]. The SD-WAN architecture is similar to the SDN architecture and consists of three architectural planes: the infrastructure plane or data plane, the control plane, and the orchestration plane.

- **The data plane.** The data plane is capable of establishing connections through private and public IP/WAN infrastructures, designed to simplify communication between geographically separated sites as well as with cloud applications and services. To do this, SD-WAN creates its own software-managed logical infrastructure on top of the existing physical infrastructure. This type of network is called an overlay, and the existing physical infrastructure is called an underlay. Although SD-WAN overlay networks are generally unified and consistent, the physical infrastructure of a primary WAN network is often heterogeneous and decentralized. Overlay networks can logically create several types of links (star, entire grid, partial grid, point-to-point, controller after branch, branch after branch, etc.). Network overlay features include support for VPN networks, which can be Layer 2 (L2 VPN) or Layer 3 (L3 VPN) VPNs. From a routing perspective, it supports IPv4 and IPv6 addressing, as well as multicast capabilities.

- **The control plane.** SD-WAN operates on a similar principle to SDN, centralizing control logic by separating the control plane from the data plane. The primary entity of this plane is the controller (or controllers), which can be located in a branch office, headquarters, data center, or the cloud. This layer controls the configuration of connected devices, while the Customer Premises Equipment (CPE) is connected to the controller via a security control connection (Southbound API). The federation and clustering of controllers can be implemented using an East-West API. This layer is also responsible for optimizing the traffic sent through the VPN tunnel to different types of services, such as branch services, data center services, and Cloud as a Service. Programming of SD-WAN services is implemented through the Northbound API interface for orchestrator entities (or managers), primarily using the Representational State Transfer Application Programming Interface (RestAPI).
- **The orchestration plane.** The orchestration plane provides a business policy framework addressing service security and corporate governance policies [63].

API is one of the most essential communication tools in SD-WAN and can be divided into three categories. Through API calls, applications communicate with controllers, or controllers communicate with CPE devices (Figure 2.9).

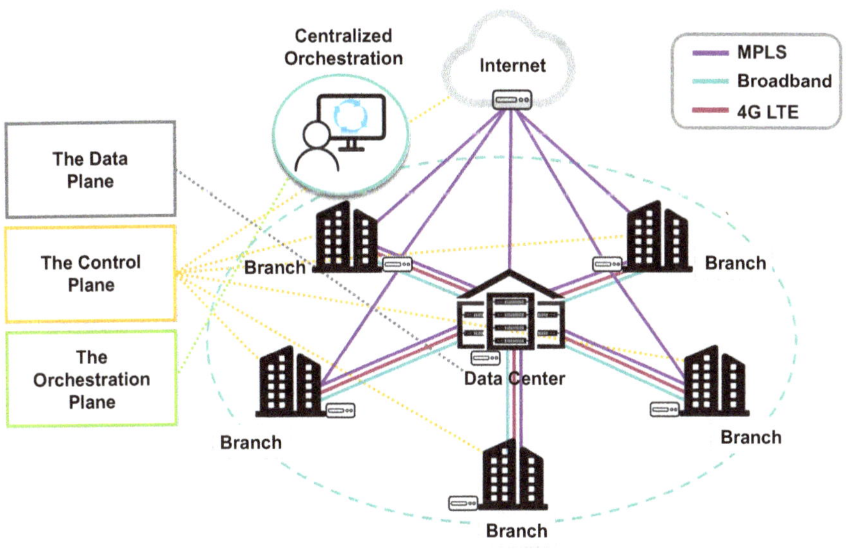

Figure 2.9 The architecture of SD-WAN

- **The Southbound API.** The communication between the CPE and the controller is called the Southbound API. From an SD-WAN vendor's perspective, Fortinet, VeloCloud, and VersaNetwork use RestAPI as the Southbound API. Cisco Viptela, Nokia, and Riverbed use their own protocols.
- **The Northbound API.** The Northbound API allows controllers to communicate with external applications. These applications can send control information to the controller or obtain state data from the controller. From the analysis of SD-WAN manufacturers, those using open Southbound API also use open Northbound API.
- **The East-West API.** The East-West API is communication between the same entity, such as between two CPEs or two controllers. For most SD-WAN solutions, there is not much information about the East-West API, with the exception that Cisco Viptela uses its own Overlay Management Protocol over Datagram Transport Layer Security/TLS for controller communication, and Nokia Nuage uses Multiprotocol Border Gateway Protocol for controller federalization.

2.5.2 Advantage of SD-WAN

From the customer's perspective, SD-WAN offers the following benefits:

- **Application visibility.** SD-WAN customers can "see" the entire infrastructure and drill down to the traffic level of a particular application. This mechanism provides an opportunity to identify issues more efficiently.
- **Alerts and notifications.** With SD-WAN, administrators can obtain end-to-end reporting of issues, such as Service Level Agreement (SLA) breaches, without tracking.
- **Cloud proxies.** SD-WAN can be used as a tool and motivation to drive further cloud migration, while providing the ability to see what is happening in the cloud environment down to the application layer.
- **Centralized control of application and security policies–greater flexibility and security.** SD-WAN provides tools to address application and security policies, configure/tune network behavior, and set or manage SLAs.
- **Production portal.** SD-WAN provides a single environment where all functions are provided centrally, rather than using multiple applications to manage existing WAN solutions.
- **High availability and resilience.** SD-WAN uses robust, dynamically resolved redundancy solutions, including device redundancy, path redundancy, application redundancy, performance tuning, and load balancing capabilities.

2.5.3 Introduction of IBN

Advanced network technologies offer a wealth of services to end users, network operators, and administrators [64]. They also make the network configuration process cumbersome to meet the needs of different stakeholders and applications. Therefore, there is a need to simplify the management and configuration of the network in a way that may be autonomous and automatic. IBN is a paradigm designed to enable flexible, agile, and simplified network configuration with minimal external intervention.

IBN is an emerging approach to loosely coupled interactions between applications and network operators, allowing applications to express desired operational goals with the utilization of more appropriate terms. On the other hand, IBN allows network operating systems the flexibility to achieve these goals according to their own optimization processes. Users can express their goals through appropriate APIs in broad, high-level specifications known as intents [65]. The original goal of IBN was to increase the automation level of network management and simplify the network configuration process [66]. Still, more recently, IBN has expanded its scope to cover different levels of intent (e.g., service intent, operational intent) to address the multi-level business relationships involved in the emerging NFV ecosystem (e.g., application providers, network operators, service providers, application developers) [67].

As depicted in Figure 2.10, the IBN approach is made possible through the mediation of the Intent Layer. The Intent Layer manages and regulates the lifecycle of intent requests emanating from the application layer, achieved through fulfillment and assurance actions [68]. More specifically, fulfillment actions deal with the intent from the user initiating the intent to its implementation in the network, including orchestrating any required coordinated configuration actions. Assurance actions ensure that the network meets the intended goals of the intent after fulfillment by collecting, aggregating, and evaluating monitoring data in real-time. These two actions are achieved through the synergistic work of the Intent Layer functional modules.

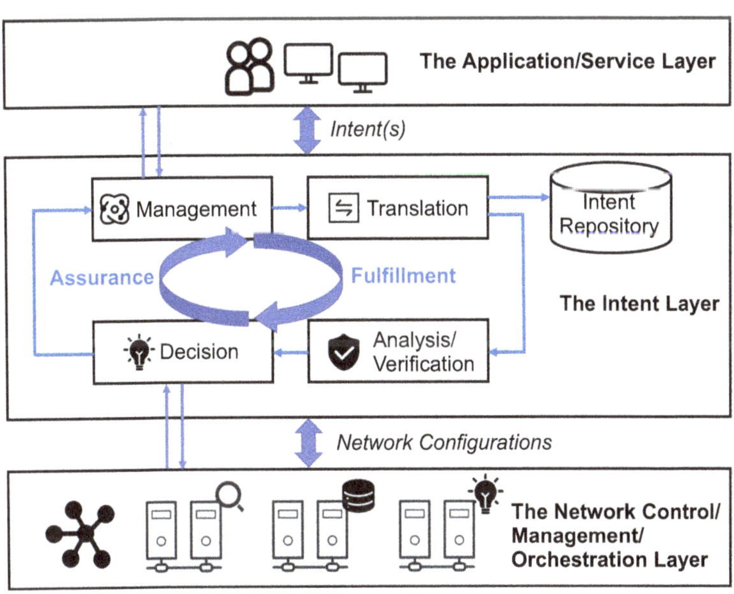

Figure 2.10 The architecture of intent-based networking

- The intent management block processes the intent issued by the user and, if eligible, forwards it to the translation block. The translation block analyzes intents, then formulates corresponding configuration and provisioning actions based on the network's state, and analysis results in the Intent Repository. The Intent Repository contains intent models that support the mapping between intents and the desired set of policies or configurations. The semantics in intent requests can be expressed in different ways depending on the user. For example, a user at the application layer may use more natural language. Therefore, intent translation may require multiple steps and splitting depending on the model. Intent translation may also involve functions and algorithms that perform optimization (e.g., path calculation algorithms, service instance selection) and be able to learn how to achieve the best results.
- Subsequently, the translation block forwards the configuration plan to the verification block to perform the verification, i.e., check whether the intent can be effectively executed based on the current network state. The verification block provides relevant information to the decision block, deciding whether the configuration plan can actually be implemented in the network. If an intent cannot be executed within the network, the decision block needs to trigger optimization procedures or remedial actions by notifying the intent management block, and cascading to trigger the translation block to take timely corrective translation measures. If the intent can be executed, the configuration plan is automatically deployed in the network by utilizing the underlying network management/control/orchestration system and coordinated by the decision block.
- After the intent is implemented and executed in the network, the validation block continuously performs validity verification, i.e., checks whether the configuration execution makes the network behave as expected based on the current network state monitoring data. If the verification fails, the translator is triggered again through the decision and intention management blocks to drive optimization or remediation solutions. The decision block is also responsible for the overall monitoring of the aggregated network state and configuration data, then reports the monitored data to the user.

Ultimately, through the above operations, IBN enables users to interact with the Intent Layer without learning the underlying system's technology-specific language. On the other hand, IBN enables network providers to improve the flexibility and availability of the network, manage the network as a whole at a higher level of abstraction, and continuously verify that user goals are being achieved. Therefore, IBN not only helps to improve network automation and flexibility, but also improves the robustness of the network through closed-loop and continuous learning, thus reducing costs through dynamic network operation and maintenance.

2.5.4 Challenges of IBN

The Internet Engineering Task Force (IETF) recently proposed the concept of IBN as a new approach to increase automation and simplify the network configuration process. However, many challenges or unresolved issues still need to be studied and addressed [64,69,70].

- **Increasing complexity.** As networks move to 6G and beyond, network operations and management complexity increase significantly, and business requirements constantly change. This phenomenon necessitates the continuous evolution of IBN systems to accommodate new scenarios and technological developments.
- **Lack of intent definition.** The lack of a formal and uniform definition of intent makes it challenging for network operators to design a practical IBN framework. Different stakeholders have different understandings of the meaning of intent (e.g., technical configurations, policies), making interpretability and translation of intent vital issues.
- **Accuracy of intent translation.** Intent translation is a critical step in the Intent Layer that translates the goals and needs expressed by the user into a form that the underlying infrastructure can understand. Errors or inaccuracies during translation can lead to network misconfigurations and performance issues. Therefore, the translation process needs to be optimized iteratively to avoid misunderstandings and configuration errors.
- **Low integration technology maturity.** Although integration with AI and Machine Learning (ML) technologies will improve the performance of IBN frameworks through increased automation and flexibility, these technologies are still in their early stages, and further research efforts are needed to reach the maturity required for integration with IBN.
- **Impact of intent dependencies on performance.** In practice, syntactically and semantically valid intents may still be infeasible due to inconsistencies or conflicts with existing intentions. Due to the complexity of service scenarios and network configurations, these dependencies are challenging to predict and detect when intent requests are received, and complex mechanisms need to be implemented to mitigate their impact.
- **Limited datasets.** Network assurance relies on ML algorithms that proactively guarantee the correct implementation of intentions and compliance with requirements. However, the datasets available for training are limited and do not contain all the necessary information (e.g., deployment details and obsolete parameters). Therefore, more complete datasets and more robust ML models must be generated to perform efficient assurance operations.

2.6 Conclusion

The development of the network is introduced first in this chapter. In order to make computer networks more programmable, SDN has been investigated. Furthermore, the architecture of SDN is discussed in the following text. As the most important part of SDN, the OpenFlow protocol is introduced, including its network architecture, the flow tables that each OpenFlow switch manages, and the work process of OpenFlow.

NFV is another architecture that improves the network and is responsible for virtualizing network functions. Then, the concept, advantage, framework, and application are also introduced. Considering the security of SDN and NFV, corresponding issues are discussed for the safe utilization of these two technologies. At the end of this chapter, the expansion of SDN and NFV, SD-WAN, and IBN, are discussed about their concepts, architectures, applications, and challenges.

References

[1] Crocker SD. The Arpanet and its impact on the state of networking. Computer. 2019;52(10):14–23.
[2] Iren S, Amer PD, and Conrad PT. The transport layer: Tutorial and survey. ACM Computing Surveys (CSUR). 1999;31(4):360–404.
[3] Scherrer JR and Spahni S. New opportunities for processing the OSI-7 layer protocols using parallel processing (transputers). International Journal of Bio-Medical Computing. 1994;34(1–4):387–398.
[4] Kessler GC. An overview of TCP/IP protocols and the internet. InterNIC Document. 2004;29:42.
[5] Chiueh SNTc and Brook S. A survey on virtualization technologies. RPE Report. 2005;142.
[6] Rose K, Eldridge S, and Chapin L. The internet of things: An overview. The Internet Society (ISOC). 2015;80(15):1–53.
[7] Burdea GC and Coiffet P. Virtual reality technology. John Wiley & Sons; 2003.
[8] Růžička V and Franchetti F. Fast and accurate object detection in high resolution 4K and 8K video using GPUs. In: 2018 IEEE High Performance extreme Computing Conference (HPEC). IEEE; 2018. p. 1–7.
[9] Holzmann GJ. Design and validation of protocols: A tutorial. Computer Networks and ISDN Systems. 1993;25(9):981–1017.
[10] Nisar K, Jimson ER, Hijazi MHA, *et al.* A survey on the architecture, application, and security of software defined networking: Challenges and open issues. Internet of Things. 2020;12:100289.
[11] Benzekki K, El Fergougui A, and Elbelrhiti Elalaoui A. Software-defined networking (SDN): A survey. Security and Communication Networks. 2016;9(18):5803–5833.
[12] Nunes BAA, Mendonca M, Nguyen XN, *et al.* A survey of software-defined networking: Past, present, and future of programmable networks. IEEE Communications Surveys & Tutorials. 2014;16(3):1617–1634.
[13] Latif Z, Sharif K, Li F, *et al.* A comprehensive survey of interface protocols for software defined networks. Journal of Network and Computer Applications. 2020;156:102563.
[14] Yang L, Ng B, Seah WK, *et al.* A survey on network forwarding in Software-Defined Networking. Journal of Network and Computer Applications. 2021;176:102947.

[15] Paliwal M, Shrimankar D, and Tembhurne O. Controllers in SDN: A review report. IEEE Access. 2018;6:36256–36270.
[16] Bondkovskii A, Keeney J, van der Meer S, *et al.* Qualitative comparison of open-source sdn controllers. In: NOMS 2016-2016 IEEE/IFIP Network Operations and Management Symposium. IEEE; 2016. p. 889–894.
[17] Song X, Xiao Z, Shao Y, *et al.* Overview of NFV Open Source Technology and Discussion on Operator Introduction Strategy (in Chinese). Guangdong Communication Technology. 2018.
[18] Zhaoxian X, Chen H, Anlin Z, *et al.* Architecture and research overview of the software defined wide area network. Fire Control & Command Control. 2017;42(12):55–60.
[19] Ford B, Srisuresh P, and Kegel D. Peer-to-peer communication across network address translators. In: USENIX Annual Technical Conference, General Track; 2005. p. 179–192.
[20] Ali FABH. A study of technology in firewall system. In: 2011 IEEE Symposium on Business, Engineering and Industrial Applications (ISBEIA). IEEE; 2011. p. 232–236.
[21] Kuźniar M, Perešíni P, and Kostić D. What you need to know about SDN flow tables. In: Passive and Active Measurement: 16th International Conference, PAM 2015, New York, NY, USA, March 19–20, 2015, Proceedings 16. Springer; 2015. p. 347–359.
[22] Lara A, Kolasani A, and Ramamurthy B. Network innovation using openflow: A survey. IEEE Communications Surveys & Tutorials. 2013;16(1):493–512.
[23] Kannan K and Banerjee S. Compact TCAM: Flow entry compaction in TCAM for power aware SDN. In: International Conference on Distributed Computing and Networking. Springer; 2013. p. 439–444.
[24] Ali AN. Comparison study between IPV4 & IPV6. International Journal of Computer Science Issues (IJCSI). 2012;9(3):314–317. Materials Science & Engineering Collection.
[25] Sun X, Sung YW, Krothapalli SD, *et al.* A systematic approach for evolving VLAN designs. In: 2010 Proceedings IEEE INFOCOM. IEEE; 2010. p. 1–9.
[26] Metcalfe RM and Boggs DR. Ethernet: Distributed packet switching for local computer networks. Communications of the ACM. 1976;19(7):395–404.
[27] Armitage G. MPLS: The magic behind the myths [multiprotocol label switching]. IEEE Communications Magazine. 2000;38(1):124–131.
[28] Langendoen K and Meier A. Analyzing MAC protocols for low data-rate applications. ACM Transactions on Sensor Networks (TOSN). 2010;7(2): 1–40.
[29] Bosshart P, Gibb G, Kim HS, *et al.* Forwarding metamorphosis: Fast programmable match-action processing in hardware for SDN. ACM SIGCOMM Computer Communication Review. 2013;43(4):99–110.
[30] Maity I, Mondal A, Misra S, *et al.* CURE: Consistent update with redundancy reduction in SDN. IEEE Transactions on Communications. 2018;66(9): 3974–3981.

[31] Yan B, Xu Y, and Chao HJ. BigMaC: Reactive network-wide policy caching for SDN policy enforcement. IEEE Journal on Selected Areas in Communications. 2018;36(12):2675–2687.
[32] Chang RK and Fung KP. Transport layer proxy for stateful UDP packet filtering. In: Proceedings ISCC 2002 Seventh International Symposium on Computers and Communications. IEEE; 2002. p. 595–600.
[33] Mijumbi R, Serrat J, Gorricho JL, *et al.* Network function virtualization: State-of-the-art and research challenges. IEEE Communications Surveys & Tutorials. 2015;18(1):236–262.
[34] Bonfim MS, Dias KL, and Fernandes SF. Integrated NFV/SDN architectures: A systematic literature review. ACM Computing Surveys (CSUR). 2019;51(6):1–39.
[35] Chiosi M, Clarke D, Donley C, *et al.* Network functions virtualisation (NFV)-network operator perspectives on industry progress. ETSI Tech. 2013. http://portal.etsi.org/NFV/NFV_White_Paper2.pdf.
[36] Pianese F, Bosch P, Duminuco A, *et al.* Toward a cloud operating system. In: 2010 IEEE/IFIP Network Operations and Management Symposium Workshops. IEEE; 2010. p. 335–342.
[37] Alwakeel AM, Alnaim AK, and Fernandez EB. Toward a reference architecture for NFV. In: 2019 2nd International Conference on Computer Applications & Information Security (ICCAIS). IEEE; 2019. p. 1–6.
[38] Pattaranantakul M, He R, Song Q, *et al.* NFV security survey: From use case driven threat analysis to state-of-the-art countermeasures. IEEE Communications Surveys & Tutorials. 2018;20(4):3330–3368.
[39] Yi B, Wang X, Li K, *et al.* A comprehensive survey of network function virtualization. Computer Networks. 2018;133:212–262.
[40] Herrera JG and Botero JF. Resource allocation in NFV: A comprehensive survey. IEEE Transactions on Network and Service Management. 2016;13(3): 518–532.
[41] Kaur K, Mangat V, and Kumar K. A review on Virtualized Infrastructure Managers with management and orchestration features in NFV architecture. Computer Networks. 2022;217:109281.
[42] Gonzalez AJ, Nencioni G, Kamisiński A, *et al.* Dependability of the NFV orchestrator: State of the art and research challenges. IEEE Communications Surveys & Tutorials. 2018;20(4):3307–3329.
[43] Bari MF, Boutaba R, Esteves R, *et al.* Data center network virtualization: A survey. IEEE Communications Surveys & Tutorials. 2012;15(2):909–928.
[44] Kiess W, Weitkemper P, and Khan A. Base station virtualization for OFDM air interfaces with strict isolation. In: 2013 IEEE International Conference on Communications Workshops (ICC). IEEE; 2013. p. 756–760.
[45] Demestichas P, Georgakopoulos A, Karvounas D, *et al.* 5G on the horizon: Key challenges for the radio-access network. IEEE Vehicular Technology Magazine. 2013;8(3):47–53.

[46] Parvez I, Rahmati A, Guvenc I, *et al.* A survey on low latency towards 5G: RAN, core network and caching solutions. IEEE Communications Surveys & Tutorials. 2018;20(4):3098–3130.

[47] Jaber M, Imran MA, Tafazolli R, *et al.* 5G backhaul challenges and emerging research directions: A survey. IEEE Access. 2016;4:1743–1766.

[48] Checko A, Christiansen HL, Yan Y, *et al.* Cloud RAN for mobile networks—A technology overview. IEEE Communications Surveys & Tutorials. 2014;17(1):405–426.

[49] Baumgartner A, Reddy VS, and Bauschert T. Mobile core network virtualization: A model for combined virtual core network function placement and topology optimization. In: Proceedings of the 2015 1st IEEE Conference on Network Softwarization (NetSoft). IEEE; 2015. p. 1–9.

[50] Liyanage M, Gurtov A, and Ylianttila M. Software defined mobile networks (SDMN): Beyond LTE network architecture. John Wiley & Sons; 2015.

[51] Berl A, Weidlich R, Schrank M, *et al.* Network virtualization in future home environments. In: Integrated Management of Systems, Services, Processes and People in IT: 20th IFIP/IEEE International Workshop on Distributed Systems: Operations and Management, DSOM 2009, Venice, Italy, October 27–28, 2009. Proceedings 20. Springer; 2009. p. 177–190.

[52] Zeadally S, Moustafa H, and Siddiqui F. Internet protocol television (IPTV): Architecture, trends, and challenges. IEEE Systems Journal. 2011;5(4): 518–527.

[53] Moreira A, Moreira J, Sadok D, *et al.* A case for virtualization of content delivery networks. In: Proceedings of the 2011 Winter Simulation Conference (WSC). IEEE; 2011. p. 3178–3189.

[54] Ageyev D, Bondarenko O, Alfroukh W, *et al.* Provision security in SDN/NFV. In: 2018 14th International Conference on Advanced Trends in Radioelecrtronics, Telecommunications and Computer Engineering (TCSET). IEEE; 2018. p. 506–509.

[55] Farahmandian S and Hoang DB. Security for software-defined (cloud, SDN and NFV) infrastructures—Issues and challenges. In: Eight International Conference on Network and Communications security; 2016.

[56] Klöti R, Kotronis V, and Smith P. OpenFlow: A security analysis. In: 2013 21st IEEE International Conference on Network Protocols (ICNP). IEEE; 2013. p. 1–6.

[57] Scott-Hayward S, O'Callaghan G, and Sezer S. SDN security: A survey. In: 2013 IEEE SDN for Future Networks and Services (SDN4FNS). IEEE; 2013. p. 1–7.

[58] Pandya B, Parmar S, Saquib Z, *et al.* Framework for securing SDN southbound communication. In: 2017 International Conference on Innovations in Information, Embedded and Communication Systems (ICIIECS). IEEE; 2017. p. 1–5.

[59] Banse C and Rangarajan S. A secure northbound interface for SDN applications. In: 2015 IEEE Trustcom/BigDataSE/ISPA. Vol. 1. IEEE; 2015. p. 834–839.

[60] Sherry J, Hasan S, Scott C, Krishnamurthy A, Ratnasamy S, and Sekar V. Making middleboxes someone else's problem: network processing as a cloud service. ACM SIGCOMM Computer Communication Review. 2012;42(4):13–24.
[61] Segeč P, Moravčik M, Uratmová J, *et al.* SD-WAN-architecture, functions and benefits. In: 2020 18th International Conference on Emerging eLearning Technologies and Applications (ICETA). IEEE; 2020. p. 593–599.
[62] Bloomberg J. SD-WAN: Entry Point For Software-Defined Everything. Forbes; 2017.
[63] Uppal S, Woo S, and Pitt D. Software defined wan for dummies. John Wiley & Sons, Ltd., Chichester, West Sussex, England; 2015.
[64] Gharbaoui M, Martini B, and Castoldi P. Intent-Based Networking: Current Advances, Open Challenges, and Future Directions. In: 2023 23rd International Conference on Transparent Optical Networks (ICTON). IEEE; 2023. p. 1–5.
[65] Zeydan E and Turk Y. Recent advances in intent-based networking: A survey. In: 2020 IEEE 91st Vehicular Technology Conference (VTC2020-Spring). IEEE; 2020. p. 1–5.
[66] Sun Q, Liu W, and Xie K. An intent-driven management framework. Internet Engineering Task Force, Internet-Draft. 2019.
[67] Li C, Havel O, Olariu A, *et al.* RFC 9316: Intent Classification. RFC Editor; 2022.
[68] Martini B, Gharbaoui M, and Castoldi P. Intent-based network slicing for SDN vertical services with assurance: Context, design and preliminary experiments. Future Generation Computer Systems. 2023;142:101–116.
[69] Wei Y, Peng M, and Liu Y. Intent-based networks for 6G: Insights and challenges. Digital Communications and Networks. 2020;6(3):270–280.
[70] Leivadeas A and Falkner M. A survey on intent-based networking. IEEE Communications Surveys & Tutorials. 2022;25(1):625–655.

Chapter 3

Transmission control protocol for message exchange

Mansi Zhang,[1] Yue Cao[1] and Bo Zhao[1]

The chapter introduces Transmission Control Protocol (TCP), presents the structure of TCP segment, TCP functionality, and implementation principles, and discusses typical security cases of TCP.

3.1 Introduction of TCP

3.1.1 End-to-end communication

End-to-end is a term often used by IT professionals today, and a label often added to many management software. However, this seemingly simple term is often interpreted in an inaccurate way.

End-to-end was introduced in the 1960s by Paul Baran and Donald Davies in their work on packet-switched networks [1]. In the 1970s, Louis Pouzin pioneered the use of end-to-end strategies in CYCLADES networks [2]. In 1981, Saltzer, Reed, and Clark first explicitly described end-to-end [3]. Thus, the end-to-end principle was born.

The basic meaning of the end-to-end principle is that the network is only responsible for providing the terminals with best-effort connections [4]. Features such as reliability and security must be provided by mechanisms and protocols located at the terminals. Therefore, network designers often ask whether a certain function should be implemented in the end system, or whether it should be implemented in the communication subsystem of the terminal.

Moreover, the end-to-end is a logical link necessary for reliable network communication [5]. It is a path that may go through a very complex physical route, but the hosts at both ends do not care the complexity and only consider that there is a connection between them. Therefore, it is far easier to obtain reliability by mechanisms in the end hosts rather than in the intermediary nodes, especially when the latter are beyond the control of, and not accountable, to the former.

The end-to-end principle has given rise to the Internet's simplicity principle, which allows hosts access to the Internet more easily by simply following the TCP/IP

[1]School of Cyber Science and Engineering, Wuhan University, China

protocol at the network layer and transport layer. The entire Internet architecture is shaped by the end-to-end principle, so Internet-based software and hardware will follow the end-to-end principle.

3.1.2 TCP/IP protocol stack

At present, the Internet is in a phase of rapid development, and various network applications are emerging. Regardless of how the Internet evolves in the future, the underlying mechanism of Internet operation, the TCP/IP model, remains unchanged. It is through the implementation of the various layers of the TCP/IP model that world-wide connectivity has been achieved and that individuals have been able to enjoy all the dividends of the Internet era.

The TCP/IP protocol stack is a model similar to the stack in data structures, it has many layers. Each layer assumes different functions and has different protocols. The protocol stack can be generally understood as a four-layer model: application layer, transport layer, network layer, and link layer [6]. Typical protocols of each layer can be seen in Figure 3.1.

- **The application layer:** It contains a number of user-oriented application-related protocols, which involve analysis and processing of data, enabling the conversion between user information and data streams.
- **The transport layer:** It is responsible for performing the conversion between data streams and segments and is the management level of data.
- **The network layer:** It involves connections with other hosts, encapsulating segments and finding suitable paths to send or receive information.
- **The link layer:** It is mainly a series of interfaces designed to implement the corresponding functions and is the bottom layer of the protocol stack. Generally speaking, user data are packaged from the application layer downwards. When

TCP/IP stack	Typical Protocols
Application layer	FTP, HTTP, TELNET, SMTP, DNS
Transport layer	TCP, UDP
Network layer	IP, ARP, ICMP, IGMP, RARP
Link layer	LAN, ARPNRT, SLIP

Figure 3.1 Protocols in TCP/IP stack

it is passed to another host, it is unpacked step by step from the link layer to application layer and finally parsed back into user data. In this process, the protocols ensure that the transmission is implemented and that the data are secure.

3.1.3 Transport layer

When data are delivered across a vast network to a destination host, similar to a post office delivery, the best-effort delivery strategy does not guarantee that the data will reach the destination host without error. Naturally, the network layer cannot guarantee that the data will reach the destination application correctly. However, for web applications, such as browsing the web, sending emails, or downloading files, the processes implementing these web applications require that the data must be transferred accurately from the source to destination application process. In order to meet this demand, the transport layer needs to provide reliable data transfer services for application processes [7]. In addition, the transport layer also needs to solve the problem of mismatch between the source and destination processes, in terms of sending and receiving data, otherwise the source may send a lot of data to overwhelm the destination application process. Therefore, the destination would inevitably discard data, because it is too late to receive the data sent by the source process.

The function of the transport layer to match the data sending and receiving capacity between processes is called the traffic control function [8]. Besides, the transport layer also takes into account that the source application process needs to restrain the rate of sending data to avoid further congestion, when a node in the network is congested. Therefore, the transport layer also needs a congestion control function [9]. In summary, it can be concluded that the main functions of transport layer are communication between application processes, reliable data transmission, traffic control, and congestion control.

Two important protocols designed at the transport layer are the TCP and the User Data Protocol (UDP) [10]. They rely on IP protocol to send packets to destinations, hence providing network services for applications and application layer protocols (e.g., HTTP, SMTP, SNMP, FTP, Telnet).

TCP is a connection-oriented protocol, which means that a reliable connection must be established with the other end before data can be formally sent or received [11]. A TCP connection has to be established after three "conversations." The brief process is as follows.

Step 1: Host A sends a connection request segment to host B: "I want to send you data, is that OK?".

Step 2: Host B sends a packet to host A agreeing to the connection and requesting synchronization (synchronization means that one of the two hosts is sending and one is receiving, coordinating their work): "Yes, when are you sending?," which is the second conversation.

Step 3: Host A sends another segment to confirm host B's request for synchronisation: "I'm sending it now, you go ahead!". This is the third conversation. The purpose of the three "conversations" is to synchronize the sending and receiving of segments, and only after the three "conversations" does host A send data to host B.

TCP can provide reliable, ordered, and error-checked delivery of data between applications. It is used for applications that require high reliability and accuracy, such as email, file transfer, and web browsing [12,13]. However, UDP is a connectionless protocol that provides unreliable delivery of data between applications [10]. UDP can send data faster to the destination than TCP, because it does not have the handshake and retransmission mechanisms of TCP. Moreover, UDP does not have congestion control mechanisms, so it can send data at a higher rate. This makes UDP better suited for applications that have high real-time requirements and can tolerate data loss or disorder.

3.2 The structure of TCP segment

The TCP segment consists of header field and data field. The data field contains content of application data, while the full functionality of TCP protocol is reflected in the role of the various fields in the header. Figure 3.2 shows the structure of TCP segment.

The TCP header can be divided into a fixed part and an optional part. The first 20 bytes of the header are fixed, while the option part can be increased by $4n$ (n is an integer) bytes. The meaning and function of each field in the header are expanded as follows.

3.2.1 Source port and destination port fields

The header includes the source and destination port numbers, which are used to multiplex/decompose data coming from or going toward the upper layer application. Processes on a computer communicate with other processes via ports, note that a computer port can only be occupied by one process at a given time. Therefore, by specifying the source and destination ports, it is possible to know which two processes need to communicate. The source and target ports are expressed in 16 bits, so the number of computer ports can be deduced by 2^{16}.

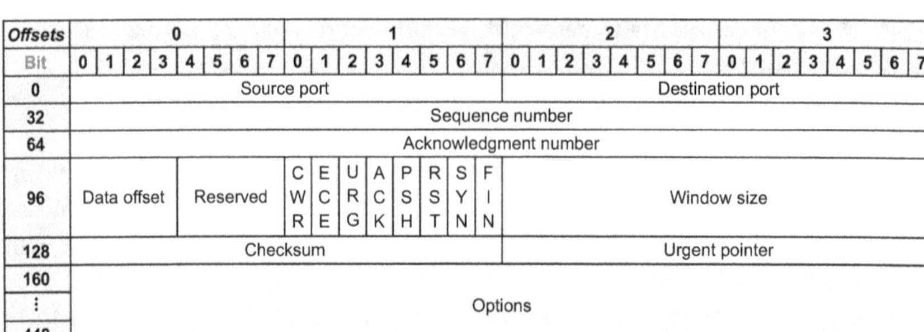

Figure 3.2 TCP segment structure

3.2.2 Sequence number and acknowledgment number fields

The bytes of data being transferred in each connection are numbered by TCP. The numbering starts with a randomly generated number. The value of sequence number field defines the number of the first data byte contained in a segment. The acknowledgment number identifies the next expected byte number of data from the other end of the connection. It is sent by the TCP receiver to indicate that it has received all bytes up to that byte number and is ready for more data.

The sequence number is used to ensure reliable data transfer between applications [14]. It enables ordered and accurate data transfer for TCP streams. The sequence number is coordinated with acknowledgment number. They are two key values during the TCP handshake, close, and while data are transferred between the client and the server.

3.2.3 Data offset

Data offset specifies the size of the TCP header in 32-bit words. The minimum size of header is 5 words and the maximum is 15 words thus giving the minimum size of 20 bytes and maximum of 60 bytes, allowing for up to 40 bytes of options in the header. The data offset is a 4-bit field in the TCP header that specifies the number of 32-bit words in the TCP header. It is used to indicate where the data begins in the TCP segment.

3.2.4 Reserved field

The 4-bit reserved for future use and should be set to zero in the current stage. The last bit was previously defined by Historic RFC 3540 as NS flag (Nonce Sum).

3.2.5 Flag field

The Congestion Window Reduced (CWR) bit is set by the sending host to indicate that it received a TCP segment with the ECE (ECN-Echo) flag set and had responded in congestion control mechanism [15].

- **The ECE bit:** It has a dual role, depending on the value of the SYN (SYNchronize) flag. (i) If SYN=1, it indicates that the TCP peer is ECN (Explicit Congestion Notification) capable. ECN is an extension to the TCP and is defined in RFC 3168 [16]. ECN allows end-to-end notification of network congestion without segment loss. (ii) If SYN=0, it means that a segment with congestion experienced flag set (ECN=11) in the IP header has been received during a transmission. This serves as an indication of network congestion (or impending congestion) to the TCP sender.
- **The URG (URGent) bit:** It indicates whether the data sent in this segment contains urgent data. URG=1 indicates that urgent data are present. The subsequent urgent pointer field is valid only when URG=1.

- **The ACK (ACKnowledgment) bit:** It indicates the preceding acknowledgement number field is valid. TCP specifies that ACK bit must be 1 when the connection is established.
- **The PSH (PuSH) bit:** It tells the other party whether the data should be pushed to the upper layer immediately upon receipt of a segment. If the PSH bit is 1, it indicates that the other party should immediately submit the data to upper layer instead of caching it up.
- **The RST (ReSeT) bit:** It indicates that there is an error for the connection to the host (e.g., the host crashed), and thus, the connection must be released and then re-established. Alternatively, it indicates that there is a problem with the last segment sent to the host but the segment has been refused to receive.
- **The SYN (SYNchronization) bit:** It is used when establishing a connection and is used to synchronize the sequence numbers. When SYN=1 and ACK=0, it means that this is a message segment requesting to establish a connection. When SYN=1 and ACK=1, it means that the other party agrees to establish a connection.
- **The FIN (FINish) bit:** It marks whether the data transmission in a TCP connection has finished. If FIN=1, it tells the other party that the connection can be released.

3.2.6 Window size field

The window size field indicates the size of the receive window, which specifies the number of window size units that the sender of this segment is currently willing to receive. The window size field takes up 16 bits and can be used for traffic control, which will be explained later.

3.2.7 Checksum field

The 16-bit checksum provides error-checking for the TCP header, the payload and an IP pseudo-header. The pseudo-header consists of the source IP address, the destination IP address, the protocol number for the TCP protocol and the length of the TCP headers and payload. The checksum is calculated by prefixing the TCP message segment with the 12-byte pseudo-header before calculating the checksum.

3.2.8 Urgent pointer field

It is used to mark the position of the last byte of the urgent data in the data field, only meaningful when URG=1. TCP must notify the receiving end when the urgent data is present and give a pointer to the end of it. The urgent pointer field takes up 16 bits.

3.2.9 Options field

Options are variable in length and their maximum length can be extrapolated from the length of the TCP header, as expressed in 4 bits. Therefore, the maximum length of the options section is: $(24 - 1) \times 4 - 20 = 40$ bytes. Options can have the following contents.

- **MSS (Maximum segment size):** It specifies the maximum length of data field, usually determined by the Maximum Transmission Unit (MTU) of the data link layer. The length of data field plus the length of the TCP header and equals the length of the entire TCP segment. The MSS value indicates the length of data field that one expects the other party to send. Both sides of communication can have different MSS values. If not filled in, the default is 536 bytes.
- **Window scaling option:** Since the window size field in the TCP header is 16 bits in length, the maximum number it represents is 65,535. However, with the creation of communications with higher latency and bandwidth (e.g., satellite communications), a larger window is required to meet performance and throughput rates, so this window scaling option was created, accounting for 24 bits [17].
- **Selective ACKnowledgements (SACK):** It is used to ensure that only the lost segments are required to be retransmitted.
- **Timestamps:** Timestamps contain a 4-byte sender timestamp value field and a 4-byte echo reply timestamp value field. They can be used to calculate Round Trip Time (RTT). When the sender sends a TCP segment, it will add the current timestamp into the sender timestamp value field. When the receiver receives the segment and sends an acknowledgement, it copies the sender timestamp value of that segment into echo reply timestamp value field, and then adds the current timestamp into sender timestamp value field. Therefore, the RTT can be calculated when the sender receives the acknowledgement. Moreover, timestamps can also be used in an algorithm known as Protection Against Wrapped Sequence (PAWS) numbers [18]. PAWS is used when the receive window crosses the sequence number wraparound boundary. It uses timestamp to distinguish different segments with the same sequence number within a connection.
- **NO-Operation (NOP):** It requires that each option must be a multiple of 4 bytes in length, and any shortfall is filled with NOP. It can also be used to split different option fields. For example, NOP is used to separate between window expansion option and SACK.

3.3 TCP functionality and implementation principles

Since the network layer services follow a best-effort delivery policy, this policy does not guarantee the successful and orderly delivery of segments, and therefore the integrity in the data. To solve such problems, TCP provides a connection-oriented and reliable byte stream service based on the IP protocol. Meanwhile, TCP also provides flow control and congestion control to eliminate the possibility of the sender overflowing the receiver's buffer and to improve segment loss due to router or link overload in the network.

3.3.1 Connection management

Connection-oriented means that two applications (usually a client and a server) using TCP must establish a TCP connection, before they can exchange segments with each other. In a TCP connection, only two parties communicate and the connection is released at the end of the communication. The process of TCP three handshakes for establishing a connection is as follows, where SEQ is the value of sequence number, and ACK is the value of acknowledgement number.

Step 1: The client sends a SYN (SEQ=x) segment to the server, entering the SYN_SEND state.

Step 2: The server receives a SYN message and responds with a SYN (SEQ=y) or ACK (ACK=x+1) segment, entering SYN_RECV state.

Step 3: The client receives a SYN segment from the server and responds with an ACK (ACK=y+1) segment to enter the Established state. With three handshakes complete, the TCP client and server have successfully established a connection and are ready to start transferring data. The whole process is shown in Figure 3.3.

The termination of a TCP connection requires four handshakes, which is caused by the semi-closing of TCP. The process is shown in Figure 3.4. Since an FIN and an ACK are required in each direction, four subsections are usually needed.

Step 1: An application process first calls close(), which is said to be an "active close" on the end. The TCP on the other end then sends a FIN subsection, to indicate that the data transmission in this TCP connection has finished.

Step 2: The other end receiving this FIN performs a "passive close," and the FIN is acknowledged by ACK.

Step 3: After a period of time, the application process that received the FIN will call close() to close its socket. This causes its TCP to send a FIN as well.

Step 4: The TCP on the original sender side (the one performing the active closure) receiving this final FIN, then acknowledges this FIN.

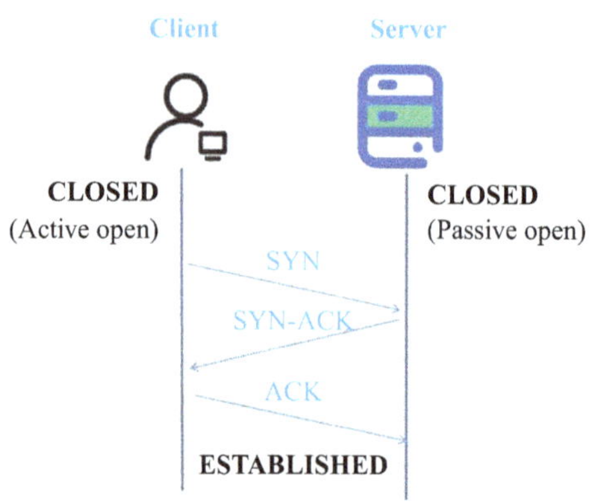

Figure 3.3 Connection establishment

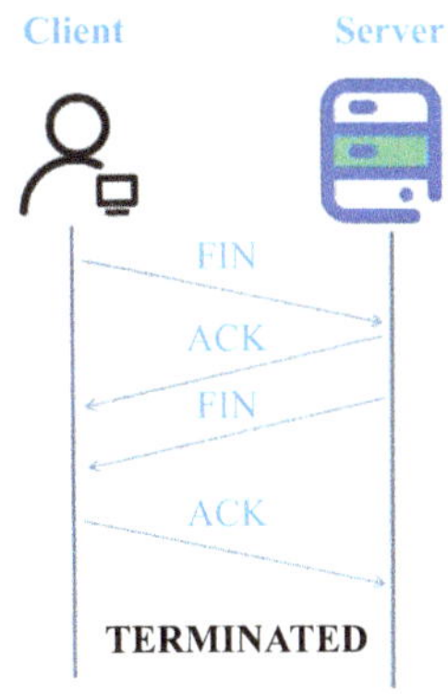

Figure 3.4 Connection termination

3.3.2 Reliable transmission

TCP is also known as the Reliable Transmission Protocol, which means that segments must be handed over to the other end in order. The reliability is achieved by data checksum, sequence number mechanism, acknowledgement, and retransmission mechanism.

- **Data checksum:** As mentioned previously, the TCP message header has a checksum, which is used to detect bit errors in a transmitted segment.
- **The sequence number mechanism:** The sequence number is used to ensure that data are handed over to the application layer in order. TCP treats data as an unstructured, ordered stream of bytes and requires a unique identifier for each byte. The sequence number is the name of the identifier. The sequence number of a segment is the identifier of the first data byte carried in that segment. Each sequence number is filled into the sequence number field in header. When there is a need from application layer for data submission, TCP will reorder received segments according to their sequence numbers. This makes sure the data handed over is in the correct order, resolving out-of-order or duplicated segments.
- **The acknowledgement number mechanism:** The acknowledgement number is the next sequence number that sender expects. TCP acknowledges correctly received segments and retransmits segments when the segment or its acknowledgement is considered lost or damaged. The bytes in the stream up to the first missing one are acknowledged cumulatively.
- **The retransmission mechanism:** The retransmission mechanism enables the sender to retransmit problematic (erroneous or missing) segments, and there are two types of retransmission mechanisms. The first type is timeout retransmission: If the timer expires and no acknowledgement is received, the corresponding segment is retransmitted. The second type is the receipt of a redundant acknowledgement: When an out-of-order segment is received, a redundant acknowledgement is sent to the sender. Once the sender receives three redundant acknowledgements, it will retransmit the corresponding segment.

For timeout retransmission, TCP uses a timeout timer to decide if it needs to retransmit an unacknowledged segment. The duration of this timer is referred to as Retransmission Time Out (RTO). RTO is determined by RTT monitored by the sender, the duration between the time slot the data is sent and the time slot the acknowledgement is received. Most TCP implementations only sample the RTT periodically to obtain a sampled RTT and approximately represent all RTTs over a period of time, rather than measuring the RTT for every segment. Due to the congestion of network, the value of sampled RTT is fluctuant and not that representable for all RTTs. To obtain a more typical RTT, initial TCP specifications adopt Smoothed Round Trip Time (SRTT). The SRTT is updated according to the following equation (3.1), in which a is a smoothing factor (usually $a = 0.125$). RTO is calculated as (3.2), in which b is a delay variance factor (usually $b = 2$).

$$SRTT = a \times RTT_{sample} + (1 - a) \times SRTT_{old} \tag{3.1}$$

$$RTO = b \times SRTT \tag{3.2}$$

However, since the weight of the latest measured RTT is only 0.125, when the RTT varies over a wide range, newly estimated SRTT cannot keep up with this variation, probably causing unnecessary retransmissions. To make estimated SRTT fit the changes of the RTTs, Round Trip Time VARiation (RTTVAR) is also defined in RFC2988 to estimate the extent to which the sampled RTT deviates from SRTT [19]. It is calculated as (3.3), where c is recommended to be 0.25

$$RTTVAR = (1 - c) \times RTTVAR + c \times |RTT - SRTT| \tag{3.3}$$

SRTT and RTTVAR are obtained as described in (3.1) and (3.3), respectively. RTTVAR is chosen as the RTO margin, which is large when fluctuations are high and small when fluctuations are low. The RTO is calculated as (3.4), where K is usually 4

$$RTO = SRTT + K \times RTTVAR \tag{3.4}$$

3.3.3 Flow control

There is a limit to how fast the receiving end can process data, and if the sender is too fast, it will fill up the buffer. At this point if it continues to send segment, it will lead to a series of chain reactions such as segment loss. Therefore, TCP supports a flow control mechanism that determines the sending speed of the sender according to the process capacity of the receiver. The receive window size value, known as Receive WiNDow (RWND), is set in the acknowledgement segment to limit the sending rate.

The receiver puts the size of the buffer it can receive into the window size field in the TCP header and notifies the sender via the acknowledgement. The larger the window size field, the higher the network throughput. Once the receiver finds its buffer is almost full, it sets the window size to a smaller value and notifies the sender. If the receiver's buffer is full, the window will be set to 0. The sender will not send any more segment, but will periodically send a window probe segment. In this case, the receiver will tell the sender regarding the latest window size.

3.3.4 Congestion control

Sending large amounts of segments without knowing the current state of the network can cause network congestion. When congestion occurs, the sender does not know the details of how the congestion occurs, but it can detect the congestion has already happened through an increase in communication latency. The congestion control is similar to traffic control in that it achieves its effect by controlling the sending rate.

The earliest TCP protocol used a simple stop and wait protocol, where each segment sent had to wait for an acknowledgement to be received, before the next segment could be sent in sequence. If a segment was lost, the sender had to wait for the retransmission timer to time out before resending the lost segment, and no effective measures were taken against network congestion. Congestive collapse was identified as a possible problem by 1984 and first observed on the early Internet in October 1986 [20,21]. However, early TCP only defines the framework, the "rules" to be followed by the sender and receiver, so its implementation and congestion control algorithm has been refined over the years in a number of different versions to solve this problem. Some of the more important ones have become widely influential RFC documents or standard options for operating systems, including Additive Increase/Multiplicative Decrease (AIMD), Tahoe, Reno, NewReno, SACK, Vegas, etc. The following is a brief description of the main differences and links between the various implementations.

3.3.4.1 Additive Increase/Multiplicative Decrease (AIMD)

The AIMD algorithm is a feedback control algorithm best known for its use in TCP congestion control [22]. AIMD combines linear growth of the congestion window with an exponential reduction when congestion is detected. The approach is to increase the transmission rate, probing for usable bandwidth until segment loss occurs.

The sender determines the sending rate based on both the receiver's ability to receive and the consideration of not congesting the network. Therefore, the TCP protocol requires the sender to maintain the two windows. One is the RWND (Receive WiNDow) used in TCP's flow control, and the other one is the CWND (Congestion WiNDow), a window size value set by the sender based on its own estimate on level of network congestion. The upper limit of the sending window should be the smaller value of RWND and CWND. This is how CWND can also influence the sending rate.

Additive-increase means increasing the CWND by a fixed amount (usually one MSS) every RTT. Multiplicative-decrease means the sender decreases (usually in half) the congestion window once congestion is detected. There are two signals for congestion, a timeout or an acknowledgement indicates a segment loss.

3.3.4.2 TCP Tahoe

The Tahoe algorithm is an early version of TCP. Its core idea is to make the CWND rapidly approach the available channel capacity in an exponential growth manner and then slowly approach equilibrium [23]. Tahoe consists of three basic congestion control algorithms: slow start, congestion avoidance, and fast retransmission.

- **Slow start algorithm:** Tahoe initializes CWND to one segment after the connection is established and then starts doubling CWND on every RTT, if no segment loss and congestion occurs. Once CWND reaches ssthresh (slow start threshold), then it goes into congestion avoidance.
- **Congestion avoidance:** CWND grows linearly in this phase until the retransmission timer times out or sender receives three duplicate acknowledgements. Then, CWND is reset to one segment size and the slow start is restarted while ssthresh is half of the current CWND.
- **Fast retransmission:** If the sender receives three duplicate acknowledgements, it performs a fast retransmission without waiting for the retransmission timer to time out, but directly resending all the unacknowledged segments in the sending window.

The shortcoming of the Tahoe algorithm is that upon receiving three duplicate acknowledgements or in the case of a timeout, it sets CWND to one and then enters a slow start phase. This causes violent oscillations in the network and reduces the network utility significantly.

3.3.4.3 TCP Reno

In response to the shortcomings of the Tahoe algorithm, the TCP Reno algorithm was proposed with the fast recovery mechanism as the main improvement [24].

- **Fast recovery phase:** After a fast retransmission, the fast recovery phase starts with ssthresh set to be half of the current CWND and CWND to be ssthresh+3. Thus, the CWND still increases linearly until a new acknowledgement is received. Then, the new acknowledgement ends the fast recovery and turns TCP Reno into the congestion avoidance phase, with CWND set to the size of ssthresh.

The Reno has become the mainstream of TCP congestion control algorithms and is widely used for its simplicity, effectiveness, and robustness. However, Reno still suffers from shortcomings [24]. First, the sender retransmits all segments already sent, during the period from the time that a segment loss to that when the lost is detected, but some of these segments are received correctly by the receiver without having to be retransmitted. Second, it is important to accurately measure the RTT. Theoretically, the RTT is a relatively simple measurement of the time between the sending of a segment and the return of the acknowledgement to the sender. Since TCP Reno uses a "cumulative" acknowledgement method, the estimation of RTT is often more complex in practice and therefore is one of the research issues. Another shortcoming of Reno is that it cannot efficiently handle the case where multiple segments are lost from a single congestion. In this case, Reno may get stuck in a loop between congestion avoidance and fast recovery. The loop makes CWND and ssthresh repeatedly halved, resulting in an exponential drop in the sending rate.

3.3.4.4 TCP NewReno

TCP NewReno modifies the fast recovery algorithm based on TCP Reno by considering the loss of multiple segments in the same sending window [25]. The fast recovery in Reno ends when the sender receives a new acknowledgement, while in the New Reno, it ends only when all segments have been answered.

NewReno TCP adds a recovery acknowledgement judgment function to enhance the ability of TCP terminals to analyze the status of segment transmission through acknowledgement information. This allows the TCP terminal to distinguish between the loss of multiple segments in a single congestion and multiple congestions, thereby increasing the robustness and throughput of TCP, by halving the congestion window only once after each congestion occurs.

TCP NewReno defines two kinds of non-redundant acknowledgements received in the fast recovery phase. The non-redundant acknowledgement received in the recovery phase of the TCP sender is assumed to ACK_x, and the most recent sent segment is assumed to PKT_y. If ACK_x is not the acknowledge of PKT_y, then the ACK_x is called partial acknowledgement. If ACK_x is exactly the acknowledge of PKT_y, then ACK_x is called recovery acknowledgement, which means all sent lost segments are correctly received by the receiver and network has recovered from the congestion. When the sender receives the first partial acknowledgement, it does not exit the fast recovery phase immediately as Reno does, but retransmits the lost segments after this partial acknowledgement, until a recovery acknowledgement is received.

3.3.4.5 TCP with SACK

TCP with SACK (Selective ACKnowledgement) is also an improvement on TCP Reno to deal more effectively with the problem of large numbers of lost segments [26]. When congestion is detected, instead of retransmitting all segments sent during the time between segments loss and the congestion detection, these segments are selectively acknowledged to avoid unnecessary retransmissions. With this method, the receiver must have the ability to hold the segments out of order in its buffer.

During the connection establishment phase, the sender and receiver negotiate whether to apply the SACK option in the TCP option field. If the SACK option is enabled, it allows the receiver selectively acknowledge a range of consecutive bytes while returning a duplicate acknowledgement segment to the sender. The interval between acknowledged bytes is the segment that has not been received by the receiver. Therefore, the sender can know which segments have been received and which are lost, so that it can selectively retransmit the lost segments.

In summary, TCP with SACK can reduce latency, increase network throughput, and fastern recovery from congestion. The SACK option has become a standard option on Linux systems and is usually already applied in current system deployments.

3.3.4.6 TCP Vegas

TCP Vegas is a TCP congestion avoidance algorithm that emphasizes transmission delay rather than segments loss. It was developed at the University of Arizona by Lawrence Brakmo and Larry L. Peterson and introduced in 1994 [27].

TCP Vegas detects congestion at an incipient stage based on increasing RTT values of the segments in the connection, unlike other flavors such as Reno, New Reno, etc., which detect congestion only after the congestion has actually happened via segment loss. The algorithm depends on accurate calculation of the RTT value. If it is too small then throughput of the connection will be less than the bandwidth available, while if the value is too large then it will overrun the connection.

A lot of research is under study regarding the fairness provided by the linear increase/decrease mechanism for congestion control in Vegas [28,29]. One caveat is when Vegas is inter-operated with other versions like Reno. In this case, the performance of Vegas degrades because Vegas reduces the sending rate earlier than Reno, as it detects congestion early and hence gives greater bandwidth to co-existing TCP Reno flows.

TCP Vegas is one of several "flavors" of TCP congestion avoidance algorithms. It is one of a series of efforts at TCP tuning that adapts congestion control and system behaviors to new challenges faced by available bandwidth increases in Internet components like Internet2 [30]. TCP Vegas has been implemented in the Linux kernel, in FreeBSD and possibly in other operating systems as well [31].

3.4 TCP security problems

3.4.1 SYN flood attack

A SYN flood is a common form of Distributed-Denial-of-Service (DDoS) attack, which sends a large amount of SYN requests to a server to overwhelm the open connections. These attacks can target any system connected to the Internet and providing TCP services (e.g., web server, email server, file transfer). A SYN flood attack is a type of TCP State-Exhaustion Attack. It attempts to consume the connection state tables present in many infrastructure components, such as load balancers, firewalls, Intrusion Prevention Systems (IPS), and the application servers themselves. This type of DDoS attack can take down even high-capacity devices capable of maintaining millions of connections [32].

3.4.1.1 Normal TCP connection establishment

Under normal circumstances, establishing a TCP connection involves three steps, also known as "the TCP three-way handshake." First, in order to establish a connection, the client sends a SYN (SYNchronize) segment to the server and enters SYN_SEND state, waiting for an acknowledgement from the server. Second, in order to acknowledge the communication, the server responds to the segment with a SYN_ACK (SYNchronize-ACKnowledge) segment and enters SYN_RECV state. Finally, the client returns an ACK (ACKnowledge) segment to the server to acknowledge the receipt of the segment. Afterwards, the client and server enter ESTABLISHED state with TCP connection established and ready to send and receive data. The whole process is shown in Figure 3.5.

3.4.1.2 Some concepts in TCP connection establishment

- **Incomplete connection queue:** Incomplete connection queue known as the SYN queue is maintained by the server. It is used for storing inbound SYN segments, responsible for sending out SYN–ACK segments and retrying them on

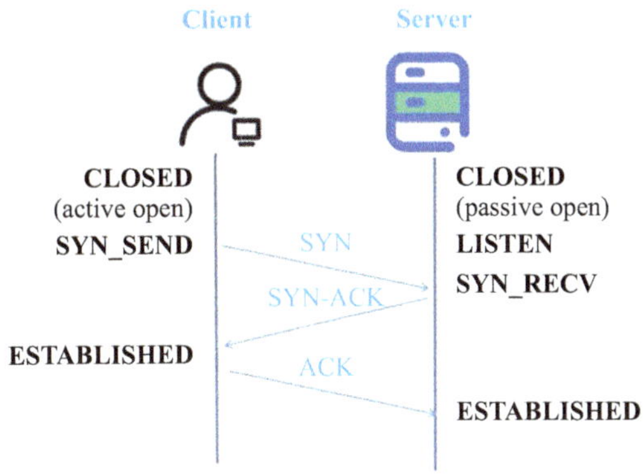

Figure 3.5 Normal connection

timeout. When an ACK segment from the client is received by the server, the corresponding SYN segments entry will be removed from the SYN queue, with the server entering the ESTABLISHED state.

- **Backlog parameter:** Backlog parameter is used for providing a limit for the maximum allowed length of the SYN queue. The backlog value controls the SYN queue size. The larger the average RTT to the client, the more queue slots are going to be used. In the case of many clients far away from the server, hundreds of milliseconds away, it makes sense to increase the backlog value.
- **SYN_RECV timeout:** SYN_RECV timeout is the lifetime of an entry in the SYN queue.

3.4.1.3 SYN flood connection

The SYN flood attack process is shown in Figure 3.6. First, the attacker sends a large number of SYN segments to a target server, with a fake source IP address. Second, the server adds entries of these SYN segments into its SYN queue. After this, the server responds to each SYN segment by sending a SYN-ACK segment back to the supposed source, waiting for a final ACK segment to complete the three-way handshake so that the entry can be removed from the SYN queue.

However, since the source IP address is fake, the ACK segment is never received, leaving the server with a large number of half-open connections waiting for timeout. These connections consume queue space, causing network congestion and ultimately overloading the system, resulting in a denial of service.

3.4.2 SYN flood attack defense

SYN flood attack prevention techniques can be categorized into two main types. One is through the reinforcement of TCP/IP stack to prevent, and the other is through firewalls protection.

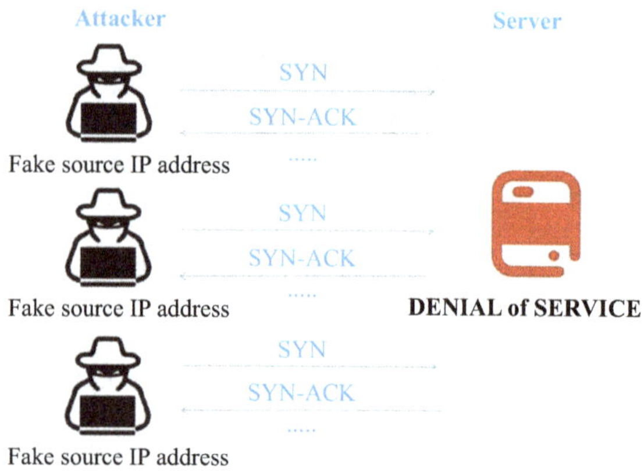

Figure 3.6 SYN flood attack

- **SYN cookies implementation:** The implementation of SYN cookies allows the server to avoid dropping connections when the SYN queue fills up [33]. Usually, the Initial Sequence Number (ISN) of the server is calculated by the server according to a certain rule or random number. However, in SYN cookies, the ISN of the server, which is called a cookie in this case, is encrypted by the hash computation of the client's IP address, the client's port number, the server's IP address, the server's port number, and other security values. When a SYN flood makes the SYN queue full, the server does not deny new SYN requests but directly replies a cookie, i.e., the server's ISN, to the client. Afterwards, if the client's ACK segment is received, the server calculates the cookie comparison number value by subtracting 1 from the value of client's acknowledgement number and performs the hash algorithm mentioned above to check whether it is equal to the cookie. If it is equal, the TCP three handshakes are completed directly.
- **Increasing the size of SYN queue:** A large number of SYN requests result in the SYN queue being full, making it impossible for normal TCP connections to complete the three handshakes. This problem can be alleviated by increasing the SYN queue space [34–36]. However, the SYN queue takes up a lot of memory resources and cannot be expanded indefinitely.
- **Reducing SYN_RECV timeout value:** The larger the SYN_RECV timeout value is, the longer the SYN queue is occupied by the incomplete connections, and the fewer SYN requests the system can handle. By reducing the SYN_RECV timeout value, the SYN queue gains more chance to store newly incoming incomplete connections [37].
- **Firewall configuration:** Firewalls can be configured to limit incoming traffic and block incoming connections from suspicious or known malicious IP addresses. The firewall sets the SYN segment timeout parameter much less than the server's SYN_RECV timeout. After the client sends the SYN segment and the server sends the SYN-ACK segment, if the firewall does not receive the ACK

segment from the client by the time when the firewall timer expires, the firewall will send an RST (ReSeT) segment to the server to make the server remove the incomplete connection entry from the SYN queue [38–40].

3.4.3 *ACK flood attack*

An ACK flood attack works in a similar mechanism as a SYN flood attack. An ACK flood attack occurs when an attacker attempts to overload a server with TCP ACK segments. Like other DDoS attacks, the goal of an ACK flood is to deny service to other clients by slowing down or crashing the target using junk data. The targeted server has to process each ACK segment received, which uses so much computing power that it is unable to serve legitimate clients.

3.4.3.1 ACK flood attack methods

After the TCP connection is established, all transmitted TCP segments are with the ACK flag bit set. When the server receives an ACK segment, first, it needs to check whether the connection indicated by the segment exists. Second, if the connection exists, the server will check whether the state indicated by the segment is legal. Finally, the server will submit the segment to application layer if the segment is legal. Otherwise, the server responds with an RST segment informing the client that the ACK segment is illegal. In summary, the server has to perform two actions: querying the connection table and responding with the ACK or RST segment. Based on this mode of operation, ACK flood can be divided into two types: ACK flood with random IP addresses and with forged IP addresses [40].

- **ACK flood with random IP addresses:** By generating random source IP addresses and source ports, the attacker sends massive illegal ACK segments to the target server. These segments induce the server to spend a lot of time querying the local connection table, causing the server busy processing these illegal requests and unable to serve normal clients. The attack process is shown in Figure 3.7.
- **ACK flood with forged IP addresses:** The attacker forges the IP address and port number of the attacked server and sets the source IP address as the server's IP address. Afterwards, it sends a large number of ACK segments to the server. When the server receives these illegal segments, the server will respond with RST segments to the source IP address, i.e., itself. When there are enough RST segments, the server will be busy processing these illegal requests and will not be able to serve normal users when they have access to the host. The attack process is shown in Figure 3.8.

3.4.4 *ACK flood attack defense*

- **Network traffic analysis:** When the attacker performs an ACK flood attack, the victim host can detect the number of receiving packets are usually abnormally larger than the sending ones. Moreover, in order to increase the speed of the attack, the attacker generally uses small segments with the same content to send.

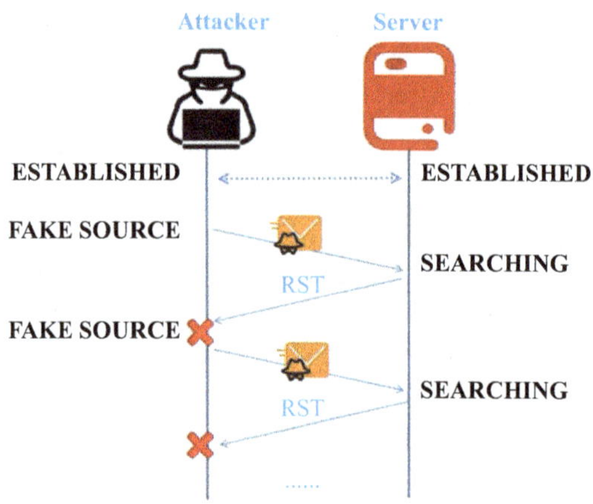

Figure 3.7 ACK flood with random IP

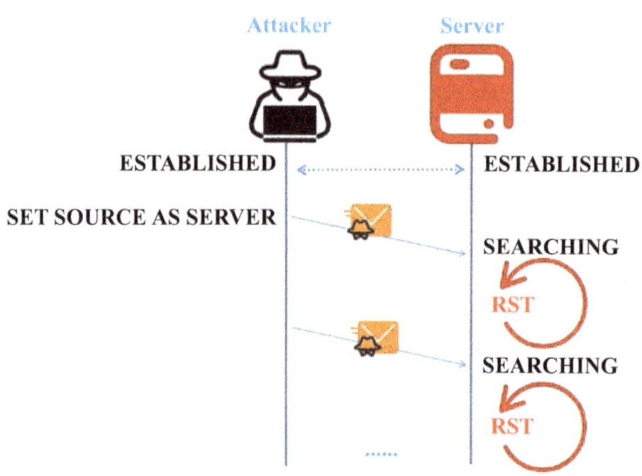

Figure 3.8 ACK flood with forged IP

These two features can be used as a basis for detecting whether ACK flood has occurred [41].

- **Firewall filtering:** Firewalls deal with ACK flood by creating a hash table to store the TCP connection state of the host, which simplifies the process of state checking compared to the host's TCP stack implementation [42]. In firewall's filtering process, there is no sequence number checking and no segments disorder processing, but only filtering the ACK segments which have the corresponding SYN-ACK segments in the connection table. Therefore, the process of the filtering reduces the resource consumption of the victim host.

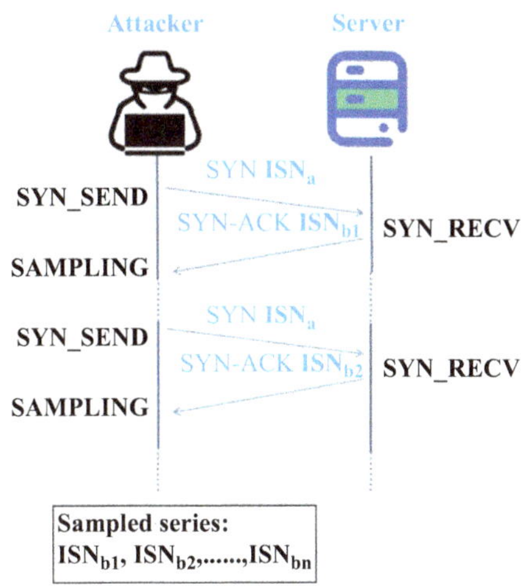

Figure 3.9 ISN sampling

3.4.5 ISN prediction attack

The TCP sequence number prediction attack was first described as a security vulnerability in 1985 by Robort. Morris [43]. He employed TCP sequence number prediction to generate a sequence of TCP segments to spoof the host on local network. Initiating TCP sequence number spoofing through predicting TCP ISN is a hidden trouble on TCP protocol. The ISN sampling process is shown in Figure 3.9.

3.4.5.1 Initial Sequence Number (ISN) prediction attack process

In the TCP protocol, whether a segment can be received by the other host depends on whether the sequence number of this segment is expected by the other host or not. If the attacker can predict the sequence number of the next segment in an established TCP connection through sampled ISN series(shown in Figure 3.8), then the attacker can forge a corresponding segment and send it to other host. When receiving the segment, the host will consider it as legitimate and thus accept and process it.

Although designed to be randomly, TCP ISN is still predictable, because it is generated by a Pseudo Random Number Generator (PRNG). After the seed of PRNG is given, each value in the generated sequence is uniquely determined by the given algorithm. However, any PRNG is predictable theoretically [44].

3.4.5.2 ISN prediction methods

- **Linear analysis:** ISN can be predicted by collecting the feedback ISN repeatedly after the TCP connection is established and analyzing the sampled ISN and the RTT (Round Trip Time); this method is simple but inexactness. However, it only works in the early version of TCP/IP where the ISN variable is incremented by a fixed number of times per second [45].
- **Combination of chaotic time series and linear regression:** Chaos is a complex behavior of a non-linear, identified low-dimensional dynamic system. Chaotic

phenomena mean the irregular movements that are widespread in nature. Chaos series prediction is based on the reconstruction theory of the phase space, which is proposed by Packard and Takens [46]. The main idea of the theory is: any component's evolution in the system is decided by its interacting components, which means that the information of related components is hidden in the development of other components. The system original rule can be withdrawn and restored from one batch of time series data of a certain component. The method of combining chaotic time series with linear regression has three main steps [47]. First, it uses a local linear approximation to perform a linear return on the sampled values. Second, a chaotic time series prediction of the difference between the sampled and regressed values is followed. Finally, the guess value can be extracted from the prediction result.

3.4.6 ISN prediction attack defense

- **The usage of encryption and authentication:** Encryption protocols can limit the consequences of introducing forged data into a connection. The attacker will not be able to interpret the data and get the connection information for ISN prediction, although the packet is hijacked. Moreover, when a legitimate receiver discovers the forged data, he can reset the TCP/IP connection. For example, IPSEC is used at the IP layer to authenticate and encrypt vulnerable TCP connections [48]. The system needs to use IPSEC to identify all connections accessing a port, preventing the attacker spoofing and hijack the TCP session.
- **The improvement of generation method of ISN:** Enhancing the robustness of the ISN PRNG (Pseudo Random Number Generator) is another way to reduce attacker's prediction accuracy of ISN. In operation systems, PRNG usually uses [source IP, destination IP, source port, destination port, hash(key)] as a random seed. This purely mathematical approach is predictable [49]. Therefore, introducing complex external random variables such as network communication information, packet arrival rate, delay time, etc., as the hash key [50,51]. The randomness of PRNG can be increased in this way.

3.5 Conclusion

This chapter presented the analysis of TCP, a cornerstone of modern networking that ensured reliable and orderly data transmission. The fundamental aspects of TCP were examined, including its segment structure and core functionalities such as reliable data transfer, flow control, and congestion control. These mechanisms enabled TCP to provide a robust connection-oriented communication model, ensuring the accurate delivery of data across complex networks. Moreover, this chapter also discussed the evolution of congestion control algorithms from early models (e.g., Tahoe and Reno) to more advanced versions (e.g., NewReno and Vegas), which addressed varying network conditions and improved overall efficiency. These advancements demonstrated TCP's adaptability to the demands of increasing traffic and diverse use cases. In addition to functionality, this chapter examined the vulnerabilities of TCP, such as SYN flood and ACK flood attacks, and outlined mitigation strategies, including SYN cookies, enhanced queue management, and firewall configurations. These measures highlighted the ongoing need for secure implementation of TCP to counteract potential threats. Overall, TCP's design and continuous improvements ensured its relevance in supporting reliable and secure communication in an ever-expanding digital ecosystem. Despite challenges, its role as a fundamental protocol in networking remained indispensable.

References

[1] Prodi C and Out T. Packet switching; 1996.

[2] Pouzin L. Presentation and major design aspects of the CYCLADES computer network. In: Proceedings of the Third ACM Symposium on Data Communications and Data Networks: Analysis and Design; 1973. p. 80–87.

[3] Saltzer JH, Reed DP, and Clark DD. End-to-end arguments in system design. ACM Transactions on Computer Systems. 1984;2(4):277–288.

[4] Devopedia. 2019. "End-to-End Principle." Version 3, October 7. https://devopedia.org/end-to-end-principle [Accessed June 25, 2024].

[5] Coates M, Rabbat M, and Nowak R. Merging logical topologies using end-to-end measurements. In: Proceedings of the 3rd ACM SIGCOMM Conference on Internet Measurement; 2003. p. 192–203.

[6] Alani MM. Guide to OSI and TCP/IP Models. Cham: Springer; 2014.

[7] Hercog D. Communication Protocols: Principles, Methods and Specifications. Springer Nature; 2020.

[8] Barbera M, Lombardo A, Panarello C, *et al.* Active window management: An efficient gateway mechanism for TCP traffic control. In: 2007 IEEE International Conference on Communications. IEEE; 2007. p. 6141–6148.

[9] Veres A and Boda M. The chaotic nature of TCP congestion control. In: Proceedings IEEE INFOCOM 2000. Conference on Computer Communications. Nineteenth Annual Joint Conference of the IEEE Computer and Communications Societies (Cat. No. 00CH37064). Vol. 3. IEEE; 2000. p. 1715–1723.

[10] AL-Dhief FT, Sabri N, Latiff NA, *et al.* Performance comparison between TCP and UDP protocols in different simulation scenarios. International Journal of Engineering & Technology. 2018;7(4.36):172–176.

[11] Shieh A, Myers AC, and Sirer EG. A stateless approach to connection-oriented protocols. ACM Transactions on Computer Systems (TOCS). 2008;26(3):1–50.

[12] Noureddine W and Tobagi F. Improving the performance of interactive TCP applications using service differentiation. Computer Networks. 2002;40(1):19–43.

[13] Sailan MK and Hassan R. Network file transfer performance: Effect of IP address, TCP window size and file size. In: 2010 Second International Conference on Network Applications, Protocols and Services. IEEE; 2010. p. 114–118.

[14] Velten D, Hinden R, and Sax J. Reliable Data Protocol. RFC Editor; 1984.
[15] Ramakrishnan K and Floyd S. A Proposal to Add Explicit Congestion Notification (ECN) to IP. RFC Editor; 1999.
[16] Ramakrishnan K, Floyd S, and Black D. RFC3168: The Addition of Explicit Congestion Notification (ECN) to IP. RFC Editor; 2001.
[17] Shang Y, Hadjitheodosiou M, and Baras J. Protocol support for a new satellite-based airspace communication network. In: Proceedings of the Fourth Integrated Communications, Navigation, and Surveillance (ICNS) Conference and Workshop; 2004.
[18] Wright GRS and Richard W. TCP/IP Illustrated, Vol. 2 (paperback): The Implementation. Addison-Wesley; 2017.
[19] Paxson V, Allman M, Chu J, *et al.* Computing TCP's retransmission timer; 2011.
[20] Nagle J. Congestion control in IP/TCP internetworks. ACM SIGCOMM Computer Communication Review. 1984;14(4):11–17.
[21] Jacobson V. Congestion avoidance and control. ACM SIGCOMM Computer Communication Review. 1988;18(4):314–329.
[22] Yang YR and Lam SS. General AIMD congestion control. In: Proceedings 2000 International Conference on Network Protocols. IEEE; 2000. p. 187–198.
[23] Waghmare S, Nikose P, Parab A, *et al.* Comparative Analysis of different TCP variants in a wireless environment. In: 2011 3rd International Conference on Electronics Computer Technology. Vol. 4. IEEE; 2011. p. 158–162.
[24] Padhye J, Firoiu V, Towsley DF, *et al.* Modeling TCP Reno performance: A simple model and its empirical validation. IEEE/ACM Transactions on Networking. 2000;8(2):133–145.
[25] Parvez N, Mahanti A, and Williamson C. An analytic throughput model for TCP NewReno. IEEE/ACM Transactions on Networking. 2009;18(2): 448–461.
[26] Fall K and Floyd S. Simulation-based comparisons of Tahoe, Reno and SACK TCP. ACM SIGCOMM Computer Communication Review. 1996;26(3): 5–21.
[27] Brakmo LS, O'malley SW, and Peterson LL. TCP Vegas: New techniques for congestion detection and avoidance. In: Proceedings of the Conference on Communications Architectures, Protocols and Applications; 1994. p. 24–35.
[28] Hasegawa G, Kurata K, and Murata M. Analysis and improvement of fairness between TCP Reno and Vegas for deployment of TCP Vegas to the Internet. In: Proceedings 2000 International Conference on Network Protocols. IEEE; 2000. p. 177–186.
[29] Bonald T. Comparison of TCP Reno and TCP Vegas: Efficiency and fairness. Performance Evaluation. 1999;36:307–332.
[30] Jin C, Wei D, Low SH, *et al.* FAST TCP. In: 57th IETF Meeting, Transport Area WG, Vienna, Austria. Available from http://netlab. caltech.edu/FAST/ [Accessed July 18, 2003], (Jul. 18, 2003); 2003.

[31] Arianfar S. TCP's congestion control implementation in Linux kernel. In: Proceedings of Seminar on Network Protocols in Operating Systems. Vol. 16; 2012.

[32] Bogdanoski M, Suminoski T, and Risteski A. Analysis of the SYN flood DoS attack. International Journal of Computer Network and Information Security (IJCNIS). 2013;5(8):1–11.

[33] Echevarria JJ, Garaizar P, and Legarda J. An experimental study on the applicability of SYN cookies to networked constrained devices. Software: Practice and Experience. 2018;48(3):740–749.

[34] Haggerty J, Berry T, Shi Q, *et al.* DiDDeM: A system for early detection of TCP SYN flood attacks. In: IEEE Global Telecommunications Conference, 2004. GLOBECOM'04. Vol. 4. IEEE; 2004. p. 2037–2042.

[35] Trammell B and Schatzmann D. On flow concurrency in the internet and its implications for capacity sharing. In: Proceedings of the 2012 ACM Workshop on Capacity Sharing; 2012. p. 15–20.

[36] Ahmed Z, Mahbub M, and Soheli SJ. Defense against SYN flood attack using LPTR-PSO: A three phased scheduling approach. International Journal of Advanced Computer Science and Applications. 2017;8(9):433–441.

[37] Trabelsi Z and Ibrahim W. A hands-on approach for teaching denial of service attacks: A case study. Journal of Information Technology Education Innovations in Practice. 2013;12:299.

[38] Safa H, Chouman M, Artail H, *et al.* A collaborative defense mechanism against SYN flooding attacks in IP networks. Journal of Network and Computer Applications. 2008;31(4):509–534.

[39] Daneshgadeh S, Baykal N, and Ertekin Ş. DDoS attack modeling and detection using smo. In: 2017 16th IEEE International Conference on Machine Learning and Applications (ICMLA). IEEE; 2017. p. 432–436.

[40] Snehi M and Bhandari A. Apprehending mirai botnet philosophy and smart learning models for IoT-DDoS detection. In: 2021 8th International Conference on Computing for Sustainable Global Development (INDIACom). IEEE; 2021. p. 501–505.

[41] Mittal M, Kumar K, and Behal S. DDoS-AT-2022: A distributed denial of service attack dataset for evaluating DDoS defense system. Proceedings of the Indian National Science Academy. 2023;89(2):306–324.

[42] Trabelsi Z, Zeidan S, Shuaib K, *et al.* Improved session table architecture for denial of stateful firewall attacks. IEEE Access. 2018;6:35528–35543.

[43] Morris RT. A Weakness in the 4.2 BSD Unix TCP/IP Software. Computing Science. AT and T Bell Laboratories. 1985.

[44] Blum L, Blum M, and Shub M. A simple unpredictable pseudo-random number generator. SIAM Journal on Computing. 1986;15(2): 364–383.

[45] Ivanovich M, Bickerdike PW, and Li JC. On TCP performance enhancing proxies in a wireless environment. IEEE Communications Magazine. 2008;46(9):76–83.

[46] Packard NH, Crutchfield JP, Farmer JD, *et al.* Geometry from a time series. Physical Review Letters. 1980;45(9):712.
[47] Zeng F, Yin K, and Chen M. Research on TCP initial sequence number prediction method based on adding-weight chaotic time series. In: 2008 The 9th International Conference for Young Computer Scientists. IEEE; 2008. p. 1511–1515.
[48] Silbersack MJ. Improving TCP/IP security through randomization without sacrificing interoperability. University of Wisconsin-Milwaukee; 2005.
[49] Murdoch SJ and Lewis S. Embedding covert channels into TCP/IP. In: International Workshop on Information Hiding. Springer; 2005. p. 247–261.
[50] Medeiros JPS, Brito AM, and Pires PSM. A new method for recognizing operating systems of automation devices. In: 2009 IEEE Conference on Emerging Technologies & Factory Automation. IEEE; 2009. p. 1–4.
[51] Zelinka I, Merhaut F, and Skanderova L. Investigation on operating systems identification by means of fractal geometry and os pseudorandom number generators. In: International Joint Conference CISIS' 12-ICEUTE' 12-SOCO' 12 Special Sessions. Springer; 2013. p. 151–158.

Chapter 4
Dynamic routing and access control lists

Zhijie Fan[1], Yue Cao[1] and Hai Lin[1]

This chapter explores dynamic routing algorithms, including link-state routing, distance vector routing, and hierarchical routing. It delves into Internet routing protocols such as Routing Information Protocol (RIP), Open Shortest Path First (OSPF), and Border Gateway Protocol (BGP). Additionally, it covers routing algorithms for ad hoc networks, encompassing proactive, reactive, hybrid, geographic, artificial intelligence-enabled, secure-aware, and blockchain-based routing. The chapter also provides an overview of access control lists, detailing their usage, operating principles, and applications.

4.1 Introduction

A router, also known as a pathfinder, is a fundamental network layer device and a vital Internet component. It performs protocol translation at the network and lower layers of the Open System Interconnection (OSI) model. This capability allows it to connect two or more networks that differ in the lower three layers. A router comprises components such as a Central Processing Unit (CPU), Random Access Memory (RAM), and interfaces. Its primary functions include determining network addresses and selecting IP paths [1].

Routers can deliver packets to their destination through a selected transmission path known as routing. Routing is the process of forwarding the packets from the device through the best path. The key to routing in a router is the presence of a routing table database that holds routing information. This routing table contains the addresses of each subnet in the interconnection network, the paths taken to reach each subnet, and the transmission overhead associated with the paths. Multiple network interfaces on each router can be connected to the network or other routers separately. For example, when node A sends a packet to node B, it first checks whether destination B is connected to the same network as source A. If so, the packet is delivered directly to node B without passing through a router. However, if they are not on the same network, the packet is sent to a router on the network where node B is located. According to the route indicated in the routing table, this router will forward the packet to the next router, called indirect delivery. When a router receives a packet on an interface, it first finds the IP address of the destination in the packet. Then,

[1] School of Cyber Science and Engineering, Wuhan University, China

it calculates the address of the network based on this IP address and looks up this address in the routing table. Each network address in the routing table corresponds to a forwarding interface. Decide which interface the packet should be forwarded to by comparing the lookup results.

The correctness of routing in the Internet depends on the correctness of the routing table. Thus, the information in the routing table needs to be updated in time. The algorithm for creating and updating the routing table is called a routing algorithm. At regular intervals or when the network changes, each router in the network updates its routing table according to the routing algorithm. The routing table maintenance is accomplished by exchanging routing information between routers. Routing can be divided into two main categories: non-adaptive algorithms (also known as static routing) and adaptive algorithms (also known as dynamic routing) [2].

The network administrator pre-sets static routing and will not vary with the network topology unless manually reset. For complex Internet topology, its adaptability could be better. The configuration of static routing can be challenging for network administrators, not only in terms of workload but also in terms of packets traveling in circles on the Internet. The main advantages of static routing include security, reliability, simplicity, and intuitiveness while also avoiding the overhead of dynamic routing. After a static route is configured, IP packets are delivered along a fixed path to the destination network. The default routing is a special kind of static routing. After the network administrator configures default routing, if no matching entry exists between the routing table and destination address, the router will send the packet to the default gateway. Among all routings, static routing has the highest priority. When a conflict occurs between dynamic and static routing, the static routing prevails.

Dynamic routing can automatically build its routing table through its learning. It can be adjusted automatically according to the changes in network topology, which is suitable for Internet environments with complex topology and large network sizes. Dynamic routing mechanisms depend on maintaining routing tables and dynamically exchanging routing information between routers.

The ultimate goal of exchanging routing information is to find the "best" route through the routing table. Its primary disadvantage is that it takes up network bandwidth, router resources, and CPU processing time. As shown in Figure 4.1, the Internet uses dynamic routing, and packets sent by node A may go through path R1→R2→R3 to node B. Once router R2 fails, the router can automatically adjust the routing table to continue sending data through the backup path R1→R4→R3. If

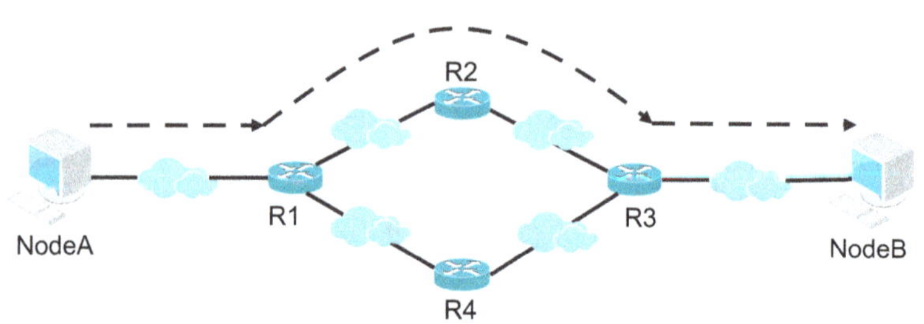

Figure 4.1 Data transmission by dynamic routing

router R2 is back to normal, the router can automatically modify the routing table again and continue to send data using path R1→R2→R3.

Routing protocols facilitate the exchange of routing information between routers. The purpose of dynamic routing protocols includes discovering remote networks, maintaining up-to-date routing information, choosing the best path to destination networks, and finding the best path if the current path is no longer available.

4.2 Routing algorithm

When packets flow from the sender to the receiver, the network layer must determine the routes or paths for these packets. The algorithm that calculates these paths is called the routing algorithm. A well-designed, ideal routing algorithm should exhibit the following key characteristics [3]:

- The algorithm must be correct, stable, and fair. Along the path guided by the routing table, packets can reach the destination from the source. When the network traffic and topology are relatively stable, the routing algorithm should converge to an acceptable solution. Once the network system is in operation, the algorithm must operate continuously and stably for a long time.
- The algorithm should be as simple as possible. The routing algorithm calculation consumes the router's computational resources and affects the packet forwarding delay. When designing routing algorithms for routers, choosing between routing effects and routing computation costs is inevitable. A good algorithm should be as computationally simple as possible, with valid results, to save computational resources and have value for use.
- The algorithm must adapt to changes in network topology and traffic, demonstrating its robustness. The topology and traffic volume of an actual network are constantly changing. When a router or a communication line fails, the algorithm should be capable of switching the route in time to bypass the failed router or link. When the network traffic volume changes, the algorithm should automatically adjust the route to balance the load on the links.
- The algorithm should be optimal, meaning it forwards packets with low overhead. The overhead can be measured by link length, capacity, security, propagation delay, and cost. Given the many factors involved, no routing algorithm is absolutely optimal. Here, "optimal" means the algorithm provides a more reasonable route based on specific conditions and requirements, such as the least number of hops or the lowest cost. Therefore, "optimal" is relative.

When discussing the routing algorithm, the following six main parameters are involved.

- **Hop count:** Hop count refers to the number of routers a packet passes through from the source to the destination. Generally, a lower hop count indicates a better path.
- **Bandwidth:** Bandwidth refers to the transmission rate of the link. For example, the transmission rate of the T1 link is 1.544 Mbps, which means that the bandwidth of the T1 link is 1.544 Mbps.

- **Delay:** It refers to the time a packet spends from the source to the destination.
- **Load:** Load is the amount of traffic per unit of time through the router or line.
- **Reliability:** Reliability refers to the packet loss rate during transmission.
- **Overhead:** Overhead usually refers to the cost of the transmission process, which is usually associated with the link length, link capacity, security, propagation delay, and cost.

Routing is a complex problem involving all hosts, routers, and communication lines in the network. At the same time, the network topology and traffic can change at any time. However, such changes cannot be known in advance. When congestion occurs in the network, obtaining the required routing information is difficult. Routing algorithms should have a specific mitigation capability. Since the routing algorithm is directly related to the congestion control algorithm, it can only find the routing that is relatively reasonable for a specific condition.

4.2.1 Link state routing algorithm

Link state routing requires global information to calculate the shortest cost path. Global information, including the network's entire router and state, is obtained through a reliable broadcast mechanism. The design idea of the link-state routing algorithm is straightforward and can be described in five parts. Each router must do the following for the algorithm to work correctly [4]:

1. Discover its neighboring nodes and know their network addresses.
2. Set the distance or cost metric to each neighbor node.
3. Construct a packet containing all the link information it learned.
4. Send this packet to all other routers and receive information packets from all other routers.
5. Calculate the shortest path to each other router.

Therefore, all routers in the network have a consistent view of the network topology and link costs. Then, the Dijkstra algorithm calculates the least cost path for each router. Since all routers use the same least-cost path algorithm and network topology to construct their routing tables, packets will be forwarded on the least-cost path in a hop-by-hop mode.

The Dijkstra algorithm computes the least-cost path from the source to all other nodes in the network, forming a minimum spanning tree. The basic idea of the Dijkstra algorithm is to find the least-cost path to all other nodes iteratively. Each iteration selects a least-cost path from the source to a destination. After k iterations, the k most minor cost paths to k destination nodes are found. Therefore, for a network with N nodes, the Dijkstra algorithm will iterate $N-1$ times before terminating. Algorithm 1 shows the pseudo-code of the Dijkstra algorithm. The following symbols are used in the pseudo-code.

- $lc(s, v)$: the link cost from node s to node v. If node s and node v are not directly connected, the link cost from node s to node v is set to infinity.
- $C(v)$: the iteration to the current node, i.e., the least-cost path from source s to node v.

- $p(v)$: the direct antecedent (successor) node along the shortest path node u.
- T: the set of nodes for which the least-cost path is known.

Algorithm 1 Dijkstra

```
for v in V − {s} do:
    if v is adjacent to s then
        C(v) = lc(s, v)
        p(v) = s
    else
        C(v) = ∞
    end if
end for
T = {s}
iteration = 0
while iteration < N − 1 do
    find w not in T s.t. C(w) is the minimum for all w in {V − T}
    T = T ∪ {w}
    for v in {V − T} do:
        C(v) = min (C(v), C(w) + lc(w, v))
        if C(w) + lc(w, v) > C(v) then
            p(v) = w
        end if
    end for
    iteration = iteration + 1
end while
```

First, the node only needs to know the link cost of its outgoing link. The cost to a neighboring node is set to the cost of the link directly connected to it. The algorithm maintains a set T of nodes in a minimum spanning tree. Initially, T contains only the source s. Each iteration selects the node w with the least cost $C(w)$ from the nodes not on the spanning tree. After adding node w to the tree (i.e., the set T), if the cost from the source to v decreases due to passing through the newly added node w, the algorithm updates the cost of the node v that is not in the tree. The while loop is guaranteed to terminate after $N-1$ iterations, and $p(v)$ is recorded as the parent node of v on the minimum spanning tree. The routing table can be built from $p(v)$.

4.2.2 Distance vector routing algorithm

The distance vector routing algorithm is another key routing algorithm used on the Internet. While the link-state algorithm is a semi-centralized algorithm that uses global information, the distance vector routing algorithm is an asynchronous, distributed algorithm that uses local information. It uses only the information exchanged from directly connected neighbors.

The distance vector routing algorithm works as follows. Each router maintains a table (i.e., a vector) that lists the best currently known distances to each destination and the links used. These tables are constantly updated by exchanging information between neighbors. Eventually, each router will know the best link to each destination. The distance vector routing algorithm is often called the distributed Bellman–Ford routing algorithm, named after its designer.

The distributed Bellman–Ford algorithm is used to compute the least cost paths asynchronously. Unlike link-state routing, it does not require all routers to exchange link-state information and compute routing tables simultaneously. Each router recalculates routes when it receives new routing information from its neighbors. After the recalculation, the new routing information is sent to its neighbors.

Algorithm 2 shows the pseudo-code of the distance vector routing algorithm. For each node, the following routing information is maintained [5]:

- $c(x, y)$: The cost from x to its neighbor v.
- $D_x = [D_x(y) : y \in N]$: A distance vector for node x, containing the estimated cost from x to all destinations y in N. N is the set of all nodes.

Algorithm 2 Distance vector

Initialization:
for all destinations $y \in N$ **do**:
    if y is not a neighbor **then**
        $c(x, y) = \infty$
    end if
    $D_x(y) = c(x, y)$
end for
for each neighbor w **do**:
    $D_w(y) =?$ for all destinations $y \in N$
end for
for each neighbor w **do**:
    send distance vector $D_x = [D_x(y) : y \in N]$ to w
end for
loop:
wait (until seeing a link cost change to some neighbor w or receiving a distance vector from some neighbor w)
for $y \in N$ **do**:
    $D_x(y) = \min_v \{c(x, y) + D_v(y)\}$
end for
if $D_v(y)$ changed for any destination y **then**
    send distance vector $D_x = [D_x(y) : y \in N]$ to all neighbors
end if

In the initialization phase, each node x starts with $D_x(y)$, and for all nodes y in the network N, the lowest path cost from itself to node y is estimated. Then, each node occasionally sends a copy of its distance vector to each neighbor. When node x receives a new distance vector from each of its other neighbors v, it saves the distance vector of v, then uses the Bellman–Ford equation $D_x(y) = \min_v \{c(x, y) + D_v(y)\}$ to update its distance vector. If an update exists, it sends a copy of its distance vector to each neighbor when it is complete. Finally, it converges to the minimum path.

4.2.3 Hierarchical routing

Since the number of routers on the Internet is enormous, the routers are not connected to a flat network for scalability. Otherwise, neither the link state nor the distance vector algorithm can scale to a network, including hundreds or tens of thousands of routers. If all the routers on the Internet were connected to a flat network, it is not hard to imagine how large the routing table would be.

The other reason for splitting the routers into groups is administrative autonomy. For example, there are many Internet Service Providers (ISPs), each with its own router and backbone. Naturally, each ISP wants complete control over the router and backbone bandwidth to prohibit traffic from other ISPs passing through its backbone. Therefore, Internet routers are organized into two layers [6].

At the lower layer, routers are divided into administrative domains or Autonomous Systems (ASes) [7]. Routers within the same AS are under the same administrative control and run the same routing protocol, called intra-domain routing protocol or Interior Gateway Protocol (IGP). A device selected from an AS, called a border router, will have physical links to the border routers of other ASes. The border routers are responsible for forwarding packets to the external AS. The inter-domain routing protocol, or External Gateway Protocol (EGP), runs between these border routers, which may differ from the intra-domain routing protocol.

Therefore, the Internet can be viewed as an interconnected AS. There are three types of ASes: stub AS, multihomed AS, and transit AS. Many users access the Internet through a campus or corporate network, typical of a stub AS. Because a stub AS has only one border router and is connected to only one ISP, no traffic is forwarded through the stub AS. A multihomed AS may have multiple border routers and be connected to multiple ISPs. However, multihomed AS also does not allow forwarding traffic to pass through. Most ISPs need to allow forwarding traffic and have many border routers to connect to other ISPs, so they are called transit ASes.

Figure 4.2 shows a simple network consisting of three ASes, A, B, and C. Each domain has multiple intra-domain routers, e.g., intra-domain routers B.1, B.2, B.3, and B.4 in domain B. These routers will run the IGP between them to build and maintain their routing tables. Besides, A.3, B.1, B.4, and C.1 are border routers that run the exterior gateway protocol to exchange routing information. Domains A and C are stub ASes because they do not allow forwarding traffic, while domain B is a transit AS. The following explains how intra-domain routing and inter-domain routing are used to send packets from hosts in domain A to destinations in domain C.

First, based on the results of intra-domain routing, all packets originating in domain A and destined for domain C need to be sent to A's border router A.3. Router A.3 forwards these packets to B.1 based on the results of inter-domain routing. Router B.1 knows to forward these packets to B.4 based on inter-domain routing and the actual path to B.4 based on intra-domain routing (i.e., routes between B.1 and B.4 are discovered based on intra-domain routing). Finally, router B.4 forwards these packets to border router C.1 in domain C, based on the results of the inter-domain

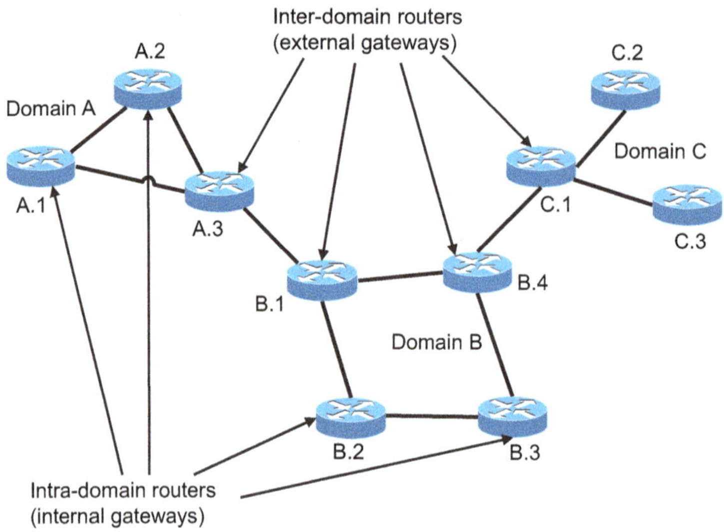

Figure 4.2 Inter-domain AS and intra-domain AS routing

route. Router C.1 then forwards these packets to the appropriate router based on the results of the intra-domain route.

Finally, revisiting the issue of Internet routing scalability. If all the routers in Figure 4.2 were viewed as a flat network, each of the ten routers would need to know the routing information of the other nine routers. However, using a two-layer hierarchical organization, each router only needs to communicate with two or three routers. The routing information for a domain is first aggregated and exchanged between border routers (or external gateways), and then the aggregated information is propagated to all internal routers. The scalability is achieved by limiting the number of routers communicating and exchanging routing information.

4.3 Routing in the Internet

The task of a routing protocol is to determine the path a packet takes between a source and a destination. The routing protocol for the Internet incorporates many of the principles mentioned earlier in this chapter. The link state, distance vector approach, and the concept of ASes all play a crucial role in the routing process of today's Internet.

4.3.1 Routing within the autonomous system: Routing Information Protocol (RIP)

The AS internal routing protocol determines how routing is performed within an AS, also known as the IGP. Historically, two routing protocols have been widely used for routing within AS on the Internet: RIP and Open Shortest Path First (OSPF) [8]. RIP is discussed first below, followed by an introduction to OSPF.

RIP [9] is one of the first Internet routing protocols within AS and is still widely used. It is created and named after the Xerox Network System (XNS) architecture. The widespread use of RIP is mainly due to its inclusion in the 1982 Berkeley Software Distribution (BSD) version of UNIX, which supports Transmission Control Protocol/Internet Protocol (TCP/IP). RIPv1 is defined in [RFC 1058], and its backward-compatible RIPv2 is defined in [RFC 2453].

RIP is a typical distance vector routing protocol. It is a straightforward routing protocol for small networks. The link cost metric RIP uses is the number of hops, i.e., all links have a cost of 1. In addition, RIP limits the maximum cost of a path to 15, i.e., a path with a cost of 16 indicates unreachability. Therefore, it is only suitable for small networks with a diameter of less than 15 hops.

In RIP, routing update information is exchanged between neighbors using an RIP response packet, which is exchanged approximately every 30 seconds. The response packet sent by a router contains a list of up to 25 destination subnets within the AS and the distance from the sender to each subnet. The response packet is also known as an RIP advertisement.

RIP uses several mechanisms to solve the stability problem of distance vector routing. First, the path cost is limited to 15 to enable rapid identification of link failures. A three-part solution to the loop problem is also used: horizontal splitting, poisoned reverse, and hold-down timers. As mentioned above, horizontal splitting suppresses updates on reverse routes. Poisoned reverse explicitly sends updates to neighbors, but with the routes learned from neighbors, toxicity reversal sets their routing metric to infinity in the update. Stabilization timers avoid sending routing updates too quickly. Once a route packet is invalidated, the route is in a suppressed state for a while, i.e., no further routing updates are received for the same destination address for a certain period.

The second version of RIP has better scalability than the first version. For example, RIPv2 supports CIDR (i.e., Classless Inter-Domain Routing), allowing route aggregation for any length of prefixes. The packet format of RIPv2 is shown in Figure 4.3. Each packet is populated with routing table entries. Each routing table entry includes information such as address family identifier, destination address, subnet mask, next hop, and distance.

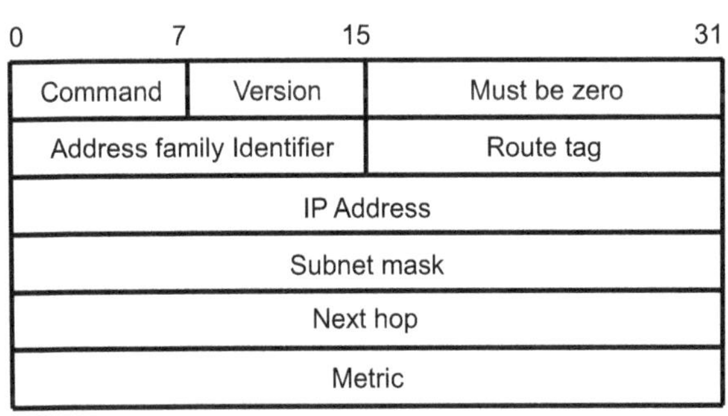

Figure 4.3 RIPv2 packet format

4.3.2 Routing within the autonomous system: OSPF

OSPF [10] is another commonly used IGP and is the dominant IGP after RIP. The OSPFv2 [11] and IPv6-based extensions of OSPF are defined in [RFC 2328] and [RFC 5340], respectively. OSPF is envisioned as a successor to RIP because of its many advanced features. However, at its core, OSPF is a link-state protocol that uses flooded link-state information and a Dijkstra shortest path algorithm. With OSPF, a router builds a complete topological map (i.e., a graph) of the entire AS. The router then runs the Dijkstra algorithm locally, which determines a tree of shortest paths to all subnets with itself as the root node.

OSPF has several unique features that make it superior to the RIP protocol. First, OSPF supports multipath routing at the exact cost of load balancing. Second, each route is described by a prefix length to support CIDR routing. Third, multicast routing can be based on the results of unicast routing. Multicast routing protocol and Multicast OSPF (MOSPF) use the same topology database as OSPF. In addition, for stability and security, a routing packet is accompanied by an 8-byte password for authentication. Finally, OSPF has a two-layer structure for scalability so that an OSPF AS can be further divided into multiple areas. An area is a set of neighboring networks and hosts. The topology of an area is invisible to the outside world. Therefore, routing within an AS is divided into two layers: intra-domain routing and inter-domain routing.

Understanding OSPF terminology is crucial for comprehending the protocol's operation. Key terms include Router_ID, overhead, link state, and neighbor [12].

- **Router_ID:** Routers running the OSPF protocol must have a unique Router_ID within the network. Duplicate IDs can prevent routers from identifying the initiator of link-state information and accurately determining network locations. Each OSPF router includes its own Router_ID in the link state it sends.
- **Overhead (Cost):** The OSPF protocol selects the best path based on bandwidth, where higher bandwidth results in lower calculated overhead. The optimal path has the lowest cumulative overhead across the links to the target network. OSPF calculates this overhead using the bandwidth of each interface. When a router must traverse multiple interfaces to reach the target network, it sums the overhead of each outgoing interface to determine the total cost.

  OSPF can automatically calculate interface overhead, but it also allows for manual specification, which takes priority over automatic calculations. For paths with equal overhead to the target network, OSPF can simultaneously enable load balancing across up to six links.
- **Link state:** In OSPF, a "link" is a router interface participating in the OSPF process. The link state describes the OSPF interface with details like IP address, subnet mask, network type, and overhead. Instead of exchanging routing tables, OSPF routers exchange link states, allowing each router to build an accurate path to each destination by gathering link-state information across the network.

  OSPF routers share their link states openly with neighbors, who then add these states to their Link State Database (LSDB) and relay them unchanged to their own neighbors. This process ensures that all OSPF routers eventually hold identical link-state information, forming a consistent view of the network topology.

Unlike RIP, which directly exchanges routing tables, OSPF's exchange of link states allows it to construct a precise network map based on each interface's link state. This approach gives OSPF a more detailed understanding of the network compared to distance-vector protocols.

- **Neighbor:** OSPF exchanges link-state information only in the neighbor state, where each router sends its complete LSDB contents to all neighbors without reservation. OSPF neighbors must first be established to enable link-state exchanges, relying on periodic Hello packets to form and maintain these relationships. Hello packets are sent at intervals specific to each network type on interfaces where OSPF is enabled. If the four times Hello interval is exceeded, the neighbor relationship will be disconnected if no Hello packet is received from the neighbor within Time-To-Live (TTL).

4.3.2.1 Working process of OSPF protocol

A router running OSPF maintains three tables: the neighbor table, the link-state table, and the routing table. The following section explores how the OSPF protocol functions by examining the process of generating these tables.

Creation of neighbor table.
A router in an OSPF area first establishes an adjacency with neighboring routers as follows: upon starting, the router sends a Hello packet every 10 seconds to discover active neighbors and assess the cost of reaching them, building a neighbor table in the process. If no Hello packet is received from a neighbor within 40 seconds, that neighbor is considered unreachable, prompting an immediate update to the LSDB and a recalculation of the routing table.

Creation of link-state table.
After generating the neighbor table, the neighboring routers must exchange the link state. When building the link-state table, the routers must go through the exchange, load, and full adjacency states.

Exchange state: OSPF lets each router exchange the link-state summary information already in this database with neighboring routers.

Load state: After exchanging database description packets with neighboring routers, the routers use link-state request packets to request from each other to send detailed information about the missing link-state items. Through this series of packet exchanges, a network-wide synchronized LSDB is established.

Full adjacency state: The synchronization of LSDB between neighbors is completed, which is judged by the neighbor link-state request list being empty and the neighbor state being loaded.

Creation of routing table.
Each router runs the shortest path first algorithm, using the established link-state table to generate the routing table to reach the destination network.

4.3.2.2 Hierarchical OSPF networks

Multiarea OSPF is implemented in a two-layer area hierarchy:

Transit area (backbone or area 0). The function of this area is the fast and efficient movement of IP packets. It interconnects with other OSPF area types and is called OSPF Area 0. All other areas must connect directly to this backbone area.

Regular (non-backbone) area. All data traffic within this area must be relayed through Area 0. A regular area does not permit traffic from another area to use its links to reach other areas.

Figure 4.4 shows the hierarchical structure of an OSPF network. There are four types of routers: two types of border routers and two types of internal routers. An area consists of multiple internal routers and one or more area border routers. The internal routers perform only intra-area routing and learn routing information about the external area from the area border router.

An area border router participates in both inter-area and intra-area routing. It aggregates routing information from other areas within and outside the AS and then broadcasts this information throughout the area. The AS border router participates in intra-area routing and inter-area routing. It runs OSPF to obtain routing information in the AS and runs external routing protocols, such as Border Gateway Protocol (BGP), to learn routing information outside the AS. The external routing information is advertised throughout the AS without modification. The backbone router is the intermediary router that contacts the AS border router and area border router.

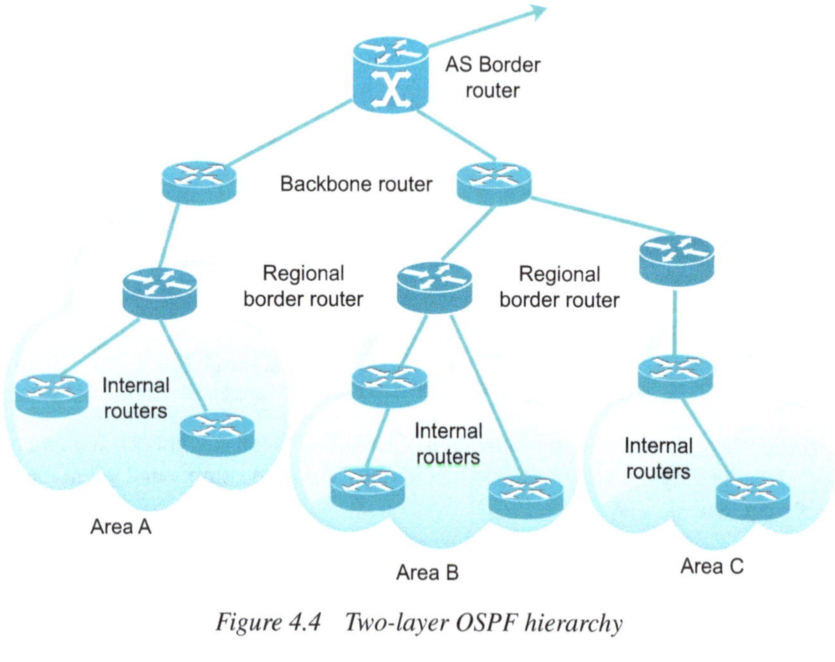

Figure 4.4 Two-layer OSPF hierarchy

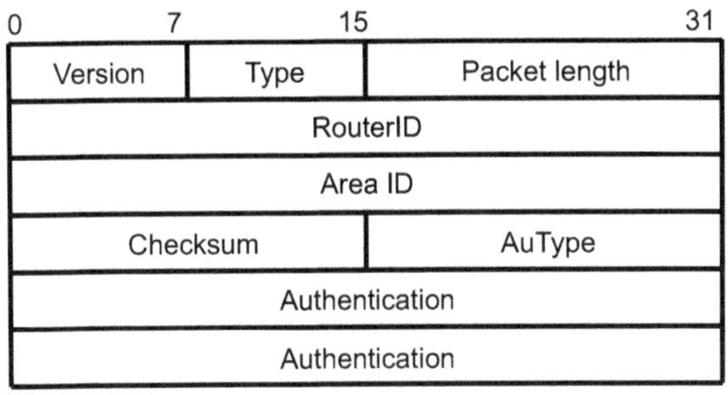

Figure 4.5 OSPF packet format

4.3.2.3 OSPF packet format

The header of an OSPF packet is shown in Figure 4.5. The type field indicates the type of the packet, and there are five types of OSPF packets:

- **Hello:** Discovers neighbors and builds adjacencies between them.
- **Link-State Update:** Sends specifically requested link-state records.
- **Link-State Acknowledgment:** Acknowledges the other packet types.
- **Database Description:** Checks for database synchronization between routers.
- **Link-State Request:** Requests specific link-state records from router to router.

Following the type field are the IP address and area ID of the source router. All packets, except for the authentication data, are protected by a 16-bit checksum, allowing types of authentication mechanisms to be applied. The authentication type indicates the mechanism used.

4.3.3 Routing between autonomous systems: BGP

The above describes how ISPs use RIP and OSPF to determine optimized paths, which are between source and destination pairs located within the same AS. The following describes how paths are determined between source and destination pairs that span multiple ASes. The BGP [13] version 4, defined by [RFC 4271] (see also [RFC 4274]), is the standard for inter-domain routing protocols on the Internet today. Commonly known as BGP4 or simply BGP, this inter-AS routing protocol [14] provides each AS with the means to do the following:

- Obtain subnet reachability information from the neighboring AS.
- Disseminate the reachability information to all routers within this AS.
- Decide on the "good" route to the subnet based on the reachability information and AS policies.

More importantly, BGP enables each subnet to announce its existence to the rest of the Internet. A subnet loudly announces, "I exist, I am here," then BGP ensures that all ASes on the Internet know about the subnet and how to get there. Without BGP, each subnet would be isolated, i.e., unknown to the rest of the Internet.

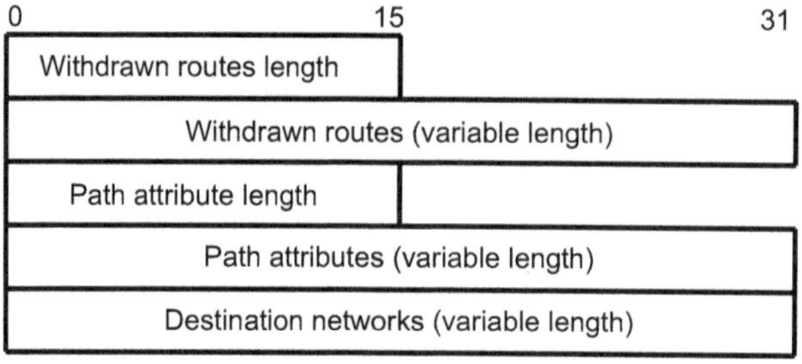

Figure 4.6 Grouping format of BGP UPDATE packet

4.3.3.1 Path vector routing

The high number of AS routers on the Internet makes the distance vector algorithm generally more suited for BGP than the link-state algorithm. However, prioritizing reachability and loop prevention, BGP uses the path vector algorithm, a variant of the distance vector approach, to establish routes between networks. The path vector algorithm exchanges routing information with neighbors and includes the full path of AS numbers to prevent loops: each AS has a unique 16-bit ID, and a loop is detected if an AS ID reappears in the path. As cost definitions vary across ASes, BGP does not exchange cost information, selecting routes instead based on priorities and AS IDs in the path.

BGP uses four packet types: OPEN, KEEPALIVE, UPDATE, and NOTIFICATION. When two BGP routers establish a TCP connection, they exchange an OPEN packet. A KEEPALIVE packet is then sent periodically to confirm the connection is active. Routing information is exchanged via UPDATE packets, which, unlike RIP, do not update the entire routing table periodically. Instead, UPDATE packets include routes and paths for specific destinations the sender wants to add or withdraw. The UPDATE packet format (Figure 4.6) includes path attributes like the source of path information (IGP, EGP, or incomplete), AS path list, next hop, Multi-Exit Discriminator (MULTI_ EXIT_ DISC, MED) for multiple AS exits, local preference (LOCAL_ PREF) for router priority within the AS, summary route, and summary AS ID. A NOTIFICATION packet signals an error if encountered.

Each BGP router reserves all feasible paths to the destination but only advertises the "best" path to its neighbors. The choice of the "best" route depends on the AS policy. However, preference is generally given to larger LOCAL_PREF, shorter paths, lower MEDs, etc. Once the "best" route is determined for a destination, the BGP speaker advertises the highest priority of each destination to neighboring BGP speakers via external BGP. Then, the BGP speaker disseminates its learned routing information to BGP routers (non-BGP speakers) via internal BGP.

4.4 Routing in ad hoc network

The former part of this chapter describes how routing works when the host is mobile and the router is fixed. Another scenario is when the router itself is mobile. This possibility occurs in several situations: emergency rescue efforts at the site of an earthquake, military vehicles on the battlefield, a fleet of ships sailing at sea, or a group of people equipped with laptops gathered in an area without an 802.11 network [15]. In these scenarios, each node communicates wirelessly and assumes the dual role of both router and host. If the network nodes are close to each other, then the network is called an ad hoc network or a Mobile Ad hoc Network (MANET) [16].

In a wired network, if a router has a valid path to a certain destination that path will remain valid (unless it fails). In ad hoc networks, the topology may change every moment, so the desirability and validity of paths change spontaneously, even without warning. These situations make ad hoc network routing more challenging than fixed routing. Many routing algorithms have been proposed for ad hoc networks. The following section will introduce them one by one.

4.4.1 Proactive routing

Proactive routing, also known as table-driven routing, includes protocols like Destination Sequenced Distance Vector (DSDV) and Optimized Link State Routing (OLSR). In this approach, the routing table is continuously updated whenever a node transmits a packet from a source to a destination or when the topology changes. The main disadvantage of proactive routing is the unnecessary table updates that occur frequently [17].

4.4.1.1 DSDV

DSDV [18] is a proactive, loop-free routing protocol that addresses the limitations of the Bellman–Ford algorithm, which is used to find the shortest path from the source to the destination. A key drawback of the Bellman–Ford algorithm is its potential to create loops. DSDV improves upon this by ensuring loop-free operation. The DSDV protocol continuously updates its routing table whenever a source sends a packet to the destination or neighboring node, ensuring that it always has access to the most current routing information.

In the DSDV protocol, there are two ways of updating the routing table:

- Full dump: Transmitting all routing information regardless of whether the routes in the routing table have changed.
- Incremental dump: Transmitting only the updated routing information can reduce network overhead and transmission delay.

By using these two update ways, the DSDV protocol can dynamically update the routing table, maintain the accuracy of routing information, and reduce the overhead associated with routing table maintenance.

4.4.1.2 OLSR

OLSR [19] is also a proactive routing protocol that optimizes the traditional algorithm. For traditional link-state routing algorithms, each node (router) in the network broadcasts its link-state information to all other nodes, a process known as flooding. Eventually, each node gets an identical network topology graph after flooding. In OLSR, each node selects some neighboring nodes to act as a MultiPoint Relay

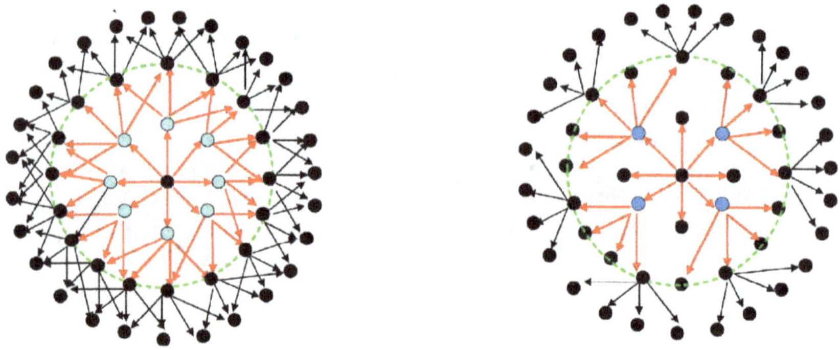

Figure 4.7 Flooding and multipoint relay

(MPR). Only MPR nodes can broadcast and propagate control packets, thus reducing the information transmitted.

The left shows the classical flooding technique as shown in Figure 4.7. Each node needs to broadcast the packet to all its neighboring nodes. The right shows the OLSR protocol, which introduces the MPR. Each node simply transmits the packet to MPR nodes, and they broadcast the packet.

4.4.2 Reactive routing

Reactive routing is on-demand routing [20]. It differs from table-based routing protocols (such as distance vector protocols and link-state protocols), which require maintaining routing tables throughout the network. In contrast, reactive routing protocols only look for and establish routes when needed.

In reactive routing, when a node needs to forward a packet to a target node, it first sends a route request into the network. Then, the request is transmitted through other nodes in the network until it reaches the target node or finds the route information of the target node. Once the routing information of the target node is found, the route is established, and the data are transmitted.

4.4.2.1 Ad Hoc On-Demand Distance Vector (AODV)

AODV [21] is a reactive routing protocol that enables mobile nodes to obtain routes to the destination quickly. Nodes need to maintain only routing information to neighbors rather than to more distant nodes. This protocol includes two processes: route discovery and route maintenance.

1. **Route Discovery:** If the source has no valid route to the destination, it will perform a route discovery process.
   Step 1: The source creates the route request packet RREQ, which contains the source address, current sequence number, destination address, destination sequence number, and broadcast ID.
   Step 2: The source node broadcasts RREQ and sets a timer to wait for the answer packet RREP.

Step 3: When a node receives an RREQ, it checks whether it has already received this RREQ.
Step 4: The node sets up a reverse route entry for the source in its routing table, with information including the source IP, sequence number, the number of hops to the source, and the IP of the neighbor who sends the RREQ.
Step 5: When the node has a valid entry for the destination in its routing table, and the sequence number associated with the destination is greater than or equal to the sequence number of the destination carried in the RREQ, the intermediate node will respond to the RREQ and transmit the RREP to the source. Otherwise, the node will continue to forward the RREQ based on the routing table.
Step 6: When the other intermediate node receives the RREP, it will set a forwarding path entry in its routing table to reach the destination. Then, it forwards the RREP to the source.
Step 7: When the source receives RREP for the first time, it starts transmitting data. If the RREQ is lost, the source rebroadcasts the RREQ to restart the route discovery process.

2. **Route maintenance:** The discovered routes will be maintained as long as the source needs them. If the source moves, the route discovery process is restarted. If the destination or intermediate node moves, a route error packet RERR is created, its predecessor node sets its route tag invalid, and the route discovery process is restarted. Neighboring nodes periodically exchange HELLO packets to monitor the link status. When one of the links in the route is broken, the intermediate node close to the source detects and sends an RERR, then restarts the route discovery process.

4.4.2.2 Dynamic source routing (DSR)

DSR [22] is a simple and efficient routing protocol designed specifically for multi-hop wireless ad hoc networks. All routes are dynamically determined and maintained by the DSR routing protocol, which provides a fast reactive service to help ensure the successful delivery of packets, even under node mobility or other changes in the network. DSR always contains the information in the packet header. In DSR, there is no need for intermediate nodes to maintain the routing information because the packet header always maintains the information.

Before transmitting the packet, the node sends a route request, and the intermediate node checks the route cache. If the route is available, then it will be selected. When the inter-node link fails, the route reply packet is sent back to the source, and the route discovery process is initiated. The advantage of DSR is that each node contains a route cache, thus minimizing the route discovery overhead [23]. However, the overhead will also increase if the network size is huge.

4.4.3 Hybrid routing

Proactive routing and reactive routing are intended for small networks to maintain information. Hybrid routing inherits both advantages and can be used for large networks. This type of protocol provides hierarchical routing with better performance. Some existing hybrid routing protocols are Zone Routing Protocol (ZRP), Zone-Based Hierarchical Link State (ZHLS), etc.

4.4.3.1 Zone Routing Protocol (ZRP)

ZRP [24] is an ad hoc network routing protocol that uses a mixture of table-driven and on-demand routing policies. ZRP divides the network into different zones according to certain rules. In order to combine the respective advantages of on-demand and table-driven routing, the ZRP protocol specifies that each node uses a table-driven routing protocol inside the zone. The on-demand routing protocol finds the routes for nodes outside the zone.

Advantages: A proactive routing approach is used within the region, which ensures that nodes have real-time access to the routing information of all other nodes in the zone. In the inter-zone, reactive routing is used to complete the route discovery between the source and destination through the route discovery process between the boundary nodes. As the topology updating process is only in a small range, it effectively reduces the system cost. At the same time, it speeds up the route discovery process and improves the response speed of the system.

4.4.3.2 Zone-Based Hierarchical Link State (ZHLS)

ZHLS [25] is based on a hierarchical representation of the network, where the network is subdivided into regions. In ZHLS, each node has its unique node ID and a zone ID. Therefore, the network inherently consists of two structural levels: (1) the zone level and (2) the node level. It also employs two types of link-state protocols: ZONE link-state protocol and NODE link-state protocol.

Before sending the packet, the source checks the routing table in the zone. If the destination is located in its zone, then the routing information already exists. Otherwise, the source broadcasts a packet through the gateway node to find the location, and the node replies with the zone ID and the unique node ID. ZHLS has its own area ID and unique node ID, so the routing overhead of ZHLS is lower compared to AODV and DSR.

4.4.4 Geographic routing

Geographic routing is a common routing technique in MANETs, which makes routing decisions based on the geographic location information of the nodes. This routing method usually depends on the distance and relative location between nodes. Common geographic routing protocols include Greedy Perimeter Stateless Routing (GPSR) and Contention-based Geographic Routing (CGR).

4.4.4.1 Greedy Perimeter Stateless Routing (GPSR)

GPSR [26] is a routing protocol designed specifically for wireless ad hoc networks. It routes packets based on location information using a greedy forwarding strategy. The GPSR features include [27]:

Statelessness: GPSR is a stateless routing protocol where each node only needs to make routing decisions based on the current geographic location, i.e., it does not need to maintain global information about the state of the network.

Greedy routing: GPSR uses a greedy routing strategy to select the nearest neighboring node to the destination in each step. This strategy reduces the routing overhead somewhat.

Adaptation to network topology changes: Since GPSR is a geolocation-based routing protocol, it is adaptive to rapid changes in network topology.

However, GPSR faces several challenges, such as inaccurate node locations and unstable routing under dynamic network conditions. To address these issues, accurate node location information is crucial. Global Positioning System (GPS) or other positioning methods are required to calculate and provide this information. Additionally, algorithms must be designed to adapt to changes in node positions and network topology to maintain routing stability and effectiveness.

4.4.4.2 Contention-based Geographic Routing (CGR)

CGR [28] is a protocol for MANET, which has two operational schemes: greedy-forwarding and void-handling.

The greedy-forwarding scheme consists of a basic mode and an optional mode. In the basic mode, when receiving a packet from the upstream node, intermediate nodes within its forwarding area contend to relay it by waiting for a Dynamic Forwarding Delay (DFD). DFD is computed based on its position relative to the upstream node and destination. The intermediate node with minimum DFD transmits the packet first, and other nodes cancel their scheduled transmission for the same packet by overhearing its packet forwarding. In the optional mode, an upstream node can send packets to its specified downstream node if the communication link between them is valid. An accurate link forecast scheme computes the valid time based on upstream and downstream nodes' location and mobility information.

In the basic mode of the greedy forwarding scheme, the upstream node should wait for the same packet broadcasted by its downstream node within Max_delay. If the upstream node (e.g., F in Figure 4.8) does not receive the packet it has sent before within Max_delay, it assumes no intermediate nodes within the forwarding area. Node F cannot deliver the packet to destination D even if a route exists among them, such as nodes F, A, B, C, and D in Figure 4.8. This undesirable phenomenon is called the communication void problem, and the upstream node is called the void node.

In the void-handling scheme, a one-hop flooding mechanism is used to solve the communication void problem. The void node broadcasts a small Neighbor

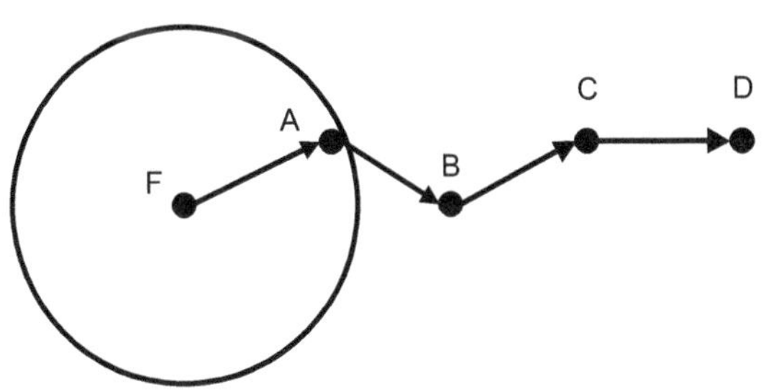

Figure 4.8 Communication Void Problem

Information Query (NIQ) packet, and all its neighboring nodes reply with Reply To Query (RTQ) packets to indicate their positions. The void node selects a neighboring node closest to the destination and unicasts the stuck packet. The void node remembers the stuck packet ID corresponding to a specific destination and refuses to accept the same packet from any of its neighboring nodes. After accepting the stuck packet, the chosen neighboring node remembers the void node ID and sends the stuck packet through a greedy forwarding scheme. If the neighboring node also does not receive any forwarding packet from a downstream node within Max_delay, it becomes a new void node. It transmits the packet through the one-hop flooding mechanism, avoiding route loops by refusing to choose the old void node as its next-hop node.

4.4.5 Artificial Intelligence (AI)-based routing protocols

AI approaches provide a novel approach to ad hoc network routing problems, which can better address the problems of limited energy, node mobility, and topology changes. These approaches can improve network performance by minimizing energy consumption, improving overheads, etc.

4.4.5.1 Biologically inspired algorithms

Most traditional optimization routing solutions are not always applicable to all network conditions, as they are designed for specific scenarios. MANETs operate under highly dynamic conditions, where nodes move at different speeds and densities are heterogeneous. Applying bio-inspired optimization techniques to developing routing protocols for MANETs can make high-performance routing possible [29].

- **Ant Colony Optimization (ACO)**

ACO [30], inspired by ant foraging techniques (which seek to achieve the optimal path from their nest to a food source), is a swarm intelligence metaheuristic technique used to compute an optimal path. ACO is a "framework for solving combinatorial optimization problems" and has been applied in MANET routing protocols. In ACO-based routing algorithms, mobile nodes create multiple ants to navigate the network and find paths between nodes. Path quality depends on the amount of "pheromone" that ants deposit based on different factors (e.g., number of hops, delay, and energy consumption).

Ant colony-based energy control routing protocol [31] balances energy consumption and increases network lifetime by considering hop counts, node and average energy, and the minimum energy of the paths to choose an optimal route. Fuzzy hierarchy ant colony optimization routing [32] is heavily influenced by the ACO routing protocol. It has four fuzzy membership functions (residual energy, mobility, buffer size, and distance) that are defined to assign a weight to nodes in a cluster. ACO is applied to the fuzzy value to choose the best cluster head.

- **Particle Swarm Optimization (PSO)**

PSO [33] is used widely to optimize MANET routing. Inspired by bird flocking and fish schooling social behaviors, PSO is a stochastic optimization technique. The algorithm is computationally inexpensive in terms of both memory and processor resources [34]. These characteristics make PSO a potential algorithm for optimizing routing in a MANET, given the limited resources of these networks.

PSO-based Bandwidth and Link Availability Prediction algorithm (PSOBLAP) [35] improved energy efficiency and link scalability using PSO and provided multi-path routing mechanisms based on bandwidth, energy level, link quality, and mobility parameters. The PSOBLAP algorithm successfully increases packet delivery ratio and path optimality while reducing end-to-end delay and link failures.

- **Cuckoo Search Algorithm**

Similar to previous research, Cuckoo Search-based routing Algorithms (CSA) [36] take inspiration from the corresponding animal. In this case, the search algorithm is based on the "brood parasitic" behavior and Levy flight pattern of cuckoo birds. Brood parasitism occurs when a bird lays an egg in the nest of another species. The host bird may discard eggs it recognizes as foreign.

As a result, the cuckoo birds can mimic the egg color and pattern of a select few species to lower the probability of their "alien" egg being abandoned. Ad hoc On-demand Distance Vector and Cuckoo Search (AODVCS) is an algorithm that uses cuckoo search to find the shortest path between source and destination, where the Levy flight is "used to generate new solutions." The protocol can increase the packet delivery rate and reduce the end-to-end delay while providing good scalability and maintaining good performance regardless of the number of nodes in the network.

- **Fungi Algorithms**

The HyphaNet algorithm proposed by [37] is inspired by fungal colony behavior. A colony is used to reference the portion that forms the body of the fungi, which will expand and allow the fungi to grow toward a nutrient source. The "filaments" that result from fungal growth form a "biological transportation network" to transport nutrients between different parts of the fungi. To help with routing, HyphaNet introduces a new metric called node attractiveness. Fungi employ this idea to choose the optimal path for distributing nutrition through filaments, and the more a filament is used for transportation, the more "attractive" it appears. This approach is intended to reduce overhead as it does not use control agents to maintain routes.

4.4.5.2 Machine Learning (ML) algorithms

Lack of adaptability is the main problem in almost all conventional routing protocols, leading to performance degradation under various conditions. To operate efficiently in dynamic environments characterized by high node mobility and frequent link changes, routing protocols must be inherently adaptable. Recently, researchers have concentrated on developing adaptive routing protocols utilizing ML techniques [38].

- **Reinforcement Learning (RL)**

RL [39], a type of dynamic programming, uses a reward or punishment system. In RL algorithms, an agent learns by receiving reward or punishment values based on its actions. These interactions with the environment guide the agent to maximize rewards and minimize penalties. The goal is to optimize various aspects of routing protocols, thereby enhancing Quality of Service (QoS), throughput, reliability, and reducing end-to-end delay.

Reinforcement Learning Routing Packet Protocol (RLRP) is a "combined routing metric, based on classical hop-count value, current Packet Loss Rate (PLR) value and received signal strength indicator or an incoming packet" [38]. The RLRP protocol introduces a reward distribution function and functions for dynamic neighbor selection. The RLRP protocol can successfully reduce PLR and recovery time value, optimizing performance and decreasing time processing overhead.

- **Learning Automata (LA)**

LA, a sub-classification of reinforcement learning, studies the environment of a learning automaton, which has a set of states, possible actions, and penalties/rewards for each action [40]. The probabilities of other actions are increased upon action selection, and the current action is decreased. LA is typically used for routing problems, especially multi-cast problems. However, they also suffer from the delay in collecting feedback, which can be a drawback.

Learning Automata-based Fault-Tolerant Routing Algorithm (LAFTRA) [41] uses the theory of LA to learn about and deal with faulty network nodes (including nodes with weak radio wave signals) and selects optimal paths while reducing routing overhead traffic and increasing network throughput. LAFTRA uses a reward and penalty strategy based on packet delivery and packet failure to calculate the "goodness" value of a path. The goodness value is then used to determine the best path.

- ***Q*-Learning**

Q-learning associates a *Q* value with each action at a given state, selecting the action with the highest *Q* as the most optimal. Similar to LA, *Q*-learning faces the drawback of delay in feedback collection. Ghaffari emphasizes the importance of maintaining high throughput in a multi-hop network for MANETs. He also identifies the unsustainable topology of MANETs as a primary challenge [42]. The author proposes an optimal solution that predicts the behavior patterns of the node to reduce packet transmission delay. The proposed method uses *Q*-learning and local information to select the best neighbor nodes to deliver the packet to the destination.

4.4.6 Secured ad hoc routing protocols

To ensure connectivity in a MANET, all nodes must engage in routing network traffic. While numerous ad hoc routing protocols, such as DSDV, OLSR, DSR, and AODV, have been proposed, they typically assume that all nodes are fully cooperative and trustworthy, overlooking the need for security mechanisms. However, MANETs often operate in less-than-friendly environments characterized by multi-hop communication and a lack of centralized management. Moreover, malicious nodes can easily join the network, leading to various performance issues, such as disrupting routing information and eavesdropping on communications.

Due to the characteristics of MANETs, they are more vulnerable to attacks than wired networks [43]. There are two main types of attacks: passive and active. Passive attacks listen for valuable information without disrupting protocol operation, while active attacks disrupt the protocol to degrade performance, gain unauthorized access, and restrict availability. Below is a brief overview of several well-known routing attacks [44].

- **Passive eavesdropping attack:** An eavesdropping attack aims to listen to the secret or confidential routing information that should be kept secret during communication. It can discover potentially sensitive topology information about the network from the information it captures.
- **Routing data manipulation attack:** A manipulation attack happens when a malicious node alters received information before forwarding it. Without integrity measures, the receiving node cannot detect tampering and may mistakenly treat the incorrect information as valid.
- **Replay attack:** A replay attack is a form of active attack in which a malicious node stores routing information and later retransmits the stored information.
- **Black hole attack:** In a black hole attack, a malicious node uses the routing protocol to advertise the shortest path to a node, thus intercepting the communicating packets passing through the malicious node. As a result, instead of normally forwarding the packets it receives, the malicious drops all packets.
- **Flooding attack:** In this attack, a malicious node aims to flood the network with many route requests in a short period to destinations in the network and then causes severe degradation of network performance.
- **Rushing attack:** This attack targets on-demand routing protocols that use duplicate suppression. The rushing node exploits this by quickly forwarding route discovery packets to include them in the discovered routes.
- **Tunnelling/wormhole attack:** The attacker circumvents the normal network path by establishing a fake "wormhole tunnel" that quickly transfers packets from one location to another.
- **Sybil attack:** In a Sybil attack, a single node presents multiple identities within the network. These false identities can be exploited to carry out various attacks. This type of attack poses a significant threat to geographic routing protocols.
- **Denial of Service:** This attack targets the availability of the node. In order to consume the network bandwidth or drain the resources of a specific node, attackers flood the network with large amounts of data.

Several proposals exist to counter the security threats mentioned above, protecting against malicious attacks and selfish behaviors. They are classified into three categories: solutions based on cryptography, solutions based on one-way hash chains, and hybrid solutions.

4.4.6.1 Routing based on cryptography

- **Symmetric cryptography solutions**

The Security-aware Ad hoc Routing (SAR) protocol [45] is an approach to ad hoc routing that incorporates security attributes as parameters into route discovery. However, traditional non-secure routing protocols find the shortest path between two nodes, while SAR can discover a path with desired security attributes. For instance, the criterion for a valid route can be when each node in the route must have a particular shared key.

SAR can be extended to any on-demand ad hoc routing protocols (such as AODV or DSR) to integrate the security metric into the route request packets. An implementation of SAR based on AODV is presented. The route request packet has an additional field (RQ_SEC_REQUIREMENT) that indicates the required security level for discovering the route. This field is only set once by the sender and does not change during the route discovery. An intermediate node that receives the packet checks if it can satisfy the security requirement. If the node can provide the required security, thus it can participate in the routing, and the route request packet is forwarded to its neighbors, updating a new field called RQ_SEC_GURANTEE to indicate the maximum level of security it can provide. If the intermediate node cannot satisfy the security requirement, it simply drops the route request packet.

When the destination receives the route request packet, it can be sure of the existence of a route from the source to the destination, and this route satisfies the security requirements defined by the sender. The destination sends a route reply packet with an additional field (RP_SEC_GUARANTEE) that indicates the maximum security available over the path. Then, the value of the RQ_SEC_GURANTEE field is copied to RP_SEC_GUARANTEE. The reply packet travels back along the reverse path. Intermediate nodes authorized to participate in routing update their routing tables per the AODV specification and record the new RP_SEC_GUARANTEE value. This value indicates the maximum security available on the cached forward path.

- **Asymmetric cryptography solutions**

Authenticated Routing for Ad hoc Networks (ARAN) [46] is a secure routing protocol built on on-demand principles. It employs cryptographic mechanisms to ensure authentication, packet integrity, and non-repudiation.

It consists of two distinct operational stages. The first stage is the preliminary certification process that requires the existence of a trusted Certificate Authority (CA). All nodes that want to connect to the network must contact the certification authority and request a certificate for its address and public key. This certification authority distributes its public key to all the nodes in the network. The second operational stage of the protocol is the route discovery process that provides end-to-end authentication. This process verifies that the intended destination has been reached.

The ARAN protocol provides both node-to-node and end-to-end authentication that guarantees protection from modification, impersonation, and fabrication attacks. However, due to heavy asymmetric cryptographic operations and large routing packets, ARAN suffers from a higher overall routing load and latency in route discovery.

4.4.6.2 Routing based on one-way hash chain

Secure Efficient Ad hoc Distance vector (SEAD) [47] is a secure ad hoc network routing protocol based on the design of the DSDV routing protocol. SEAD uses a hash chain to authenticate hop counts and sequence numbers, eliminating the need for asymmetric cryptographic operations.

In SEAD, each node creates its hash chain by applying a one-way hash function to a random value. When a node sends or transmits a routing update, it includes one value from the hash chain for each entry in that update. Nodes receiving a routing update verify the authentication of each entry by hashing the received hash value. This hashed value is then compared to the previously authenticated hash value. According to this comparison, the routing update is either accepted as authenticated or discarded.

Additionally, to avoid routing loops, SEAD employs two methods to authenticate the source of each routing update packet. The first method requires clock synchronization among nodes and uses broadcast authentication mechanisms. The second method relies on a shared secret key between each pair of nodes, utilizing a packet authentication code (e.g., MAC) to authenticate routing update packets.

SEAD is robust against multiple attackers attempting to create incorrect routing states in other nodes, even if some nodes are compromised, or active attackers are present. However, SEAD does not protect against wormhole attacks.

4.4.6.3 Hybrid solutions

The Secure Ad hoc On-demand Distance Vector protocol (SAODV) extends the AODV routing protocol [48]. It uses cryptographic signatures to authenticate the immutable fields of packets and a one-way hash chain to secure the hop-count field in RREQ and RREP packets, the only mutable field in AODV. Additionally, the protocol requires a key management mechanism that enables each node to obtain public keys from other nodes in the ad hoc network.

The information associated with the signature and hash chain is transmitted with the AODV packet as an extension packet, called a signature extension. These SAODV extensions consist of the following fields. The hash function field indicates which hash function has to be used. The field max hop count specifies the maximum number of nodes a packet is allowed to go through. The field hash is a randomly generated number called a seed. Finally, the top hash field is calculated by hashing the value in the Hash field Max Hop Count times. The format of the SAODV signature extensions is shown in Figure 4.9.

When a node sends a route request or reply in AODV, it includes a random number as a seed in the hash field. It also sets the max hop count field and specifies the hash function. After that, it applies the hash function to the seed max hop count times, and the calculated result is set to the top hash field. Furthermore, the node signs all fields except the max hop count and hash fields. An intermediate node checks

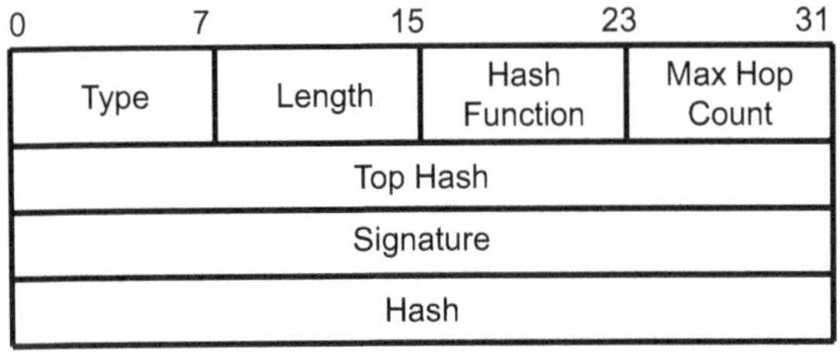

Figure 4.9 SAODV protocol header

the hop count field upon receiving a route request or reply. If the check fails, the packet will be dropped. The node then hashes the old hash value before forwarding the packet.

The security features provided by SAODV include integrity, authentication, and non-repudiation. Nevertheless, due to the use of asymmetric cryptography, SAODV suffers from performance degradation. Moreover, a hop count authentication using hash chains is not perfect, and malicious nodes might forward packets without increasing the hop count.

4.4.7 Blockchain-based routing protocols

Blockchain-based routing protocols in MANETs aim to address the security and trust issues inherent in traditional routing protocols. These protocols utilize blockchain's decentralized, tamper-proof security to improve routing reliability and safety.

Typically, blockchain-based routing protocols operate as follows:

- **Decentralized control:** Blockchain technology enables nodes in the network to participate in routing decisions without relying on centralized routers or controllers. Each node can become part of the blockchain network, validating and forwarding routing information.
- **Trust establishment:** Through the consensus mechanism of blockchain, nodes in the network can establish trust and validate routing information provided by other nodes. This approach reduces the impact of malicious nodes and enhances the overall security of the network.
- **Routing information storage:** Routing information is stored in the form of a blockchain among nodes in the network, ensuring the integrity and reliability of the information. Each new routing update is added to the blockchain, validated, and synchronized by nodes in the network.
- **Enhanced security:** Blockchain technology provides encryption and digital signature mechanisms, ensuring that routing information is not tampered with or forged during transmission. This mechanism helps prevent routing attacks such as deception and denial of service.

Blockchain-based routing protocols offer potential advantages in MANETs, including improved reliability of routing information, reduced trust costs in the network, and enhanced security.

4.4.7.1 Blockchain-based multi-hop routing protocol for non-cooperative MANETs

MANET is an infrastructure-less extended scenario of Blockchain Radio Access Network (B-RAN). Meanwhile, the decentralization of B-RAN befits MANETs. In the framework of B-RAN, Data Broker [49] is proposed as a blockchain-based multi-hop routing protocol for non-cooperative MANETs.

To incentivize collaboration among selfish peers, the authors record the identity information of participating brokers on a ledger list. However, blockchain cannot guarantee the integrity of such a routing ledger directly. Therefore, a ledger safeguard mechanism is designed, along with reward policies, to avoid the ledger list being tampered with or modified by dishonest brokers. The experimental results show that Data Broker can significantly improve the network performance of non-cooperative MANETs in terms of latency and loss rate.

4.4.7.2 Blockchain-based authentication for AODV

The reactive routing protocol AODV, as described earlier in this chapter, is efficient in MANETs due to its low overhead and reduced message exchanges by using limited information. However, this efficiency creates a weakness: nodes have limited knowledge about other nodes' identities beyond their immediate neighbors (nodes within transmission range). This limitation hinders the ability to authenticate other nodes and verify the integrity of exchanged information. To address this issue, additional message exchanges would be required, which would undermine AODV's core principles and increase overhead, potentially depleting the limited battery power of portable devices in the network.

The Blockchain AODV Routing Protocol (BAODV) [50] enhances routing by incorporating blockchain concepts. It generates a hashed identifier from each node's IP address, which is exchanged during route discovery to verify node identities and maintain information integrity. Simulation results using Riverbed/Opnet demonstrate that BAODV effectively prevents impersonation and black-hole attacks by eliminating paths involving malicious nodes, resulting in a 4 ms increase in route discovery time.

4.4.7.3 Modification of DSDV using blockchain

The original DSDV routing protocol lacks security, making it vulnerable to attacks that can disrupt its operation in MANETs. To address this, the work in [51] proposes modifications to DSDV that incorporate blockchain technology for enhanced security. Instead of allowing all nodes to create their own routing tables, a designated miner node generates a common routing table with all-pair shortest paths using the Floyd-Warshall algorithm. This table is then publicly distributed to all nodes. A group of trusted nodes serves as miners, with only one acting as the miner at any given time to manage power consumption. The authors analyze the protocol's security and performance, concluding that MANETs using the modified DSDV with blockchain are effectively protected.

4.5 Access Control Lists (ACLs)

4.5.1 Overview

ACL is an access control technique based on packet filtering, which allows packets on an interface to be filtered and allowed to be received or rejected based on set conditions. Acceptance or rejection of packets can depend on criteria such as source address, destination address, and port number. ACLs are commonly used in routers and layer three switches, enabling effective control over user access to the network and enhancing overall network security [52].

The user can make a set of rules based on specific information in the packet. Each rule describes the action taken on packets matching certain information: permit or deny. Users can apply these rules to the entry or exit direction of a network device port. So that data flows in a particular direction on a particular port and must enter or exit the switch in accordance with the specified ACL rules. With ACLs, it is possible to restrict the Internet activity of PCs with a certain IP address or PCs in certain network segments. In this way, it is used for network management.

ACLs can be categorized into standard and extended types based on their functionality. Standard ACLs, numbered in the range 1–99, match only the source address. Extended ACLs, numbered from 100 to 199, offer more advanced capabilities than standard ACLs. They can match not only the source address but also the source port, destination address, destination port, and network protocol. Extended ACLs are essential for achieving precise control. By default, ACLs deny all access.

4.5.2 Usage

Using ACLs is generally a two-step process [53]:

- **Step 1:** Write ACL statements.
- **Step 2:** Apply the ACL to the specified direction of the relevant interface or network service.

General guidelines for creating ACLs:

- Use ACLs in firewall routers positioned between internal networks and external networks such as the Internet.
- Configure ACLs on border routers, which are positioned at the edges of networks.
- Configure ACLs for each network protocol on the border router interfaces.

The three postscripts:

- *One ACL per protocol.* To control traffic flow on an interface, an ACL must be defined for each protocol enabled on the interface.
- *One ACL per direction.* ACLs manage traffic in one direction at a time on an interface, so two separate ACLs are required to control inbound and outbound traffic.
- *One ACL per interface.* ACLs control traffic for an interface, for example, GigabitEthernet 0/0.

ACL is top-down to match statements. When the above does not meet the requirements, automatically match the next statement. So, the order is significant, and each interface can only apply an ACL. Each ACL should be placed where it has the greatest impact on efficiency. The basic rules are:

- *Standard ACLs.* Because standard ACLs do not specify destination addresses, place them as close to the destination as possible.
- *Extended ACLs.* Locate extended ACLs as close as possible to the traffic source to be filtered.

- Placement of the ACL may also depend on the extent of the network administrator's control, bandwidth of the networks involved, and ease of configuration.

4.5.3 Operating principle

- **Inbound ACL logic:** When a packet enters a port, the router checks if the packet is routable. (1) If an inbound packet matches an ACL statement with a permit, it is sent to be routed. (2) If an inbound packet matches an ACL statement with a deny, it is dropped and not routed. (3) If an inbound packet does not meet any ACL statements, then it is "implicitly denied" and dropped without being routed.
- **Outbound ACL logic:** The router checks the destination port for the presence of ACL-controlled outbound packets. Packets are checked for a route before being sent to an outbound interface. (1) If there is no route, the packets are dropped. (2) If an outbound interface has no ACL, the packets are sent directly to that interface. (3) If there is an ACL on the outbound interface, packets are tested before being sent to that interface. (4) If an outbound packet matches an ACL statement with a permit, it is sent to the interface. (5) If there is no match, packets are dropped.

In summary, an inbound packet is processed by the router, which reads the packet header (e.g., target IP address) and searches the routing table to find a matching entry. If so, it is forwarded from the routing table's selected interface (if not, the packet is discarded), and the data enters the interface's ACL (if there are no access control rules, it is forwarded directly). Then filtered according to the conditions [54].

When the ACL processes a packet, once the packet matches an ACL statement, it skips the rest of the statements remaining in the list and decides to allow or reject the packet based on the content of that matching statement. If the packet content does not match the ACL statement, the packet will be tested using the next statement in the ACL in turn. The matching process continues until it reaches the end of the list. The last implied statement applies to all packets that do not satisfy any of the previous conditions. This final test condition matches these packets and usually implies a directive to reject all packets. At this point, the router will not allow these data to enter or be sent out of the interface but will simply discard it. This last statement is often called the implicit "deny any" statement. Because of this statement, there should be at least one PERMIT statement included in the ACL. Otherwise, by default, the ACL will block all traffic [55].

To effectively manage network security and access control, understanding the decision processes of ACLs is essential. The following sections will cover two fundamental ACL decision processes.

Standard ACL Decision Process: Standard ACLs only examine the source IPv4 address. The destination of the packet and the ports involved are not considered. The first match determines whether the software accepts or rejects the address. Because the software stops testing conditions after the first match, the order of the conditions is critical. If no conditions match, the address is rejected.

Extended ACL Decision Process: The ACL first filters on the source address, then on the port and protocol of the source. It then filters on the destination address, then on the port and protocol of the destination, and makes a final permit or deny decision.

4.5.4 Applications

ACLs can be applied to a variety of situations. The most common application scenarios are as follows [56]:

- Filters routing information delivered between neighboring devices.
- Control switching access to prevent illegal access to the device, such as control of the Console interface, Telnet, or SSH access.
- Control traffic and network access across network devices.
- Protect the router by restricting access to certain services on the router, such as HTTP, SNMP, and NIP.
- Define flows of interest for DDR and IPSeC VPNs.
- The capability to implement QoS features in IOS in various ways.
- Extended applications in other security technologies, such as TCP interception and IOS firewalls.

4.6 Conclusion

This chapter first introduces the definition of routing options, as well as static routing versus dynamic routing. Second, routing algorithms are presented, including link state routing algorithm, distance vector routing algorithm, and hierarchical routing. Then, the routing on the Internet is described in detail, i.e., RIP, OSPF, and BGP. In addition, a detailed description of routing in ad hoc networks is given, including proactive routing, reactive routing, AI-based routing, and secured routing. Finally, ACLs techniques and applications are introduced.

References

[1] Peterson LL and Davie BS. Computer Networks: A Systems Approach. 6th ed. Morgan Kaufmann. 2021.

[2] Gutiérrez J, Cuevas R, Riaz T, Pedersen JM, and Madsen OB. Characterization of static/dynamic topological routing for grid networks. 2009 Eighth International Conference on Networks. 2009; p. 367–373.

[3] Zhang Q. Principles and Applications of Computer Networks (in Chinese). Nanjing University Press. 2019.

[4] Lin Y-D, Hwang R-H, and Baker F. Computer Networks: An Open Source Approach. 1st ed. McGraw-Hill Education. 2011.

[5] Kurose J and Ross K. Computer Networking: A Top-Down Approach. 7th ed. Pearson. 2016.

[6] Al-Karaki JN and Kamal AE. Routing techniques in wireless sensor networks: a survey. IEEE Wireless Communications. 2004;11(6):6–28.

[7] Halsall F. Data Communications, Computer Networks, and Open Systems. 4th ed. Pearson. 1996.

[8] Verma A and Bhardwaj N. A review on routing information protocol (RIP) and open shortest path first (OSPF) routing protocol. International Journal of Future Generation Communication and Networking. 2016;9(4):161–170.

[9] Hedrick CL. RFC1058: Routing information protocol. 1988.
[10] Moy J. RFC2328: OSPF Version 2. 1998.
[11] Katz D, Kompella K, and Yeung D. Traffic engineering (TE) extensions to OSPF version 2. No. rfc3630. 2003.
[12] Han L, Han L, Wang Y, and Ma Q. Deep Dive into Computer Networks (in Chinese). People's Posts and Telecommunications Press. 2021.
[13] Rekhter Y, Li T, and Hares S. RFC 4271: A border gateway protocol 4 (BGP-4). 2006.
[14] Nicholes MO and Mukherjee B. A survey of security techniques for the border gateway protocol (BGP). IEEE Communications Surveys & Tutorials. 2009;11(1):52–65.
[15] Tanenbaum A and Wetherall D. Computer Networks. 5th ed. Pearson. 2010.
[16] Corson S and Macker J. RFC2501: Mobile ad hoc networking (MANET): Routing protocol performance issues and evaluation considerations. 1999.
[17] Chauhan A and Sharma V. Review of performance analysis of different routing protocols in MANETs. International Conference on Computing, Communication and Automation (ICCCA). 2016; p. 541–545.
[18] Perkins CE and Bhagwat P. Highly dynamic destination-sequenced distance-vector routing (DSDV) for mobile computers. ACM SIGCOMM Computer Communication Review. 1994;24(4):234–244.
[19] Clausen T and Jacquet P. RFC3626: Optimized link state routing protocol (OLSR). 2003.
[20] Perkins CE, Royer EM, Das SR, and Marina MK. Performance comparison of two on-demand routing protocols for ad hoc networks. IEEE Personal Communications. 2001;8(1):16–28.
[21] Das SR, Perkins CE, and Belding-Royer EM. RFC3561: Ad hoc on-demand distance vector (AODV) routing. 2003.
[22] Johnson DB, Maltz DA, and Broch J. DSR: The dynamic source routing protocol for multi-hop wireless ad hoc networks. Ad Hoc Networking. 2001;5(1):139–172.
[23] Boukerche A, Turgut B, Aydin N, Ahmad MZ, Boloni L, and Turgut D. Routing protocols in ad hoc networks: A survey. Computer Networks. 2011;55(13):3032–3080.
[24] Beijar N. Zone routing protocol (ZRP). Networking Laboratory, Helsinki University of Technology. 2002;9(1):12.
[25] Hamma T, Katoh T, Bista BB, and Takata T. An efficient ZHLS routing protocol for mobile ad hoc networks. 17th International Workshop on Database and Expert Systems Applications (DEXA'06). 2006; p. 66–70.
[26] Karp B and Kung HT. GPSR: Greedy perimeter stateless routing for wireless networks. Proceedings of the 6th Annual International Conference on Mobile Computing and Networking. 2000; p. 243–254.
[27] Ko YB and Vaidya NH. Geocasting in mobile ad hoc networks: Location-based multicast algorithms. Proceedings WMCSA'99 Second IEEE Workshop on Mobile Computing Systems and Applications. 1999; p. 101–110.
[28] Li X, Zhang J, and Shi X. CGR: Contention-based geographic routing protocol for mobile ad hoc networks. 2008 4th International Conference

on Wireless Communications, Networking and Mobile Computing. 2008; p. 1–4.

[29] Blazevic L, Le Boudec J-Y, and Giordano S. A location-based routing method for mobile ad hoc networks. IEEE Transactions on Mobile Computing. 2005;4(2):97–110.

[30] Meng X and Deng Y. A time-aware resource search strategy with the ant colony optimization in MANETs. Peer-to-Peer Networking and Applications. 2019;12:1013–1027.

[31] Zhou J, Tan H, Deng Y, Cui L, and Liu DD. Ant colony-based energy control routing protocol for mobile ad hoc networks. International Conference on Wireless Algorithms, Systems, and Applications, Springer. 2015; p. 845–853.

[32] Kandan JM and Sabari A. Fuzzy hierarchical ant colony optimization routing for weighted cluster in manet. Cluster Computing. 2019;22(4):9637–9649.

[33] Manickavelu D and Vaidyanathan RU. Particle swarm optimization (PSO)-based node and link lifetime prediction algorithm for route recovery in MANET. EURASIP Journal on Wireless Communications and Networking. 2014; p. 1–10.

[34] Ali H, Shahzad W, and Aslam Khan F. Energy-efficient clustering in mobile ad-hoc networks using multi-objective particle swarm optimization. Applied Soft Computing. 2012;12(7):1913–1928.

[35] Harold Robinson Y, Balaji S, and Golden Julie E. PSOBLAP: Particle swarm optimization-based bandwidth and link availability prediction algorithm for multipath routing in mobile ad hoc networks. Wireless Personal Communications. 2019;106(4):2261–2289.

[36] Kout A, Labed S, Chikhi S, and Bourennane EB. AODVCS, a new bio-inspired routing protocol based on cuckoo search algorithm for mobile ad hoc networks. Wireless Networks. 2018;24:2509–2519.

[37] da Costa Bento CR and Wille ECG. Bio-inspired routing algorithm for MANETs based on fungi networks. Ad Hoc Networks. 2020;107:102248.

[38] Dugaev DA, Matveev IG, Siemens E, and Shuvalov VP Adaptive reinforcement learning-based routing protocol for wireless multihop networks. 2018 XIV International Scientific-Technical Conference on Actual Problems of Electronics Instrument Engineering (APEIE). 2018; p. 209–218.

[39] Sutton RS and Barto AG. Reinforcement learning: An introduction. Robotica. 1999;17(2):229–235.

[40] Karunaratne S and Gacanin H. An overview of machine learning approaches in wireless mesh networks. IEEE Communications Magazine. 2019;57(4):102–108.

[41] Misra S, Venkata Krishna P, Bhiwal A, Chawla AS, Wolfinger BE, and Lee C. A learning automata-based fault-tolerant routing algorithm for mobile ad hoc networks. Journal of Supercomputing. 2012;62:4–23.

[42] Ghaffari A. Real-time routing algorithm for mobile ad hoc networks using reinforcement learning and heuristic algorithms. Wireless Networks. 2017;23(3):703–714.

[43] Khan MS, Jadoon QK, and Khan MI. A comparative performance analysis of MANET routing protocols under security attacks. Mobile and Wireless Technology. 2015; p. 137–145.

[44] Saeed A, Raza A, and Abbas H. A survey on network layer attacks and AODV defense in mobile ad hoc networks. IEEE Eighth International Conference on Software Security and Reliability-Companion. 2014; p. 185–191.

[45] Yi S, Naldurg P, and Kravets R. Security-aware ad hoc routing for wireless networks. Proceedings of the 2nd ACM International Symposium on Mobile Ad Hoc Networking & Computing. 2001; p. 299–302.

[46] Sanzgiri K, Dahill B, Leviney BN, Shields C, and Belding-Royer EM. A secure routing protocol for ad hoc networks. 10th IEEE International Conference on Network Protocols. 2002; p. 78–87.

[47] Hu Y-C, Johnson DB, and Perrig A. SEAD: Secure efficient distance vector routing for mobile wireless ad hoc networks. Ad hoc Networks. 2003;1(1):175–192.

[48] Zapata MG and Asokan N. Securing ad hoc routing protocols. Proceedings of the 1st ACM Workshop on Wireless Security. 2002;1(1):1–10.

[49] Ling X, Chen P, Wang J, and Ding Z. Data broker: Dynamic multi-hop routing protocol in blockchain radio access network. IEEE Communications Letters. 2021;25(12):4000–4004.

[50] Jarjis A and Kadir G. Blockchain authentication for aodv routing protocol. 2020 Second International Conference on Blockchain Computing and Applications (BCCA). 2020; p. 78–85.

[51] Biswas AK and Dasgupta M. Modification of DSDV and secure routing using blockchain technology. 2020 4th International Conference on Electronics, Materials Engineering & Nano-Technology (IEMENTech). 2020; p. 1–5.

[52] Li X and Zheng Y. Network Engineering Design and Project Training (in Chinese). Southeast University Press. 2016.

[53] Zheng L, Zhu S, and Zhou Y. Practical Technology Tutorial of Computer Networks (in Chinese). Northwest University Press. 2010.

[54] Li J, Chen R, Shen Q, and Zhao Y. Computer Network Technology and Applications (in Chinese). China Railway Publishing House. 2013.

[55] Zhang Y, Pan R, Wang N, and Pang S. Internet of Things Laboratory Manual (in Chinese). China Railway Publishing House. 2014.

[56] Yin S, Yu R, and Wang L. Network Security Technology Tutorial (in Chinese). Wuhan University Press. 2014.

Chapter 5
Deterministic networks for real-time applications

Sifan Li[1], *Yue Cao*[1] *and Yuan Zhuang*[2]

This chapter includes the introduction of deterministic networks (applications: automotive industry, IoT, Industrial IoT, industrial automation, and control systems), the equipment of deterministic networks (time synchronization hardware and hard real-time system), flow management (flow scheduling algorithms, bandwidth allocation and flow control), data and control (machine learning-based packet filtering and classification), the technology of switch (time-sensitive scheduling and congestion management), and the frontier of deterministic networks.

5.1 The introduction of network basics

5.1.1 Basic concept of network

The network is the integration of the entire Internet into a massive supercomputer, achieving comprehensive sharing of computing resources, storage resources, data resources, information resources, knowledge resources, and expert resources. The fundamental characteristic of the network is not necessarily its scale but rather the sharing of resources, eliminating resource isolation. Networks provide people with the tools to access the Internet, transmit data, and engage in communication.

A network is a system formed by multiple nodes, including computers, devices, sensors, etc., connected through communication links such as cables, optical fibers, radio waves, etc. These nodes can exchange data, share resources, and provide services within the network.

The fundamental components of a network include hardware (such as routers, switches, terminal devices), software (including operating systems, application software), and protocols (such as TCP/IP, HTTP, FTP). These components collaborate to facilitate data transmission, manage communication, and implement various application functionalities within the network. Here, networks can be categorized based on different criteria, such as topology (e.g., star, ring, bus), coverage (e.g., LAN, MAN, WAN), transmission media (e.g., wired, wireless), and purposes (e.g., enterprise network, campus network, Internet of Things (IoT)). Within any type of network,

[1]School of Cyber Science and Engineering, Wuhan University, China
[2]State Key Laboratory of Information Engineering in Surveying, Mapping and Remote Sensing, Wuhan University, China

protocols play a crucial role in achieving network interoperability, providing a set of rules and agreements to coordinate communication between nodes [1]. Common network protocols include the TCP/IP protocol suite, HTTP, FTP, SMTP, etc.

The applications of network are extensive, encompassing activities such as email communication, online chatting, web browsing, e-commerce, remote work, etc. With technological advancements, the scope of network applications has expanded from traditional computing to fields like the IoT and Artificial Intelligence (AI).

5.1.2 Classification of network topology

As shown in Figure 5.1, networks can be classified based on their topology, primarily into star networks, ring networks, and bus networks [2]:

5.1.2.1 Star topology

In a star network structure, each node is connected to the network using its own cable. Therefore, if a node encounters a failure, it does not affect the overall network operation. In the star structure, each workstation is connected to a hub through a dedicated twisted-pair cable, making it easy to maintain. Identifying network faults is straightforward with the use of switched cables or a simple method at the workstation. Additionally, with channel separation, the entire network remains unaffected by a single node failure, and the addition or removal of network nodes is convenient. Therefore, the star network structure is the most commonly used network topology today.

5.1.2.2 Ring topology

In a ring network structure, all nodes are connected to form a closed loop through communication media. Ring networks are easy to install and monitor, but they have limited capacity (nodes). Once the network is established, adding new nodes becomes difficult. In the ring structure, each node is connected to form a closed loop, and the data in the ring is transmitted in one direction. Its characteristics include simple structure, easy implementation, and deterministic transmission delay. If any node in the ring encounters a line failure, the entire network will be paralyzed. Therefore, the use of ring network structures for building Local Area Networks (LANs) has been abandoned now. In a ring network, each node is connected to a closed loop communication line through a ring interface. Any node on the ring can request to

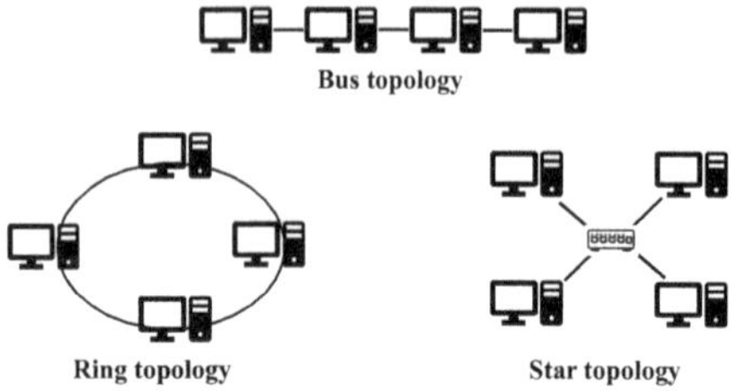

Figure 5.1 Three network topologies

send data. Once approved, the data can be sent to the ring. Data in the ring network can be transmitted in either one direction or both directions. Due to the ring line being shared, data from one node must pass through all the ring interfaces in the loop. When the destination address in the data flow matches the address of a node on the ring, the data is received by that node's ring interface. From there, the data continues to circulate through the ring until it eventually returns to the original generator.

5.1.2.3 Bus topology

In a bus network structure, all nodes share a single data channel. Bus networks are easy to install, with the shortest cable to be laid and low cost. Generally, a failure at one node will not affect the entire network, but a failure in the medium can cause network paralysis. Because of the low security, the bus network is relatively difficult to monitor, and adding new nodes is not as easy as in a star network. The bus topology is one of the most economical, simplest, and effective network structures. It has the characteristics of a wide bandwidth and resistance to interference during data transmission. However, since all devices are connected by a single cable in a bus structure, a break in any segment of the cable will cause the entire network to fail, resulting in poor stability. Therefore, the bus network structure has been abandoned.

The network topology management plays a crucial role in computer network operation and maintenance. Its specific functions include optimizing network performance, enhancing network stability, strengthening network security, simplifying network management, supporting business requirements, improving network scalability, and reducing resource waste [3]. Through rational planning and management of network topology structure, it is possible to minimize data transmission path length, thereby improving network transmission speed and response efficiency. The proper design and maintenance of network topology can reduce the impact range of network single point failures, improving network reliability.

5.1.3 Common network protocols and communication modes

Common network protocols and communication modes are essential components of computer networks, enabling reliable data transmission and smooth network communication. The TCP/IP protocol serves as the basis of Internet communication, with TCP (Transmission Control Protocol) ensuring reliable data transmission and IP (Internet Protocol) responsible for transmitting data packets [4]. The HTTP (Hypertext Transfer Protocol) is used to transmit hypertext documents over the network, forming the basis of web browsing [5]. The FTP (File Transfer Protocol) supports file upload/download operations and is commonly used for file transfer [6]. The SMTP (Simple Mail Transfer Protocol) is a standard protocol used for sending emails over the network, while the POP3 and IMAP protocols are used for retrieving emails from mail servers on client computers [7].

In addition to the above protocols, the DNS protocol (Domain Name System) is responsible for resolving domain names to corresponding IP addresses, enabling the translation of web addresses into IP addresses, which is essential for the normal operation of the Internet. The DHCP protocol (Dynamic Host Configuration Protocol) automatically assigns IP addresses and other network configuration parameters to client devices, simplifying network management and configuration [8].

In terms of communication modes, synchronous and asynchronous communication are two common data transmission methods. The synchronous communication requires sending and receiving ends to remain synchronized, usually coordinated using clock signals. In asynchronous communication, the clock signal is not used for data synchronization, and some synchronization signal bits are directly inserted into the data signal. Additionally, communication modes include simplex communication, half-duplex communication, and full-duplex communication. Here, simplex communication allows data transmission in only one direction, such as one-way broadcasting. Half-duplex communication allows data transmission in two directions but not simultaneously, such as walkie-talkies. Full-duplex communication allows data transmission in two directions simultaneously, such as telephone calls or Internet communication.

5.2 The introduction of deterministic network

5.2.1 Definition and characteristics of deterministic networks

Deterministic networks are a type of network architecture where the paths and timing of data transmission are predetermined rather than being based on randomness [9]. Deterministic networks provide an effective solution for real-time communication by offering predictable data transmission paths, lower latency, and higher reliability. These networks are characterized by

- Explicit routing: Deterministic networks have predefined routing paths, where the transmission path of data is established in advance, rather than relying on dynamic routing protocols.
- Precise transmission timing: Data in deterministic networks is transmitted according to precise timing, with predictable arrival times for data. This feature is beneficial for real-time applications and control over communication latency.
- Low latency and high reliability: Due to fixed routing paths, deterministic networks typically exhibit lower transmission latency and higher reliability, making them suitable for applications with stringent latency and reliability requirements.
- Efficient resource utilization: Deterministic networks can effectively utilize network resources since routing paths and transmission timing are predetermined, avoiding additional overhead and resource wastage during the routing process.

5.2.2 Evolution and applications of deterministic networks

The concept and technical foundation of Deterministic Networking (DetNet) can be traced back to the early standardization efforts by IEEE. These efforts focused on time synchronization and network real-time performance. In 2000, the establishment of the IEEE 1588 committee marked the birth of the high-precision time synchronization standard [10]. This standard, in conjunction with the work of IEEE 802, made it possible to develop standardized Ethernet interfaces and software that support enterprise-level network time synchronization with an accuracy exceeding 1 μs. This laid the groundwork for time synchronization, a critical component for the subsequent development of DetNet.

Following this, the IEEE 802.1 working group established the Audio Video Bridging (AVB) task group in 2007, with the goal of replacing HDMI, speaker cables, and coaxial cables in home environments with Ethernet, thereby achieving real-time transmission in the audio and video domains [11]. The AVB standards primarily applied to bridged Layer 2 networks and found successful applications in studios, sports venues, and entertainment facilities. This success attracted the attention of the industrial and automotive sectors, providing momentum for the further development of DetNet technologies.

In 2012, the IEEE 802.1 AVB task group renamed as the Time-Sensitive Networking (TSN) task group, signaling a new phase in the evolution of DetNet. The TSN standards extended the technologies of AVB, becoming a new generation of Ethernet-based network standards. These standards incorporate features such as time synchronization and guaranteed latency to ensure real-time performance [12]. TSN standards defined a suite of network protocols covering aspects such as time synchronization, traffic scheduling, reliability, and configuration management, providing comprehensive support for the application of DetNet within LANs.

However, with the rise of applications such as the Industrial Internet and telemedicine, the demand for DetNet has expanded beyond LANs to WANs. To address this, the Internet Engineering Task Force established the DetNet working group in 2015, focusing on implementing deterministic paths across Layer 2 bridged segments and Layer 3 routed segments [13]. The goal of the DetNet working group is to extend DetNet to WANs using technologies like IP/MPLS, thereby enabling a broader scope of deterministic services. DetNet technology provides deterministic performance guarantees for network transmission by setting worst-case bounds on latency, packet loss, and jitter.

Meanwhile, with the development of 5G technology, the application of DetNet in mobile networks has garnered widespread attention. Mobile network standards bodies, represented by 3GPP, have begun researching 5G support for IEEE TSN protocols and 5G LAN technology to promote the application of DetNet in mobile networks [14]. Operators like China Mobile are also actively advancing network slicing technology, offering network services with deterministic Quality of Service (QoS) through resource isolation, quality assurance, and functional customization for different industry users.

Due to their ability to provide reliable communication, deterministic networks have seen significant development and find applications across various fields [15]. As shown in Figure 5.2, the application areas of deterministic networks are as follows.

5.2.2.1 Industrial automation and control systems

Deterministic networks, such as TSN and Deterministic Ethernet, have been extensively adopted in Industrial Automation and Control Systems (IACS). These networks ensure precise timing and low latency communication, crucial for real-time

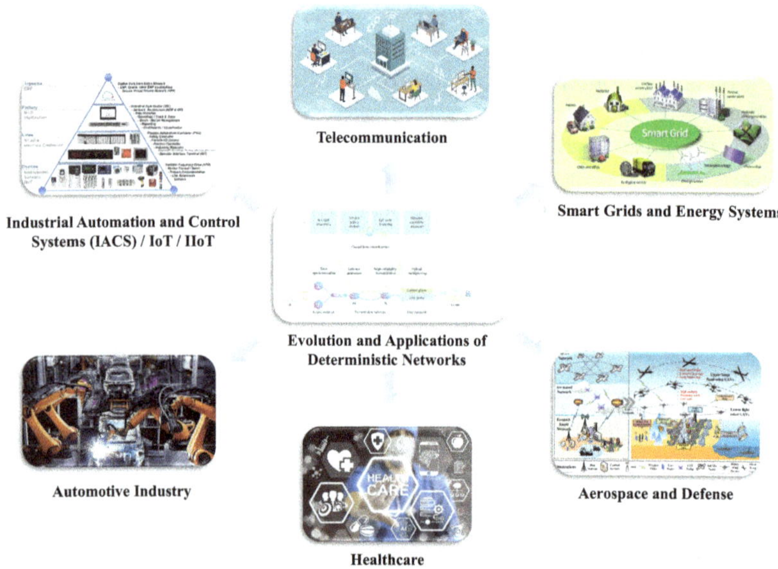

Figure 5.2 Evolution and applications of deterministic networks

control of industrial machinery. They enable synchronized data transmission, allowing for seamless integration of various devices and systems in industrial environments.

5.2.2.2 Automotive industry

Deterministic networks play a vital role in modern automotive systems, particularly in the context of Connected and Autonomous Vehicles. Time-sensitive communication is essential for Vehicle-to-Vehicle (V2V) communication, Vehicle-to-Infrastructure communication, collision avoidance and cooperative driving applications. Deterministic networks ensure reliable and low-latency data exchange, contributing to improved efficiency in automotive systems.

5.2.2.3 Telecommunications

In telecommunications networks, DetNet technologies are used to meet the stringent requirements of services such as Voice over IP (VoIP), video conferencing, and real-time multimedia streaming. By guaranteeing predictable data transmission paths and timing, these networks ensure QoS, enhancing the user experience for time-sensitive applications.

5.2.2.4 Smart grids and energy systems

Deterministic networks are employed in smart grid infrastructures to monitor and control power distribution systems. These networks enable precise synchronization of data transmission among substations, sensors, and control centers, supporting applications such as demand response, fault detection, and grid optimization.

5.2.2.5 Aerospace and defense

DetNet technologies are utilized in aerospace and defense applications, including unmanned aerial vehicles, military communications, and control systems. These networks provide reliable communication for mission-critical operations, ensuring timely delivery of data and commands in challenging environments.

5.2.2.6 Healthcare

In healthcare systems, deterministic networks are used to support telemedicine, remote patient monitoring, and real-time medical imaging applications. These networks enable timely transmission of patient data and diagnostic information, facilitating remote consultations and healthcare delivery in distributed environments.

5.2.2.7 IoT and Industrial IoT (IIoT)

DetNet solutions are increasingly deployed in IoT and IIoT to support time-sensitive applications such as process control, predictive maintenance and asset tracking. These networks ensure deterministic behavior and low-latency communication, enabling efficient data exchange among IoT devices and systems. Overall, deterministic networks continue to evolve and explore applications across diverse domains. In these domains, reliable, low-latency, and predictable communication is essential for supporting critical operations and enabling innovative services.

5.3 Equipment of deterministic network

5.3.1 Time synchronization hardware

In deterministic networks, time synchronization hardware is essential for ensuring precise synchronization among network nodes. It achieves this by providing accurate clocks and advanced timestamping capabilities. [16]. As shown in Figure 5.3, this section will introduce six main types of time synchronization hardware. Here is a detailed overview of the various types of time synchronization hardware commonly used in deterministic networks.

5.3.1.1 Global Positioning System (GPS) receivers

GPS receivers are widely used time synchronization hardware in deterministic networks. These receivers capture time signals from satellites and provide a reference

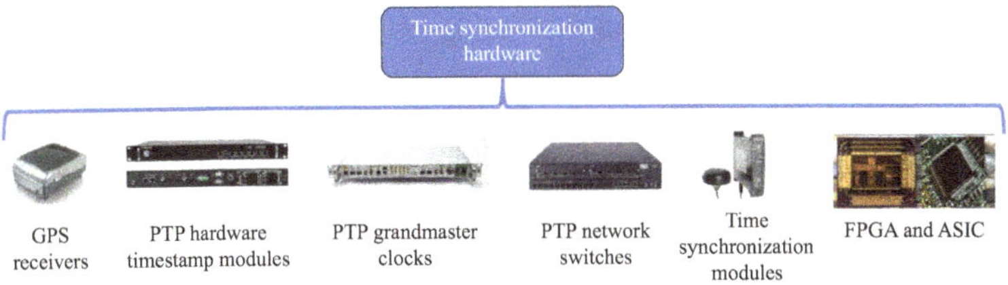

Figure 5.3 Six main time synchronization hardwares

for synchronizing time across network nodes. They offer high accuracy and stability, making them suitable for applications requiring precise time synchronization.

5.3.1.2 IEEE 1588 Precision Time Protocol (PTP) hardware timestamp modules

IEEE 1588 PTP relies on hardware support to achieve high-precision timestamping and clock synchronization. Hardware timestamp modules can timestamp data packets at the hardware level, and ensure clock synchronization with other nodes in the network.

5.3.1.3 PTP Grandmaster Clocks

PTP Grandmaster Clocks are devices equipped with high-precision clocks, which serve as the primary clock source in a network. They distribute time synchronization information to other nodes in the network, ensuring time synchronization across the entire network. Grandmaster Clocks typically integrate high-precision oscillators and clock correction mechanisms to maintain synchronization.

5.3.1.4 IEEE 1588 PTP network switches

Some network switches feature built-in IEEE 1588 PTP functionality, allowing for time synchronization at the switch level. These switches support hardware timestamping and precise clock synchronization, reducing latency among network nodes.

5.3.1.5 Time synchronization modules

Certain hardware devices integrate dedicated time synchronization modules designed to achieve time synchronization among network nodes. These modules offer high-precision clock and timestamping capabilities, ensuring accurate data transmission and processing within the network.

5.3.1.6 Field-Programmable Gate Array (FPGA) and Application-Specific Integrated Circuit (ASIC) chips

Custom hardware platforms (such as FPGA and ASIC chips) can be employed to implement high-performance and customized time synchronization functions. These chips facilitate high-speed data processing and precise clock synchronization, making them suitable for complex network applications.

5.3.2 Design of hard real-time system

Designing a hardware Real-Time Operating System (RTOS) for deterministic networks involves several key components and considerations [17]. As shown in Figure 5.4, there is a detailed overview of the elements typically included in the design of a hardware RTOS for deterministic networks.

5.3.2.1 Real-time task scheduler

In the RTOS, the real-time task scheduler is a critical component responsible for managing the execution of tasks based on their timing constraints and priorities. Unlike

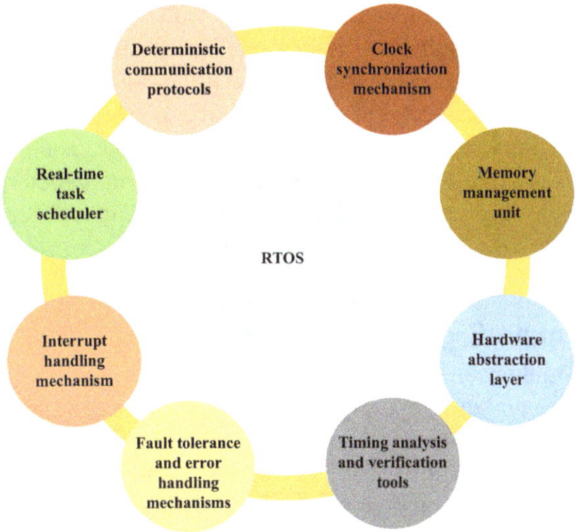

Figure 5.4 Design of hard real-time system

traditional task schedulers, which may focus on maximizing throughput or minimizing latency, the real-time task scheduler is designed to ensure that tasks meet their deadlines [18].

The scheduler typically supports different types of tasks, such as periodic, aperiodic, and sporadic tasks, each with its own timing requirements. It employs various scheduling algorithms, such as Rate Monotonic Scheduling (RMS), Earliest Deadline First (EDF), or Least Laxity First, to determine the order of task execution. The choice of algorithm depends on the specific requirements of the application, such as whether hard real-time guarantees are needed or if the system can tolerate occasional deadline misses. The real-time task scheduler also incorporates mechanisms for priority inversion prevention, such as priority inheritance or priority ceiling protocols, ensuring that high-priority tasks are not unduly delayed by lower-priority ones.

5.3.2.2 Interrupt handling mechanism

In the RTOS, the interrupt handling mechanism manages the system's response to external and internal events that require immediate attention. When an interrupt occurs, the RTOS must quickly interrupt the current execution flow to handle the event, ensuring minimal latency and maintaining the real-time constraints of the system.

The interrupt handling process typically involves an Interrupt Service Routine (ISR), which is a specialized, high-priority task designed to execute with minimal delay. The RTOS must manage the ISR execution carefully to avoid excessive blocking of other real-time tasks, which could endanger the ability of system to meet critical deadlines [19].

To optimize interrupt handling, RTOSs often employ techniques such as interrupt prioritization, where higher-priority interrupts can preempt lower-priority ones.

Another technique is nested interrupt handling, which allows the system to handle multiple interrupts simultaneously without significant overhead. Additionally, the RTOS may use deferred processing, where the most time-sensitive part of the interrupt is handled immediately, and less critical processing is deferred to a later time, reducing the impact on the overall system performance. The interrupt handling mechanism is designed to ensure that the RTOS can maintain deterministic behavior even under high interrupt load, which is essential for applications where timing predictability and reliability are paramount.

5.3.2.3 Deterministic communication protocols

Deterministic communication protocols are essential for ensuring predictable and reliable data exchange between tasks, devices, or subsystems. These protocols are designed to guarantee that messages are delivered within a predefined time window, adhering to the stringent timing requirements of real-time applications [20].

Deterministic communication protocols, such as Time-Triggered Protocol, TSN, and Controller Area Network, achieve determinism by employing mechanisms like Time Division Multiple Access (TDMA). The TDMA prevents collisions and ensures that each entity can transmit data at precise intervals, maintaining temporal predictability.

Additionally, these protocols often incorporate features like synchronous data transmission, where communication is synchronized with a global clock. They also provide bounded latency, which sets an upper limit on the time it takes for a message to traverse the network. This is critical in systems where delayed or out-of-order messages could lead to system instability or failure.

5.3.2.4 Clock synchronization mechanism

The clock synchronization mechanism is a vital process that ensures all components within the system maintain a consistent and accurate sense of time. This synchronization is crucial for coordinating time-sensitive operations across distributed tasks, devices, or subsystems, especially in environments where precise timing is critical, such as industrial automation, avionics, and telecommunications [21].

The clock synchronization mechanism typically employs algorithms like PTP, defined by IEEE 1588, or Network Time Protocol (NTP), to achieve microsecond or sub-microsecond accuracy. These protocols synchronize the local clocks of different devices to a master clock, ensuring that all entities within the system operate on a common time base.

In systems requiring extremely high precision, hardware-assisted synchronization methods are often used, where timestamping occurs at the hardware level to minimize jitter and latency introduced by software processing. This can involve specialized network interfaces or dedicated synchronization circuits. The clock synchronization mechanism is designed to compensate for clock drift, which can occur due to variations in clock frequencies across different devices. It ensures that all tasks and communications within the RTOS adhere to the timing constraints necessary for deterministic behavior, enabling the system to perform coordinated actions with the required temporal accuracy.

5.3.2.5 Memory Management Unit (MMU)

The MMU ensures that tasks are allocated memory efficiently while adhering to the stringent timing constraints of real-time applications. Unlike general-purpose operating systems, where memory management prioritizes flexibility and efficiency, the MMU in an RTOS is optimized for predictability and determinism. The MMU typically supports real-time memory protection, which isolates tasks to prevent them from interfering with each other's memory spaces, thereby ensuring system stability and security. This is crucial in real-time environments where a memory violation by one task could lead to system-wide failures or missed deadlines.

To maintain timing predictability, the MMU in an RTOS often avoids complex memory management techniques such as paging or swapping, which could introduce non-deterministic delays. Instead, it relies on static memory allocation and pre-configured memory regions to ensure that memory access times are consistent and bounded. The MMU may also employ techniques like memory locking, where critical memory regions are kept in physical memory to prevent page faults during real-time operations [22].

Additionally, the MMU supports fast context switching by managing memory access permissions and translating virtual addresses to physical addresses with minimal overhead. This ensures that real-time tasks can be swiftly and efficiently switched in and out of execution, maintaining strict adherence to timing constraints.

5.3.2.6 Hardware Abstraction Layer (HAL)

The HAL serves as a crucial interface between the system's hardware components and its software, enabling the RTOS to operate across different hardware platforms with minimal modification. The HAL abstracts the specifics of the underlying hardware, providing a standardized set of APIs. This allows the operating system and application software to interact with hardware devices such as processors, timers, interrupts, and I/O peripherals in a consistent and predictable manner.

In the context of an RTOS, the HAL is designed to maintain the deterministic behavior required for real-time applications. It ensures that hardware interactions, such as interrupt handling, timing, and Direct Memory Access (DMA), are managed with minimal latency and maximum predictability. The HAL achieves this by providing low-level routines optimized for real-time performance, such as precise control over timer hardware for task scheduling and synchronization, and efficient interrupt management to meet strict timing constraints.

Furthermore, the HAL in an RTOS supports hardware independence, allowing the same real-time software to run on different hardware platforms without requiring extensive rewrites [23]. This is particularly important in embedded systems where hardware variations are common, and real-time performance must be maintained consistently across different devices. By abstracting hardware details, the HAL simplifies the development and portability of real-time applications, while ensuring that the underlying hardware can meet the stringent timing requirements of the RTOS.

5.3.2.7 Timing analysis and verification tools

Timing analysis and verification tools are essential for ensuring that the system meets its stringent temporal constraints. These tools are designed to analyze, verify, and validate the timing behavior of real-time tasks, ensuring that they adhere to their specified deadlines and that the overall system performs predictably under all conditions [24].

Timing analysis tools typically perform Worst-Case Execution Time analysis, which calculates the maximum time a task or ISR might take to execute. This analysis is crucial for scheduling and resource allocation, as it helps ensure that all tasks can be completed within their deadlines, even under the worst-case scenario.

Verification tools, on the other hand, focus on schedulability analysis. This analysis determines whether the task set, given their priorities, execution times, and periodicity, can be scheduled on the available processors without violating any timing constraints. These tools often support various scheduling algorithms, such as RMS or EDF, and allow for the evaluation of system performance under different conditions.

Advanced timing analysis tools may also include simulation and model checking capabilities, where the system's temporal behavior is modeled and tested under different scenarios to detect potential timing violations or bottlenecks. These tools are vital for identifying and mitigating risks related to timing, such as priority inversion or resource contention, which could lead to missed deadlines or system instability.

5.3.2.8 Fault tolerance and error handling mechanisms

Fault tolerance and error handling mechanisms are designed to detect, isolate, and recover from faults. These mechanisms minimize disruption to real-time tasks and preserves the system's timing guarantees. Fault tolerance in an RTOS typically involves redundancy techniques, such as hardware redundancy (e.g., multiple processors or communication paths) and software redundancy (e.g., task duplication or voting algorithms). These techniques allow the system to continue functioning correctly even if one or more components fail. For instance, if a primary task or hardware module fails, a backup task or module can take over without missing critical deadlines [25].

Error handling mechanisms in an RTOS include exception handling, where the system is equipped to manage unexpected conditions like hardware malfunctions, memory violations, or task overruns. The RTOS must handle these exceptions swiftly to prevent cascading failures. This is often achieved through graceful degradation, where non-critical functions are reduced or disabled to ensure that critical real-time tasks continue to execute. Another key component is watchdog timers, which monitor the system for anomalies such as task hangs or missed deadlines. If a task fails to complete within its expected timeframe, the watchdog timer triggers corrective actions, such as task reinitialization or system reboot, to restore normal operation.

5.4 The technology of flow management

5.4.1 Classification of flow scheduling algorithms

Flow scheduling algorithms are used in computer networks to efficiently allocate network resources and manage the transmission of data flows [26]. These algorithms determine how packets are routed through the network, taking into account factors such as link capacity, traffic load, and QoS requirements. Here are several common flow scheduling algorithms:

5.4.1.1 First Come, First Served (FCFS)

FCFS is a basic and non-preemptive scheduling strategy where network flows are processed in the exact order they arrive, without consideration for their priority or urgency. Under FCFS, each flow is queued and handled sequentially, meaning that the first flow to arrive is the first to be served, and subsequent flows must wait until all preceding flows have been fully processed.

While FCFS is straightforward to implement and ensures fairness by treating all flows equally, it is generally not suitable for real-time or DetNet environments where timing guarantees are critical. This is because FCFS does not account for the varying latency requirements of different flows. As a result, high-priority or time-sensitive traffic experiences significant delays due to the presence of earlier, lower-priority flows in the queue.

5.4.1.2 Round Robin (RR)

RR is a flow scheduling algorithm used in network traffic management that allocates equal time slices or processing intervals to each flow in a cyclic order. In this non-preemptive algorithm, flows are placed in a circular queue, and each flow is served in turn, moving from one to the next until all flows have received service. Once a flow has been served, it is placed back at the end of the queue if it still requires additional processing, and the next flow in line is served [27]. RR is designed to ensure fairness by giving each flow an equal opportunity to access the network resources, regardless of its priority or urgency. This approach is simple to implement and works well in scenarios where all flows have similar requirements and the primary goal is to avoid starvation.

However, in deterministic or real-time networking environments, RR may not be the optimal choice because it does not account for the varying deadlines or latency requirements of different flows. As a result, critical or time-sensitive flows might experience delays if they are forced to wait for their turn in the queue. For applications requiring strict timing guarantees, more advanced algorithms such as Weighted Round Robin (WRR), which assigns different weights to flows based on their priority, or EDF, which prioritizes flows based on their deadlines, are often preferred.

5.4.1.3 Weighted Round Robin (WRR)

WRR extends the basic Round Robin approach by assigning different weights to each flow, allowing for proportional allocation of network resources based on the assigned weights. In WRR, each flow is assigned a weight that reflects its priority or required bandwidth [28]. The scheduler then cycles through the flows in a Round-Robin manner, but instead of serving each flow equally, it serves each flow a number of times proportional to its weight. As shown in Figure 5.5, w_i, w_j, and w_k represent different weights for each flow.

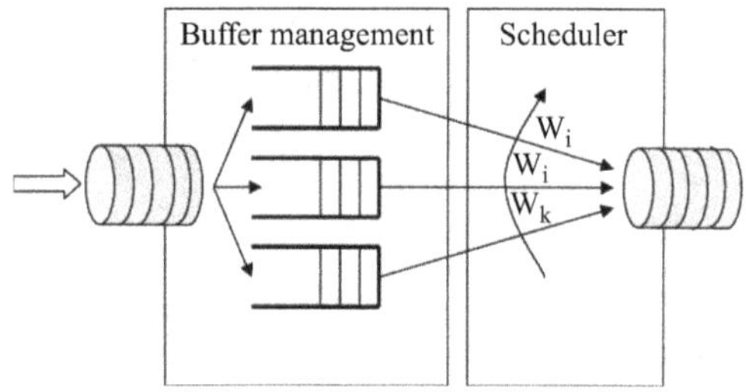

Figure 5.5 Weighted Round Robin (WRR)

WRR is particularly useful in environments where flows have different priorities or bandwidth requirements, such as in QoS scenarios, where certain types of traffic (e.g., video or voice) must be prioritized over others. By adjusting the weights, WRR allows for fine-grained control over resource allocation, ensuring that critical traffic meets its performance requirements while still allowing lower-priority traffic to be processed.

5.4.1.4 Weighted Fair Queuing (WFQ)

WFQ is used in networking to provide fair bandwidth distribution among multiple traffic flows. It also accounts for their different priorities or bandwidth requirements. WFQ extends the basic Fair Queuing (FQ) algorithm by assigning a specific weight to each flow, which determines the proportion of the total bandwidth that the flow will receive. The weight reflects the priority or importance of the flow, with higher-weighted flows receiving more bandwidth compared to lower-weighted ones.

As shown in Figure 5.6, WFQ works by calculating the finish time for each packet in the system, based on its assigned weight and the flow's current state. The packets are then scheduled for transmission in order of their calculated finish times [29]. This ensures that all flows receive a fair share of the network resources according to their weights, while also ensuring that higher-priority flows are given more timely access to the network.

WFQ is widely used in scenarios where different types of traffic with varying QoS requirements coexist, such as in IP networks that handle a mix of voice, video, and data traffic. By providing a balanced approach to resource allocation, WFQ helps ensure that critical traffic meets its performance requirements without completely starving lower-priority traffic.

5.4.1.5 Class-Based Weighted Fair Queuing (CBWFQ)

CBWFQ provides differentiated service levels by categorizing flows into different classes. Each class is assigned a specific weight, which determines the proportion of the available bandwidth that the class will receive [30]. Within each class, flows are scheduled using a fair queuing mechanism, ensuring that all flows within the same class are treated equitably.

CBWFQ extends the traditional WFQ by allowing network administrators to define multiple classes of traffic, each with its own bandwidth allocation. As shown

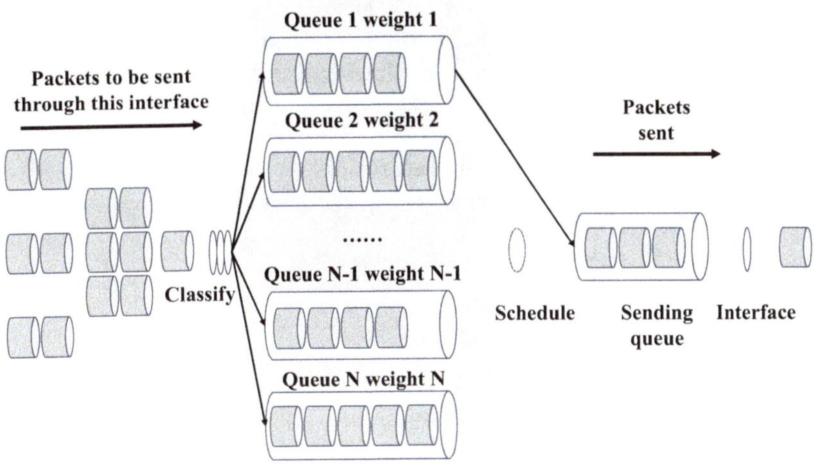

Figure 5.6 Weighted fair queuing

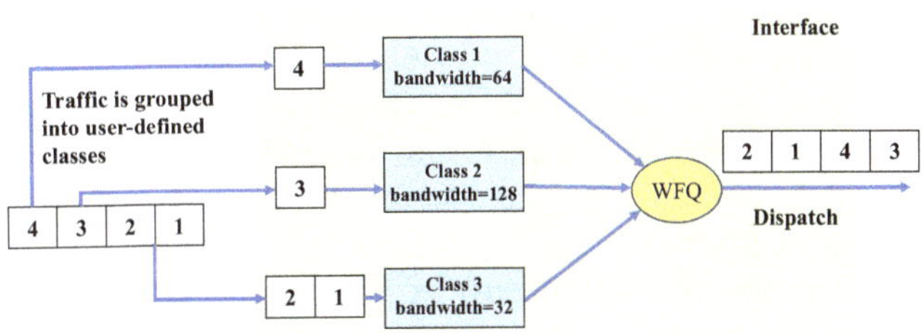

Figure 5.7 Class-based weighted fair queuing

in Figure 5.7, the bandwidth of Classes 1, 2, and 3 is 64, 128, and 32. This enables precise control over network resources, ensuring that critical traffic (such as voice or video) receives the necessary bandwidth to meet performance requirements, while less critical traffic is allocated proportionally based on its assigned weight. The key advantage of CBWFQ is its ability to support QoS by providing predictable and controlled bandwidth allocation, making it well-suited for networks that need to handle a mix of real-time and non-real-time traffic.

5.4.1.6 Deficit Round Robin (DRR)

DRR is an advanced flow scheduling algorithm that builds on Round Robin by efficiently managing variable packet sizes. DRR addresses the limitations of simple Round Robin, which can be unfair to flows with larger packets, by introducing a deficit counter for each flow. This counter keeps track of the "credit" or "deficit" accumulated by each flow based on the size of the packets that have been served [31].

In DRR, each flow is assigned a quantum, which is the amount of data (in bytes) that the flow is allowed to send during each round. If a flow's packet size exceeds its current quantum, the packet is held back, and the deficit counter is incremented by the quantum value minus the packet size. In the next round, the flow's quantum is increased by the deficit counter value, allowing it to send the remaining packet. This process continues until the entire packet is transmitted, ensuring fairness among flows of varying packet sizes.

DRR is particularly effective in scenarios where network traffic consists of packets of different sizes, as it provides fair queuing without the need for complex computations or packet fragmentation. It is widely used in networking devices that need to balance efficiency and fairness in packet scheduling.

5.4.1.7 Token bucket algorithm

Token bucket algorithm is commonly used in networking to control the amount of data that is transmitted over a network in a given time period. The algorithm operates by generating tokens at a constant rate, where each token represents permission to send a specific amount of data (typically one packet or a certain number of bytes) [32]. These tokens are accumulated in a "bucket," which has a fixed capacity. If the bucket is full, additional tokens are discarded, meaning that if the bucket is empty, the data flow must wait until enough tokens are available.

When a packet is ready to be sent, the algorithm checks if there are enough tokens in the bucket to cover the packet's size. If sufficient tokens are available, the packet is transmitted, and the corresponding number of tokens is removed from the bucket. If not, the packet is held until enough tokens accumulate.

The token bucket algorithm is effective in controlling bursty traffic while allowing for flexibility in data transmission. It allows short bursts of traffic to be sent at higher rates while ensuring that the long-term average rate of data transmission does not exceed a specified limit. This makes it ideal for applications requiring both bandwidth control and the ability to handle occasional high traffic loads.

5.4.1.8 Shortest Remaining Processing Time (SRPT)

SRPT prioritizes network flows based on the remaining amount of processing time required to complete them. Under SRPT, the flow with the SRPT is given priority over others, meaning that the scheduler dynamically selects the flow that can be completed the quickest [33]. This approach aims to minimize the overall response time of the system by reducing the average time flows spend in the queue.

In practice, SRPT can significantly improve system efficiency, especially in environments where processing time varies widely among flows. By completing shorter tasks more quickly, SRPT reduces the overall waiting time for all flows, leading to higher throughput and better resource utilization.

However, SRPT may introduce a risk of starvation for longer flows, as shorter flows continually preempt them. To mitigate this, SRPT can be combined with other strategies, such as setting a minimum service guarantee for longer flows to ensure they eventually receive processing time.

5.4.2 Bandwidth allocation and flow control method

In deterministic networks, bandwidth allocation and traffic control methods are used for managing network resources effectively [34]. Typical common bandwidth allocation and traffic control methods in deterministic networks are as follows:

5.4.2.1 Time-Division Multiple Access (TDMA)

As shown in Figure 5.8, TDMA divides data stream into frames. Each frame contains multiple time slots of equal duration. Users or devices are assigned specific time slots in which they can transmit their data. During each assigned time slot, only one user sends data, thereby preventing interference from other users. Accurate time synchronization is crucial to ensure that each user's transmission aligns with their allocated time slot. The receiver then captures and decodes the data based on these time slots, allowing multiple users to share the same frequency channel efficiently while avoiding collisions [35].

5.4.2.2 Token bucket

As shown in Figure 5.9, the token bucket algorithm limits the rate at which nodes can send data by assigning each node a fixed capacity token bucket. Nodes must acquire tokens from the token bucket to send data, where the transmission can only occur when tokens are available [36]. Token bucket algorithm controls the rate of traffic, preventing network congestion and ensuring reliable data transmission.

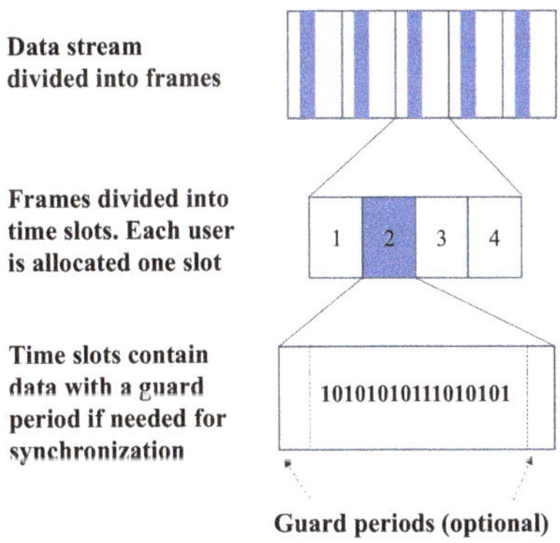

Figure 5.8 Time-division multiple access

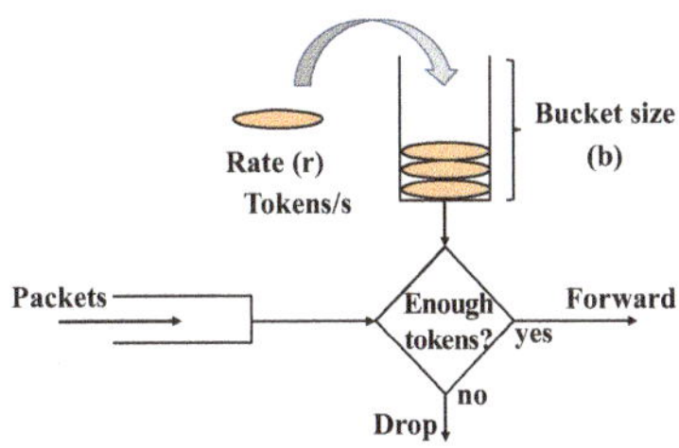

Figure 5.9 Token bucket

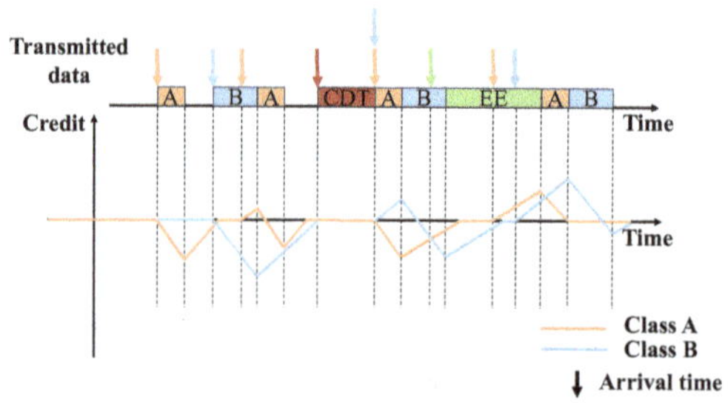

Figure 5.10 Credit-based shaper

5.4.2.3 Credit-Based Shaper (CBS)

The IEEE 802.1Qav standard defines the CBS, which ensures soft real-time guarantees for two traffic classes, labeled A and B. As illustrated in Figure 5.10, each traffic class is allocated a specific credit that decreases with each transmitted frame. When the credit of one class is depleted (becomes negative), its traffic must pause until the credit is replenished. During this time, traffic from the other class can continue transmission, provided its credit remains positive. This system effectively prevents starvation and manages the end-to-end delay for soft real-time traffic. [37,38].

5.4.2.4 Frame Preemption (FP)

FP allows high-priority data frames to interrupt the transmission of low-priority frames, to ensure timely delivery of high-priority data [39]. When high-priority data needs to be transmitted, FP suspends the transmission of low-priority frames and allows high-priority data frames to be transmitted immediately.

5.4.2.5 QoS classes

Deterministic networks often categorize traffic into different QoS classes, each with different priority and QoS requirements. Based on QoS classes, the network can implement various bandwidth allocation and traffic control strategies to meet the specific requirements of different data streams [40].

These bandwidth allocation and traffic control methods can be used individually or in combination to ensure efficient data transmission in deterministic networks while meeting real-time requirements [41]. The choice of method depends on the network characteristics, application scenarios, and performance requirements.

5.5 Data and control

5.5.1 Clock synchronization management

In deterministic networks, clock synchronization management techniques are essential for ensuring synchronized operation among network nodes, facilitating efficient coordination of data transmission and real-time communication [42]. There is a detailed description of typical common clock synchronization management techniques:

5.5.1.1 IEEE 1588 Precision Time Protocol (PTP)

IEEE 1588 PTP is a standard protocol used for time synchronization in networks, enabling precise time synchronization between master and slave clocks (The master clock is responsible for unified management, control and synchronization of the slave clock. The slave clock depends on the master clock to obtain accurate time information). PTP utilizes synchronization and delay measurement to calculate clock offsets in the network, calibrating slave clocks to remain synchronized with the master clock. Meanwhile, it supports various clock synchronization modes, including unicast, multicast, and hybrid modes, suitable for different application scenarios.

5.5.1.2 GPS

The GPS is a commonly used time synchronization technology, synchronizing clocks of network nodes by receiving time signals from satellites. GPS receivers are installed on network nodes, receiving time signals and using them as a reference for local clocks. GPS provides high-precision time synchronization, which is suitable for wide-area networks and mobile environments.

5.5.1.3 White Rabbit (WR)

White Rabbit is an open network protocol for clock synchronization in distributed systems, suitable for applications such as particle physics and industrial control. WR achieves high-precision clock synchronization using fiber optic Ethernet and the PTP protocol, providing low latency and high reliability.

5.5.1.4 Network Time Protocol (NTP)

The NTP is a protocol used to synchronize computer clocks over the Internet, typically employed for achieving relatively lower precision clock synchronization. NTP utilizes a hierarchical structure of time servers to provide time signals, calculate clock offsets and adjust local clocks through multiple round-trip measurements.

5.5.1.5 IEEE 802.1AS Precision Time Protocol (PTP)

IEEE 802.1AS is a network clock synchronization standard based on IEEE 1588 PTP, specifically designed for real-time applications in Ethernet networks. 802.1AS imposes stricter time synchronization requirements, including shorter synchronization intervals and higher synchronization accuracy, to meet the demands of real-time applications.

5.5.2 Packet filtering and classification

In deterministic networks, packet filtering and classification techniques involve definition of appropriate rules to filter, identify, and allocate network packets, thereby achieving control of network traffic. Common packet filtering and classification technologies are used as follows:

5.5.2.1 Rule-based packet filtering

Rule-based packet filtering employs a predefined set of rules to filter and classify incoming/outgoing packets. Each rule consists of a set of conditions, such as source IP address, destination IP address, port number, etc., along with associated actions like allow, deny, or redirect packet. This technology is commonly used in network devices such as firewalls and routers, to control traffic [43].

5.5.2.2 Machine learning-based packet filtering and classification

Machine Learning (ML)-based packet filtering and classification utilizes ML algorithms to analyze network traffic and make decisions about packet forwarding/categorization [44]. By leveraging ML techniques, such as supervised learning or deep learning, these systems can adaptively learn from incoming traffic patterns and make intelligent decisions in real-time, enhancing network security and performance.

5.5.2.3 Deep Packet Inspection (DPI)

DPI technology allows network devices to inspect the content of packets beyond header information. DPI analyzes the payload of packets to identify applications, protocols and content types, then utilizes these for packet filtering or classification purposes [45]. The DPI is widely used in traffic management, network security, and application performance optimization.

5.5.2.4 Traffic marking and tag-based classification

Traffic marking techniques involve adding tags or labels to packet headers to identify different types of traffic. Tags can be set based on different criteria or policies such as priority, QoS class, or security policies. Tag-based classification techniques classify and process packets based on these tags, allowing network devices to implement specific operations or policies based on tags.

5.5.2.5 Load balancing and traffic scheduling

Load Balancing refers to the process of distributing incoming network traffic across multiple servers to prevent any single server. This not only improves the overall responsiveness of the network but also provides redundancy, enhancing system reliability. Load balancing algorithms can be static or dynamic, with dynamic algorithms making real-time decisions based on current network conditions.

Traffic scheduling, on the other hand, involves prioritizing and managing the sequence of packet transmissions across the network. This ensures that packets are delivered in a manner that meets the required QoS levels, particularly in environments with varying traffic types and priorities. Traffic scheduling algorithms, such as WFQ or Round Robin, are employed to ensure that high-priority traffic receives the necessary bandwidth and minimal latency, while lower-priority traffic is appropriately managed.

5.5.2.6 Port and protocol-based classification

Port and protocol-based classification is a method used to categorize and manage network traffic based on the destination port numbers and the specific protocols. Each network service or application is typically associated with a standard port number (e.g., HTTP uses port 80, HTTPS uses port 443), and protocols such as TCP, UDP, or ICMP define the rules for data transmission. By analyzing the port numbers and protocols in the packet headers, network devices can classify traffic into different categories, allowing for more granular control over how data is routed, prioritized, or filtered.

This type of classification is essential in implementing security policies, QoS mechanisms, and traffic management strategies. For example, network administrators can use port and protocol-based classification to prioritize VoIP traffic (which might use the RTP protocol over specific ports) over general web traffic. They can also block certain types of traffic (such as unauthorized applications or services) at the network perimeter.

5.5.2.7 Application layer proxies and gateways

Application layer proxies and gateways perform packet parsing at the application layer, enabling deep identification and control of specific application layer protocols. These proxies and gateways are commonly used in firewalls, proxy servers, and application accelerators for fine-grained traffic filtering.

- First, these technologies help network administrators enforce security policies to safeguard the network against malicious attacks and unauthorized access. By identifying potential network threats such as malware, viruses, botnets, and Denial of Service (DoS) attacks, they ensure the security of the network.
- Second, by filtering and classifying network traffic, they control the flow of data, preventing network congestion and bandwidth overload. According to business requirements, administrators can optimize traffic to ensure the priority of critical business and applications.
- Third, packet filtering and classification technologies classify data streams according to QoS requirements. By tagging packets or applying specific traffic control policies, they optimize QoS parameters such as latency, packet loss, bandwidth, and throughput, thereby enhancing network performance.
- Finally, by analyzing and optimizing network traffic, they identify performance bottlenecks, improving network efficiency. Optimization and improvement of the network are achieved by filtering out unnecessary traffic, optimizing data transmission paths, and reducing network latency.

5.5.3 Security measures

In deterministic networks, various security measures are implemented to protect against potential threats and vulnerabilities. These security measures include the following.

5.5.3.1 Access control

Access control regulates who or what can view or use resources within a network environment. In the context of deterministic networks, access control ensures that only authorized devices, users, or applications can access certain parts of the network or specific data flows.

Access control mechanisms can be implemented using various methods, including Role-Based Access Control, Mandatory Access Control, and Discretionary Access Control. These methods define policies based on roles, attributes, or identities to enforce strict rules about who can access what resources and under what conditions. In deterministic networks, where low-latency and highly predictable data transmission are crucial, access control must be carefully managed to prevent unauthorized access while ensuring that legitimate traffic is not delayed or disrupted.

Additionally, access control in DetNet often involves network-level enforcement mechanisms such as Access Control Lists (ACLs). More advanced technologies like Zero Trust Architecture (ZTA) are also used, where each request for access is verified regardless of the requester's location within the network.

5.5.3.2 Encryption

Encryption techniques, such as SSL/TLS (Secure Sockets Layer/Transport Layer Security), are used to secure data transmission by encrypting communication between network nodes. This ensures that data remains confidential and cannot be intercepted or tampered with by unauthorized parties.

In the context of DetNet, encryption must be carefully managed to avoid introducing latency or jitter that could disrupt the network's deterministic properties. This is particularly important in applications such as industrial automation, autonomous vehicles, or critical infrastructure, where even minimal delays can lead to significant issues. There are two primary types of encryption used in deterministic networks: symmetric encryption, which employs the same key for both encryption and decryption, and asymmetric encryption, which uses a pair of keys—a public key and a private key. The choice of encryption method depends on the specific requirements for security, performance, and the deterministic nature of the network.

5.5.3.3 Firewalls

Firewall acts as a barrier between a trusted internal network and untrusted external networks, such as the internet. In the context of deterministic networks, where predictable performance and security are paramount, firewalls are used to enforce strict security policies by monitoring, filtering, and controlling network traffic based on predefined rules.

Firewalls operate at various layers of the network stack, including the application, transport and network layers. In deterministic networks, firewalls must be carefully configured to ensure that they do not introduce latency, jitter, or packet loss, which could affect the network's deterministic properties.

5.5.3.4 Intrusion Detection and Prevention Systems (IDPS)

IDPS can be divided into two parts based on functionality: IDS (Intrusion Detection System) and IPS (Intrusion Prevention System). IDS monitors network traffic for suspicious activities or known attack patterns. If an intrusion is detected, the system generates an alert, allowing administrators to take appropriate action. However, IDS alone does not take direct action to stop the intrusion. IPS, on the other hand, not only detects but also actively prevents identified threats by blocking or mitigating malicious traffic in real-time. In deterministic networks, IPS must be carefully designed to avoid introducing delays or disruptions that could affect the network's deterministic properties.

IDPS can be implemented at various points within the network, such as at the perimeter, on individual devices, or within specific segments of the network. Advanced IDPS solutions may use techniques like DPI, anomaly detection, and signature-based detection to identify threats. In DetNet environments, the deployment of IDPS ensures that security is maintained without sacrificing the predictability and reliability of critical network services.

5.5.3.5 Network segmentation

Network segmentation divides the network into smaller segments to contain security breaches. Each segment operates independently, with specific security policies and controls tailored to its unique requirements. This approach helps to contain potential security breaches, restrict unauthorized access, and limit the spread of threats within the network.

In deterministic networks, where precise timing and low-latency communication are essential, network segmentation ensures that sensitive or critical traffic can be isolated and prioritized without interference from less critical data flows. This isolation helps maintain the deterministic properties of the network, such as predictable latency and bandwidth, while also enhancing overall security.

Network segmentation can be implemented using various techniques, such as Virtual Local Area Networks (VLANs), firewalls, and ACLs. By segmenting the network, administrators can enforce more granular security policies, reduce the attack surface, and improve traffic management.

5.5.3.6 Security policies and compliance

Security policies and compliance are fundamental components of safeguarding deterministic networks, ensuring that network operations adhere to established security standards and regulatory requirements. Security policies are a set of rules and guidelines that define how data and resources within a network should be protected, specifying what actions are permissible and what controls must be in place to mitigate risks. These policies encompass various aspects, including access control, encryption, authentication, data integrity, and incident response.

In deterministic networks, where predictability and reliability are crucial, security policies must be designed to prevent unauthorized access, data breaches, and other security incidents without compromising the network's deterministic properties. Compliance, on the other hand, involves adhering to industry standards, regulations, and legal requirements, such as GDPR, HIPAA, or ISO/IEC 27001. Ensuring compliance helps organizations avoid legal penalties and maintain trust with stakeholders.

Implementing security policies and ensuring compliance in deterministic networks requires continuous monitoring, regular audits, and updates to the policies in response to evolving threats and regulatory changes. This proactive approach helps maintain the security and integrity of the network, ensuring that it operates within the boundaries of both internal policies and external regulations.

5.5.3.7 Patch management

Patch management involves regularly updating software, firmware, and operating systems to address known vulnerabilities. Effective patch management in deterministic networks includes identifying relevant patches, testing them in a controlled environment to assess their impact, and scheduling their deployment during maintenance windows to avoid disrupting critical network services. It also involves keeping an accurate inventory of all network components, ensuring that no devices or systems are overlooked during the patching process. Given the importance of maintaining both security and performance in deterministic networks, patch management must balance the need to quickly address vulnerabilities with the requirement to maintain the deterministic properties of network, such as low latency and high availability.

5.5.3.8 Physical security

Physical security is a fundamental aspect of safeguarding deterministic networks, focusing on protecting the physical components of the network infrastructure from unauthorized access, damage, or tampering. This includes securing hardware devices such as routers, switches, servers, and network cables, as well as ensuring the integrity of data centers, network rooms, and other critical facilities.

In deterministic networks, where precise timing and reliability are crucial, physical security measures are essential to prevent disruptions caused by physical threats. These measures can include controlled access to network infrastructure through the use of access control systems, surveillance cameras, and security personnel. Additionally, environmental controls such as climate regulation and fire suppression systems are implemented to protect the hardware from environmental hazards.

Physical security also involves implementing measures to protect against physical attacks, theft, or vandalism. This can include secure enclosures for network equipment, tamper-evident seals, and robust locking mechanisms. Ensuring the physical security of network components is maintained helps to prevent unauthorized modifications or damage.

5.6 The technology of switch

5.6.1 Introduction of switch equipment

In deterministic networks, switches play a pivotal role in facilitating efficient data exchange and communication among network devices within a LAN. These devices are engineered to swiftly forward data packets based on their destination addresses, ensuring seamless connectivity and high-speed transmission. Typically equipped with multiple ports, switches vary in port count and speed, ranging from a few ports to

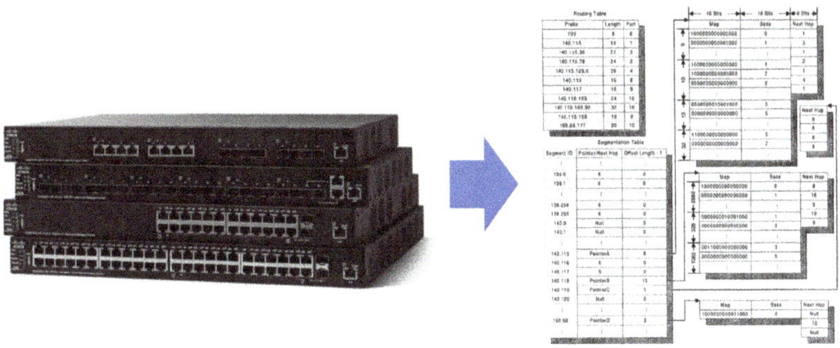

Switch **Forwarding tables**

Figure 5.11 Switch equipment and forwarding tables

several dozen ports, with common rates including 10/100/1000 Mbps Ethernet ports and 10 Gigabit Ethernet ports.

As shown in Figure 5.11, one of the key functionalities of switches lies in their forwarding mechanisms, where they utilize forwarding tables to store destination address and associated port information, allowing for exact packet forwarding. Switches employ various forwarding methods such as store-and-forward, cut-through and fast forwarding, with fast forwarding being the most prevalent method used in most scenarios. Modern switches often offer an array of management features including remote management, VLAN support, QoS configuration, traffic monitoring, and security functionalities.

Reliability and redundancy are paramount in deterministic networks, prompting switches to incorporate redundant power supplies, redundant ports, and hot-swappable modules to ensure uninterrupted service in the event of equipment failures. These devices find widespread application across enterprise networks, data centers, campus networks and industrial networks. They also provide high-speed, reliable data exchange, and communication services in these applications [46]. The performance and scalability of switches are critical considerations, influencing their deployment for network environments. Additionally, switches often include security features such as ACLs, port security, 802.1X authentication and user authentication to safeguard networks against malicious attacks, further enhancing the overall security posture of deterministic networks.

5.6.2 Clock synchronization technology

In deterministic networks, clock synchronization among switches is important for ensuring accurate timing and coordination, which is essential for applications requiring precise timing, such as industrial automation, financial trading, and telecommunication systems. Clock synchronization techniques in deterministic networks typically aim to achieve tight synchronization between switches, minimizing packet transmission delays and ensuring consistent network performance [16]. As shown in Figure 5.12, clock synchronization techniques are mainly classified into IEEE 1588

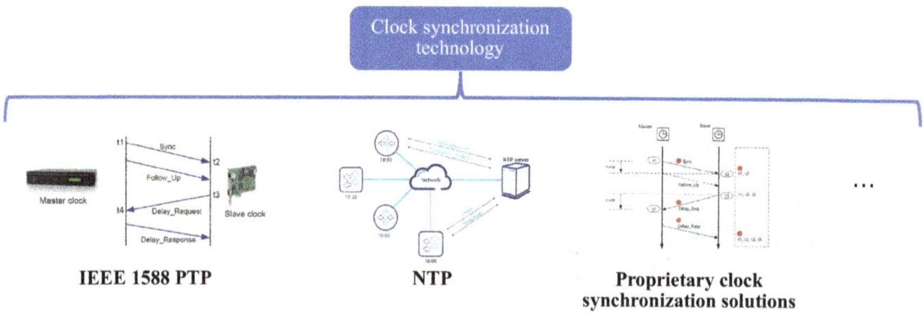

Figure 5.12 Clock synchronization technology

PTP, NTP, and other proprietary clock synchronization solutions. One commonly used clock synchronization protocol in deterministic networks is the PTP, standardized by the IEEE 1588 standard. PTP enables switches to synchronize their clocks with high precision by exchanging timing information packets over the network. These packets contain timestamps that allow switches to accurately determine the propagation delay and offset between their clocks, enabling them to adjust their local clocks accordingly.

Another widely adopted clock synchronization technique is the NTP, which is commonly used for synchronizing clocks in traditional IP-based networks. While NTP offers good accuracy for general time synchronization purposes, it may not provide the level of precision required for deterministic networks due to inherent network latency and variability. However, NTP can still be utilized as a secondary synchronization method in conjunction with PTP for redundancy and failover purposes.

In addition to PTP and NTP, other deterministic networks may employ proprietary clock synchronization solutions specifically tailored to their requirements. These solutions may leverage specialized hardware or algorithms optimized for low-latency synchronization, providing enhanced performance in demanding network environments.

Furthermore, advanced features, such as transparent clocking and boundary clocking, are implemented in switches to further enhance clock synchronization accuracy. Transparent clocking enables switches to compensate for network delay variations introduced by intermediate network devices, while boundary clocking allows switches to act as intermediate timekeepers, reducing the overall synchronization errors in the network. Overall, clock synchronization plays a critical role in ensuring precise timing and coordination in deterministic networks, enabling switches to operate effectively in applications where timing accuracy is paramount. By utilizing protocols such as PTP, NTP, and proprietary synchronization solutions, deterministic network switches can achieve tight synchronization, facilitating reliable and efficient network operation.

5.6.3 Time-sensitive scheduling

In deterministic networks, time-sensitive scheduling techniques in switches are used for ensuring predictable and controlled data transmission, particularly in real-time communication scenarios. Below are some common time-sensitive scheduling techniques.

5.6.3.1 Time-Aware Scheduler (TAS)

TAS is a technology implemented in switches to achieve time-sensitive scheduling. It allows administrators to assign strict transmission times to different types of traffic, ensuring that high-priority real-time traffic gets transmission opportunities within specified time windows. TAS identifies data streams of different priorities, queuing and scheduling data according to their timing requirements [47]. This helps to reduce network latency and jitter, thereby enhancing the quality of real-time communication.

5.6.3.2 Time-aware traffic shaping

Time-aware traffic shaping refers to the process of controlling and adjusting data traffic based on its time requirements. By implementing time-aware traffic shaping algorithms in switches, administrators can effectively manage the transmission time and bandwidth allocation of real-time data streams. This technology enables network administrators to precisely schedule and control data flows in the network according to the specific requirements of real-time applications, ensuring the reliability of data transmission [48].

5.6.3.3 Queue-based time scheduling

In deterministic networks, queue-based time scheduling techniques allow administrators to place data streams of different priorities into separate transmission queues and schedule data based on their timing requirements [49]. By scheduling transmission queues, switches can ensure that high-priority real-time data streams receive timely transmission in the network, meeting the timing sensitivity requirements of real-time communication.

These time-sensitive scheduling techniques, coupled with clock synchronization mechanisms and traffic control algorithms, provide precise time management for real-time communication in deterministic networks. They ensure that real-time data streams are transmitted on time, meeting the stringent timing and reliability requirements of real-time communication applications.

5.6.4 Congestion management

In deterministic networks, switches employ various congestion control strategies to manage and mitigate network congestion effectively. By implementing these congestion control strategies, switches can effectively manage network congestion and ensure reliable data transmission in deterministic networks, even under challenging conditions. Some common congestion control strategies include the following.

5.6.4.1 Priority-based queuing

Priority-based queuing is a congestion management technique used in networking to manage traffic by assigning different priorities to packets or flows. In this approach, packets are placed into different queues based on their assigned priority levels.

Higher-priority packets are processed and transmitted first, while lower-priority packets are delayed until the higher-priority queues are empty. This method ensures that critical or time-sensitive traffic, such as real-time communication or control signals, receives the necessary bandwidth and low-latency treatment, even during periods of network congestion [50].

5.6.4.2 QoS

QoS is a key concept in congestion management that involves prioritizing and managing network traffic to ensure optimal performance for different types of data. QoS mechanisms allocate network resources based on the specific needs and requirements of various traffic types, such as voice, video, and data. By defining policies for bandwidth allocation, latency, jitter, and packet loss, QoS ensures that critical applications receive the necessary resources to function properly, even under conditions of high network load or congestion.

In deterministic networks, QoS plays a vital role in maintaining predictable performance by providing guarantees on the performance characteristics of different traffic flows. This is accomplished through techniques such as traffic classification, marking, and scheduling, which effectively manage network resources and ensure that critical services meet their performance objectives [40].

5.6.4.3 Traffic policing and shaping

Traffic policing and shaping techniques are used to control the rate of traffic flows. Traffic policing involves monitoring network traffic to ensure it adheres to predefined policies and thresholds. This technique checks the traffic against specified criteria, such as rate limits and traffic profiles. If traffic exceeds these limits, policing actions such as packet dropping, remarking, or congestion notification are applied to bring the traffic back within acceptable bounds.

Traffic shaping, on the other hand, involves adjusting the traffic flow to smooth out bursts and ensure a steady stream of data. This technique uses mechanisms such as buffering and scheduling to control the rate at which packets are sent into the network. By delaying packets to conform to a specified traffic profile or rate, traffic shaping reduces the likelihood of congestion and ensures that traffic is transmitted more evenly. This approach helps in managing network load and improving overall performance by avoiding sudden spikes [51].

5.6.4.4 Explicit Congestion Notification (ECN)

ECN is a mechanism that allows switches and routers to notify end hosts of impending congestion before packet loss occurs [52]. ECN-capable switches mark packets instead of dropping them when congestion is detected, and end hosts respond by adjusting their transmission rates accordingly.

When ECN is implemented, network devices such as routers and switches monitor the network for signs of congestion. Instead of dropping packets when congestion is detected, these devices set an ECN mark in the packet header. The sender and receiver use this mark to adjust their transmission rates and alleviate congestion. This proactive approach helps to maintain network performance and reduce the need for retransmissions caused by packet loss.

ECN is particularly useful in networks where maintaining high performance and low latency is critical. By providing early congestion feedback, ECN helps to prevent congestion from escalating and ensures a more stable and efficient network operation.

5.6.4.5 Load balancing

Load balancing distributes traffic across multiple network paths to optimize resource utilization and prevent individual links from becoming overloaded. Switches can dynamically adjust traffic distribution based on factors such as link utilization, network topology and traffic patterns to alleviate congestion [13].

In practice, load balancing involves using algorithms to dynamically allocate traffic based on various criteria, such as current load, response time, or capacity. These algorithms distribute incoming traffic across multiple servers or network paths, balancing the load and minimizing the risk of congestion.

Load balancing can be implemented at different layers of the network. For example, in the application layer, it might involve distributing user requests across multiple servers hosting the same application. At the network layer, it could involve routing packets over multiple paths to avoid overloading any single path. By effectively managing the distribution of traffic, load balancing enhances the network's ability to handle high volumes of traffic and maintain optimal performance under varying conditions.

5.6.4.6 Flow control

Flow control mechanisms regulate the flow of data between network devices to prevent congestion and buffer overflow. Techniques such as pause frames and buffer management allow switches to control the rate of data transmission, reducing the likelihood of packet loss and network congestion [53].

In networking, flow control mechanisms operate at various levels, including the data link layer and transport layer. At the data link layer, protocols such as stop-and-wait and sliding window control the flow of data between adjacent nodes by managing the number of unacknowledged packets. At the transport layer, flow control is managed through mechanisms such as TCP's window-based flow control, which dynamically adjusts the rate of data transmission based on the ability of receiver to process incoming data.

Effective flow control prevents network congestion by ensuring that data is transmitted at a rate that the network can handle, reducing the likelihood of packet loss and retransmissions. This improves overall network performance and reliability, especially in scenarios with variable network conditions and diverse traffic patterns.

5.7 The introduction of deterministic network frontier

5.7.1 Development trend of deterministic network

The development of deterministic networks is driven by the increasing demand for reliable, low-latency communication in various industries such as industrial automation, automotive, telecommunications, and healthcare. As technology advances and new applications emerge, several trends are shaping the future of deterministic networks:

1. Integration of TSN Standards: TSN standards, such as those defined by the IEEE 802.1 Time-Sensitive Networking Task Group, are becoming more prevalent in deterministic networks. These standards provide mechanisms for achieving precise time synchronization, low-latency communication, and deterministic behavior over Ethernet networks. As TSN gains widespread adoption, it is expected to become a fundamental technology in enabling deterministic communication in diverse applications.
2. Emergence of Edge Computing and Fog Networking: With the proliferation of IoT devices and the rise of edge computing, there is a growing need for deterministic communication at the network edge. Fog networking, which extends cloud computing capabilities to the edge of the network, enables real-time processing and analysis of data closer to the data source [54]. DetNet technologies will play a crucial role in enabling low-latency, high-reliability communication in edge and fog computing environments.
3. Integration of AI and ML: AI and ML technologies are increasingly being integrated into deterministic networks to enhance network management, optimization, and security. AI algorithms can analyze network traffic patterns, predict potential congestion, and dynamically adjust network configurations to ensure deterministic behavior. ML algorithms can also be used for anomaly detection, intrusion detection, and threat mitigation, further improving the security of deterministic networks.
4. Deployment of 5G networks: The rollout of 5G networks is expected to accelerate the adoption of deterministic communication in mobile and wireless networks. 5G networks offer higher bandwidth, lower latency, and greater reliability compared to previous generations of cellular networks, making them well-suited for time-critical applications such as autonomous vehicles, remote surgery, and industrial automation. DetNet technologies will play a vital role in ensuring predictable communication and QoS in 5G networks.
5. Standardization and interoperability: As DetNet technologies mature, there is a growing emphasis on standardization and interoperability. Industry organizations and standards bodies are working to develop common standards/protocols for deterministic communication, enabling seamless integration of diverse devices and systems from different vendors. Interoperability will be essential for realizing the full potential of deterministic networks and enabling widespread adoption across various industries.
6. Security and resilience: With the increasing connectivity and digitization of critical infrastructure, security is paramount concerns for deterministic networks. Future developments in DetNet will focus on enhancing security mechanisms, such as encryption, authentication, and access control, to protect against cyber threats. Additionally, efforts will be made to improve network resilience through redundancy, fault tolerance, and rapid recovery mechanisms, ensuring uninterrupted operation even in the face of disruptions or attacks.

In conclusion, the future of deterministic networks is characterized by the integration of TSN standards, edge/fog computing, AI/ML technologies, 5G networks, standardization, security, and resilience. These trends will drive the evolution of deterministic networks, enabling reliable, low-latency communication in a wide range of applications and industries.

5.7.2 Related standards of deterministic network

The development of deterministic networks is supported by a range of standards aimed at providing unified technical specifications and guidelines. These standards are useful to ensure that network communication meets stringent requirements for timeliness, reliability, and predictability. Some key standards related to deterministic networks are as follows:

5.7.2.1 IEEE 802.1 standards series

The IEEE 802.1 series of standards form the foundation for DetNet. It encompasses several sub-standards such as IEEE 802.1AS (time synchronization), 802.1Qbv (time-aware traffic scheduling), 802.1Qbu (bandwidth reclamation), 802.1Qca (stream reservation and synchronization), 802.1Qcc (stream control and management), and others. These standards define protocols, mechanisms, and algorithms for achieving time-sensitive communication, providing technical support for the design and implementation of deterministic networks [55].

5.7.2.2 IEEE 802.3 standards series

The IEEE 802.3 series of standards define the physical layer and data link layer technologies for Ethernet, which are crucial for the deployment of deterministic networks [56]. These standards encompass Ethernet rates, media types, interface specifications, and more, providing the foundation for hardware design in deterministic networks.

5.7.2.3 IEC 61508 and ISO 26262

These standards are functional safety standards for safety-critical systems and electronic systems. While not directly aimed at deterministic networks, they provide guidance and frameworks for ensuring the reliability aspects when implementing deterministic networks in industries such as automotive and industrial sectors [57].

5.8 Conclusion

In conclusion, this chapter has comprehensively introduced the multifaceted landscape of deterministic networks, highlighting their pivotal applications across the automotive industry, IoT, IIoT, and IACS. By delving into the essential equipment comprising time synchronization hardware and hard real-time systems, this chapter underscores the foundational infrastructure required for deterministic performance. Furthermore, it has explored flow management strategies, encompassing flow scheduling algorithms, bandwidth allocation, and flow control, which are crucial for maintaining efficient and predictable network behavior. The integration of

ML for packet filtering and classification represents a significant advancement in data and control mechanisms, enhancing the intelligence and adaptability of deterministic networks. Additionally, this chapter has shed light on the innovative technology of switches, emphasizing time-sensitive scheduling and congestion management to further bolster network reliability and responsiveness. Lastly, by presenting the frontiers of deterministic networks, this chapter has painted a vision of the future, where ongoing research and development will continue to push the boundaries of what is achievable in DetNet, ensuring their relevance and impact in an increasingly interconnected world.

References

[1] Espina J, Falck T, Panousopoulou A, *et al.* Network topologies, communication protocols, and standards. In: Body Sensor Networks. Springer; 2014. p. 189–236.

[2] Karris S. Networks: Design and management. Orchard Publications; 2009.

[3] Liu Q and Liu Q. A study on topology in computer network. In: 2014 7th International Conference on Intelligent Computation Technology and Automation. IEEE; 2014. p. 45–48.

[4] Goralski W. The illustrated network: How TCP/IP works in a modern network. Morgan Kaufmann; 2017.

[5] Berners-Lee T, Fielding R, and Frystyk H. Hypertext transfer protocol–HTTP/1.0. RFC Editor; 1996.

[6] Ranie L, Narula P, and Panchal N. FTP—The File Transfer Protocol. International Journal of Research (IJR). 2014;1(9):1029–1031.

[7] Riabov VV. SMTP (simple mail transfer protocol). River College; 2005.

[8] Aitchison R. An Introduction to DNS. Pro DNS and BIND. Apress; 2005. p. 3–19.

[9] Bradley GH. Survey of deterministic networks. AIIE Transactions. 1975;8(1):222–234.

[10] Zhen N, Chen X, Wang Y, *et al.* Research on high precision time synchronization scheme of power system based on network. In: 2018 2nd International Conference on Applied Mathematics, Modelling and Statistics Application (AMMSA 2018). Atlantis Press; 2018. p. 336–342.

[11] Imtiaz J, Jasperneite J, and Schriegel S. A proposal to integrate process data communication to IEEE 802.1 Audio Video Bridging (AVB). In: ETFA2011. IEEE; 2011. p. 1–8.

[12] Gavriluţ V and Pop P. Scheduling in time sensitive networks (TSN) for mixed-criticality industrial applications. In: 2018 14th IEEE International Workshop on Factory Communication Systems (WFCS). IEEE; 2018. p. 1–4.

[13] Chen S, Leguay J, Martin S, *et al.* Load balancing for deterministic networks. In: 2020 IFIP Networking Conference (Networking). IEEE; 2020. p. 785–790.

[14] Nasrallah A, Thyagaturu AS, Alharbi Z, *et al.* Ultra-low latency (ULL) networks: The IEEE TSN and IETF DetNet standards and related 5G ULL research. IEEE Communications Surveys & Tutorials. 2018;21(1):88–145.

[15] Grossman E. Deterministic networking use cases. RFC Editor; 2019.

[16] Hu B and Gharavi H. A hybrid wired/wireless deterministic network for smart grid. IEEE Wireless Communications. 2021;28(3):138–143.

[17] Mooney VJ and Blough DM. A hardware–software real-time operating system framework for SoCs. IEEE Design & Test of Computers. 2002;19(6): 44–51.

[18] Yoo M. Real-time task scheduling by multiobjective genetic algorithm. Journal of Systems and Software. 2009;82(4):619–628.

[19] Wada R and Yamasaki N. Fast interrupt handling scheme by using interrupt wake-up mechanism. In: 2019 Seventh International Symposium on Computing and Networking Workshops (CANDARW). IEEE; 2019. p. 109–114.

[20] Raja FR, Chen D, and Hexel R. A flexible communication protocol with guaranteed determinism for distributed, safety-critical real-time systems. IEEE Access. 2022;10:48049–48070.

[21] Lévesque M and Tipper D. A survey of clock synchronization over packet-switched networks. IEEE Communications Surveys & Tutorials. 2016;18(4):2926–2947.

[22] Awad A, Hammond SD, Voskuilen GR, *et al.* Samba: A detailed memory management unit (MMU) for the sst simulation framework. Sandia National Lab. (SNL-NM), Albuquerque, NM; 2016.

[23] Popovici K and Jerraya A. Hardware abstraction layer: Introduction and overview. In: Ecker W, Müller W, and Dömer R (eds.), *Hardware-dependent Software: Principles and Practice*. Dordrecht: Springer, 2009. p. 67–94.

[24] Ferdinand C, Heckmann R, Kästner D, *et al.* Integration of code-level and system-level timing analysis for early architecture exploration and reliable timing verification. In: ERTS2 2010, Embedded Real Time Software & Systems; 2010.

[25] Shajahan MA. Fault tolerance and reliability in AUTOSAR stack development: Redundancy and error handling strategies. Technology & Management Review. 2018;3(1):27–45.

[26] Nayak NG, Dürr F, and Rothermel K. Incremental flow scheduling and routing in time-sensitive software-defined networks. IEEE Transactions on Industrial Informatics. 2017;14(5):2066–2075.

[27] Mustafa ME. Load balancing algorithms round-robin (RR), least connection, and least loaded efficiency. Computer Science & Telecommunications. 2017;51(1):25–29.

[28] Saidu I, Subramaniam S, Jaafar A, *et al.* A load-aware weighted round-Robin algorithm for IEEE 802.16 networks. EURASIP Journal on Wireless Communications and Networking. 2014;2014:1–12.

[29] You G and Zhao Y. A weighted-fair-queuing (WFQ)-based dynamic request scheduling approach in a multi-core system. Future Generation Computer Systems. 2012;28(7):1110–1120.

[30] Zakariyya I and Rahman MNA. Bandwidth guarantee using class based weighted fair queue (CBWFQ) scheduling algorithm. International Journal of Digital Information and Wireless Communication (IJDIWC). 2015;5(3): 152–157.

[31] Lenzini L, Mingozzi E, and Stea G. Tradeoffs between low complexity, low latency, and fairness with Deficit Round-Robin schedulers. IEEE/ACM Transactions on Networking. 2004;12(4):681–693.
[32] Tang PP and Tai TY. Network traffic characterization using token bucket model. In: IEEE INFOCOM'99. Eighteenth Annual Joint Conference of the IEEE Computer and Communications Societies. The Future is Now (Cat. No. 99CH36320). Vol. 1. IEEE; 1999. p. 51–62.
[33] Lin M, Wierman A, and Zwart B. Heavy-traffic analysis of mean response time under shortest remaining processing time. Performance Evaluation. 2011;68(10):955–966.
[34] Lee A, Wang P, Lin SC, *et al.* Dynamic bandwidth allocation in SDN based next generation virtual networks: A deterministic network calculus approach. In: Proceedings of the 2018 Conference on Research in Adaptive and Convergent Systems; 2018. p. 80–87.
[35] Norden S, Balaji S, Manimaran G, *et al.* Deterministic protocols for real-time communication in multiple access networks. Computer Communications. 1999;22(2):128–136.
[36] Zhang E and Xu L. Capacity and token rate estimation for networks with token bucket shapers. Computer Networks. 2015;88:1–11.
[37] Maile L, Hielscher KSJ, and German R. Delay-guaranteeing admission control for time-sensitive networking using the credit-based shaper. IEEE Open Journal of the Communications Society. 2022;3:1834–1852.
[38] Álvarez I, Moutinho L, Pedreiras P, *et al.* Comparing admission control architectures for real-time ethernet. IEEE Access. 2020;8:105521–105534.
[39] Hellmanns D, Falk J, Glavackij A, *et al.* On the performance of stream-based, class-based time-aware shaping and frame preemption in TSN. In: 2020 IEEE International Conference on Industrial Technology (ICIT). IEEE; 2020. p. 298–303.
[40] Chen YJ, Wang LC, Lin FY, *et al.* Deterministic quality of service guarantee for dynamic service chaining in software defined networking. IEEE Transactions on Network and Service Management. 2017;14(4):991–1002.
[41] Li E, He F, Zhao L, *et al.* A SDN-based traffic bandwidth allocation method for time sensitive networking in avionics. In: 2019 IEEE/AIAA 38th Digital Avionics Systems Conference (DASC). IEEE; 2019. p. 1–7.
[42] Pravda M, Vodrazka J, and Lafata P. Simulations and measurements of packet network synchronization by precision time protocol. In: 2012 35th International Conference on Telecommunications and Signal Processing (TSP). IEEE; 2012. p. 116–120.
[43] Tongaonkar AS. Fast pattern-matching techniques for packet filtering. Citeseer; 2004.
[44] Chebrolu CS, Lung CH, and Ajila SA. Dynamic packet filtering using machine learning. In: 2022 IEEE 23rd International Conference on Information Reuse and Integration for Data Science (IRI). IEEE; 2022. p. 206–211.

[45] El-Maghraby RT, Abd Elazim NM, and Bahaa-Eldin AM. A survey on deep packet inspection. In: 2017 12th International Conference on Computer Engineering and Systems (ICCES). IEEE; 2017. p. 188–197.

[46] Song F, Li L, You I, *et al.* Enabling heterogeneous deterministic networks with smart collaborative theory. IEEE Network. 2021;35(3):64–71.

[47] Min J, Kim Y, Kim M, *et al.* Reinforcement learning based routing for time-aware shaper scheduling in time-sensitive networks. Computer Networks. 2023;235:109983.

[48] Stüber T, Osswald L, Lindner S, *et al.* A survey of scheduling algorithms for the time-aware shaper in time-sensitive networking (TSN). IEEE Access. 2023;11:61192–61233.

[49] Zhou B and Cheng L. TSN-VM: A real-time and distributed algorithm for scheduling-violation mitigation in time-sensitive networking. Authorea Preprints; 2023.

[50] Rahouti M, Xiong K, Xin Y, *et al.* QoSP: A priority-based queueing mechanism in software-defined networking environments. In: 2021 IEEE International Performance, Computing, and Communications Conference (IPCCC). IEEE; 2021. p. 1–7.

[51] Kasiolas A. Intelligent control in multimedia traffic policing, shaping and congestion avoidance over broadband networks. National Library of Canada= Bibliothèque nationale du Canada, Ottawa; 2000.

[52] Teymoori P, Hayes DA, Welzl M, *et al.* Estimating an additive path cost with explicit congestion notification. IEEE Transactions on Control of Network Systems. 2021;8(2):859–871.

[53] Ryu HK and Chong S. Deterministic packet marking for max-min flow control. IEEE Communications Letters. 2005;9(9):856–858.

[54] Peng G, Wang S, Huang Y, *et al.* Enabling deterministic tasks with multi-access edge computing in 5G networks. IEEE Communications Magazine. 2022;60(8):36–42.

[55] Stanton KB. Distributing deterministic, accurate time for tightly coordinated network and software applications: IEEE 802.1 AS, the TSN profile of PTP. IEEE Communications Standards Magazine. 2018;2(2):34–40.

[56] Ethernet Rt. IEEE TSN (Time-Sensitive Networking): A Deterministic Ethernet Standard; 2015.

[57] Reddy GP, Leburu R, Rajireddy K, *et al.* Achieving ISO 26262 & IEC 61508 objectives with a common development process. In: Computer-Aided Developments: Electronics and Communication. CRC Press; 2019. p. 247–255.

Chapter 6
Delay-tolerant network

Yujie Song[1], *Xinyu Li*[1] *and Yue Cao*[1]

This chapter introduces several aspects of Delay-Tolerant Networks (DTN), including background, representative characteristics, architecture, advantages and disadvantages, technologies, security, and applications.

6.1 Introduction

With the development of wireless radio frequency technologies, wireless networks are employed in numerous scenarios, such as military communications, broadcast communications, Wireless Local Area Networks (WLAN), Cellular Networks (CN), etc. The traditional communication networks establish links among their participators (e.g., routers, switches, base stations) to provide data transmission services for terminal users (e.g., smartphones, personal laptops, vehicles), including Transmission Control Protocol/Internet Protocol (TCP/IP) [1], Routing Information Protocol (RIP) [2], Open Shortest Path First (OSPF) [3], and Ad hoc On-demand Distance Vector (ADOV) routing [4]. Those networks construct complete and reliable paths (i.e., a group of relay devices) from sources to destinations to transmit data, but fail to address the frequent network interruptions problem, causing data transmission interruptions. Furthermore, with the development of information technologies, terminal users can also provide data services for other users, e.g., the person-to-person network. Unfortunately, the ad hoc network constructed by mobile users cannot provide reliable data transmission services because of the intermittent connectivity caused by the mobility of users, which results in frequent topology changes [5]. Therefore, how to provide consistent data services in frequent network interruption scenarios becomes a major requirement of developing networks (e.g., high reliability and bandwidth, low latency).

To overcome network interruptions and satisfy developing network requirements, originating from Interplanetary Networks (IPNs), Delay-Tolerant Networks (DTN) is focused on by academia and industry. DTN represents the special networks without sufficient connectivity among participators and cannot employ the traditional communication protocols (e.g., TCP/IP, RIP, OSPF, and AODV), such as Mobile Ad-hoc Networks (MANETs) [6], Vehicular Ad-hoc Networks (VANETs) [7], and

[1] School of Cyber Science and Engineering, Wuhan University, China

Wireless Mesh Network (WMN) [8]. DTN is considered to address the frequent network interruption problem and provide consistent data transmission services thanks to the Store-Carry-Forward (SCF) mechanism [9]. A node with SCF mechanism stores data in its buffer, carries data until it encounters a suitable node, and forwards data to the suitable encounters. For instance, there are no vehicles within the communication range of an observed vehicle. The observed vehicle stores and carries data while moving along roads. When the observed vehicle encounters other vehicles, it establishes connectivities with others and forwards data (messages) to them.

In addition, message-oriented DTN utilizes the mobility of nodes to establish dynamic connectivity with other nodes. Thanks to the SCF mechanism in DTN, the process of data delivery does not rely on the complete and consistent path from sources to destinations. Nodes try to transmit data to encounters based on the dynamically established connectivity while moving. Furthermore, the routing protocol employed in nodes determines whether to transmit data to an encounter and which encounter is the suitable recipient, such as quantitative utility-based routing protocols, social relationship-based routing protocols, prediction-based routing protocols, topological routing protocols, and geographic routing protocols [10]. Various routing protocols focus on different indicators to evaluate the data transmission probability, service capability of encounters, and the End-to-End (E2E) latency, such as moving speeds, buffer spaces, moving directions, social properties, locations, geographic information, etc.

6.2 The presentative characteristics of DTN

6.2.1 Nodes

6.2.1.1 Limited resource

Due to mobile nodes are designed to be a small volume in DTN, their storage and processing capabilities are limited by the equipped devices with a low power. Specifically, numerous data are stored in nodes in a long time because of the frequent network interruption, causing the buffer of nodes to be occupied and nodes cannot receive new data. The frequent interruption of data transmission consumes much bandwidths and decreases the data delivery ratio, resulting in low Quality of Services (QoS) for users.

6.2.1.2 Limited lifespan

DTN is usually deployed in harsh environments, such as military battlefields, underwater communication, disaster rescue, etc. The cost, size, and quality of nodes are limited by various application scenarios, and the battery capacity of nodes is also finite. Furthermore, the working time of nodes is affected by energy consumption, environment changes, and the quality of communication channels. In scenarios where the transmission time of a message exceeds the lifespan of nodes, nodes cannot provide data transmission services for users.

6.2.1.3 Low occupancy ratio

The occupancy ratio represents the ratio of consistent working time to the lifespan of nodes. When the total energy is finite, nodes always cannot be charged. They will switch to the lower power status to reduce energy consumption for long-term services, causing low occupancy ratio.

6.2.2 Connectivities

6.2.2.1 Low transmission speed and high latency

In DTN, the transmission speed of communication channels is limited by the power of equipped devices, interference, distance, and environment (e.g., trees, buildings, pedestrians). For instance, the transmission speed of underwater devices is approximately 10 kbps, and thus, the limited transmission speed causes high latency. Furthermore, since the distance between ground stations and satellites exceeds 500 km in IPNs, data transmission takes more time between ground stations and satellites, resulting in high transmission latency.

6.2.2.2 Frequent transmission interruption

Due to the high-speed mobility of nodes, communication interference caused by obstacles, and short-term dormancy of nodes with low energy, DTN is more prone to connectivity interruptions than traditional networks. Furthermore, connectivity interruptions can be predicted according to the mobility of nodes in a special scenario, such as satellite constellations. Unfortunately, most ad hoc networks cannot provide regular networking paradigms, such as Internet of Vehicles (IoVs), Wireless Sensor Networks (WSNs), and Pocket Switched Networks (PSNs).

6.2.2.3 High queuing latency

The waiting latency in output queues (i.e., queuing latency) is a major factor that affects the E2E latency in a multi-hop network. Specifically, in traditional core networks (e.g., Internet and local area networks with wired cables), the queuing latency is usually lower than 1 s, thanks to their reliable connectivities. On the contrary, nodes store data in their buffers and seek the next hop node to address network interruptions caused by the mobility of nodes. Due to the randomness of encounters in DTN, the queuing latency cannot be precisely evaluated, and its value is larger in most cases. Therefore, how to reduce the high queuing latency in DTN has become a significant challenge in improving the performance of data delivery.

6.2.3 Networks

6.2.3.1 Interoperability

Media Access Control Protocols (MACPs) are the component of architecture in DTN. MACPs with simple structures are different from traditional protocols, such as TCP/IP. Specifically, TCP/IP provides the abstract layered protocol stack to divide the network into five layers, i.e., physical layer, data link layer, network layer, transport layer, and application layer, but lacks cross-layer cooperation and interoperability. For instance, several special application formats reduce the extensibility of networks and increase the difficulty of network congestion control, such as restricted addresses of nodes, regular data size, etc. In the view of MACPs, they focus on transmitting data between two nodes by controlling the data transmission rule, allocating addresses, and avoiding data transmission conflict.

6.2.3.2 Security

To provide security data transmission services, it is necessary for DTN to utilize authentication and control access technologies because of the leakage of communication resources and the problem of malicious attacks between nodes. However, due to the intermittent connectivity in DTN, key exchange and access control technologies are difficult to employ by E2E connection methods. Based on several conventional methods (e.g., cryptography), the cooperation of trusted Roadside Units (RSUs) and mobile nodes is an available way to improve the security of DTN.

6.3 The architecture of DTN

6.3.1 Overall architecture

Figure 6.1 shows the protocol stacks of TCP/IP and DTN. Specifically, the protocol stack of TCP/IP consists of five layers, i.e., the physical layer, data link layer, network layer, transport layer, and application layer. Based on this, the protocol stack of DTN adds a bundle layer between the transport and application layers. Furthermore, the SCF mechanism is implemented in the bundle layer to improve the performance of data delivery.

6.3.2 Protocol stack

The protocol stack of DTN is shown in Figure 6.2. Different from the protocol stack of traditional networks (e.g., TCP/IP), DTN introduces a bundle layer to manage data transmission. The bundle layer is data-oriented and responsible for virtual message forwarding rather than packet switching.

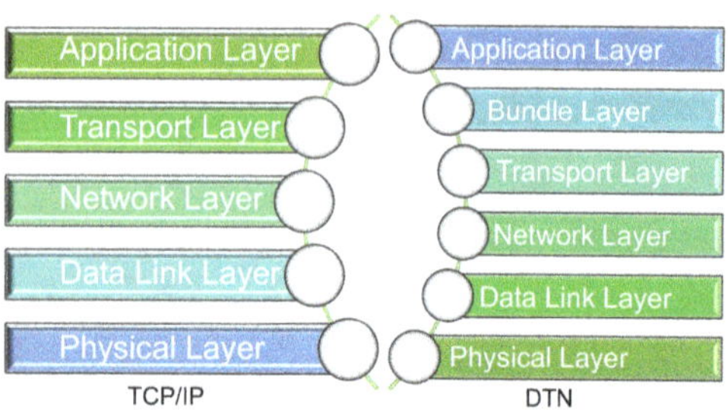

Figure 6.1 The architectures of TCP/IP and DTN.

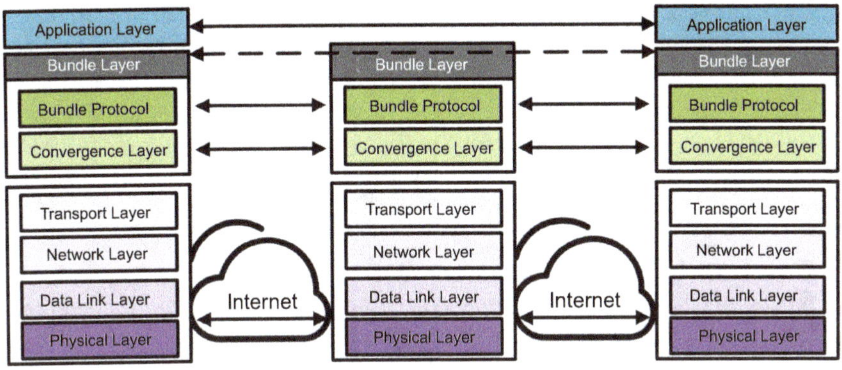

Figure 6.2 The protocol stack of DTN

6.3.2.1 Physical layer

The physical layer focuses on the following three characteristics:

- Undifferentiated data transmission for various protocols and communication types in upper layers.
- Physical link establishment, maintenance, and release.
- Uniquely identifies data circuits between two neighboring systems.

Furthermore, the physical layer provides reliable transmission links to transmit various types of messages, and its details are shown as follows:

- **Transmission links:** The link is constructed by a physical device at least. Usually, this link represents a physical cable or wireless channel between two devices.
- **Data transmission services:** The physical layer converts data frames into binary signals for data transmission.

Several characteristics of the physical layer are shown as follows:

- **Mechanical property:** (1) The shape and size of connectors utilized for an interface. (2) The number and arrangement of leads. (3) Fixing and locking devices, etc.
- **Electrical property:** The range of voltages that appear on each line of the interface cable, such as the description of circuit characteristics, identification of signals, electrical parameters, etc.
- **Functional property:** It depicts the meaning of voltage at a certain level on links, such as the interface function, signal control, timing signal line, etc.
- **Regulation:** The interface of process of a bit stream and event orders are introduced, including execution order of events and data transmission methods.

6.3.2.2 Data link layer

The data link layer defines how data are transmitted over a single link. Its main functions consist of data allocation (i.e., encapsulating data as blocks, namely frames), frame transmission, error processing, and link management. Furthermore, to ensure the accuracy of data transmission and improve the utilization of transmission channels, the data link layer maintains a logical line based on various protocols and regularities (e.g., the logical link control, media access control, point-to-point protocol, high-level data link protocol, frame relay, asynchronous transfer mode). Moreover, the fundamental functions of this layer include frame synchronization, error correction, traffic control, and link management.

- **Frame synchronization:** To retransmit data when an error occurs during the process of data transmission, frame synchronization is responsible for organizing frames and identifying them from the bitstream received at the physical layer, i.e., distinguishing the beginning and tails of frames. Furthermore, the popular methods include byte counting, character padding, bit-filling, and Manchester coding methods.
- **Error correction:** To ensure the accuracy of data transmission, the data link layer tries to detect and correct the occurred error, keeping errors as small as possible. Furthermore, parity code and cyclic redundancy checks are employed to detect and correct errors.
- **Traffic control:** It is different from the traffic control mechanisms of upper layers, i.e., the traffic control in the data link layer focuses on the frame stream between two nodes by controlling the number of frames in the sliding window of senders and receivers.
- **Link management:** It provides connection-oriented services for users. Before the nodes at both ends of the link can communicate, they must first confirm that the other side is in a ready state and exchange some necessary information, to initialize the frame sequence number before the connection can be established and maintained during transmission. In case of errors, the connection needs to be reinitialized and re-established automatically. Furthermore, when the transmission is complete, the connection is released. The establishment and maintenance of data link layer connections and their release are called link management.

6.3.2.3 Network layer

The main mission of network layer is to interconnect the networks, thus enabling data transmission between networks. The purpose of this layer is to provide transparent data transmission services, with specific functions such as addressing, routing, connection establishment, retention, and termination. Furthermore, different from the data link layer, the network layer is responsible for transmitting data among homogeneous/heterogeneous networks, focusing on utilizing networking topologies, communication media, and switching technologies.

In addition, the functions of the network layer are shown as follows:

- **Packet and packet switching:** The data received from the transport layer is encapsulated into packets and transmitted to the data link layer.
- **Routing:** According to routing algorithms, the network layer selects an optimal path among various networks for packets to reduce the E2E latency and

avoid network congestion (i.e., numerous packets are stored in a buffer space and waiting for transmission).

- **Network link multiplexing:** Logical links are constructed for packets in networks to improve the performance and QoS of data transmission. Based on this, multiple logical links pass through a section of the common physical link to maximize the utilization of bandwidths, which is called network link multiplexing. Then, this technology is also employed to improve the utilization of physical links by time/space-division multiplexing techniques.
- **Error detection and correction:** To ensure the accuracy and continuity of data transmission, error detection is usually performed with the header checksum in packets. Then, error correction acknowledges and retransmits packets based on the information of received packets.
- **Service selection:** The network layer provides two services for the transport layer, i.e., datagram and virtual circuit services. Specifically, the datagram represents the unit of packets, including a header and data content. The virtual circuit represents the logical connection between nodes.
- **Network management:** The network layer manages the process of data transmission, i.e., transmitting data from its source to destinations. To improve the performance of networks and alleviate the overhead of networks, the network balancing technology focuses on arranging the transmission paths and managing relay rules.
- **Traffic control:** It is implemented through traffic shaping techniques to prevent numerous traffic from degrading the performance of communication subnets.
- **Congestion control:** When the data traffic of networks exceeds the rated capacity, it will trigger network congestion and results in a sharp decrease in the throughput capacity of networks. Therefore, several congestion control mechanisms are employed to alleviate traffic congestion, such as buffer pre-allocation, packet discard, quota control methods, etc.
- **Network interconnection:** Several networks are connected to provide cross-networks communication services in heterogeneous networks, considering network types, protocols, fault tolerance, etc.
- **Fragmentation and reassembly:** If the packet exceeds the allowed length of the data unit in a protocol, the network layer of senders will fragment the packet. Then, fragments of packets will be reassembled again in the network layer of receivers.

6.3.2.4 Transport layer

The transport layer provides communication services proceeding between two nodes. The proceeding represents an instance of a computer program that is being executed. Furthermore, since a node executes several programs simultaneously, the transport layer should provide multiplexing and diversion functions to ensure the quality of experience for users, thanks to the powerful computing of central processing unit. In addition, the most important definition in the transport layer is the “port”, i.e., the channel of data transmission between the transport layer and the upper layer. Different from the network layer, the transport layer identifies various data and conveys them to specific ports according to the type of applications.

To provide reliable communication services and avoid error, loss, repetition, and disorder of fragments, the transport layer employs several functions between application processes of nodes, such as splitting data, reorganizing data, addressing by port number, connection management, error control, flow control, and error correction. For instance, the classical protocols of transport layer are TCP and User Datagram Protocol (UDP). Specifically, as shown in Figure 6.3, TCP splits data into numerous fragments with a reasonable length and a serial number to ensure the order of fragments during data transmission. Receivers store fragments and reorganize them according to their serial numbers. Then, the corresponding data is conveyed to specific ports according to the types of applications.

As shown in Figure 6.4, UDP is a noncontinuous protocol that provides simple transaction-oriented unreliable data transmission services to support high-speed data transmission, e.g., multimedia data streaming, audio data streaming, game, and industrial Internet of Things (IoTs). The fundamental idea of UDP is to transmit data as rapidly as possible and to tolerate transient loss of data. Specifically, thanks to the mode of connectionless data transmission, it is unnecessary to maintain connection status, including the size of moving windows, sending speed, and receiving speed. Then, a sender can rapidly transmit data without confirmation from receivers. Furthermore, the packet header of UDP is only eight bytes, and its communication cost is lower than TCP. Based on this, throughput is unregulated by the congestion control algorithm and is limited only by the rate at which the application generates data, bandwidth, and the performance of nodes. Thus, UDP can provide high-speed data transmission services thanks to a few limitations of protocol construction.

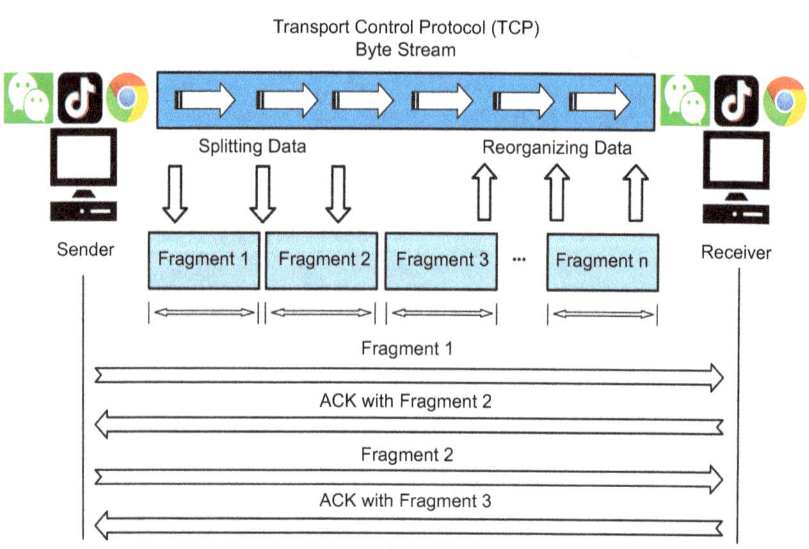

Figure 6.3 The paradigm of TCP

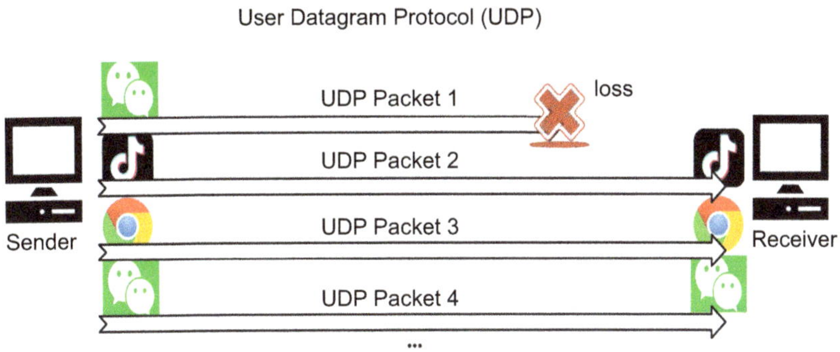

Figure 6.4 The paradigm of UDP

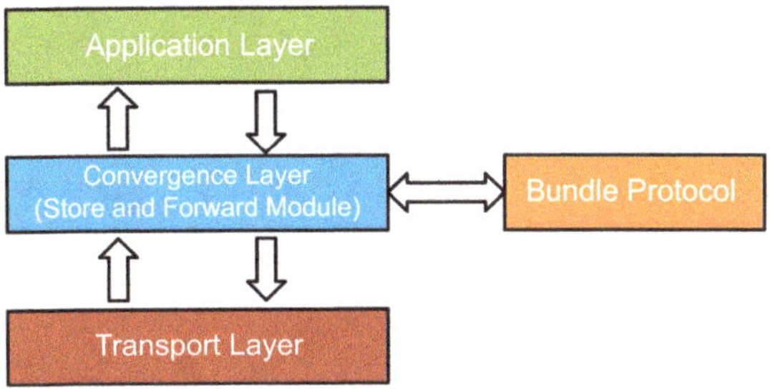

Figure 6.5 The architecture of bundle layer

6.3.2.5 Bundle layer

Figure 6.5 depicts the architecture of the bundle layer. The bundle layer consists of the convergence layer and bundle protocols. Specifically, the convergence layer stores and forwards data according to bundle protocols. The bundle protocol is responsible for generating the data transmission strategy and organizing the data order.

The bundle layer provides several services to address the connection interruption problem, including custody delivery, receiving replies, custody delivery notice, bundle forwarding and notification, delivery priority classification, authentication, etc.

- **Custody delivery:** The node has the function of saving data and passing data to other DTN nodes.
- **Receive reply:** After the destination node receives data, it sends an acknowledgment message to the source node.
- **Custody delivery notice:** After receiving the data from the previous hop, the intermediate node sends an acknowledgment notification to the previous hop.
- **Bundle forwarding and notification:** When data need to be forwarded, an acknowledgment message is sent to the next hop node.
- **Delivery priority classification:** DTN provides different delivery priorities based on the urgency of data.
- **Authentication:** Identity and data integrity of senders are verified.

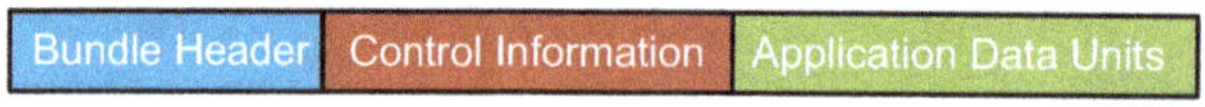

Figure 6.6 The data architecture in the bundle layer

In addition, the data architecture in the bundle layer is shown in Figure 6.6. First, the bundle header consists of several basic information, such as node identity, creation timestamp, Time-To-Live (TTL), and dictionary length. Second, the control information consists of control flag bit information that depicts how to address, store, and discard data. Third, the application data unit represents the data generated by applications. Based on the above architecture, DTN minimizes the number of packet interactions and improves the communication capability under limited connectivities.

Similar to the data processing of the IP protocol, the bundle protocol splits data into several fragments, and the receiver will reorganize fragments according to the preset configuration of the bundle protocol. Furthermore, the convergence layer provides the Licklider Transmission Protocol (LTP) and the Saratoga protocol. Both LTP and Saratoga are based on a transmission mechanism, namely Automatic RepeatreQuest (ARQ). The core theory of ARQ derives from the transmission protocol [11] of consultative committee for space data systems.

- **LTP [12]:** It selects an appropriate transmission way for data according to the attributes of files. For instance, to transmit important and secret data, LTP provides data transmission without negotiation. When a data transmission interruption occurs, LTP suspends the communication process until the connectivity is recovered. However, LTP without text validation and error detection mechanisms cannot provide reliable data transmission services.
- **Saratoga [13]:** To improve the reliability of data transmission in DTN and detect errors during data transmission, the selective negation of automatic retransmission mechanism is employed by Saratoga. This retransmission mechanism addresses the asymmetrical communication status problem among nodes. Furthermore, Saratoga supports unidirectional transmission services to transmit various files with different sizes by selecting file offset descriptors.

Moreover, when the source node queries its routing table and seeks an available next-hop node (i.e., the node with an active status), it transmits packets to the available next-hop and starts a retransmission timer to confirm time. If the source node has not received the confirm packets from the next-hop until the timer has expired, the corresponding packets will be retransmitted. However, if there are no available nodes, the source node will store packets and wait for the next transmission opportunity.

Based on the protocols of underlying layer, the bundle protocol utilizes the reliability of data transmission to relay data step by step. The intermediate node is selected to retransmit data when data transmission interruption occurs, facilitating data transmission over networks with high latency or unstable connectivities.

6.3.2.6 Application layer

The application layer bridges data and applications, providing numerous network application services, e.g., multi-process parallel communication management. Furthermore, the detailed function of application layer consists of the Common Application Service Element (CASE) and Special Application Service Element (SASE).

- **CASE:** It provides the fundamental services to construct application entities for users, such as process communication and distributed system control mechanisms.
- **SASE:** It is designed for specific applications and provides customized services, such as file transfer, access management, job transfer, bank transactions, order entry, etc. SASE involves virtual terminals, job transfer, job manipulation, file transfer, access management, remote database access, graphics core systems, open system interconnection management, etc.

With the rapid development of application concepts and protocols, it brings complexity and difficulty to the standardization of application functionality. Based on this, the application layer requires more standards to evolve its technologies and provides interfaces among applications according to functional characteristics of the application layer, e.g., transfer access and management, email, virtual terminal, directory services, remote job entry, graphic and information communication, etc. Moreover, several application protocols are utilized to apply the above functions, such as Domain Name System (DNS), Hyper Text Transfer Protocol (HTTP), and File Transfer Protocol (FTP).

- **DNS:** It is utilized to improve the sense of user experience of human–computer interactions. Specifically, DNS maps an IP address to a domain name, thus users are more convenient to remember the IP address of service providers.
- **HTTP:** It is a simple require-response protocol based on the TCP, illustrating what kind of message the client may send to the server and what kind of response it gets. The request and response message headers are given in ASCII form.
- **FTP:** It provides standardization to transmit files in various networks and heterogeneous architectures of computers. FTP focuses on authentication, client-service model, file upload and download, etc.

6.4 The advantages and disadvantages in DTN

6.4.1 Advantages

Thanks to the mobility of nodes and SCF mechanism, DTN exhibits better flexibility, scalability, and robustness than traditional networks. Especially, DTN is inherently employed to address the intermittent connectivity problem. Based on this, advantages of DTN are shown as follows:

- **Flexibility:** Due to the mobility of nodes, the network topology constructed by nodes is dynamically changed during nodes moving. Specifically, nodes establish connectivities among themselves through wireless communication channels. When the distance between two nodes exceeds the communication range of

On-Board Units (OBUs), the connectivity between nodes is disconnected, thus the two nodes cannot exchange data anymore. On the contrary, nodes establish connectivities among themselves when they move into their communication ranges.

- **Autonomy:** In various scenarios, nodes establish connectivities according to their various requirements, such as fast data transmission, emergency communication, disaster relief, etc. For instance, in the disaster relief scenario, nodes establish connectivities with each other when they move into their communication ranges to construct a full-connection network for reliable data transmission. The high probability of successful data transmission is ensured by multiple connectivities in ad hoc networks, improving the survival rate of victims indirectly.
- **Robustness:** Thanks to the mobility of nodes and various wireless communication protocols, nodes can establish connectivities with various types of equipment, e.g., RSUs, base stations, mobile phones, vehicles, traffic lights, satellites, etc. There may be differences in the protocols carried out by a pair of connected nodes. DTN utilizes a buffer to alleviate the gap in transmission rate between nodes based on the SCF mechanism, thus various devices can establish connectivities and exchange data in different types of equipment, improving the robustness.

6.4.2 Disadvantages

Although the mobility of nodes improves the characteristics of flexibility, autonomy, and robustness for DTN, it results in high E2E latency, unstable connectivity, and unpredictability simultaneously.

- **High E2E latency:** In DTN, the E2E latency is extremely challenging to be limited in an ultra-low value, because the process of data delivery relies on the moving speeds and directions of encounters. Specifically, a node cannot ensure that the moving direction of encounters is always similar to the transmission direction of data (i.e., a vector constructed by the destination of data and source node). In the worst case, the encounter received data moves to the opposite direction of transmission direction of this data, causing high E2E latency or even destination unreachability (i.e., data cannot be delivered to its destination).
- **Unstable connectivity:** Due to the mobility of nodes, the network topology is dynamically changed when nodes enter or run out of their communication ranges, resulting in data transmission interruptions and the inefficiency of data transmission.
- **Unpredictability:** Since the unstable connectivity of networks and random encounters, the network topology and the pre-transmission trajectory are difficult to predict. On the one hand, to predict the change of network topology and encounters, the system needs numerous status information of nodes to extract and calculate key elements, e.g., moving speed, moving direction, moving trajectory, buffer space, encounter time, etc. It will improve the computing cost of whole system. On the other hand, the prediction precision of change of

network topology and encounters is a key indicator and affects the validity of decision-making of data transmission.

For instance, in VANETs, suppose the network topology in period t is denoted as G_t, the predicted network topology in period $t + 1$ is denoted as G_{t+1}, and the actual network topology in period $t + 1$ is denoted as G^*_{t+1}. If G_{t+1} has a low similarity level to G^*_{t+1}, i.e., $|G_{t+1} \cap G^*_{t+1}| < \alpha$, where α represents a threshold which is utilized to identify the similarity level of predicted network topology, the low similarity level represents several elements (e.g., vehicles) of G_{t+1} cannot provide services in period t, thus data will be allocated to a non-existent vehicle in G^*_{t+1}. Then, those data need to be reallocated, and the process of reallocation consumes numerous computational and storage resources, increasing the E2E latency. Unfortunately, previous works cannot address the above problem, and the unpredictability still plays a disadvantageous role in DTN. Therefore, how to efficiently improve the prediction precision of network topology becomes an important problem for a predictable network in the future.

6.4.3 Challenges

Due to the characteristics of DTN (e.g., unstable connectivities, mobility of nodes, dynamical topology change), several challenges have emerged, such as energy constraints, limited bandwidth, buffer management, data organization, dynamical routing, etc. The detail of the above challenges is shown as follows:

- **Energy constraints [14]:** Energy drives devices to receive data, send data, perceive device status, and respond to the requirements of users. Since mobile devices (nodes) with limited volumes cannot embed infinite batteries with energy, energy management plays an important role in maximizing the resource utilization of nodes without considering battery replacement/charging. For instance, nodes cannot replace/charge batteries in extreme environments (e.g., interplanetary, underwater, high altitude, etc.). Therefore, energy-efficient routing is focused on by industry and academics.
- **Limited bandwidth [15]:** The mobile device with energy constraints employs the equipment with limited power, thus resulting in limited bandwidth for data transmission in DTN. When two nodes exchange all generated data without traffic control, some data will be lost because of unequal transmission and receiving rates which causes data collisions and network congestion. Furthermore, numerous data are aborted because of data collisions, resulting in wasting communication resources. Therefore, bandwidth can be utilized efficiently by prioritizing data during data pre-transmission.
- **Buffer management [16]:** In DTN, the transmission rate usually has a gap with the receiving rate because of various OBUs of nodes. The buffer management is utilized to store and organize data with non-confirmed status. Furthermore, numerous routing protocols of DTN are multiple copy-based, e.g., Epidemic, Spray and Wait (SaW), Binary Spray and Wait (BSaW). They flood with data and occupy their buffers for data transmission. However, redundant copies stored in nodes have occupied a large amount of buffer space, resulting in the subsequent

dropping of incoming data. To improve the success ratio of data delivery, buffer management is considered to organize data and maintain the utilization of buffer space.

- **Data organization [17]:** Numerous data are stored in the buffer of nodes and are waiting to be transmitted or reorganized. The non-optimized prioritization of output queues for data transmission causes TTL expiration, data transmission interruption, low buffer utilization, and low communication channel utilization problems. For instance, a node ignores the priority of data and transmits it by First-In-First-Out (FIFO), thus data with a high priority needs to be transmitted in buffers. Unfortunately, this data is expired (i.e., its TTL does not exceed zero) and discarded, resulting in wasting of storage resources. Moreover, if two nodes transmit data simultaneously, the data transmission collision and interruption will occur, causing high communication resource waste. Therefore, data organization is focused on improving the data transmission capability and buffer space utilization.
- **Dynamical routing [18]:** Due to the dynamic change of network topology and data transmission status, traditional works cannot perceive the above dynamical changes, resulting in a high transmission interruption ratio, low utilization of communication resources, and high overhead. For instance, when the network topology is changed, several data cannot be transmitted to the disconnected node, thus the data transmission occurs. Those data need to be reorganized to seek a next-hop node, causing the waste of computing resources. Therefore, to reduce the cost of communication, energy, and storage, it is necessary for DTN to design dynamical routing algorithms to perceive the frequent change of network status and adjust the generated data arrangement strategy.

6.5 Technologies in DTN

6.5.1 Store-carry-forward mechanism

Thanks to the SCF mechanism, DTN addresses several problems that the traditional network cannot deal with, e.g., connectivity interruption, high latency, and asymmetrical transmission rate problems. Specifically, a node encounters another node and decides whether the data will be transmitted to the encounter. The two nodes with mobility replace the traditional nodes fixed on a place. Furthermore, since the mobility of nodes results in uncertain encounters and buffer time, DTN belongs to opportunity networks. Based on this, the SCF is probability based when node interactions are related to their historical records.

6.5.2 Routing category

In addition, according to various focus of researchers, as shown in Table 6.1, DTN can be divided into several classes, i.e., copy-based routing, forwarding-based routing, replication-based routing, coding-based routing, social-based routing, geographic-based routing, etc.

Table 6.1 Related works

Category	Purpose	Articles
Copy-based	Data is replicated into multiple copies to control the maximal network overhead and avoid network congestion.	[19–27]
Forwarding-based	In single-copy based routing protocols, data is never replicated and forwarded step by step.	[28–32]
Replication-based	Nodes can replicate the received data and transmit them.	[33–37]
Coding-based	Coding is utilized to improve the efficiency of data transmission by splitting, encoding, and reorganizing data.	[38–42]
Social-based	Social relationships provide the contact information among nodes and are utilized to evaluate the reliability and availability of nodes.	[43–50]
Geographic-based	The geographic information is utilized to locate nodes and evaluate the space relationship among nodes for data transmission.	[51–58]

6.5.2.1 Copy-based routing protocols

Copy-based routing protocols are divided into two types according to the number of copies, i.e., single-copy and multiple-copy models.

The single-copy model represents nodes that only generate and forward data, but fail to replicate data. Each data is unique during data transmission. Furthermore, several single-copy-based routing protocols are introduced in detail as follows:

- The work [19] is a classical routing protocol to address the intermittent connectivity problem for DTN, and it also belongs to the forwarding-based routing protocol because there is only one copy of data. Each data with only one copy exists in the network during the process of data transmission. The single-copy model effectively controls the network overhead, but fails to provide high reliability and low latency. Specifically, the low network overhead benefits from a limited number of copies. Unfortunately, due to the mobility of nodes in DTN, the unique data is always transmitted to an unsuitable node that cannot move to the destination of data, increasing the E2E latency and the destination unreachable risk of data transmission.
- The work [20] presented a routing scheme called Single-Copy Replication (SCR) routing based on a time interval protocol. According to the time interval of senders and receivers, as shown in Figure 6.7, the opportunistic value can be predicted to schedule the connectivities among nodes. SCR selects the node with a minimal time interval value as the next-hop node to transmit data.
- The work [21] presented a domain-based single copy routing algorithm in the BirdNet designed to research mobility and cluster moving schemes of birds. Specifically, nodes are divided into several clusters according to their locations,

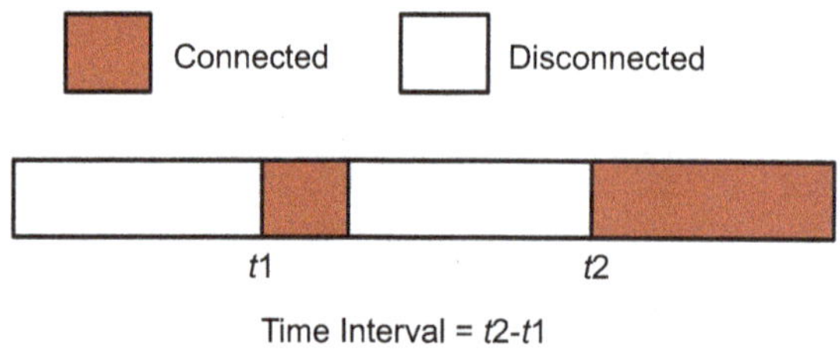

Figure 6.7 The illustration of time interval

and the data forwarding process can be classified as domain forwarding or inter-domain forwarding. Furthermore, thanks to the intermittent nodes, the domain forwarding is predictable. For instance, three nodes in a domain (e.g., A, B, C) have established connectivities, i.e., $A \leftrightarrow B, B \leftrightarrow C$. If A plans to transmit data to C, the probability of successful direct delivery (i.e., $A \rightarrow C$) is lower than that of the forwarding path in a domain (i.e., $A \rightarrow B \rightarrow C$). Moreover, similar to the data forwarding strategy in the same domain, the inter-domain forwarding is based on a domain path list to construct predictability. Therefore, the predictability of forwarding paths is beneficial to increase the reliability of data forwarding based on the established connectivity.

- The work [22] proposed a centralized optimal formulation and developed a distributed routing algorithm with the delay constraint in the mobile opportunistic networks. First, a binary transmission matrix is maintained to quantify the single-copy multi-path optimization problem with delay constraints. Second, delay and communication costs are considered to work as optimization indicators. Third, to improve the calculation efficiency and achieve a close-to-optimal solution, a distributed routing algorithm is proposed based on the above constraints.

In multiple-copy models, nodes replicate the generated data into multiple copies. The number of copies can be customized according to the requirements (e.g., high reliability and efficiency) of users. It is usually set to $[10\% * N, 15\% * N]$ (N represents the total number of nodes) [23]. Furthermore, several multiple-copy-based routing protocols are introduced in detail as follows:

- Epidemic [24], the classical multi-copy routing protocol, was proposed to improve the probability of successful data delivery in DTN thanks to the unlimited number of copies. Specifically, nodes replicate a copy and transmit it to the encounters. However, Epidemic without a copy control strategy causes heavy network overhead and congestion because of the amount number of copies, reducing the efficiency of data delivery and increasing the E2E latency.
- To reduce the network overhead and alleviate network congestions caused by numerous copies, SaW and BSaW [25] were proposed based on a copy control strategy. SaW and BSaW focus on how many copies will be transmitted to the encounters under the constraint with a limited number of copies, and both their data transmission processes are divided into two phases, i.e., the spray phase and the wait phase. In the spray phase, each data is replicated to L copies. A node

encounters other nodes (namely, neighbors) and transmits a certain number of copies to its neighbors according to the data spray strategy. For instance, when the number of copies exceeds 1, a node-embedded SaW transmits one copy to its neighbors, while a node with the BSaW routing protocol transmits $\lfloor L/2 \rfloor$ copies to its neighbors. In the wait phase, if data has not been delivered to its destination, L nodes carry and transmit data until they encounter the destination of data.

- Probability Routing Protocol using History of Encounters and Transitivity, namely PROPHET [26], was proposed to evaluate the encounter probability among nodes, based on the historical interactions and the predictable moving trajectory. The fundamental principle is that nodes may encounter each other in a certain location at an approximate time because of routine and predictable human activities. Furthermore, PROPHET can be divided into two phases, i.e., the encounter probability calculation and the forward strategy. In the encounter probability calculation phase, nodes calculate and update the corresponding encounter probability according to several indicators, e.g., time attenuation factor, initial probability, update interval, etc. In the forward strategy phase, the data with a high probability is transmitted first.
- The work [27] presented an optimization strategy for different DTN routing algorithms based on utility functions, considering energy consumptions, the Bayesian signaling game, and behaviors of nodes. Specifically, the behavior strategy of nodes is utilized to evaluate the willingness to receive messages with energy classes. The Bayesian equilibrium with those behavior strategies is approaching according to Bayes's rules, to evaluate the confidence degree. Based on this, the payoff equation is constructed to integrate gains and costs and evaluate the data transmission capability of nodes. Then, the node with the maximum of payoff is selected as the optimal relay node.

6.5.2.2 Forwarding-based routing protocols

The fundamental principle of forwarding-based routing protocols is that several intermittent nodes carry and deliver data to the destination of data. The major problem for data delivery is the selection of relay nodes in DTN. To address the above problem, utility forwarding-based algorithms are focused on.

- Spray and Focus (SaF) routing protocol [28] is an improved version based on SaW and BSaW. SaF selects relay nodes by a utility function, and the process can be divided into the spray phase and focus phase. Specifically, in the spray phase, L message copies generated by nodes are initially spread to L distinct relay nodes (encounters). In the focus phase, nodes select the relay node with a maximum of utility functions.
- Random and Encounter Time (RET) based forwarding mechanism [29] was proposed to evaluate the data transmission capability of vehicles according to a utility forwarding mechanism. Furthermore, RET is divided into the random forwarding phase and the utility-based forwarding phase. In the random forwarding phase, nodes randomly transmit data to encounters because utility-based mechanisms without sufficient interactions cannot work effectively. In the utility-based

forwarding phase, data is forwarded from the node with a low utility value to the node with a higher one based on the timer utility.

- The work [30] presented a utility-based routing protocol to address the high network overhead caused by numerous copies, considering the node density, encounter probability, and locations. Specifically, each node estimates the node density at a certain location according to a Gaussian kernel function. According to the node density threshold, data is allocated to a corresponding forwarding probability, like a utility function, based on the PROPHET routing protocol.
- The work [31] proposed an Energy Efficient Greedy Forwarding (EEGF) routing protocol to reduce energy consumption and prolong the network lifetime. Based on the evaluation of distance between nodes and remaining energy, EEGF greedily selects the optimal node as an intermittent node.
- A Virtual-range-Forwarding-Based Opportunistic Routing (VFBOR) method [32] was proposed to transmit data in a mine goaf sensor network that belongs to IoTs. The mine goaf represents a loose coal-rock mass area formed after the collapse of the remnant cavity in the process of coal mining. VFBOR focuses on improving the performance of data transmission by constructing a virtual-range-forwarding strategy with energy limitations. Based on this, VFBOR defines a recovery mechanism to address the void region problem caused by the mine goaf.

6.5.2.3 Replication-based routing protocols

The replication-based routing protocols overcome disadvantages exist in single-copy-based routing protocols, such as the low delivery ratio and the high E2E latency by increasing the number of data copies. They focus on controlling the number of data copies to reduce the E2E latency and increase the probability of successful data delivery. Specifically, nodes with replication-based routing protocols replicate data and transmit it to encounters, thus data has a high probability of being delivered to its destination. For instance, Epidemic, SaW, BSaW, and PROPHET are the conventional replication-based routing protocols. To improve the performance of data transmission in DTN, various enhanced routing protocols improve their resource utilization by managing their buffer space and choosing an optimal intermittent node.

- To improve the efficiency of routing protocols and avoid the abuse of buffer space, the work [33] drops expired messages based on a timer scheme and TTL. To prevent bundles from being discarded prematurely caused by improper TTL values, the authors dynamically change the value of TTL.
- The work [34] proposed a Markov-based routing protocol with a buffer space management to address the problem of quantifying the buffer size of nodes. First, this work utilizes the Large Deviations Theory (LDT) [35] to describe the buffer size in terms of the tail distribution of overflow probability. Second, the authors focus on evaluating the bounding buffer problem by using LDT and Markov modulated process. Third, the constant service rate queue is modeled to reflect the effective bandwidth in two scenarios (no relay nodes, with relay nodes).
- Based on erasure coding technology, Replication-based Efficient data Delivery routing protocol (RED) [36] was proposed to deliver data and manage messages.

According to the delivery probability, RED decides the optimal erasure coding parameters, such as the number of data blocks and the requirement of redundancy. Furthermore, RED selects the intermittent node with a minimum delivery probability that is no less than the desired message delivery probability, to reduce the communication overhead.

- The work [37] addressed the problem of deriving the optimal closed-loop control for replication strategy in opportunistic networks based on the Markov Chain. Specifically, the authors model the spreading dynamics of messages with mobility and paths, considering the hop count, mobility parameter, infection mode, and replication probability. To improve the utilization of buffer spaces, buffer occupancy is considered to control the buffer space of nodes by evicting messages.

6.5.2.4 Coding-based routing protocols

Different from the traditional routing protocols, the coding-based routing protocols focus on coding and decoding multi-path networks, messages, data flows, etc. Furthermore, the unique view is considered to address the routing loop problem thanks to the high efficiency and simplification of coding strategies. Various coding-based routing protocols are shown as follows:

- The work [38] proposed a decode-and-forward strategy to find an optimal route for data transmission. Specifically, single-hop and multi-hop coding strategies are analyzed to maximize the possible route rate. The decode-and-forward cooperative coding is utilized to evaluate the reception rate of nodes in route, considering co-channel interference and noise.
- The work [39] proposed an interference model in VANETs, considering the average number of transmissions, computational complexity, network topology with a maximal clique, etc. First, the authors define the average number of transmissions that a message is delivered from the source node to its destination. Second, the computational complexity of coding problem is analyzed to demonstrate the high efficiency of coding scheme in theory. Finally, a maximal clique is constructed to seek the optimal path for data delivery.
- Connected Domaining Set (CDS)-based and Flow-oriented Coding-aware Routing (CFCR) mechanism [40] was proposed to avoid coding collision in WMN and improve network performances. Specifically, to select the CDS, the authors construct a graph based on the relationship between nodes thanks to the graph theory. Then, the flow-oriented coding type is chosen, and the multi-hop coding awareness is considered for CFCR. Moreover, the authors solve the coding collision and packet loss problems by a potential coding opportunity confirmation mechanism in the process of route selection.
- The work [41] proposed a Cumulative Coded ACKnowledgment (CCACK) routing protocol based on the network coding to avoid duplicate transmissions and overcome the new challenge (i.e., how many coded packets should each forwarder transmit). Specifically, CCACK utilizes the feedback scheme to acknowledge network-coded traffic from upstream nodes, solving the collective space problem and the false-positive problem. Then, CCACK can control

the transmitting rage by a differential backlog function thanks to the cumulative coded feedback scheme.
- The work [42] proposed a cooperative routing protocol based on the Positive Orthogonal Coding (POC) method, to address the broadcast storm problem in multi-hop vehicle networks. Specifically, POC-based Medium Access Control (MAC) focuses on avoiding collision during data transmission thanks to the unique codeword with location.

6.5.2.5 Social-based routing protocols

In the real community, the social relationship is established among participants (e.g., people, vehicles, places) and utilized to depict the connectivity between things. Based on this, the social relationship is also employed to deliver data in DTN and provide various reliable services, such as the ultra-low latency of data transmission, reliable trust management, and high utilization of bandwidths.

- The work [43] proposed a community-based Epidemic forwarding scheme to explore the stable relationship between nodes, considering network topology, community structure, similarity metrics, and local information. First, the Gaussian similarity function [44] is utilized to normalize the value of average separation period which consists of frequency and length of encounters. Second, to identify the underlying communities, a neighboring graph-based scheme is considered, including virtual links and local communities. Finally, multiple forwarding plans are adopted for inter- and intra-community data forwarding to improve the efficiency of data delivery.
- The work [45] explored the social-based efficient replica allocation mechanism in Ad-hoc social network, to improve the performance with different metrics, such as consistency, relocation cost, and read cost. The authors have proposed a Community-Partition Aware replica Allocation method (ComPAS) to exploit the social relationship during the process of replication, considering location histogram, storage space, write query cost, and read query cost.
- The work [46] proposed a Privacy-preserving Social-assisted content Dissemination (PSaD) scheme for data transmission in DTNs to improve the data delivery performance, such as family photo transmission, video clips transmission, and the process of content dismission. Specifically, PSaD is divided into two parts, i.e., attribute verification and content dissemination. In the attribute verification phase, a certificate is utilized to check the attribute similarity between two nodes. In the content dissemination phase, a node with a certificate accesses the attribute verification of another node, then they can transmit data to each other.
- The work [47] proposed a Social-Attraction-based data delivery routing protocol with Infrastructure Support (SAIS) to address two main problems, i.e., space-crossing community detection and its influence on data delivery in DTNs. First, SAIS utilizes the similarity attraction to evaluate the similarity between neighbors and the destination of data, considering time slots, the local activity of nodes, and network topologies. Second, the infrastructure support phase focuses on transmitting data to access points within common connected components.

- To improve the efficiency of traditional routing protocols using greedy schemes, the work [48] builds and utilizes the social relationship to select the optimal intermittent nodes for data delivery. Then, a multi-agent learning mechanism with centralized training is utilized to generate the collaboration strategy, improving the intelligence of routing protocols.
- The work [49] proposed a social-based buffer management scheme to improve the efficiency of data transmission and alleviate network congestion. Specifically, the proposed scheme evaluates the routing cost and probability of successful data delivery according to the value of TTL.
- The work [50] proposed a Routing protocol based on overlapping hierarchical community detection to build a social graph and route data by generating a tree structure, considering social properties, contact time, contact frequency, and contact regularity.

6.5.2.6 Geographic-based routing protocols

To improve the efficiency and reliability of data delivery, various routing protocols utilize geographic information, the moving direction of nodes, and trajectories. Specifically, thanks to the location and moving trajectory of nodes, the data pre-transmission path and the position of nodes can be predicted, so that the predicted routing mechanism will become an important research domain. Furthermore, several representative geographic-based routing protocols are shown as follows:

- The work [51] proposed a SCF-based reliable data forwarding mechanism, considering multiple copies, geographic information, and the moving direction of nodes. Specifically, the positioning information and moving direction of nodes are utilized to control the direction of data transmission, so that it can reduce the network overhead.
- The work [52] proposed an energy-aware dual-path geographic routing protocol to reduce the energy consumption of nodes and improve the delivery ratio of data. Specifically, the authors establish an energy model that integrates the Euclidian distances and path loss. Then, an anchor list is utilized to arrange the data transmission path based on right-hand rules to save energy.
- To address problems of low converging speed and inefficient resource utilization caused by the dynamic scale of Q-value table, the work [53] proposed an adaptive geographic-based routing protocol for unmanned aerial vehicles. Specifically, the routing protocol is divided into two phases, i.e., aerial and ground phases. In the aerial phase, based on the fuzzy logic, the depth-first-search method, and the location information of nodes, the global routing path is generated to route data. In the ground phase, vehicles maintain a Q-table and seek the optimal intermittent node according to a reward function and the generated global routing path.
- Reward Function Learning for Q-learning-based Geographic routing (RFLQGeo) [54] was proposed to address the unstable connectivity problem in unmanned robotic networks. Specifically, RFLQGeo integrates local information maintenance, Q-learning, and reward function learning to energize the routing protocol with intelligence.

- The work [55] proposed a Road Weight Evaluation (RWE) routing protocol based on geographic information to alleviate network congestion. First, the urban area is depicted as a weighted directed graph according to its geographic information. Second, a channel model, node movement model, vehicular traffic model, channel contention model, and link connection model are constructed to simulate the communication environment, including the fading of radio wave propagation, the received signal power, path-loss exponent, the Poisson distribution, the minimum contention window size, and link connection time. Third, the authors analyze the E2E latency to quantify the network performance of RWE.
- A Multilevel-scenario-oriented Greedy Opportunity Routing protocol (M-GOR) [56] was proposed to address the problem of unreliable connectivity and complicated transmission conditions. Specifically, M-GOR is employed to provide the flow-forwarding service in the two-level scenario. M-GOR considers the transmission range of nodes and connectivity probability between vehicles to evaluate the communication conditions. Based on this, M-GOR evaluates the probability of hop count increase and delivery ratio decrease to provide the data support for a greedy algorithm, so that it can select the optimal intermittent node.
- The work [57] proposed a Geographic-based Spray-and-Relay (GSaR) routing protocol to assist decision-making of nodes. Specifically, GSaR evaluates the movement range of destination according to the historical geographic information, and selects several intermittent nodes that carry messages for data delivery.
- The work [58] proposed a fuzzy logic-based routing protocol with geographic information to coordinate and analyze contradicting metrics for data delivery, e.g., vehicle location, direction, link quality, and bandwidth. Specifically, the proposed protocol calculates the distance to the destination, the direction in relation to the destination, link quality, and available bandwidth to evaluate the data forwarding capability of neighbors. Then, fuzzy logic is utilized to seek the optimal intermittent node for data delivery.

6.6 DTN security

The traditional host-based security mechanisms cannot satisfy the requirement of DTN because of the large computation cost, high detection latency, and deep security checking. Due to the unique bundle layer employed by DTN, DTN suffers from traditional and novel security problems, such as resource security, bundle security, and privacy leakage problems. Furthermore, the characteristic of wireless transmission enables DTN to suffer from various attacks according to different functions in each layer. Moreover, various security requirements are proposed to overcome the above problems and improve the reliability of DTN.

6.6.1 Physical layer security

The physical layer is responsible for beta stream transmission by changing the voltage magnitude, the frequency of radio waves, and the amplitude of radio waves. Due to the openness of data transmission, several attack models can steal, tamper, and interfere with data transmission, such as physical damage, node capture, node simulation, signal interference, message stealing, and message tampering.

6.6.1.1 Physical damage

Physical damage is the most effective but most difficult method to block communication among nodes. One the one hand, the extremist way is that devices can be damaged by destroying and dismantling, i.e., nodes cannot work anymore. On the other hand, the communication media is damaged, such as wired links.

6.6.1.2 Node capture and simulation

Node capture and simulation focus on recovering the encryption key of nodes to compromise the confidentiality and integrity of data, e.g., Sybil attack. Specifically, this type of attack refers to a single node with multiple IDentities (IDs) in DTN. Attackers utilize a few nodes to control multiple false IDs and impersonate/forge legitimate nodes to send information, thus controlling or affecting numerous normal nodes. Due to the node mobility in DTN, the influence range of attacks is expanding.

6.6.1.3 Signal interference

Signal interference focus on utilizing noise to reduce the quality of right information because of the addition of wireless waves, including same frequency interference, intermodulation interference, spurious emission interference, and adjacent channel interference.

- **Same frequency interference:** It indicates that two adjacent nodes (e.g., vehicles, base stations) have been set to the same frequency, thus receivers cannot parse the received signal because of different transmission distances and phase differences.
- **Intermodulation interference:** When two or more interfering signals are added to the receiver at the same time, the combination of various interfering frequencies will be exactly equal to or close to the required frequency due to the role of nonlinearity.
- **Spurious emission interference:** It is a system outside the frequency band of spurious radiation falling into another system within the receiving band caused by interference.
- **Adjacent channel interference:** It is caused by two adjacent or close wireless wave channels that transmit a signal that exceeds the width of wave channels, thus interfering with the signal propagated by adjacent wave channels.

6.6.1.4 Message stealing and tampering

Message stealing and tampering usually occur during the process of data transmission, and it can be divided into two classes, i.e., active attacks and passive attacks.

- **Active Attacks:** The integrity and availability of messages are focused on by active attacks. The classical active attacks include replay, tampering, impersonation, forgery, and blocking attacks.
- **Passive Attacks:** Passive attacks do not change the data context, but focus on stealing data context. Then, the leaked data will be utilized to perform other active attacks.

6.6.2 Data link layer security

Data link layer security focuses on ensuring the integrity and confidentiality of data, thus preventing data from being eavesdropped on and tampered with during data transmission. However, the data link layer suffers from the risk of resource depletion, link collision, and non-fair competition.

6.6.2.1 Resource depletion risk

The efficient utilization of resources can provide reliable service and low latency, reducing the rental cost of servers and increasing the QoS of services. However, several attackers control a large number of machines and send numerous required messages to servers, thus servers with limited resources cannot respond to each request in a finite time. The classical attack of resource depletion is a Distributed Denial of Service (DDoS) attack.

6.6.2.2 Link collision risk

In the data link layer, when two nodes simultaneously send messages through the same link, the link collision will occur and messages cannot be analyzed by receivers. Although several protocols of the data link layer monitor and detect the availability of links to avoid collisions (e.g., the binary retreat algorithm, probability contentions), malicious attackers send massive messages at ultra-small intervals to benign nodes, thus causing frequent link collisions.

6.6.2.3 Non-fair competition risk

Malicious attackers abuse high-priority messages to occupy channels, thus benign users cannot send messages. The abuse of communication links limits the performance of data transmission and blocks benign users from normal requests.

6.6.3 Network layer security

The network layer focuses on delivering messages and provides numerous interfaces for different network protocols, e.g., Local Area Network (LAN), Metropolitan Area Network (MAN), and Wide Area Network (WAN). Those networks consist of numerous nodes and protocols, but suffer from several security risks, such as unauthorized access, malicious gateway, DDoS, bluejacking, packet sniffing, etc. Based on this, several classical attacks are shown as follows:

- **False routing information:** Based on spoofing, tampering, and retransmitting routing information, attackers can create routing loops, block network transmission, and send false error messages to increase the E2E latency of data.
- **Selective forwarding attack [59]:** A malicious node probabilistically forwards or drops specific messages so that packets cannot be delivered to their destinations, causing network confusion.
- **Sink hole attack [60]:** The goal of attackers is to receive as much traffic as possible in an area through a malicious node. Then, the malicious node can tamper with the context of data, and can lead to many other types of attacks.
- **Sybil attack [61]:** A single node with multiple IDs controls multiple nodes to reduce the performance of distribution networks. Based on multiple IDs, the malicious node can sniff packets, disguise them as other nodes with forged IDs, and send false packets to other nodes.
- **Wormhole attack [62]:** Two malicious nodes establish a wormhole link, thus packets transmitted through the wormhole link can save a lot of time. Furthermore, the fast track for packets reduces the E2E latency and increases the weight of paths. According to the design of routing protocols, numerous packets will be routed to the wormhole link, so that malicious nodes can sniff and tamper the context of packets.

6.6.4 Transport layer security

Transport Layer Security evolves from a secure socket layer and provides encryption service for data transmission, to prevent data from sniffing and tempering. The message privacy, integrity, and mutual authentication are focused on and need to be solved. First, message privacy is responsible for protecting the context of messages based on encryption algorithms, so that malicious nodes cannot sniff those messages. Second, the message integrity indicates that communicators will know the message is been leaked and tampered with. Third, mutual authentication ensures that communicators cannot be pseudo. However, due to the design of transport layer protocols, those protocols suffer from several security problems, such as flooding attacks, lose-step attacks, and session hijacking.

- **Flooding attacks [63]:** Malicious nodes control other nodes and send uncountable request information to the destination node. Due to those requests exceeding the service capability of destination node, this node cannot address numerous requests and respond to benign users. DoS and DDoS are the classical flooding attacks.
- **Lose-step attacks [64]:** Attackers send replayed false information to a node, causing the node to request retransmission of the lost data frames. Then, the attacker can weaken or even completely chip away at the node's ability to perform data change and waste energy, shortening the node's lifecycle.
- **Session hijacking [65]:** Attackers disturb the synchronization status of communication between clients and servers, thus the session established by them will be changed.

6.6.5 Bundle layer security

The bundle layer is a unique design and is employed to cache data, operate custodial transmission, and retransmit data. Based on the mechanism of bundle layer, attackers focus on operating and changing the context of data, i.e., data security attacks. Several types of attacks have shaken up the foundations of data security (e.g., privacy, integrity, and availability), including forging bundle sources, tamping with bundle purpose and control fields, modifying load content, copying or leaking bundle data, etc. Furthermore, to address the above problems and avoid various types of attacks, the fundamental method is encrypting data during transmission. Unfortunately, due to the special application environment of DTN, several existing security protocols requiring multiple interactions and high resource consumption are not applicable, thus it is difficult to distribute and manage keys in DTN.

6.6.6 The security requirements

Due to the unique operating scheme of DTN (i.e., SCF), several specially designed attacks focus on sniffing messages and tampering with their contexts in the bundle layer. Since the different security threats between DTN and traditional networks, various security requirements with differences follow, including confidentiality, integrity, authentication, and reliability.

- **Confidentiality:** It refers to malicious nodes that cannot decrypt the ciphertext. For special applications of DTN (e.g., military command and deep space communications), the context of data needs to be high-level security, thus the malicious node cannot decrypt it. Therefore, based on reliable key distribution and management mechanisms, confidentiality can be provided during data transmission in DTN.
- **Integrity:** It indicates that the context of data should not be tampered with or damaged, thus the destination node of data can receive the complete commands. Therefore, it is generally ensured that the messages are not tampered with during transmission, over the wireless network or radio frequency link utilizing key-protected hashing algorithms, etc.
- **Authentication:** It refers to the trustworthiness of data, including information such as the identity of senders. Due to the intermittency of communications between nodes, they cannot ensure the legitimacy of data transmission, causing unauthenticated node access. To ensure the security of data transmission, communications are merely employed after checking the authentication of nodes based on their signatures.
- **Reliability:** It indicates that authenticated users access and legitimately utilize the required resource. The requirement of reliability is urgent in DTN, because nodes are usually limited in storage space, computing power, and communication capabilities. Unfortunately, the deployment environment of DTN further increases the lack of above resources. To address the above problem, the unauthenticated nodes are denied to access limited resources, increasing the reliability of DTN.

6.7 Applications in DTN

DTN is employed to adapt to harsh communication environments and provide the available data delivery services, thanks to the SCF mechanism and the mobility of nodes. Various DTN applications have emerged and are shown as follows:

- **Emergency wireless communication:** When the connectivity of network is damaged by disasters or man-made damages, messages cannot be transmitted to their destinations. In this case, DTN-based emergency wireless communication is extremely important. Therefore, future emergency wireless communication networks and terminal devices will support DTN and act as host or intermittent devices at any time.
- **Mobile vehicle communication:** With the development of VANETs and the increasing number of vehicles, how to provide a safe traffic service becomes a significant problem for VANETs. Specifically, due to the mobility of vehicles, it is difficult to maintain a stable communication channel between vehicles similar to a wired link. Therefore, based on the SCF mechanism, vehicles store, carry, and forward data while moving.
- **Interstellar network communication:** It mainly relies on ultra-long-range wireless communication between satellites and ground stations. The data transmission latency increases with the increase of communication distances. Furthermore, due to the mobility of satellites, the connectivity between satellites and ground stations is intermittent. Therefore, DTN can be employed to deal with the above problems, i.e., increasing the reliability of communications and reducing the data transmission latency.
- **Wildlife tracking:** It is difficult to provide constant power in a wild field. To track the wildlife and record their action trajectories or living habits, power control and wireless communication are focused. In this case, DTN provides mobile wireless communication, vehicular base stations, and fixed base stations to transmit significant information.
- **Remote area communication:** In some remote and isolated areas, such as some large desert areas, due to economic or natural environmental constraints, it is not suitable for the construction of basic communication networks. The residents of these areas also need access to communication services, mainly due to environmental and cost considerations, so that they can carry wireless access points through public transportation systems or other transportation systems to collect messages along the way and thus communicate them. Furthermore, due to the problems of intermittent random communication and large experiments, DTN can also be utilized for communication in various mobile scenarios.

6.8 Conclusion

To compensate for the weak performance of traditional networks in dynamically changing network topology scenarios, DTN was designed and employed thanks to the SCF mechanism. First, this chapter introduced the background of DTN. Second, the presentative characteristics of DTN were analyzed. Third, the architecture of DTN was introduced in detail, and the difference between DTN and traditional networks was demonstrated. Fourth, the advantages, disadvantages, and challenges of DTN were listed. Fifth, numerous technologies were introduced, including the SCF mechanism and routing protocols. Sixth, the security problems were analyzed to introduce the requirements of DTN in each layer. Finally, applications in DTN were shown to illustrate the utilization value of DTN.

References

[1] Lakshman T and Madhow U. The performance of TCP/IP for networks with high bandwidth-delay products and random loss. IEEE/ACM Transactions on Networking. 1997;5(3):336–350.
[2] Hedrick CL. Routing Information Protocol. IETF; 1988.
[3] Wollman WV and Barsoum Y. Overview of open shortest path first, version 2 (OSPF V2) routing in the tactical environment. In: Proceedings of MILCOM'95. Vol. 3. IEEE; 1995. p. 925–930.
[4] Perkins C, Belding-Royer E, and Das S. Ad hoc on-demand distance vector (AODV) routing. RFC Editor; 2003.
[5] Song Y, Cao Y, Jiang K, *et al.* MP-VRCR: A multi-dimension and priority-based vehicle-road collaborative routing protocol. IEEE Transactions on Vehicular Technology. 2023;72(8):10797–10812.
[6] Chen K, Shen H, and Zhang H. Leveraging social networks for P2P content-based file sharing in disconnected MANETs. IEEE Transactions on Mobile Computing. 2012;13(2):235–249.
[7] Song Y, Jiang K, Cao Y, *et al.* STALB: A spatio-temporal domain autonomous load balancing routing protocol. IEEE Transactions on Network and Service Management. 2022;20(1):73–87.
[8] Rong B, Qian Y, Lu K, *et al.* Mobile-agent-based handoff in wireless mesh networks: Architecture and call admission control. IEEE Transactions on Vehicular Technology. 2009;58(8):4565–4575.
[9] Wang Y, Liu Y, Zhang J, *et al.* Cooperative store–carry–forward scheme for intermittently connected vehicular networks. IEEE Transactions on Vehicular Technology. 2016;66(1):777–784.
[10] Cao Y and Sun Z. Routing in delay/disruption tolerant networks: A taxonomy, survey and challenges. IEEE Communications Surveys & Tutorials. 2012;15(2):654–677.
[11] Unnikrishnan E, Ravichandran V, Sudhakar S, *et al.* Delay tolerant network for space. In: 2016 3rd International Conference on Signal Processing and Integrated Networks (SPIN). IEEE; 2016. p. 591–595.
[12] Yang Z, Wang R, Yu Q, *et al.* Analytical characterization of licklider transmission protocol (LTP) in cislunar communications. IEEE Transactions on Aerospace and Electronic Systems. 2014;50(3):2019–2031.
[13] Wood L, Eddy WM, Ivancic W, *et al.* Saratoga: A Delay-Tolerant Networking convergence layer with efficient link utilization. In: 2007 International Workshop on Satellite and Space Communications. IEEE; 2007. p. 168–172.

[14] Banerjee N, Corner MD, and Levine BN. Design and field experimentation of an energy-efficient architecture for DTN throwboxes. IEEE/ACM Transactions on Networking. 2010;18(2):554–567.

[15] Chen K and Shen H. DTN-FLOW: Inter-landmark data flow for high-throughput routing in DTNs. IEEE/ACMs Transactions on Networking. 2014;23(1):212–226.

[16] Dimitriou S and Tsaoussidis V. Effective buffer and storage management in DTN nodes. In: 2009 International Conference on Ultra Modern Telecommunications & Workshops. IEEE; 2009. p. 1–3.

[17] Tajima S, Asaka T, and Takahashi T. Priority control using multi-buffer for DTN. In: The 16th Asia-Pacific Network Operations and Management Symposium. IEEE; 2014. p. 1–6.

[18] Lu Y, Zhao Y, Sun F, *et al.* Dynamic fault-tolerant routing based on FSA for LEO satellite networks. IEEE Transactions on Computers. 2012;62(10):1945–1958.

[19] Jain S, Fall K, and Patra R. Routing in a delay tolerant network. In: Proceedings of the 2004 Conference on Applications, Technologies, Architectures, and Protocols for Computer Communications; 2004. p. 145–158.

[20] Yin L, Lu H-m, and Cao Y-d. A novel single copy replication routing strategy for delay tolerant networks. In: 2009 5th International Conference on Wireless Communications, Networking and Mobile Computing. IEEE; 2009. p. 1–5.

[21] Chen Y, Xiao C, and Zhang Q. Domain based routing algorithm for DTN (the single copy case). In: 2010 International Conference on Information, Networking and Automation (ICINA). Vol. 2. IEEE; 2010. p. V2-76–V2-79.

[22] Han Y, Wu H, Yang Z, *et al.* Delay-constrained single-copy multi-path data transmission in mobile opportunistic networks. In: 2014 Eleventh Annual IEEE International Conference on Sensing, Communication, and Networking (SECON). IEEE; 2014. p. 37–45.

[23] Spyropoulos T, Psounis K, and Raghavendra CS. Spray and focus: Efficient mobility-assisted routing for heterogeneous and correlated mobility. In: Fifth Annual IEEE International Conference on Pervasive Computing and Communications Workshops (PerComW'07). IEEE; 2007. p. 79–85.

[24] Vahdat A and Becker D. Epidemic Routing for Partially Connected Ad hoc Networks. Technical Report CS-200006, Duke University; 2000.

[25] Spyropoulos T, Psounis K, and Raghavendra CS. Spray and wait: An efficient routing scheme for intermittently connected mobile networks. In: Proceedings of the 2005 ACM SIGCOMM workshop on delay-tolerant networking; 2005. p. 252–259.

[26] Lindgren A and Doria A. Probabilistic Routing Protocol using History of Encounters and Transitivity (PRoPHET). RFC 6693, IETF Document; 2012.

[27] Maia SL, Silva ÉR, and Guardieiro PR. A new optimization strategy proposal for multi-copy forwarding in energy constrained DTNs. IEEE Communications Letters. 2014;18(9):1623–1626.

[28] Spyropoulos T, Psounis K, and Raghavendra CS. Efficient routing in intermittently connected mobile networks: The multiple-copy case. IEEE/ACM Transactions on Networking. 2008;16(1):77–90.

[29] Shu J, Yu K, Liu L, *et al.* RET: A random and encounter time based forwarding mechanism for opportunistic network. In: 2010 Third International Symposium on Information Processing. IEEE; 2010. p. 50–53.
[30] Kimura T, Matsuura T, Sasabe M, *et al.* Location-aware utility-based routing for store-carry-forward message delivery. In: 2015 International Conference on Information Networking (ICOIN). IEEE; 2015. p. 194–199.
[31] Singh P and Chen YC. Energy efficient greedy forwarding based on residual energy for wireless sensor networks. In: 2018 27th Wireless and Optical Communication Conference (WOCC). IEEE; 2018. p. 1–6.
[32] Yang X, Xu Y, Wang D, *et al.* Virtual-range-forwarding-based opportunistic routing for mine goaf sensor networks. IEEE Sensors Journal. 2022;22(22):22244–22254.
[33] Feng Z and Chin KW. A unified study of epidemic routing protocols and their enhancements. In: 2012 IEEE 26th International Parallel and Distributed Processing Symposium Workshops & PhD Forum. IEEE; 2012. p. 1484–1493.
[34] Mahendran V and Murthy CSR. Buffer dimensioning of DTN replication-based routing nodes. IEEE Communications Letters. 2012;17(1):123–126.
[35] Ganesh AJ. Big Queues. Springer; 2004.
[36] Wang Y and Wu H. Replication-Based efficient data delivery scheme (RED) for Delay/Fault-Tolerant mobile sensor network (DFT-MSN). In: Fourth Annual IEEE International Conference on Pervasive Computing and Communications Workshops (PERCOMW'06). IEEE; 2006. p. 5.
[37] Ippisch A, Sati S, and Graffi K. Optimal replication based on optimal path hops for opportunistic networks. In: 2018 IEEE 32nd International Conference on Advanced Information Networking and Applications (AINA). IEEE; 2018. p. 251–258.
[38] Ong L and Motani M. Optimal routing for decode-and-forward based cooperation in wireless networks. In: 2007 4th Annual IEEE Communications Society Conference on Sensor, Mesh and Ad Hoc Communications and Networks. IEEE; 2007. p. 334–343.
[39] Tang X and Tang Z. Coding based opportunistic routing in ad hoc networks. In: 2012 2nd International Conference on Consumer Electronics, Communications and Networks (CECNet). IEEE; 2012. p. 3136–3139.
[40] Chen J, He K, Du R, *et al.* Dominating set and network coding-based routing in wireless mesh networks. IEEE Transactions on Parallel and Distributed Systems. 2013;26(2):423–433.
[41] Koutsonikolas D, Wang CC, and Hu YC. Efficient network-coding-based opportunistic routing through cumulative coded acknowledgments. IEEE/ACM Transactions on Networking. 2011;19(5):1368–1381.
[42] Zhang L, Hassanabadi B, and Valaee S. Cooperative positive orthogonal code-based forwarding for multi-hop vehicular networks. IEEE Transactions on Wireless Communications. 2014;13(7):3914–3925.
[43] Li F and Wu J. LocalCom: A community-based epidemic forwarding scheme in disruption-tolerant networks. In: 2009 6th Annual IEEE Communications

Society Conference on Sensor, Mesh and Ad Hoc Communications and Networks. IEEE; 2009. p. 1–9.

[44] Von Luxburg U. A tutorial on spectral clustering. Statistics and Computing. 2007;17:395–416.

[45] Xia F, Ahmed AM, Yang LT, *et al.* Exploiting social relationship to enable efficient replica allocation in ad-hoc social networks. IEEE Transactions on Parallel and Distributed Systems. 2014;25(12):3167–3176.

[46] Guo L, Zhang C, Yue H, *et al.* PSaD: A privacy-preserving social-assisted content dissemination scheme in DTNs. IEEE Transactions on Mobile Computing. 2014;13(12):2903–2918.

[47] Li Z, Wang C, Yang S, *et al.* Space-crossing: Community-based data forwarding in mobile social networks under the hybrid communication architecture. IEEE Transactions on Wireless Communications. 2015;14(9):4720–4727.

[48] Han C, Yao H, Mai T, *et al.* QMIX aided routing in social-based delay-tolerant networks. IEEE Transactions on Vehicular Technology. 2021;71(2): 1952–1963.

[49] Majeed MR, Naeem F, Salam A, *et al.* Enhanced buffer management scheme to avoid congestion in delay tolerant social network. In: 2018 IEEE 21st International Multi-Topic Conference (INMIC). IEEE; 2018. p. 1–7.

[50] Meng X, Xu G, Guo T, *et al.* A novel routing method for social delay-tolerant networks. Tsinghua Science and Technology. 2018;24(1):44–51.

[51] Ohta Y, Ohta T, Kohno E, *et al.* A store-carry-forward-based data transfer scheme using positions and moving direction of vehicles for VANETs. In: 2011 Tenth International Symposium on Autonomous Decentralized Systems. IEEE; 2011. p. 131–138.

[52] Huang H, Yin H, Min G, *et al.* Energy-aware dual-path geographic routing to bypass routing holes in wireless sensor networks. IEEE Transactions on Mobile Computing. 2017;17(6):1339–1352.

[53] Jiang S, Huang Z, and Ji Y. Adaptive UAV-assisted geographic routing with Q-learning in VANET. IEEE Communications Letters. 2020;25(4):1358–1362.

[54] Jin W, Gu R, and Ji Y. Reward function learning for Q-learning-based geographic routing protocol. IEEE Communications Letters. 2019;23(7): 1236–1239.

[55] Chen C, Liu L, Qiu T, *et al.* Delay-aware grid-based geographic routing in urban VANETs: A backbone approach. IEEE/ACM Transactions on Networking. 2019;27(6):2324–2337.

[56] Zhu L, Li C, Li B, *et al.* Geographic routing in multilevel scenarios of vehicular ad hoc networks. IEEE Transactions on Vehicular Technology. 2015;65(9):7740–7753.

[57] Cao Y, Sun Z, Wang N, *et al.* Geographic-based spray-and-relay (GSaR): an efficient routing scheme for DTNs. IEEE Transactions on Vehicular Technology. 2014;64(4):1548–1564.

[58] Alzamzami O and Mahgoub I. Fuzzy logic-based geographic routing for urban vehicular networks using link quality and achievable throughput estimations. IEEE Transactions on Intelligent Transportation Systems. 2018;20(6):2289–2300.

[59] Chae Y, DiPippo LC, and Sun YL. Trust management for defending on-off attacks. IEEE Transactions on Parallel and Distributed Systems. 2014;26(4):1178–1191.

[60] Sheela D, Kumar CN, and Mahadevan G. A non cryptographic method of sink hole attack detection in wireless sensor networks. In: 2011 International Conference on Recent Trends in Information Technology (ICRTIT). IEEE; 2011. p. 527–532.

[61] Wei W, Xu F, Tan CC, and Li Q. SybilDefender: A defense mechanism for sybil attacks in large social networks. IEEE Transactions on Parallel and Distributed Systems. 2013;24(12):2492–2502.

[62] Sasirekha D and Radha N. Secure and attack aware routing in mobile ad hoc networks against wormhole and sinkhole attacks. In: 2017 2nd International Conference on Communication and Electronics Systems (ICCES). IEEE; 2017. p. 505–510.

[63] Zhi T, Luo H, and Liu Y. A Gini impurity-based interest flooding attack defence mechanism in NDN. IEEE Communications Letters. 2018;22(3):538–541.

[64] Xing M, Wang Y, Pang Q, *et al.* Dynamic-memory event-based asynchronous attack detection filtering for a class of nonlinear cyber-physical systems. IEEE Transactions on Cybernetics. 2022;53(1):653–667.

[65] Hu Q, Du B, Markantonakis K, *et al.* A session hijacking attack against a device-assisted physical-layer key agreement. IEEE Transactions on Industrial Informatics. 2019;16(1):691–702.

Chapter 7
Mobile and wireless networks

Shuohan Liu[1,2]*, Junqiao Gao*[2]*, Yue Cao*[2] *and Hai Lin*[2]

This chapter introduces the evolution of mobile networks from 1G to 6G, highlighting key technologies, performance metrics, and applications. In addition, it describes cellular network architecture, spectrum management, mobility solutions, and key security challenges in 3G, 4G, as well as 5G networks. Finally, this chapter discusses future trends, including the integration of Artificial Intelligence (AI) and blockchain, shaping the next generation of secure and intelligent networks.

7.1 Mobile networks

7.1.1 Introduction to mobile networks

Mobile networks, also known as wireless networks, enable devices to communicate without the need for fixed wiring or local connections, relying instead on Radio Frequency (RF) waves to transmit and receive data. These networks have underpinned the rise of mobile phones, smartphones, tablets, and various Internet-of-Things (IoT) devices, creating a connected fabric that spans the globe.

The history of mobile communications is a chronicle of humanity's quest for seamless connectivity. From the launch of first-generation analog mobile networks in the 1980s to the impending advent of sixth-generation (6G) networks, each evolutionary step has unlocked new capabilities, from simple voice transmission to high-definition multimedia streaming, paving the way for a digitally interconnected society.

The cornerstone concepts of mobile networking—such as frequency reuse, handover mechanisms, and the structure of mobile network architecture—form the foundation upon which mobile services are built. These concepts are critical to ensure continuous connectivity, efficient bandwidth utilization, and scalability of the network to accommodate growing numbers of users and devices.

The ubiquity of mobile networks has transformed them into a critical infrastructure for modern society. They support an ecosystem of services that drive economic

[1]Shandong Computer Science Center, Qilu University of Technology, China
[2]School of Cyber Science and Engineering, Wuhan University, China

growth, enable social interactions, and provide vital links for emergency services, making them indispensable in today's fast-paced world.

7.1.2 Key Performance Indicators (KPIs)

KPIs serve as the quantifiable benchmarks that network operators and engineers use to evaluate the operational effectiveness of a mobile network. These metrics are vital for assessing Quality of Service (QoS), guiding network improvements, and aligning performance with consumer expectations and industry standards. KPIs are essential for ensuring that the network delivers on the promise of connectivity, speed, and reliability that users have come to expect. The below explores some of the most crucial KPIs in the industry:

- **Throughput** is the amount of data transferred over a network in a given amount of time, typically measured in bits per second (bps). High-throughput rates are indicative of a robust network capable of handling intensive data demands. For example: typically in real-world throughput, a 4G network may offer throughput of around 20 Mbps, while a 5G network could provide speeds exceeding 1 Gbps, illustrating a significant improvement in data handling capacity. The throughput (*Th*) is often calculated by measuring the total amount of data (*D*) transferred over a period of time (*t*), which can be represented by the formula:

$$\text{Throughput } (Th) = \frac{\text{Total Data Transferred } (D)}{\text{Time } (t)} \tag{7.1}$$

  For instance, if a mobile network transfers 2 GB of data in 10 s, the throughput would be

$$Th = \frac{2\text{ GB}}{10\text{ s}} = 200 \text{ megabytes per second (MBps)} \tag{7.2}$$

- **Latency** measures the time it takes for a packet of data to travel from one point to another in the network. It is critical for time-sensitive applications like online gaming or video conferencing. For instance, in a 4G network, the latency may be around 50–100 ms, whereas, in a 5G network, latency could be reduced to as low as 1 ms, thereby significantly enhancing the user experience for real-time applications. Latency (L) is typically measured in milliseconds and can be calculated using network testing tools that measure the Round-Trip Time (RTT) for a packet:

$$\text{Latency } (L) = \frac{\text{Round Trip Time } (RTT)}{2} \tag{7.3}$$

  For example, if the RTT is 100 ms, the latency would be 50 ms.
- **Availability** is a measure of a network's operational performance and its ability to provide continuous service. It is defined as the ratio of time that the service is available to the total time it is expected to be available. A mobile network that has an availability of 99.9% (also known as "three nines") is considered highly reliable, indicating that it is down for no more than 8.76 h in a year. Availability

(A) is calculated as the percentage of time a system is functioning and available. It is formulated as

$$\text{Availability } (A) = \frac{\text{Total Operational Time Downtime}}{\text{Total Operational Time}} \times 100\% \quad (7.4)$$

For example, if a network is operational for 8,760 h in a year and experiences 8 h of downtime, the availability is

$$A = \frac{8760 - 8}{8760} \times 100\% \approx 99.91\% \quad (7.5)$$

- **Reliability** refers to the network's ability to perform consistently under varying conditions and to maintain a certain level of performance over time. It can be exemplified by the stability of connection during high-traffic periods or in dense urban environments where signals might be obstructed. For instance, a reliable network should maintain stable call quality and data rates even during peak usage times or in areas with physical barriers. Reliability can be modeled using different statistical methods, but one simple measure is the Mean Time Between Failures (MTBF). For networks, this can be calculated by dividing the total operational time by the number of failures occurred

$$\text{Mean Time Between Failures } (MTBF) = \frac{\text{Total Operational Time}}{\text{Number of Failures}} \quad (7.6)$$

- **Mobility** measures the network's ability to maintain a user's active sessions while they move geographically, including the capability to handle handoffs between cells seamlessly. For example, a user on a train traveling at high speeds should be able to maintain a voice call without drops. The success rate of handovers between cells without call drops or session interruptions is a direct indicator of the network's mobility performance. Mobility metrics such as handover success rate can be calculated by

$$\text{Handover Success Rate} = \frac{\text{Number of Successful Handovers}}{\text{Total Number of Handover Attempts}} \times 100\% \quad (7.7)$$

This metric serves as a key performance indicator for evaluating the mobility management efficiency of the network. In modern Long-Term Evolution (LTE) and 5G networks, a handover success rate above 98% is considered indicative of high service reliability.

7.1.3 Overview of mobile network generations

Figure 7.1 shows the journey of mobile communications technology, which began with 1G in the 1980s and has progressed through to the emerging 6G technology. Each generation is marked by significant improvements.

- **1G: The first wave of mobile communications:** The advent of 1G in the 1980s marked the inception of mobile telecommunications. Being predominantly analog, 1G networks laid the foundation for mobile voice communication, with

Figure 7.1 Mobile network technology journey

systems like Advanced Mobile Phone System (AMPS) being among the most prominent. Although limited to voice with speeds barely reaching 2.4 kbps (peak data rate of early AMPS implementations), 1G revolutionized communication, liberating phones from the confines of homes and offices.

- **Transitioning to 2G:** The digital leap: As the 1990s approached, 2G replaced analog signals with digital, bolstering security through encryption and introducing data services with the Global System for Mobile Communications (GSM) standard. Speeds increased modestly to 64 kbps, and for the first time, services like Short Message Service (SMS) and basic Multimedia Messaging Service (MMS) became possible. Moreover, 2G heralded the advent of General Packet Radio Service (GPRS) and Enhanced Data rates for GSM Evolution (EDGE), providing internet access and signifying a critical move toward data-centric mobile usage.
- **3G: Broadening the mobile Internet:** With the new millennium, 3G networks brought substantial improvements in data speeds (initially up to 384 kbps) and services. This era witnessed the introduction of video calling and mobile internet access, transitioning the mobile phone into a multimedia device. Technologies such as Universal Mobile Telecommunications System (UMTS) and later High-Speed Packet Access (HSPA) pushed speeds into multiple Mbps, fostering the growth of mobile applications and content consumption.
- **4G: The age of mobile broadband:** The release of 4G in the 2010s marked the true arrival of mobile broadband, with speeds exceeding 100 Mbps. The transition to LTE technology enabled not just faster internet access but also the birth of new digital ecosystems, streaming services, and cloud applications. 4G's high capacity and low latency supported unprecedented growth in mobile data consumption. This era introduced the concept of mobile devices becoming the primary internet access point for many users.
- **5G: A quantum leap in connectivity:** The ongoing deployment of 5G networks is a quantum leap in mobile network technology. 5G is set to unlock multi-gigabit speeds and single-digit millisecond latency under ideal conditions. It introduces network slicing and edge computing, enhancing the IoT, autonomous vehicles, smart cities, and virtual reality applications. By enabling massive Machine Type Communications (mMTC) and Ultra-Reliable Low-Latency Communication (URLLC), 5G is envisioned to catalyze the fourth industrial revolution.

- **Anticipating 6G: The future horizon:** Looking toward the horizon, 6G is anticipated to emerge in the 2030s as the successor to 5G, pushing boundaries further into terabit-per-second speeds and microsecond latency. Planned improvements for future networks involve advanced Multiple Input Multiple Output (MIMO) technologies, networks operated by AI, and the smooth combination of space-based network components. Even though it is still early in development, 6G is expected to support groundbreaking applications.

The evolution from 1G to 6G is not merely a series of technological increments but a transformative journey that has seamlessly connected generations of networks. Each new generation has built upon the accomplishments of its predecessors while setting the stage for future advancements. This ever-evolving landscape highlights the telecommunications industry's drive toward creating a more interconnected and intelligent world.

The following sections will delve into the network structure and technological transformations that have characterized the evolution from 1G to 6G. The examination will encompass the fundamental shifts in communication paradigms, the advancements in hardware and software that have facilitated these shifts, and the corresponding socio-economic impacts that each generation of mobile networks has engendered. By examining each generation's advancements, it can be better understood how every new technology has changed the way people connect and broadened the possibilities of mobile communication.

7.2 Cellular networks

The foundational knowledge of mobile networks presented in the previous chapter leads naturally to an in-depth examination of cellular networks, the backbone of mobile communications. These networks, predicated on the principles of cellular architecture, have enabled the scaling and availability of mobile services on a global scale. This chapter delves into the operational dynamics of cellular networks, the complexities of their infrastructure, and the critical aspects of security in an interconnected landscape.

7.2.1 Fundamentals of cellular network

The essence of cellular network operation resides in its design philosophy, which partitions regions into multiple, defined areas or "cells," each served by a transmitter known as a base station. This cellular structure creates a network capable of covering large geographic areas and supporting a vast number of simultaneous users.

Figure 7.2 illustrates the cellular network structure, which visually differentiates between rural, urban, and dense urban areas, showcasing how cell density and size vary in response to differing demands for network coverage and capacity. At the core of a cellular network's design is the division of service area into multiple cells, each served by its transmitter known as a base station. The illustration employs hexagons to represent these cells–an idealized shape that simplifies the concept of coverage

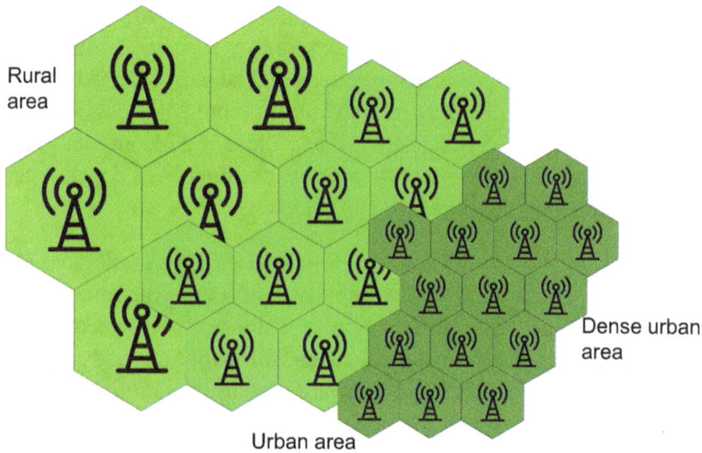

Figure 7.2 Cellular network structure

areas, though in practice, cell coverage areas are often irregular due to natural terrain and human-made obstructions.

It should be noted that cell sizes are not uniform and are strategically varied to optimize service delivery and resource use. In rural areas, where user density and traffic are lower, cells are larger to maximize coverage with a limited number of Base Stations (BS). Conversely, in urban and particularly dense urban areas, cells are smaller due to a higher population density and increased demand for services. This allows more users to be served effectively and efficiently.

The seamless exchange of signals between mobile devices and BS forms the foundation of cellular networks. This communication is facilitated through RF that transmits data through the air. The allocation of these frequencies is a complex task, typically regulated by governmental bodies to ensure organized distribution and to prevent interference between services.

7.2.2 Spectrum management methodologies

Spectrum management is the process of regulating the use of RF to prevent interference among users. It involves assigning frequency bands to different services, allocating specific frequencies within these bands, and coordinating the use of frequencies across borders. Spectrum management methods must consider the propagation characteristics of radio waves, the coverage area required, and the capacity demands of network.

In managing the spectrum, regulators first divide the available frequencies into bands. Each band is further subdivided into channels or frequency blocks assigned to different operators or services. To avoid interference, allocations are based on geographic region, signal overlap, and adjacent-band compatibility. Table 7.1 shows a simplified spectrum allocation table for China.

Table 7.1 Spectrum allocation

Frequency band (MHz)	Allocation	Service type	Notes
700	Commercial cellular	LTE, 5G	Used for wide coverage, especially in rural areas
800	Commercial cellular	Code Division Multiple Access (CDMA), LTE	Formerly allocated for CDMA, currently repurposed for LTE deployments
900	Commercial cellular	GSM, LTE	Traditional band for GSM, also repurposed for LTE
1,800	Commercial cellular	GSM, LTE	High capacity for urban areas, also used for LTE
2,100	Commercial cellular	UMTS, LTE	Main band for 3G services, also used for LTE
2,300	TD-LTE	LTE	TD-LTE, specifically used in China
2600	Commercial cellular	LTE, 5G	Frequency-Division Duplex (FDD) and TDD LTE, newly allocated for 5G
3,300–3,600	5G	5G	Primary band for 5G services, focusing on capacity
4,800–5,000	5G	5G	Auxiliary band for 5G services to provide additional capacity

- **LTE:** A standard for wireless broadband communication, widely used in China for 4G services.
- **GSM:** A standard developed to describe the protocols for 2G digital cellular networks, widely adopted in China.
- **UMTS:** A 3G mobile cellular system for networks based on the GSM standard.
- **CDMA:** A channel access method used by various radio communication technologies, was used for 3G services in China.
- **TD-LTE:** China has been a proponent of TD-LTE for its 4G services, which uses the Time-Division Duplex (TDD) technology.

However, it should be noted that the behavior of radio waves varies with frequency. Lower frequencies have longer wavelengths and can cover greater distances and penetrate through obstacles more effectively, making them ideal for rural coverage. Higher frequencies, with shorter wavelengths, offer more bandwidth and higher data rates, suited for dense urban environments where the demand for high-speed data services is greater.

Thus, spectrum management also involves balancing coverage and capacity. Coverage relates to the area that a network can reach, while capacity refers to the volume of data traffic it can handle. Lower frequencies provide broader coverage but are limited in capacity. Conversely, higher frequencies offer greater capacity but have limited reach, necessitating a denser network of BS.

7.2.3 Handover processes in cellular networks

Handover, also known as handoff, occurs when a mobile device's connection is transferred from one base station to another without disrupting the ongoing communication. This process is vital for mobile communication, as it ensures service continuity, which is essential for user satisfaction and operational integrity. Handovers in cellular networks can be categorized based on different criteria.

Figure 7.3 shows the two most common forms of handovers. In practice, there are many other forms of handovers:

- **Hard handover:** This is a break-before-make process where the connection to the old base station is broken before a new connection is established, which is commonly used in 2G networks.
- **Soft handover:** Soft handovers follow a make-before-break principle, where the new connection is established before the old one is released. The mobile device

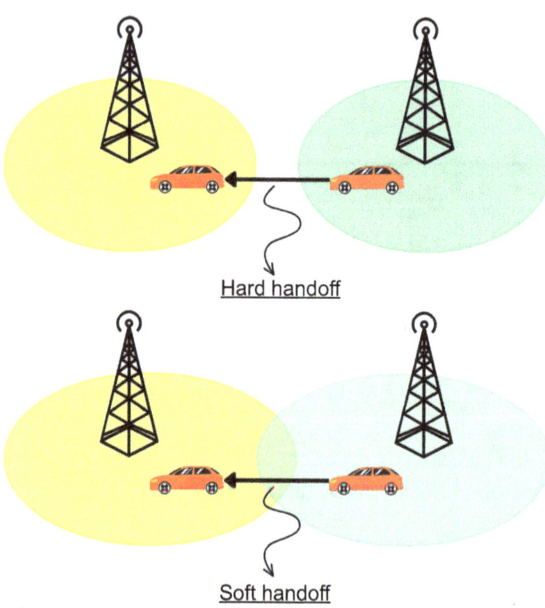

Figure 7.3 Types of handovers

connects to the new base station before disconnecting from the current one. This is typical of CDMA-based 3G networks.

- **Inter-frequency handover:** This happens when the handover is between different frequency bands within the same network, often necessitated by capacity and coverage optimization.
- **Inter-system handover:** Occurs when a device moves between different types of networks, such as from a 3G network to a 4G LTE network.

The ability to switch connections reliably between cells or networks is imperative for several reasons:

- It maintains call and data session continuity, which is critical for the user experience.
- It optimizes network resource utilization by freeing up resources on one cell while allocating them on another.
- It ensures optimal connectivity and service quality by connecting the user to the best available network.

7.2.4 Cellular network infrastructure components

Cellular network infrastructure consists of a complex web of interconnected components that function cohesively to provide seamless mobile communication services. This network is typically structured in hierarchical layers, from the radio access network to the core network, each layer serving a distinct role in the overall operation.

Figure 7.4 shows the basic components of a simple cellular network:

- **Base Stations (BS)**: Also known as cell sites, BS house the radio transceivers that communicate directly with mobile devices. They are connected to the mobile network's core via backhaul link (either fiber or microwave).

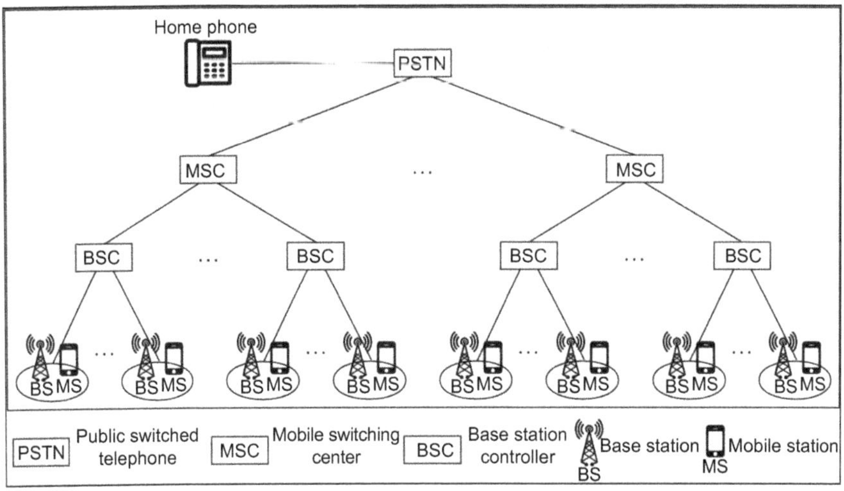

Figure 7.4 Components of cellular network infrastructure

- **Mobile Switching Center (MSC)**: The MSC is responsible for routing calls and data and for managing mobile services such as SMS and voicemail.
- **Base Station Controller (BSC)**: The BSC manages the resources and handover (the process of transferring an ongoing call or data session from one channel to another) for multiple BS.
- **Public Switched Telephone Network (PSTN)**: The PSTN is the traditional telephone network that uses circuit-switched telephony to provide voice communication services worldwide. It consists of a combination of fiber optic cables, microwave transmission links, satellites, and undersea telephone cables connected by switching centers, which allow telephones around the world to communicate with each other.

Besides, Radio Access Network (RAN) in a cellular network consists of the BS and their controllers (such as BSCs in 2G or radio network controllers in 3G networks). It connects mobile devices to the core network and manages the radio communications between them. The RAN is a critical interface that determines the quality and coverage of mobile network.

In LTE networks, the Evolved Packet Core (EPC) is responsible for data routing and mobility management. It is the backbone that enables high-speed data transfer for mobile broadband. The EPC handles user authentication, session management, and the seamless transfer of data across the network.

7.2.5 First-generation mobile networks (1G)

The genesis of mobile communication can be traced back to the first generation of mobile networks, commonly referred to as 1G, which was commercially introduced in the early 1980s. This era heralded the transformation from stationary communication to mobile telephony, providing users with the revolutionary ability to communicate while on the move. The adoption and spread of 1G technology were rapid and impactful, setting a precedent for personal communication and paving the way for the mobile-centric lifestyle that is prevalent today.

1G networks were based on analog technology and were primarily designed for voice communication with little to no consideration for data services or text messaging, which would become ubiquitous in later generations. During this period, different countries developed their own systems without much concern for interoperability or global standards, which resulted in a variety of 1G technologies, such as the Advanced Mobile Phone System (AMPS) in the United States and the Nordic Mobile Telephone (NMT) system in Scandinavian countries.

The primary technology underpinning 1G networks was Frequency Division Multiple Access (FDMA), which allocated separate frequency bands to users for the duration of their calls. This method of access was relatively straightforward but inefficient by today's standards, as it could only support a limited number of simultaneous users per channel.

In terms of specific systems, the NMT was among the first to be deployed and offered better sound quality, international roaming within the Nordic countries, and

Table 7.2 Key technical aspects of NMT

Feature	Description
Technology type	Analog cellular network
Frequency bands	NMT-450 used 450 MHz, NMT-900 used 900 MHz
Access method	FDMA
Duplex method	Full-duplex using frequency pairs
Channels	NMT-450 had 180 channels; NMT-900 had 1,990 channels
Channel bandwidth	25 kHz for NMT-450, 12.5 kHz for NMT-900
User capacity	Higher than previous systems but limited by FDMA
Coverage	Designed for rural and urban areas with robust coverage
International roaming	Roaming agreements among Scandinavian countries
Security	Basic, with no encryption; susceptible to eavesdropping
Voice encoding	Analog modulation, susceptible to noise and interference
Data services	Minimal, primarily for signaling and not for user data
Expansion	Upgrades to the system allowed for some flexibility

higher capacity compared to contemporaries. Table 7.2 outlines the key technical aspects of NMT system:

Despite their groundbreaking status, 1G networks had several limitations. The analog signals were susceptible to noise and interference, which could degrade voice quality. Security was another significant concern because analog communications were easy to intercept and eavesdrop on, raising privacy issues. Furthermore, the capacity constraints became increasingly evident as the number of mobile phone users grew. The transition to the second generation of mobile networks, or 2G, was primarily driven by the need for better voice quality, increased capacity, and the desire to incorporate digital services into mobile communication. This shift marked the move from analog to digital technology, with the introduction of systems like GSM, which offered improved sound quality, higher capacity, and encrypted communication, addressing many of the security concerns inherent in 1G networks.

The evolution to 2G also facilitated the first steps toward international standards, which significantly enhanced roaming capabilities and interoperability between different networks and countries. This transition laid the groundwork for future innovations and the explosive growth of mobile communication, setting the stage for the data-driven generations to come.

7.2.6 2G network: analog-to-digital communications

The inception of 2G mobile networks marked the transition from analog to digital communications in the 1990s. This digital leap introduced two main technologies: GSM and CMDA.

GSM emerged as the most popular 2G standard globally, characterized by its use of Time Division Multiple Access (TDMA) and FDMA for channelizing users. GSM was officially launched in 1991 in Finland, rapidly expanding across the globe due to its robust standards and interoperability between different network providers.

On the other hand, CDMA utilized a different approach known as spread spectrum technology, where it encoded each caller's data with a unique key, allowing multiple users to be multiplexed over the same physical channel. This technique enhanced privacy and allowed for a more efficient use of the available spectrum.

2G networks introduced several key features that were not present in 1G networks:

- **Encryption:** 2G networks introduced end-to-end encryption, significantly improving privacy and security over the unencrypted analog signals of 1G.
- **SMS:** Often dubbed as "text messaging," this feature became a revolutionary communication tool, allowing users to send and receive text messages.
- **Data Services:** Although initially limited, 2G networks provided data services such as fax and email.
- **Subscriber Identity Module (SIM):** This innovation allowed users to switch between devices while retaining their mobile identity.
- **International Roaming:** Enhanced by the widespread adoption of GSM, roaming agreements facilitated international use of mobile phones.

The evolution of 2G networks saw the introduction of packet-switched data transmission technologies, which provided users with internet access and the beginning of mobile data services. Here, GPRS Launched in the late 1990s, it allowed for a more efficient use of the network's resources by sending data in packets and providing an "always-on" data service. It significantly increased data rates over the previous circuit-switched systems, reaching speeds of up to 114 kbps.

7.2.7 3G network: voice-centric to data-centric services

The advent of the third generation (3G) of mobile telecommunications introduced a paradigm shift from voice-centric services, which dominated 2G networks, to data-centric services. This was facilitated by the enhancement in data transmission capabilities, enabling not just clearer voice services but also the accommodation of high-speed internet and multimedia services. The introduction of technologies such as UMTS and CDMA2000 marked this transition, offering a substantial increase in data bandwidth:

- **UMTS:** UMTS uses Wideband Code Division Multiple Access (W-CDMA) as the underlying standard, a marked difference from 2G's TDMA and CDMA. It is an evolution of the GSM standards with a core network evolution, that allows for higher data speeds and more data-intensive services. The architecture of UMTS consists of the core network, UMTS Terrestrial Radio Access Network (UTRAN), and user equipment. The UTRAN allows for connection between the user and the core network, handling all radio-related functionalities.
- **CDMA2000:** This standard is an evolution of the 2G CDMA. It is divided into several phases, such as 1XRTT and EV-DO (Evolution-Data Optimized), each providing progressively faster data rates. CDMA2000 networks are characterized by their core network, which is connected to the Packet Data Serving Node (PDSN) for handling data traffic and to the MSC for voice traffic.

Besides, a key innovation, as shown in Figure 7.5, of 3G was the introduction of the Internet Protocol (IP) multimedia subsystem. This architectural framework allows for the delivery of multimedia and voice services over an IP-based network. It integrates with the existing cellular standards and allows users to access services across wireless and wired networks seamlessly. IP Multimedia Subsystem (IMS) is access independent as it supports multiple access types, which provides a vast range of services like video calling, and rich messaging, over IP.

Figure 7.5 illustrates the layered architecture of IMS, a framework designed to deliver multimedia and voice services over IP-based networks. The architecture is divided into several pivotal components, categorized across different layers, to facilitate the provisioning of services:

- **Access/devices layer:** This foundational layer comprises an assortment of end-point devices such as mobile phones, tablets, or other devices capable of connecting to the network. These devices gain access to IMS services through underlying connectivity options, which may encompass cellular networks, Wi-Fi, or wired links.
- **Transport layer:** The intermediary layer facilitates the conveyance of data via the IP network, which can represent a dedicated data backbone or the broader internet. This layer includes gateways to other network systems like the PSTN, enabling interoperability between IMS and traditional voice communication infrastructures.
- **Control layer:**
  - **Home Subscriber Server (HSS)**: A central repository maintaining subscriber data, this server handles user information, service profiles, such as subscriptions, identities, locations, and security credentials.
  - **Call Session Control Function (CSCF)**: Acting as the signaling control nexus, the CSCF orchestrates the initiation, management, and termination of communication sessions, representing the linchpin of control layer within IMS.

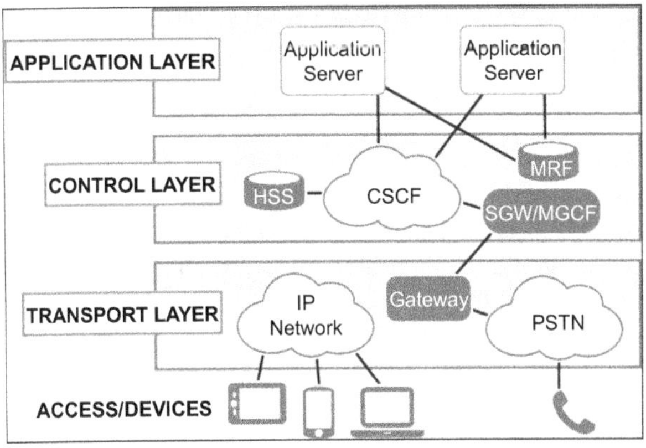

Figure 7.5 IP multimedia subsystem

  - **Media Resource Function (MRF)**: This function encompasses the provisioning of media resources, involving processing capabilities for voice and video, which may include transcoding and conferencing controls.
  - **Signaling Gateway/Media Gateway Control Function (SGW/MGCF)**: These components enable connectivity and communication between the IMS network and traditional voice and multimedia networks, bridging new IP-based services with established communication frameworks.
- **Application layer:** At the zenith of architecture lies a suite of application servers, delivering a spectrum of IP-based services such as voice telephony, multimedia messaging, and video conferencing. These servers administer the business logic and delivery of services, granting users access to diverse functionalities through their interconnected devices.

IMS plays a critical role in the convergence of data and telecommunication services, enabling operators to offer a new breed of services while simplifying the network architecture and reducing costs. As we continue to progress into more advanced networks like 4G and 5G, the principles of IMS remain fundamental in ensuring seamless service continuity and network efficiency.

7.2.8 4G network: evolution and architectural mastery

The fourth generation (4G) of mobile networks marks a significant leap in wireless communication, characterized by its robust data transmission capabilities and enhanced network efficiencies.

LTE, often considered the first true 4G standard, introduced a simplified, IP-based network architecture that significantly reduced latency compared to previous generations. The core network was streamlined, with enhanced spectral efficiency and bandwidth flexibility. LTE-Advanced (LTE-A) built upon these foundations, offering carrier aggregation, advanced antenna techniques, and increased peak data rates, fulfilling the ITU's IMT-Advanced criteria.

Orthogonal Frequency-Division Multiple Access (OFDMA) forms the cornerstone of 4G downlink air interface. It enhances data rates by splitting the transmission bandwidth into numerous narrowband sub-frequencies, which reduces interference and improves efficiency. MIMO technology leverages multiple transmitter and receiver antennas to boost network capacity and the speed of data transfer, allowing for multiple simultaneous data streams.

Integration with IMS facilitated the advent of Voice over LTE (VoLTE), enabling High-Definition (HD) voice calling over LTE networks. VoLTE transmits voice calls as data flows within the LTE data bearer, which means that voice service as traditionally implemented through a Circuit-Switched (CS) voice network is now carried through an all-IP network based on LTE, with enhanced quality and reliability.

Table 7.3 highlights the major technological advancements and capabilities of each generation:

The amalgamation of these elements not only underscores the profound transformations within the 4G landscape but also highlights the architectural brilliance that

Table 7.3 Major technological advancements and capabilities of each generation

Generation	Standard	Key technologies	Max data speeds	Core network	Notable features
2G	GSM, CDMA	TDMA, CDMA	Up to 384 kbps	Circuit-switched	SMS, MMS, basic data services
2.5G	GPRS	2G with packet-switched data	Up to 114 kbps	Mixed	Improved data services over 2G
3G	UMTS, CDMA2000	W-CDMA, CDMA2000	Up to 42 Mbps	Packet-switched	Video calling, mobile internet
3.5G	HSPA	High-Speed Packet Access	Up to 168 Mbps	Packet-switched	Improved data rates over 3G
4G	LTE	OFDMA, MIMO, SC-FDMA (uplink)	Up to 1 Gbps DL[a]	All-IP	HD voice/video, high-speed mobile web
4G Advanced	LTE-Advanced	Carrier aggregation, MIMO, relay nodes	Up to 1 Gbps UL[a], 3 Gbps DL[a]	All-IP	Enhanced peak speeds, increased capacity

[a]DL: Downlink, UL: Uplink.

enables an array of sophisticated services, marking a watershed in the telecommunications industry. The fruition of 4G networks has redefined mobile connectivity, establishing a robust foundation for the future development of mobile communications and setting the stage for the eventual transition to 5G and beyond.

7.2.9 5G network: industrial revolution with high-speed connectivity

5G networks represent a significant leap forward in wireless technology, designed to meet the growing data demands of modern world. They incorporate various cutting-edge technologies that enable faster speeds, lower latency, and more reliable connections across a multitude of devices. Below is a summary of the key features and advancements of 5G networks:

5G New Radio (NR) is the global standard for a new air interface designed for 5G networks. It is built on Orthogonal Frequency-Division Multiplexing (OFDM) with a wider bandwidth, capable of supporting a vast array of frequencies from low-band spectrum (<1 GHz) to millimeter waves (>24 GHz). 5G NR aims to provide greater efficiency, lower latency, and increased capacity compared to its predecessors.

Massive MIMO involves the deployment of a large number of antennas at the base station to support a greater number of concurrent users. Beamforming is a technology that focuses a wireless signal toward a specific receiving device, rather than having the signal spread in all directions, as with a traditional antenna. Together, these technologies dramatically improve signal directionality, strength, and network capacity.

5G networks are designed to support the burgeoning IoT, facilitating the connection of billions of devices. 5G introduces URLLC, which is essential for mission-critical applications requiring uninterrupted and robust data exchange. This includes remote surgery, autonomous vehicles, and industrial automation, where a delay of even milliseconds could be detrimental.

The integration of these technologies within the 5G framework promises to unlock a plethora of new applications and services, from enhanced mobile broadband experiences to new industrial use cases that were not feasible with previous generations of cellular technology. Furthermore, 5G technology is poised to revolutionize various industrial sectors with its high speed, low latency, and the ability to connect a vast number of devices simultaneously. Here are some examples of industrial applications of 5G:

- **Smart manufacturing (Figure 7.6):** 5G enables smart factories by facilitating the connection of machines, sensors, and control systems in real-time. This allows for greater automation, real-time monitoring, and data analytics, leading to improved efficiency, predictive maintenance, and flexible production practices.
- **Autonomous vehicles (Figure 7.7):** In the automotive industry, 5G is essential for the deployment of autonomous vehicles. The technology's low latency

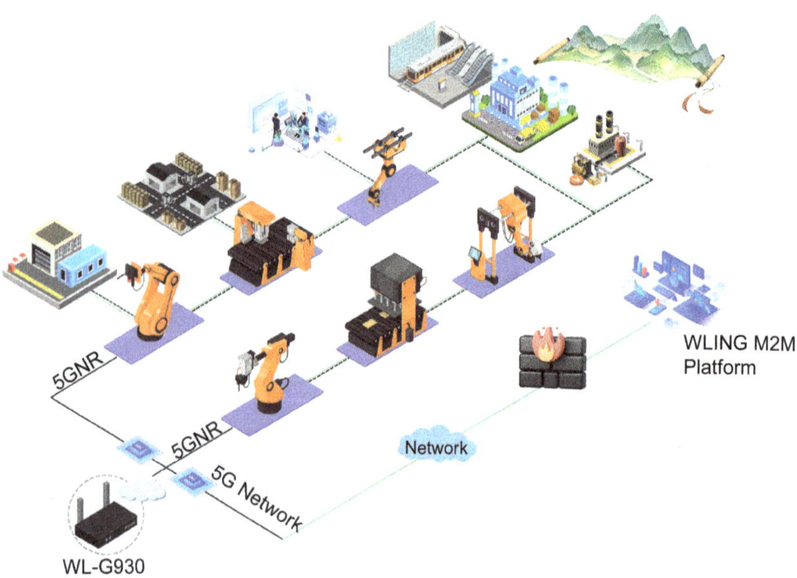

Figure 7.6 5G smart manufacturing

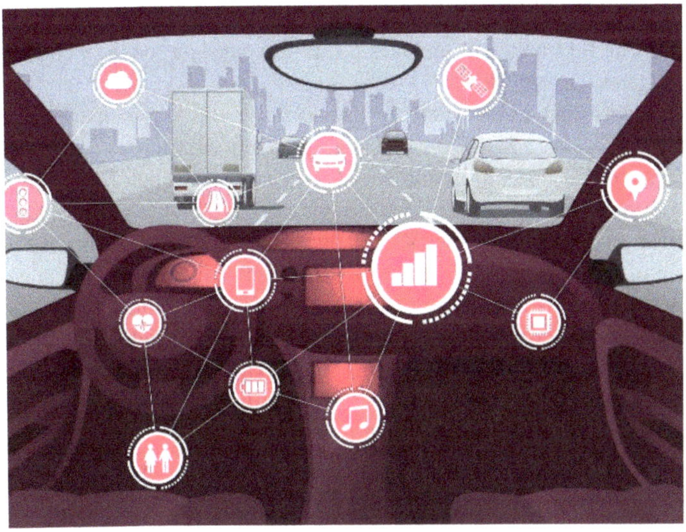

Figure 7.7 5G autonomous vehicles

allows for instantaneous communication between vehicles and their environment, which is critical for safety and traffic management.

- **Healthcare:** 5G can transform healthcare delivery through telemedicine, remote monitoring, and even remote surgery. The high reliability and low latency of 5G are crucial for transmitting real-time medical data and supporting telesurgery where precision and quick response times are vital.
- **Agriculture:** Precision agriculture can be significantly enhanced with 5G by enabling real-time data collection from various sensors and drones. This allows for more precise crop monitoring, efficient use of resources, and automated equipment operations.

7.2.10 6G network: the next frontier of connectivity

6G, the next generation of wireless communication technology following 5G, is expected to be commercialized by 2030. Not only does 6G deliver higher data rates and lower latency, it can also support entirely new applications and services, such as holographic communications, tactile Internet, and highly automated industrial applications. In addition, the development of 6G will be driven by lifestyle and societal changes, including a high-fidelity holographic society, the Internet of Everything, and time-sensitive or time-engineered applications [1]. The following is a description of the key features of 6G [2]:

- **High security, secrecy, and privacy:** Although 4G and 5G have improved network performance, the security of wireless communications remains a critical concern. To address security challenges, 6G will employ Physical Layer Security (PLS) techniques and quantum key distribution via Visible-Light Communications (VLC) to enhance data security [3,4]. Meanwhile, to protect user privacy, 6G network plans to achieve anonymity, decentralization, and untraceability through blockchain technology to prevent data leakage and ensure user information security [5].

- **High affordability and full customization:** 6G will allow customers to choose a service model based on their personal preferences, such as a low-rate reliable service or a low-cost unreliable service. In addition, customers can choose to focus on the energy consumption of device or give up the smart features due to privacy and security concerns. 6G will ensure that customer rights are not limited by technology and will make customer experience a core performance metric.
- **Low energy consumption and long battery life:** To reduce charging frequencies, 6G will shift computing tasks through smart BS or radio space [6], utilizing cooperative relaying and network densification to reduce transmission power [7]. In addition, the 6G will employ energy-harvesting technology to capture energy from ambient signals, micro-vibrations and sunlight [8].
- **High intelligence:** The high intelligence of 6G networks will bring innovation in three areas: operations, environment, and services. First, 6G achieves optimal allocation of resources and improves network performance through deep learning and other technologies [9]. Second, with the smart radios and materials, 6G networks will have self-organizing and self-healing capabilities, enhancing intelligent communication between devices [10]. Finally, 6G service intelligence will enhance the customer experience through personalization and precision services [11].

Furthermore, 6G provides major enhancements and changes in other features and KPIs compared to past technologies. A detailed comparison of 1G to 6G is shown in Table 7.4 [2,12]. Thanks to its outstanding performance, 6G not only expands new application areas, but also pushes society into a new generation of highly interconnectedness and intelligence. The following are examples of potential application scenarios for 6G [13]:

- **Holographic communications:** 6G will support high-fidelity holographic communications, allowing users to interact with 3D images. This immersive experience is revolutionary for areas such as teleconferencing, online education, entertainment, and healthcare.
- **Smart cities:** 6G networks will interconnect various devices and services in cities, including traffic management systems, public safety monitoring and environmental monitoring. This connectivity will enable the optimized allocation and management of resources, enhance the efficiency of urban operations. Meanwhile, it will reduce energy consumption and improve the quality of life for residents.
- **Connectivity for everything:** The Internet of everything is applicable to a wide range of scenarios, such as real-time monitoring of buildings, cities, environments, transportation, and infrastructure. Additionally, 6G will drive the development of smart wearables and the Internet of in-body sensors (Internet of Biological Things), which will exceed the existing need for mMTC.

Table 7.4 Detailed comparison of 1G to 6G networks

Features	**1G**	**2G**	**3G**	**4G**	**5G**	**6G**
Period	1980–1990	1990–2000	2000–2010	2010–2020	2020–2030	2030–2040
Maximum Rate	2.4 kb/s	144 kb/s	2 Mb/s	1 Gb/s	35.46 Gb/s	100 Gb/s
Maximum frequency	894 MHz	1,900 MHz	2,100 MHz	6 GHz	90 GHz	10 THz
Service level	Voice	Text	Picture	Video	3D VR/AR	Tactile
Standards	MTS, AMPS, IMTS, PTT	GSM, IS-95, CDMA, EDGE	UMTS, WCDMA, IMT2000, CDMA2000, TD-SCDMA	WiMAX, LTE, LTE-A	5G NR, WWWW	–
Multiplexing	FDMA	FDMA, TDMA	CDMA	OFDMA	OFDMA	Smart OFDMA plus IM
Architecture	SISO	SISO	SISO	MIMO	Massive MIMO	intelligent surface
Core network	PSTN	PSTN	Packet N/W	Internet	Internet, IoT	Internet of everything
Highlight	Mobility	Digitization	Internet	Real-time streaming	Extremely high rate	Security, secrecy, privacy
Experienced data rate	–	–	–	10 Mb/s	20 Gb/s	$\geq$ 1 Tb/s
Spectrum efficiency	–	–	–	1$\times$	3$\times$ that of 4G	5–10$\times$ that of 5G
Network energy efficiency	–	–	–	1$\times$	10–100$\times$ that of 4G	10–100$\times$ that of 5G
Connectivity density	–	–	–	10^5 Devices/km^2	10^6 Devices/km^2	10^7 Devices/km^2
Latency	–	–	–	10 ms	1 ms	10–100 μs
Mobility	–	–	–	350 km/h	500 km/h	$\geq 1,000$ km/h

7.3 Mobile IP and mobility in cellular networks

7.3.1 Mobile IP: concept

Mobile IP is a critical enhancement to the IP that allows users to maintain a constant IP address while moving between different networks. This ensures ongoing Internet sessions remain uninterrupted, which is particularly vital for modern applications that demand persistent connectivity, such as video conferencing, mobile gaming, and various enterprise services.

The basic operation of Mobile IP involves two main processes: registration and tunneling. When a mobile device moves to a new network, it registers with a Foreign Agent (FA) on that network. The FA communicates with the home agent to establish a tunnel for forwarding packets. The home agent then redirects packets meant for the mobile device's IP address through the tunnel, allowing for seamless data transfer regardless of the device's location.

The home agent is responsible for maintaining information about the mobile device's current location and for packet forwarding during mobility. The FA provides the necessary CoA—a temporary IP address—to the mobile device on the visited network and assists in the registration process. The interplay between these agents is crucial to provide the mobility support in Mobile IP, enabling users to roam across networks without changing their IP address.

Here is a simplified example to illustrate how Mobile IP works (Figure 7.8): Imagine a business professional named Alex, who is traveling from their office in New York to a conference in Tokyo. Alex is participating in a critical, ongoing online collaboration session that must not be interrupted, even while they are in transit. Alex's device, a smartphone, is equipped with Mobile IP technology, enabling a persistent connection.

Figure 7.8 Mobile IP example

1. **Home network setup:** In New York, Alex's smartphone is connected to the office network with a permanent IP address provided by the office's network, known as the home network. The Home Agent (HA) on this network keeps track of Alex's device location.
2. **Movement and discovery:** Upon arriving in Tokyo, Alex's smartphone detects a new network and attaches to it. This new network is the foreign network where the FA is located.
3. **Registration with FA:** Alex's smartphone sends a registration request to the FA in Tokyo. The FA assigns a Care-of Address (CoA), which is a temporary IP address for use while on the foreign network.
4. **FA communicates with HA:** The FA sends the registration request, including the CoA, to the HA in New York. The HA updates its records, noting that any communication sent to Alex's permanent IP address should now be forwarded to the CoA in Tokyo.
5. **Tunneling of data:** The HA establishes a tunnel from the home network to the CoA. This tunnel is a virtual pipe through which data packets can be sent securely and directly to Alex's device in Tokyo, even though the packets still bear the home IP address.
6. **Seamless communication:** As the meeting continues, data packets destined for Alex's device are intercepted by the HA in New York, encapsulated, and sent through the tunnel to the FA in Tokyo, which then delivers them to Alex's smartphone.
7. **Continuity of service:** To the collaboration software and the rest of Alex's team in New York, it appears as if Alex has never left the office. The session continues seamlessly, without any interruption or the need for Alex to log in again or change settings.

This process allows Alex to travel across the globe without losing connectivity to important services, demonstrating the power and utility of Mobile IP in maintaining uninterrupted internet sessions during mobility.

7.3.2 Mobile IP: indirect routing

Indirect routing is a fundamental aspect of Mobile IP that enables a device to receive data via a route that is different from the one used in standard IP routing. This mechanism is particularly crucial for maintaining an active internet session as a mobile node moves across various networks.

Indirect routing in Mobile IP is anchored in the protocol's ability to abstract the mobile node's physical location from its logical IP address, technically:

1. **Agent discovery:** When a mobile node enters a new network, it performs an agent discovery process to identify the local FA. It does this by listening for Agent Advertisement messages or by sending an Agent Solicitation message.
2. **Registration process:** After discovering the FA, the mobile node registers its new CoA with its HA back in the home network. This process involves a secure exchange of messages that update the HA with the current location of mobile node.

3. **Tunnel establishment:** Upon successful registration, the HA establishes a tunnel to the current CoA of mobile node. This tunnel is typically facilitated using IP-in-IP encapsulation, Generic Routing Encapsulation (GRE), or other tunneling mechanisms like Layer Two Tunneling Protocol (L2TP) or Multi-Protocol Label Switching (MPLS).
4. **Packet encapsulation and decapsulation:** Data packets sent to the mobile node's home address are intercepted by the HA, which then encapsulates these packets and sends them through the tunnel. When the packets arrive at the FA, they are decapsulated and forwarded to the mobile node.
5. **Maintaining active sessions:** For active sessions, the HA continually routes packets to the FA, which ensures that the mobile node can maintain an ongoing session, such as a Voice over Internet Protocol (VoIP) call or a Virtual Private Network (VPN) connection, even as it moves between networks.

7.3.3 Mobile IP: Agent Discovery

The process of Agent Discovery in Mobile IP is a critical step that allows a mobile node to identify an FA when it moves to a new network. This mechanism ensures that the MN can establish a new point of attachment and maintain uninterrupted internet connectivity. Here is a detailed overview:

Agent Discovery is the process through which a mobile node becomes aware of the CoA that it should use in a new network. This process is facilitated by two types of messages defined in the Mobile IP protocol: Agent Advertisement and Agent Solicitation.

- **Agent Advertisement:** Periodically, each FA and HA broadcasts an Agent Advertisement message on its network. This message contains information about the agent's services and one or more care-of addresses that a mobile node may use to receive packets while attached to this network.
- **Agent Solicitation:** If a mobile node requires services more immediately than the next scheduled advertisement, it may broadcast an Agent Solicitation message. This solicitation prompts agents within the network to issue an Agent Advertisement message out of their normal sequence, allowing the MN to quickly ascertain the availability of mobile services and a CoA.

When a mobile node turns on or enters a new network, it listens for Agent Advertisement messages to determine if it has moved to a new network. These messages are sent by both home and foreign agents, informing mobile nodes of their presence.

- **In the home network:** If the mobile node receives an advertisement from its HA, it realizes it is in the home network and uses its home address for all communications.
- **In the foreign network:** If the mobile node recognizes the advertisement from a foreign agent, it knows it is in a foreign network. It then obtains a CoA from the FA's advertisement, which it will use for communications while in this network.

Once the mobile node receives a CoA through the Agent Discovery process, it proceeds with the registration process to inform its HA of the new location so that the HA can tunnel the MN's packets to the new CoA.

7.3.4 Mobility in cellular network

Mobility in cellular networks refers to the ability of mobile devices to maintain seamless communication while moving across different geographical areas and network coverage zones. This capability is crucial for providing users with uninterrupted service as they travel, ensuring that voice calls, text messages, and data services remain accessible.

A key aspect of mobility is switching, i.e., the transfer of an ongoing call or data session from one base station to another while the user moves from one coverage area to another. There are various types of switching mechanisms, including hard switching (disconnect then connect) and soft switching (connect then disconnect). Each method has its own advantages and disadvantages in terms of call quality and latency.

Additionally, mobility management in cellular networks includes several functions such as location tracking, user authentication, and resource allocation. The Mobility Management Entity (MME) plays a vital role in managing user sessions, tracking the location of devices, and ensuring that users remain connected to the most suitable network resources.

With technologies such as 5G, mobile management has become more complex. Functions such as network slicing and dynamic resource allocation are implemented. These innovations not only enhance the user experience but also improve the overall efficiency and performance of network.

In summary, mobility in cellular networks is essential to provide continuous connectivity and high quality of service while users are moving. Thanks to advanced management protocols and technologies, it is possible to adapt to changing environments and user requirements.

7.4 Security in mobile networks

The above sections describe the principles and evolution associated with mobile networks, whose technical characteristics have led to their widespread application. However, with the widespread application of cellular networks, they still face many challenges in security. Compared to wired networks, cellular networks have more security concerns in an open wireless access environment, which makes the network vulnerable to various attacks. This section analyzes the main limitations of cellular networks and explores different types of attack models as well as security defenses.

7.4.1 Limitation of cellular networks

Cellular networks offer significant advantages in providing a wide range of mobile communication services, but there are still some limitations compared to wired networks. The following are detailed limitations [14]:

- **Open wireless access medium:** Cellular networks utilize wireless channels for communication, and there is no physical isolation to prevent attackers from accessing the network.

- **Limited bandwidth:** Although wireless communication technology is continuously improving, the bandwidth of wireless channels remains limited. Since cellular networks employ shared channels, multiple users compete for bandwidth on the same frequency band, resulting in insufficient bandwidth and affecting network throughput and user experience.
- **System complexity:** Cellular network systems are complex, especially with the introduction of mobility and wireless resource management, which makes the design and maintenance of systems more difficult. Increased system complexity introduces potential security vulnerabilities and failure points, which may result in degraded network performance or security risks.
- **Limited power:** Wireless devices (e.g., cell phones, IoT devices) typically rely on battery power, resulting in limited battery life. Prolonged communication or high power operation may cause devices to drain quickly, requiring users to recharge frequently and making energy management a challenge.
- **Limited processing power:** The computational power of wireless devices is relatively low, especially when compared to traditional wired network devices (e.g., servers, routers). Although the processing power of wireless devices is increasing, it is still insufficient for complex cryptographic calculations, large-scale data processing, etc., which limits the application of wireless networks in high-intensity computing scenarios.
- **Relatively unreliable network connection:** Wireless channels in cellular networks are susceptible to interference and attenuation, resulting in less stable connections. Compared to wired networks, wireless networks have lower communication stability and are more susceptible to data loss, transmission errors, or interruptions, especially when facing electromagnetic interference, weather changes, and physical barriers.
- **Security challenges:** Due to the transmission characteristics of wireless signals, cellular networks are more susceptible to various security attacks, such as signal jamming, fake base station attacks, identity theft, etc. The susceptibility of wireless signals to tampering and their propensity for attacks pose additional challenges to the security of wireless networks.

7.4.2 Security issues in 3G network

3G networks have greatly enriched the scope of mobile communications with their high-speed data transmission and multimedia service capabilities. However, the openness and complexity of 3G networks also introduce new security challenges, including data leakage, privacy violation, and unauthorized access. These security issues not only threaten the security of users' information, but also affect the trust of users in 3G services.

- **Insufficient confidentiality of user identity:** A key weakness in the security architecture of 3G networks is the backup procedure for Temporary Mobile Subscriber Identity (TMSI) reallocation [15]. When the Service Network (SN) or the Visitor Location Register (VLR) is unable to associate the TMSI with the user's International Mobile Subscribers Identity (IMSI) due to corruption of the TMSI, 3G will require users to use the IMSI to identify themselves through the wireless path. This practice causes the user's IMSI to be transmitted in clear text over the wireless interface, which violates the confidentiality of the users' identity and can be exploited by attackers.

- **Network Domain Security (NDS) issues:** In earlier versions of UMTS, especially R99, NDS functionality was not fully implemented. This means that signaling switching protection, including IP and SS7 technologies, was not fully considered in the wireline network architecture, leaving a potential security hole [16].
- **Limitations of traditional network security technologies:** Traditional network security technologies can no longer meet the needs of 3G networks. First of all, firewalls are designed for fixed networks, so they are not perfectly suited for mobile network scenarios. Firewalls cannot effectively defend against inside threats and attacks, as well as not being able to distinguish between services, limiting their security. In addition, static VPNs lack flexibility. VPNs are suitable for fixed connections between large organizations and mobile operators, but not for individual users on an on-demand basis. As a result, it limits the need for dynamic, flexible, and secure connectivity for mobile users.

7.4.3 Security issues in 4G network

LTE and WiMAX, the key technologies for achieving 4G performance goals, bring significant data rate improvements to 4G networks. These technologies not only support broadband performance and multimedia applications, but also operate entirely on the TCP/IP architecture, which reduces costs while increasing the complexity of security issues. In addition, the openness and IP infrastructure of 4G networks make them more challenging to secure compared to 2G and 3G networks. The following are security issues in 4G networks [17]:

- **Physical layer issues:** Both WiMAX and LTE have critical vulnerabilities in the physical layer. By deliberately inserting artificial interference into the communications medium, attackers can disrupt the normal operation of the communications system. There are two main forms of such interference: noise and multicarrier. Noise interference can be performed with White Gaussian Noise (WGN). For multicarrier interference, attackers identify the carriers utilized by the system and inject very narrowband signals on those carriers [18].
- **WiMAX MAC layer issues:** In WiMAX networks, the IEEE 802.16 standard defines seven steps for a mobile station to establish an initial connection with a base station [19]: (1) Initial Ranging and Time Synchronization, (2) UL Parameter Acquisition, (3) Basic Capabilities Negotiation, (4) Scanning and Synchronization, (5) MS Authorization and Key Exchange, (6) Registration with the Serving BS, and (7) Connection Establishment. The first five of these steps involve non-secure traffic, which can increase security risks [20]. Also, the management MAC messages are not encrypted in transit, which provides an opportunity for attackers to listen in on traffic and potentially gain access to sensitive information.

- **Wi-Fi security issues:** As the application of Wi-Fi becomes more and more widespread, its security issues should not be ignored. The original security mechanism of Wi-Fi, Wired Equivalent Privacy (WEP), has multiple security vulnerabilities due to improper cryptographic application. For example, Wi-Fi uses RC4 stream ciphers and CRC-32 authentication [21].

7.4.4 Security issues in 5G network

5G networks are leading the revolution in communication technology with their high speed and low latency characteristics. However, as 5G networks are rapidly deployed and widely applied, their security concerns are becoming increasingly prominent. The complexity of 5G networks, their interoperability with existing technologies, and the need for new and emerging services have created new challenges for network security [22].

- **User identity and confidentiality:** The security mechanism of 5G is similar to that of 4G, which mainly protects users from passive attacks, but provides insufficient protection against active attacks.
- **New trust models:** 5G needs to introduce new trust models for authentication, responsibility attribution and non-repudiation to adapt to evolving usage scenarios.
- **5G radio network security:** A larger threat space and new low-cost technologies have led to an increase in attacks on radio networks. While LTE provides reasonable encryption mechanisms against eavesdropping attacks, there is no protection against modification or injection of user traffic.
- **Security for new service delivery models:** 5G will leverage cloud computing and virtualization to optimize services, which raises new security concerns. When service providers host third-party applications in their clouds, these applications execute on the same hardware as the service provider's services, increasing the need for virtualization with strong security.
- **5G drivers:** Drivers in mobile networks are mainly utilized to improve latency and throughput. However, drivers in 5G will introduce some critical factors that may affect security [23].

7.4.5 Security defense in cellular networks

The security of cellular networks is vital to protect users' data, ensure service availability, and prevent unauthorized access. To address various threats and ensure secure communication, cellular networks implement defense mechanisms that focus on four core aspects: confidentiality, integrity, availability, and authentication [24]. Below are the security defense measures for each of these areas:

7.4.5.1 Confidentiality

Confidentiality encompasses both data confidentiality and privacy protection. Data confidentiality ensures that access to data is restricted to authorized users only, preventing unauthorized access and protecting data from passive attacks. Privacy protection, on the other hand, focuses on safeguarding traffic information of users from being analyzed by attackers, such as the locations of senders and receivers.

- **Data encryption:** Data encryption has been widely applied to prevent unauthorized users from extracting useful data from broadcast messages, in order to ensure data confidentiality. For example, symmetric key cryptography [25] is commonly employed to encrypt and decrypt data in order to provide user anonymity.
- **PLS:** As the computational power of attackers increases, traditional cryptographic methods face new challenges. Therefore, PLS [26] techniques can be utilized as a complement to traditional encryption mechanisms. PLS can enhance data confidentiality by resisting jamming and eavesdropping attacks.
- **Privacy protection technology:** In addition, as 5G networks become more widespread, privacy protection becomes especially important. Common privacy protection techniques include **anonymity services**, **differential privacy algorithms** [27], and **group communication privacy protection** [28].

7.4.5.2 Integrity

Integrity ensures that the data transmitted over the network remains unaltered and accurate during transit, preventing unauthorized modifications. Data integrity can be compromised by malicious internal attacks, such as message injection or data modification. These attacks are difficult to detect because insider attackers have valid identities. Common defenses are described as follows:

- **Message Authentication Codes (MACs):** MACs are utilized to verify the integrity of messages [29]. They generate a unique identifier for each message, and the recipient can check whether the message was altered during transmission.
- **Digital signatures:** Digital signatures allow the sender to sign a message or piece of data utilizing their private key [30]. The recipient can then verify the integrity of message by checking the signature using the sender's public key, ensuring that the data has not been altered.

7.4.5.3 Availability

Availability ensures that legitimate users can access and run cellular network services when needed, while network resources are not compromised by malicious attacks. In addition, availability evaluates the robustness of a system in the face of various attacks and is a key performance metric in 5G cellular networks.

- **Redundancy and backup systems:** Cellular networks implement redundancy at various levels (e.g., backup BS, alternative routing paths, and redundant servers), in order to ensure that services remain available even in the event of hardware or software failures.
- **DoS protection:** To defend against DoS or Distributed DoS attacks, traffic filtering techniques, rate limiting, and anomaly detection systems are utilized to identify and block malicious traffic, preventing service disruption.

7.4.5.4 Authentication

Authentication ensures that only authorized users and devices can access the network, protecting against unauthorized access and fraudulent activities. It requires users to provide credentials to prove their identity, including passwords, digital certificates, biometric information, security tokens, etc. The following are popular authentication techniques:

- **Mutual authentication:** Mutual authentication verifies both the identity of users and networks. In cellular networks, both the mobile device and base station authenticate each other to prevent attackers from impersonating legitimate devices or networks [31].
- **Handover authentication:** Handover authentication refers to the process of authenticating a user device when it switches BS [32]. It ensures that the network continues to provide secure communication services when the device of users is moving.
- **Three-factor authentication:** The scheme can be divided into three main categories: **smart cards**, **passwords**, and **biometrics**. In addition, these three different data types can be utilized together in authentication protocols to provide more secure authentication [33].

7.4.6 Future security trends in mobile networks

As technology continues to evolve, the security of mobile networks faces new challenges and opportunities. Future mobile network security will be influenced by several important trends. First, there is the application of emerging technologies (e.g., AI and blockchain) in security. AI can analyze large volumes of data through machine learning techniques to identify potential security threats and respond in real time, thereby enhancing intrusion detection and defense capabilities. Meanwhile, blockchain technology, with its decentralized and immutable characteristics, increases data security and transparency, providing more secure identity verification and transaction records.

Second, the proliferation of IoT and Vehicle-to-Everything (V2X) technologies brings new security challenges. Due to the large number of IoT devices and their relatively weak security measures, hackers can utilize these devices as entry points for attacks. The application of V2X technology also faces security threats, including communication between vehicles and connections to infrastructure. Therefore, it is especially important to develop more robust security protocols and standards to ensure traffic safety.

Finally, future security technologies will trend toward intelligence and automation. Researchers are exploring solutions that leverage deep learning and big data analytics to enhance security measures. Meanwhile, adaptive security policies are researched in order to respond quickly to the changing threat environment. In addition, zero-trust architecture will be the new security model, emphasizing that no device or user should be trusted by default under any circumstances, thus enhancing overall network security.

7.5 Conclusion

The rapid evolution of mobile networks, from the analog era of 1G to the transformative potentials of 6G, underscores the pivotal role that wireless communication has played in shaping modern society. Each generation of mobile networks has addressed previous limitations while introducing groundbreaking technologies that have fundamentally altered the way we connect and interact. The transition from voice-centric services to data-driven ecosystems has enabled applications such as IoT, autonomous vehicles, and smart cities, reflecting the integration of communication networks into every facet of daily life.

However, alongside these advancements, security challenges have grown in complexity. The shift to open wireless environments, reliance on IP-based architectures, and increasing device heterogeneity have introduced vulnerabilities that necessitate innovative defenses. Addressing these challenges requires a multi-faceted approach, integrating PLS security, advanced cryptographic protocols, and real-time threat detection systems.

Looking ahead, the future of mobile networks lies not only in technical excellence but also in their ability to address societal needs such as affordability, sustainability, and inclusivity. Technologies like AI, blockchain, and energy-efficient designs will be instrumental in realizing the vision of a seamlessly connected and secure global network infrastructure. The journey toward 6G represents an opportunity to redefine connectivity and create a foundation for a more intelligent, secure, and interconnected world.

References

[1] FG-NET-2030. Network 2030—A blueprint of technology, applications and market drivers towards the year 2030 and beyond. ITU-T; 2019.

[2] Dang S, Amin O, Shihada B, *et al.* What should 6G be? Nature Electronics. 2020;3(1):20–29.

[3] Shiu YS, Chang SY, Wu HC, *et al.* Physical layer security in wireless networks: A tutorial. IEEE Wireless Communications. 2011;18(2):66–74.

[4] Obeed M, Salhab AM, Alouini MS, *et al.* On optimizing VLC networks for downlink multi-user transmission: A survey. IEEE Communications Surveys & Tutorials. 2019;21(3):2947–2976.

[5] Henry R, Herzberg A, and Kate A. Blockchain access privacy: Challenges and directions. IEEE Security & Privacy. 2018;16(4):38–45.

[6] Van Huynh N, Hoang DT, Lu X, *et al.* Ambient backscatter communications: A contemporary survey. IEEE Communications Surveys & Tutorials. 2018;20(4):2889–2922.

[7] Yunas SF, Valkama M, and Niemelä J. Spectral and energy efficiency of ultra-dense networks under different deployment strategies. IEEE Communications Magazine. 2015;53(1):90–100.

[8] Ulukus S, Yener A, Erkip E, *et al.* Energy harvesting wireless communications: A review of recent advances. IEEE Journal on Selected Areas in Communications. 2015;33(3):360–381.
[9] Mao Q, Hu F, and Hao Q. Deep learning for intelligent wireless networks: A comprehensive survey. IEEE Communications Surveys & Tutorials. 2018;20(4):2595–2621.
[10] Yang L and Wang FY. Driving into intelligent spaces with pervasive communications. IEEE Intelligent Systems. 2007;22(1):12–15.
[11] Belmonte-Hernández A, Hernández-Peñaloza G, Gutiérrez DM, *et al.* SWiBluX: Multi-sensor deep learning fingerprint for precise real-time indoor tracking. IEEE Sensors Journal. 2019;19(9):3473–3486.
[12] Zhang Z, Xiao Y, Ma Z, *et al.* 6G wireless networks: Vision, requirements, architecture, and key technologies. IEEE Vehicular Technology Magazine. 2019;14(3):28–41.
[13] Tataria H, Shafi M, Molisch AF, *et al.* 6G wireless systems: Vision, requirements, challenges, insights, and opportunities. Proceedings of the IEEE. 2021;109(7):1166–1199.
[14] Gardezi AI. Security in Wireless Cellular Networks. Washington University; 2006.
[15] Xenakis C. Security in UMTS 3G mobile networks. In: Handbook of Research on Wireless Security. IGI Global; 2008. p. 318–338.
[16] Xenakis C and Merakos L. Security in third generation mobile networks. Computer Communications. 2004;27(7):638–650.
[17] Mohapatra SK, Swain BR, and Das P. Comprehensive survey of possible security issues on 4G networks. International Journal of Network Security & Its Applications. 2015;7(2):61.
[18] Park Y and Park T. A survey of security threats on 4G networks. In: 2007 IEEE Globecom Workshops. IEEE; 2007. p. 1–6.
[19] Seddigh N, Nandy B, Makkar R, *et al.* Security advances and challenges in 4G wireless networks. In: 2010 Eighth International Conference on Privacy, Security and Trust. IEEE; 2010. p. 62–71.
[20] Berkmann J, Carbonelli C, Dietrich F, *et al.* On 3G LTE terminal implementation-standard, algorithms, complexities and challenges. In: 2008 International Wireless Communications and Mobile Computing Conference. IEEE; 2008. p. 970–975.
[21] Gupta A and Buthmann T. The Bell Labs security framework: Making the case for end-to-end Wi-Fi security. Lucent Technologies 2006;11:15.
[22] Ericsson A. 5G Security-Scenarios and Solutions. White Paper. 2015.
[23] Baraković S, Kurtović E, Božanović O, *et al.* Security issues in wireless networks: An overview. In: 2016 XI International Symposium on Telecommunications (BIHTEL). IEEE; 2016. p. 1–6.
[24] Fang D, Qian Y, and Hu RQ. Security for 5G mobile wireless networks. IEEE Access. 2017;6:4850–4874.
[25] Chen CM, Wang KH, Wu TY, *et al.* A scalable transitive human-verifiable authentication protocol for mobile devices. IEEE Transactions on Information Forensics and Security. 2013;8(8):1318–1330.

[26] Trappe W. The challenges facing physical layer security. IEEE Communications Magazine. 2015;53(6):16–20.

[27] Farhang S, Hayel Y, and Zhu Q. PHY-layer location privacy-preserving access point selection mechanism in next-generation wireless networks. In: 2015 IEEE Conference on Communications and Network Security (CNS). IEEE; 2015. p. 263–271.

[28] Abd-Elrahman E, Ibn-Khedher H, and Afifi H. D2D group communications security. In: 2015 International Conference on Protocol Engineering (ICPE) and International Conference on New Technologies of Distributed Systems (NTDS). IEEE; 2015. p. 1–6.

[29] Black Jr JR. Message Authentication Codes. University of California, Davis; 2000.

[30] Boneh D. Digital signature standard. In: van Tilborg, H.C.A. and Jajodia, S. (eds.), Encyclopedia of Cryptography and Security. Boston, MA: Springer; 2011.

[31] Haddad Z, Mahmoud M, Taha S, *et al.* Secure and privacy-preserving AMI-utility communications via LTE-A networks. In: 2015 IEEE 11th International Conference on Wireless and Mobile Computing, Networking and Communications (WiMob). IEEE; 2015. p. 748–755.

[32] Cao J, Li H, and Ma M. GAHAP: A group-based anonymity handover authentication protocol for MTC in LTE-A networks. In: 2015 IEEE International Conference on Communications (ICC). IEEE; 2015. p. 3020–3025.

[33] Fan CI and Lin YH. Provably secure remote truly three-factor authentication scheme with privacy protection on biometrics. IEEE Transactions on Information Forensics and Security. 2009;4(4):933–945.

Chapter 8

Edge computing

Zhenning Wang[1], Yue Cao[1], Hai Lin[1] and Bo Zhao[1]

This chapter includes the development of edge computing, the architectures of edge computing (fog/cloud/multi-cloud networks, three tire architectures, multi-cloud networking), optimization solutions (basic model, optimization problems, optimization objectives, optimization methods), applications (digital twin, smart cities, healthcare, intelligent transportation, etc.), and edge computing technology challenges (security and privacy, dynamic, model and architecture, etc.).

8.1 Development of edge computing

First, this part briefly outlines the origins and development of edge computing. Then, an overview of the basic content of edge computing is provided.

8.1.1 The origin of edge computing

With the rapid development of mobile networks, various intelligent devices have become an indispensable part of daily life. Meanwhile, with the advancement of Internet of Things (IoT) technology, it has opened up many computing-intensive application fields, such as intelligent transportation, medical care, online interactive games, Augmented/Virtual Reality (AR/VR), etc [1]. These complex applications place higher demands on the computing power and resources of smart devices [2].

Over the past two decades, cloud computing has emerged as a new computing paradigm. Cloud computing is a cost-effective model that can provide a rich set of applications and services. Moreover, cloud computing greatly alleviates the conflict between IoT applications and resource-constrained mobile users. By centralizing computing, storage and network management in the cloud, it can ensure sufficient computing resource requirements for terminal devices. However, in recent years, most IoT services have placed higher requirements on transmission bandwidth, latency, energy consumption, application performance, and reliability. For some latency-sensitive IoT services, cloud computing is undesirable. This is because long transmission distances in cloud processing cause additional transmission costs and delays.

[1]The School of Cyber Science and Engineering, Wuhan University, China

In this context, Mobile Edge Computing (MEC) emerged [3]. As a key component in IoT architecture to handle computing-intensive tasks, it moves cloud computing services from centralized remote clouds to distributed edge networks. Specifically, by setting up MEC servers, mobile users' workloads can be shifted closer to the users. This not only meets the computing power requirements of mobile users, but also improves the Quality of Service (QoS) of IoT applications while significantly reducing cost and latency. At present, MEC technology has been well applied in system architecture, energy efficiency, and computing resource optimization [4].

8.1.2 The overview of edge computing

Many emerging mobile applications benefit from MEC, by offloading compute-intensive tasks to Edge Servers (ES) for execution. The following example illustrates the basic principles of MEC. For example, face recognition applications typically consist of five main computing components, including image acquisition, face detection, pre-processing, feature extraction, and classification. Here, the image acquisition component needs to be executed on the terminal device. However, other components can be offloaded to ES for processing, including complex calculations such as signal processing and machine learning algorithms. In this way, the computing burden of the terminal device can be effectively reduced [5].

In MEC, computing resources are distributed at the edge of the network close to mobile users. Typically, MEC infrastructure may include dozens of large cloud data centers. In addition, it also includes thousands of small ES with limited computing capabilities. It can offload the tasks of mobile users received from different locations to ES for processing [6]. This scalable and flexible architecture enables MEC to provide the following benefits. (1) Highly distributed and heterogeneous resources: Since ES are distributed in different geographical locations, they have different scales in processing and storing network resources. (2) Support low-latency real-time applications: By migrating computing-intensive tasks to nearby ES instead of central servers, potential network congestion is reduced and application responses are accelerated. (3) Lower mobile energy consumption: Mobile users can migrate computing tasks to ES, which can significantly reduce device energy consumption and extend battery life. (4) Improve security: The distributed deployment and small-scale characteristics of ES in MEC make them less vulnerable to security attacks. Additionally, MEC prevents critical data from being uploaded to remote data centers. (5) Interoperability with traditional centralized clouds: In some cases, obtaining resources from remote centralized clouds with greater computing and storage capabilities is much cheaper than MEC. Therefore, mobile cloud computing and MEC can collaborate with each other to handle computing tasks [7].

8.2 Development of edge computing

This part first introduces the basic computing paradigms of edge computing. Then, the three-layer basic architecture is introduced. Based on this, four collaboration methods in edge computing are also introduced.

8.2.1 Computing paradigm

As an emerging computing framework, edge computing has attracted much attention because it can provide ultra-low latency services for terminal devices. Here, system architecture related to edge computing includes three different paradigms, namely, Cloudlet, fog computing, and MEC. The different computing paradigms are introduced in detail below.

8.2.1.1 Cloudlet computing

Cloudlet is a computing architecture that combines mobile computing and cloud computing. It is a trusted cluster of computers that provides cloud services at the edge of the network. Typically, Cloudlet acts as the middle layer of a three-tier architecture, namely, terminal device, Cloudlet, and cloud. Here, Cloudlet can often be thought of as a micro data center, deployed near end devices to support offloading and caching. In addition, Cloudlets are ideally located at the edge of the network to provide high-bandwidth access to terminal devices. With Cloudlet, terminal devices can offload latency-sensitive or compute-intensive applications, thereby reducing latency and system overhead. Clearly, Cloudlets enhance the ability of mobile cloud computing to solve latency-related issues between end devices and the cloud [8].

8.2.1.2 Fog computing

As a distributed computing architecture, fog computing was launched by Cisco in 2012. Similar to MEC, the main idea of fog computing is to migrate large-scale processing tasks from cloud computing centers to servers close to terminal devices. Since fog computing fills the gap in providing location awareness and real-time response for IoT systems, it is also a new computing architecture. Therefore, fog computing is more suitable for IoT systems [9]. In fog computing, a group of medium-sized computing units aggregated as a fog layer is placed between edge devices and the cloud, where a single computing unit is defined as a fog computing node. Typically, fog computing nodes can provide a medium-sized set of services (e.g., computing, storage, networking) to edge devices. It is worth noting that the above fog computing nodes are along the routing path. Since large-scale processing tasks are mostly executed in fog computing nodes, the delay of task processing and the network transmission load are greatly reduced. In addition, since fog computing nodes are closer to terminal devices, terminal devices can obtain various benefits, such as real-time transmission of data, pre-analysis of data sources, etc.

8.2.1.3 MEC

MEC can provide computing power and IT service environment within the wireless access network near mobile users [10]. Its main idea is to allocate highly complex and heavy computing tasks to adjacent ES, thereby achieving ultra-low latency computing services, higher transmission bandwidth, lower energy consumption, etc. In addition, by applying MEC technology, the battery life of user equipment (such as industrial IoT equipment) can be significantly extended while its storage space can be significantly expanded. In view of the above advantages, MEC undoubtedly eliminates the disadvantages of fog computing and mobile cloud computing. With the vigorous development of the IoTs, MEC will support more applications.

8.2.2 Three-tier network architecture

Due to bandwidth congestion and overloaded core networks in traditional cloud computing, it is difficult to meet users' high requirements for real-time response and low energy consumption. Although edge computing has obvious advantages in the above aspects, it cannot directly replace cloud computing. This is because edge computing does not have the powerful resource capabilities of cloud computing. In some cases, the advantages of edge computing can be used to offload computing services, from the cloud to the edge to improve the user's Quality of Experience (QoE). Therefore, cloud computing and edge computing are complementary to each other. On this basis, the following describes the most common three-layer network architecture in edge computing, which mainly includes the end layer (user layer), edge layer, and cloud layer (shown in Figure 8.1) [11]. The basic three-layer network architecture has been used in numerous studies.

(1) End layer: The end layer is also called the user layer and consists of various terminal devices, such as drones, smartphones, AR devices, surveillance cameras, and other intelligent IoT devices. In different studies, various terminal devices have certain storage and computing capabilities. Here, devices are constantly generating and collecting multiple types of data. Then, depending on the QoE and QoS requirements of the device, the data can be processed locally or offloaded to the edge and cloud.

(2) Edge layer: As the core of the three-layer architecture, the edge layer is the middle layer between the end layer and the cloud layer. The edge layer consists of various computing devices such as cell towers, ES, road side units, gateways, etc. On the one hand, the edge layer provides connection services to terminal devices through various wireless access technologies. Basically, the edge layer can provide more powerful storage and computing power than the end layer. On the other hand, the edge layer has edge management capabilities that can provide service management and invocation. The edge layer can process the data flow from the terminal layer, thereby enabling functions such as intelligent sensing and data analysis. In addition, since edge and cloud are complementary, services in the cloud can be offloaded to the edge layer to achieve load balancing and better QoE.

(3) Cloud layer: The cloud layer consists of existing cloud computing infrastructure, such as Cloud Service Centers (CSC), and is connected to the edge layer through the core network. In the three-tier architecture, the cloud layer has the most powerful data processing and storage capabilities. Although the edge layer can handle large amounts of data to reduce latency or energy consumption, the computing and storage capabilities of the cloud are still necessary to handle huge computing tasks. In addition, the cloud layer can also serve as a

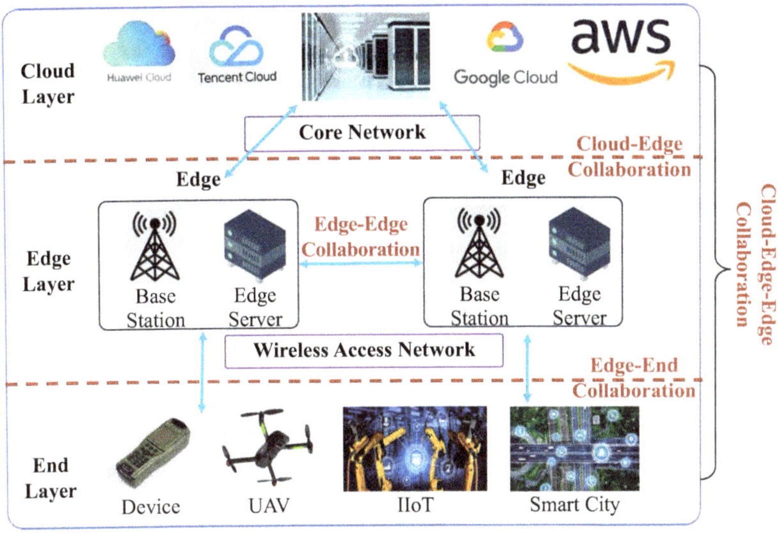

Figure 8.1 Architecture of edge computing

central decision-maker to dynamically adjust global deployment strategies and algorithms based on network resource distribution.

Based on the three-layer network architecture, four different collaboration methods in edge computing are briefly introduced below, namely, end-edge collaboration, end-edge-cloud collaboration, edge-edge collaboration, and edge-cloud collaboration (shown in Figure 8.1).

(1) End-edge collaboration: End-edge collaboration mainly involves the end layer and edge layer [12]. Tasks generated by smart devices can be processed locally or transferred to ES for processing. Whether to transfer these tasks depends on the IoT collaboration strategy or the QoS and QoE requirements of smart devices.

(2) End-edge-cloud collaboration: Although end-edge collaboration can efficiently handle computing tasks, it ignores the huge computing resources of cloud computing centers. As the number of smart devices and resource-consuming applications increases, it will become increasingly difficult to rely solely on the edge layer to meet the needs of smart devices. Therefore, the end-edge-cloud collaboration method is particularly important, which can give full play to the advantages of edge computing and cloud computing [13]. This can provide better offloading performance and good scalability for computing tasks on smart devices.

(3) Edge-edge collaboration: Typically, edge-to-edge collaboration in edge computing does not exist in isolation. Instead, it is often accompanied by end-edge collaboration or end-edge-cloud collaboration. Tasks generated by the device can be scheduled between different edge devices and executed collaboratively. This not only balances the load between different edge devices, but also makes

full use of the computing resources of the edge devices. Through edge-to-edge collaboration, computing tasks can be processed more efficiently [14].

(4) Edge-cloud collaboration: In some scenarios, mobile users subscribe to various services in the CSC. At this time, most computing tasks are performed in the CSC, which will cause a long delay and cannot meet the user's QoE. Here, the latency problem can be improved by offloading some or all tasks of the CSC to the edge through edge-cloud collaboration [15].

8.2.3 Multi-cloud networking

As an important support for edge computing, cloud computing plays an important role in services, control, etc. Cloud computing services can be provided by multiple cloud providers, thus forming a multi-cloud networking. Accordingly, Multi-Cloud Network Services (MCNS) are also generated.

Multi-cloud networking refers to the use of multiple cloud computing services in a single architecture, thereby leveraging the strengths of each service. This approach helps organizations avoid vendor lock-in, enhance redundancy, and improve performance by selecting the best service from different cloud providers. It has many advantages, as described below.

(1) Vendor diversity and avoidance of lock-in: By using services from multiple vendors, the risks associated with vendor-specific issues or changes are reduced. In addition, the best service from each provider can be selected, optimizing performance and costs.
(2) Redundancy and high availability: Distributing workloads across multiple cloud providers can enhance resiliency. If one provider experiences an outage, the others can take over, minimizing downtime.
(3) Performance optimization: By using multi-cloud, resources can be deployed closer to end users, thereby reducing latency and improving performance. In addition, workloads can be dynamically balanced across different clouds to optimize performance and effectively manage traffic peaks.
(4) Cost management: It is possible to choose cost-effective services from different suppliers and avoid the price increases of a single supplier. Meanwhile, having multiple suppliers can provide leverage in negotiations, potentially leading to better pricing and terms.

MCNS is a solution that provides integration and management services for multi-cloud environments. It can efficiently connect and manage network resources between multiple cloud service providers. Specifically, MCNS provides a unified network architecture that enables enterprises to easily establish connections between multiple cloud environments, ensuring that data and applications can be seamlessly transferred between different clouds. Meanwhile, through optimized network routing and high-bandwidth connections, MCNS ensures low latency and high throughput across cloud environments. In general, MCNS provides strong support for enterprises to manage network resources in a multi-cloud network environment. By leveraging MCNS, enterprises can optimize their multi-cloud strategies, reduce operating costs, enhance business continuity, and simplify operational processes.

8.3 Optimization-oriented edge computing

Finally, this section explains the methods to solve these problems and the optimization objectives respectively.

8.3.1 Basic model overview

In a typical edge computing scenario, various computing tasks are generated by user devices [16]. Generally, a typical computing task T can be described by $T = \{D, c, \alpha, \gamma, \tau\}$. Here, D is the data amount of task T, c represents the calculation amount of task T (in CPU cycles/bits), $\alpha(0 \leq \alpha \leq 1)$ represents the parallelizable part of T, γ represents the proportion of task completion, and τ represents the delay constraint of T. The generated task T can be processed locally or offloaded (such as to an edge server or the cloud). Here, corresponding offloading decisions are taken based on different factors such as energy consumption, delay, cost, calculation rate, etc. It can be known that γ denotes the offloading decision variable, which represents the ratio of the offloaded data size to the total data size of task T.

The generated task T can be processed locally or offloaded to the edge or cloud for processing. Here, corresponding offloading decisions are taken based on different factors such as energy consumption, delay, cost, calculation rate, etc. Let γ denote the offloading decision variable, which represents the ratio of the offloaded data size to the total data size of task T. Generally, there are two offloading methods in edge computing, $0-1$ offloading and partial offloading. In $0-1$ offloading, tasks are indivisible, either all processed locally or all processed at the edge. Here, $\gamma = \{0, 1\}$ exists. If $\gamma = 0$, task T will be processed locally, if $\gamma = 1$, task T will be processed at the edge. In partial offloading, tasks can be split, with part executed locally and part executed at the edge. Here, there exists $0 \leq \gamma \leq 1$, indicating the proportion of task offloading. If $\gamma = 1$, task T will be completely offloaded. Otherwise, data of size γD will be offloaded and data of size $(1-\gamma)D$ will be processed locally. The specific content of computing offloading will be introduced in detail later.

In the process of offloading tasks, another important issue is studied, which is resource allocation [4]. For example, how much computing resources are allocated by the edge server to process tasks, how much bandwidth is allocated for transmission tasks, etc. These decisions also affect the efficiency of task completion and the cost of consumption. In addition, in order to reduce the overhead of all parties, the edge server may cache the database or related applications used to process computing tasks in advance. Thus, edge caching technology was introduced [17]. Through edge caching, all parties can save operating costs, reduce latency, and reduce energy consumption.

8.3.2 Optimization problems in edge computing

This part mainly introduces common research issues in edge computing from three aspects: computing offloading, resource allocation, and edge caching. The specific structure and classification of this part are shown in Figure 8.2.

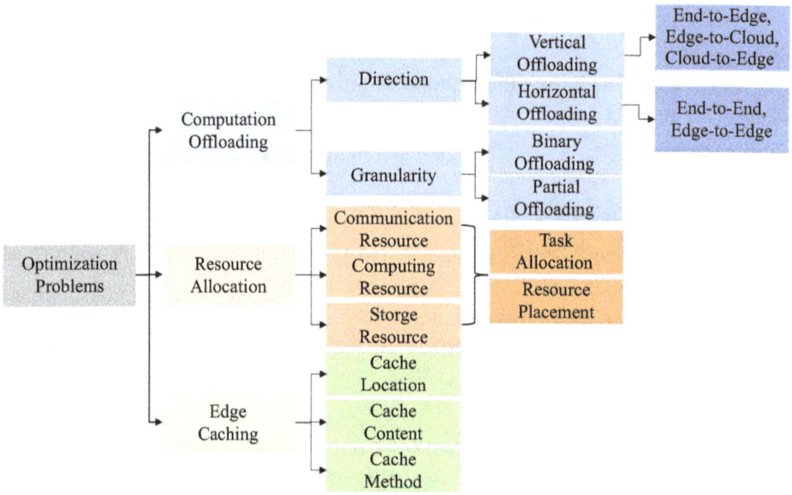

Figure 8.2 Classification of optimization problems

8.3.2.1 Computation offloading

Computation offloading is a very important research issue in edge computing, which transfers computing tasks to more appropriate locations for execution [18]. At present, computing offloading can be roughly divided into the following two categories. First, it is classified according to the offloading direction, including from device to edge, from edge to cloud, from cloud to edge, from device to device, and from edge to edge. The second is to classify based on the granularity of offloading, including binary offloading and partial offloading. The specific offloading diagram is shown in Figure 8.3.

Direction

Since most terminal devices at the end layer have limited resources, resource-intensive tasks need to be offloaded in whole or in part to ES with powerful computing resources [19]. In this way, the limitations of terminal devices in computing performance, storage, and energy efficiency can be alleviated. Moreover, offloading computing tasks from terminal devices to ES can reduce the load on CSC and reduce delays caused by transmission. For example, video data can be offloaded from surveillance cameras to ES for execution. Compared to offloading to CSC, low-latency analysis and processing can be performed while protecting data privacy. In addition, the vehicle's real-time sensing application data needs to be offloaded to edge services for rapid processing and then guide the vehicle to take correct driving behavior. Similarly, if the edge server cannot process the computing tasks offloaded from the terminal device in time, it can be offloaded to the CSC. The computing offloading method from the terminal device to the edge server, and from the edge server to the CSC, can be called upward offloading. Computation offloading also applies to downward offloading, that is, offloading from the CSC to the edge. For example, this

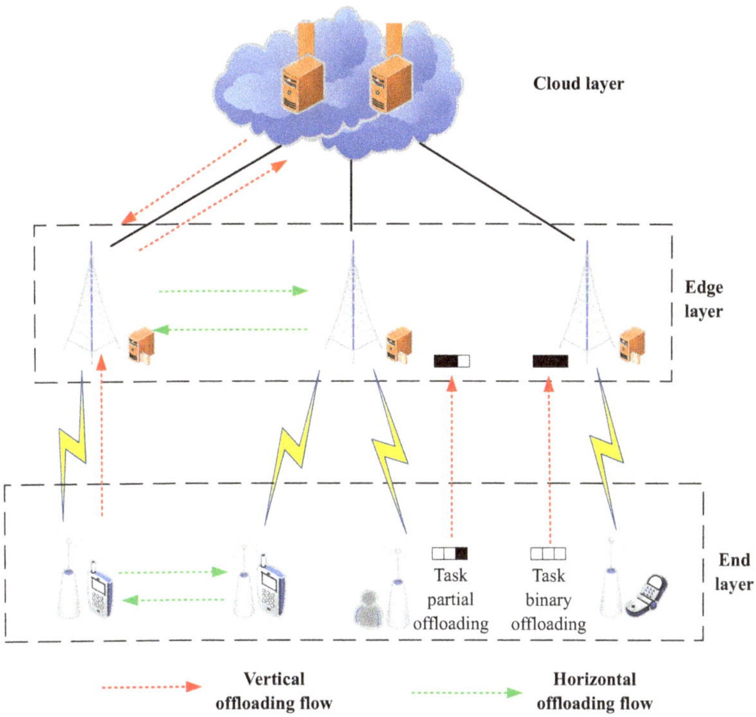

Figure 8.3 The offloading of edge computing

offloading method is used in the edge-cloud collaboration introduced earlier. Here, both upward offloading and downward offloading are regarded as vertical offloading.

In addition to vertical offloading, computation offloading also includes horizontal offloading [20]. In horizontal offloading, there are two offloading methods. The first is that end devices can offload their resource-intensive tasks to other end devices with free computing resources. The second is that an ES can also migrate the computing tasks that need to be processed to other ES for processing. In this way, there are a total of five different offloading directions for vertical offloading and horizontal offloading, which are discussed separately below.

(a) Device-to-edge: For applications that require powerful computing resources or are latency-sensitive, various terminal devices will offload their tasks to ES for execution. This offloading method is the focus of computing offloading and operates in the end-edge collaboration mode. The offloading method from the terminal device to the edge server can realize the different QoS and QoE requirements from the terminal device [21]. These requirements include reducing task processing delays, reducing energy consumption, minimizing task execution costs, etc.

(b) Edge-to-cloud: Typically, tasks offloaded from end devices are processed by computing nodes at the edge layer. Computing nodes include cloudlets, ES, base stations, mini data centers, etc., which can provide different computing resources. If the task data at the edge layer cannot be processed by the computing node in time, it can be further offloaded to the CSC to achieve load balancing [22]. This offloading method from edge to cloud is carried out in the edge-cloud collaboration mode. In this way, the system execution efficiency can be effectively improved.

(c) Cloud-to-edge: This offloading direction also operates in edge-cloud collaborative mode, which brings computing tasks from distant clouds to the edge [23]. This allows for lower data transfer latency and faster application response times. Typical problems of cloud-to-edge offloading mainly include: (i) video transcoding on ES, (ii) application caching from cloud to edge to provide users with better QoE, (iii) edge data replication, and (iv) edge discovery and management, offloading workloads from the cloud to specific ES and assessing differences in workloads between different ES.

(d) Edge-to-edge: Edge-to-edge offloading actually operates in edge-to-edge collaboration mode. It can relieve the work pressure of overloaded ES by offloading (or migrating) some computing tasks to nearby ES [24]. Typical issues with edge-to-edge offloading include: (i) Task scheduling, which can coordinate task allocation among different edge services. (ii) Service migration, which can dynamically migrate services between multiple heterogeneous edge services. (iii) Offloaded forwarding, where a certain edge server can be regarded as a relay node that forwards workloads to other adjacent ES.

(e) Device-to-device: Device-to-device offloading can be performed in the end-edge collaboration mode and the end-edge-cloud collaboration mode. Here, the workload is offloaded from one terminal device to another by making full use of idle resources [25]. For example, in vehicular edge computing, the cooperative task data scheduling problem can be studied. Specifically, the vehicle's computing tasks can not only be processed locally, or offloaded to the ES near the road, but can also be migrated to other vehicles with idle computing resources.

Granularity

In addition to considering the direction of computing offloading, it is also necessary to focus on whether and how much computing tasks are offloaded. Depending on whether the computing task can be split, it can be divided into two offloading methods: (a) binary offloading and (b) partial offloading.

(a) Binary offloading: Binary offloading, also known as "0-1 offloading", means that the entire computing task is either completely processed locally or completely offloaded [26]. Typically, computing tasks in this state are indivisible. Here, "0" and "1" are indicators of whether the task is to be unloaded. In general, "0" means the entire task is completed locally, "1" means it is offloaded elsewhere. When a task is completed locally, the computing time, energy consumption, and cost to complete the task are determined by the computing power of the local device. When tasks are offloaded to other nodes for completion, the computing time mainly includes task transmission time and task completion time. Here, energy consumption mainly includes task transmission energy consumption and task execution energy consumption. Likewise, cost mainly includes transmission cost and execution cost. From this perspective, factors that affect offloading efficiency include wireless channel conditions, wireless bandwidth, and the computing power of the destination node (i.e., the node to which the task is offloaded). The main research on binary offloading involves the association between tasks and target nodes, that is, determining to offload a specific task to the target node among various tasks and target nodes.

(b) Partial offloading: Partial offloading allows flexible splitting of tasks, which means tasks can be divided into separate parts. The study of partial offloading is to determine how much of the entire task can be offloaded and how it can be offloaded to the destination node [27]. Generally, a ratio called "offload ratio" is set to represent the proportion of offloading some tasks. Partial offloading involves two parts of task processing, the local processing part and the offloading part. Therefore, task processing performance is determined by the computing time, energy consumption and cost of processing tasks locally as well as at the destination. Usually, various incentive mechanism methods such as game theory, auction theory, etc., are applied in the research of partial offloading. The purpose is to determine the optimal offloading strategy and maximize the interests of all parties. In fact, in addition to determining and optimizing offloading strategies to achieve various QoS requirements, research on partial offloading also involves the association between task offloading and target nodes. In most existing research, binary offloading or partial offloading problems cannot be solved alone and thus are usually jointly studied with other issues such as resource allocation, edge caching, etc.

8.3.2.2 Resource allocation

Resource allocation is also an important research issue in edge computing [28]. By reasonably allocating resources, computing tasks can be accomplished more effectively. Generally, research on resource allocation mainly involves the allocation of computing resources, communication resources, and storage resources. Here, computing resources usually refer to CPU cycles and resource blocks. Communication resources refer to wireless resources used for data transmission during computing offloading, including bandwidth, spectrum, power, links, etc. Storage resources cache resources related to computing tasks (such as video on demand, AR/VR, road monitoring, etc.) to the edge of the network, thereby reducing service response time and network burden. Here, the allocation of storage resources also corresponds to edge caching. Currently, a few studies only focus on allocating one resource, while most studies consider joint resource allocation.

(1) Single resource: Existing work involving single resource allocation mainly focuses on the allocation of computing or communication resources. For example, in studies that consider communication resource allocation, most of them focus on optimal transmission power or bandwidth allocation strategies, so that system overhead can be minimized during task offloading [29].

(2) Computing and communication resource: The offloading process usually involves the joint allocation of communication and computing resources. For example, in the process of task offloading, in addition to considering the optimal communication resource allocation decision, the optimal computing resource allocation decision also needs to be considered [30]. In other words, communication resource allocation usually determines the transmission efficiency of tasks, while computing resource allocation determines the execution efficiency of tasks.
(3) Computing, communication, and storage resource: Many works consider communication, computing, and storage resources simultaneously in the resource allocation problem [31]. In recent years, the popularity of edge intelligence has attracted extensive attention from academia and industry. In the edge intelligence framework, the allocation optimization of computing, communication and cache resources has been discussed by many researchers.

Since the user's resources requirements are uncertain, the workload of the edge computing system will also fluctuate. The workload uncertainty may lead to problems such as over-allocation or under-allocation of computing resources. If too many computing resources are allocated, the resources provided to users will be greater than their actual needs, which will generate unnecessary additional overhead. In addition, if computing resources are insufficiently allocated, the resources allocated to users are less than their actual needs, which may result in incomplete tasks and poor QoS. Therefore, dynamically provisioning (allocating) appropriate amounts of computing resources to users is an important issue. The purpose is to minimize system costs and meet users' QoS requirements.

Currently, research on resource provisioning in edge computing can be divided into two categories: (a) task allocation. From the user's perspective, it is a passive resource provisioning. The task allocation problem in edge computing refers to the optimal resource provisioning problem between users and edge devices [32]. (b) Resource placement. From the perspective of the resource provider, this is a proactive resource provisioning. Resource placement mainly includes the decentralization of cloud services to the edge, optimal deployment of ES, allocation of edge resources, and placement of virtual edge resources [33].

8.3.2.3 Edge caching

Edge caching is also one of the common research issues in edge computing [34]. Usually, edge caching uses the storage resources of ES to store relevant content, which can be directly applied without downloading directly from the cloud. Without edge caching, content requests from mobile users are typically served by the remote content servers (e.g., web servers). When mobile users retrieve the same popular content from remote servers, they need to send the same file repeatedly, which may cause duplicate traffic and network congestion. Therefore, by caching popular content that users need at the edge closer to users, the delay in transmission can be reduced and repeated transmissions can be avoided. Additionally, as storage costs decrease, deploying cache at the edge becomes more cost-effective.

Currently, edge caching has the following advantages. First, with edge caching, content is placed closer to the user at the edge of the network, so it reduces the latency for users to request content. Second, edge caching avoids large amounts of repeated data transmission, thereby reducing traffic overhead. Third, mobile edge caching helps reduce energy consumption. For example, when the requested data is cached at the micro base station, the energy consumption of the macro base station for sending the data can be avoided. Fourth, spectral efficiency can be improved through edge caching. For example, when multiple users request the same content, the base station can transmit cached files via multicast sharing the same spectrum. Fifth, edge caching can use network information collected by ES (such as user preferences, file popularity, user social information, etc.) to improve caching efficiency. In this way, cached content can be kept popular and highly available, improving the performance advantages of edge caching [35].

Importantly, where, how, and what to cache at the edge are key research questions that often need to be addressed.

(1) Where to cache refers to choosing the most appropriate cache location to cache content. Typically, content caching can be done by leveraging the mobile device's own storage space. This cached content can then be shared between end devices via Device-to-Device communication. In addition, popular content can also be cached at base stations, such as Small Base Stations and Macro Base Stations, etc.

(2) How to cache involves the selection of cache standards and the design of cache solutions. In order to improve the performance of mobile edge cache, the following goals should be ensured. First, a high cache hit rate needs to be ensured. Cache hit rate refers to the ratio of the number of cached files requested by the user to the total number of files in the cache. Second, the caching scheme should be designed to improve both energy efficiency and spectral efficiency. Third, consideration should be given to minimizing content retrieval delays, which directly affect users' QoE. Fourth, caching popular content at the edge can offload traffic from the backhaul link, so maximizing traffic offloading can also be one of the goals of caching.

Several caching schemes have been studied recently. Depending on whether content is cached after or before the user requests it, it can be divided into responsive and active caching. According to the location of content cache, it can also be divided into centralized cache and distributed cache. Centralized caching uses a central controller to determine all content caching options. Instead, distributed caching makes decisions for local caching based on information from neighboring user equipment or base stations. In addition, since edge nodes have limited cache space, designing a cache strategy for each node individually may result in underutilization of the cache. Thus, collaborative caching solves this problem, which allows different cache nodes to share content with each other.

(3) Deciding what to cache requires understanding content request patterns. Content types include multimedia files (such as videos and documents) or IoT data, which have more dimensions and shorter life cycles. Making decisions in the

optimal manner without understanding the request patterns is challenging. In order to increase the probability that a specific content will be requested, the popularity of the content and user preferences need to be predicted.

In fact, the edge caching process is divided into the following stages: (a) Content request stage: The request is initiated by the mobile user. (b) Content exploration phase: Search the system network for the requested content to determine whether the content has been cached. (c) Content delivery stage: Deliver the requested content to mobile users. (d) Content update stage: According to the popularity of cached content, cached content with low request rate is replaced with more popular cached content [36].

8.3.3 Optimization objectives in edge computing

Generally, optimization objects in edge computing include latency, energy consumption, cost, utility, etc. They will be introduced one by one below. The specific classification of this part is shown in Figure 8.4.

8.3.3.1 Latency

From the perspective of the optimization goal of the current study, latency is a key performance indicator that affects user QoE [37]. For delay-sensitive applications, designing a resource allocation algorithm to reduce latency is one of the main research directions. Typically, edge systems have limited computing, communication, and storage resources. If multiple latency-sensitive task requests are sent to the edge simultaneously, not only the latency requirements must be considered, but also the constraints of resource capacity and energy consumption must be weighed. This will be a complex optimization problem. In resource allocation, the delay of a task usually includes (a) local computing time; (b) transmission time for task offloading; (c) edge or cloud processing time; and (d) transmission time for result return. In general, since the data volume of task results is small, the time for result return is usually ignored in actual calculations. Currently, most research focuses on establishing latency models for specific application scenarios. Then, the optimization problem is formulated by

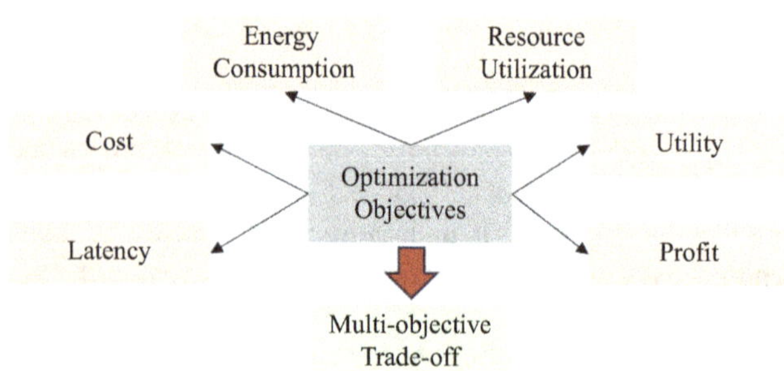

Figure 8.4 Classification of optimization objectives

considering various constraints to reduce the latency, and finally solved by different algorithms.

8.3.3.2 Energy consumption

Energy consumption is one of the important performance indicators of user QoE in edge computing, especially for small smart devices [38]. The energy consumption generated in edge computing scenarios mainly includes (a) energy consumption of local computing; (b) offloading energy consumption; (c) energy consumption of processing tasks at the edge or cloud; and (d) energy consumption of transmitting results back. This corresponds to the latency incurred during task processing. Therefore, in addition to several studies aimed at reducing energy consumption, there are also some studies aimed at reducing both latency and energy consumption. Furthermore, recent studies consider the terminal device to have energy harvesting and wireless charging functions while minimizing energy consumption. For example, combining edge computing with wireless power transfer technology can fully utilize energy.

8.3.3.3 Cost

In edge computing, cost minimization is also one of the performance indicators studied. This is generally a comprehensive performance index established on the premise of satisfying user service quality [39]. From the perspective of task completion, energy consumption and time overhead will be incurred during task offloading and calculation. However, from the perspective of the system or resource provider, the resources occupied by transmission and processing tasks will incur costs. Specifically, when tasks are offloaded, their costs include energy costs (transmitting and processing tasks), costs of using communication channels for transmission, and costs of processing tasks at the edge. Current research generally targets cost minimization and then seeks the best solution by establishing different cost models.

8.3.3.4 Utility

Utility in edge computing refers to the satisfaction that users or other entities obtain under a certain design solution [40]. Usually, there are different utility function design methods for different entities. Specifically, according to different optimization goals, different indicators can be incorporated into the utility function through various mathematical transformations, such as data transmission rate, latency, energy consumption, cost, etc. Here, mathematical transformations mainly include reciprocals, logarithms, weighted sums, etc. Finally, an effective optimization algorithm is usually designed with the goal of maximizing utility.

8.3.3.5 Profit

In general, profits are measured from the perspective of edge service providers deploying, allocating, and scheduling resources for users [41]. Profit is calculated by subtracting the service provider's operating costs from the fees paid by users. Usually, under the conditions of satisfying user QoS, the profit maximization problem can be solved, and then specific solutions (such as game theory, matching theory, auction) can be proposed. Similar to the profit maximization problem, several studies also aim at maximizing social welfare in edge computing systems.

8.3.3.6 Resource utilization

Resource utilization is measured by edge resource providers. Since edge resources are limited compared with resources in the cloud, the utilization of edge resources becomes important as the number of users increases [42]. Therefore, appropriate resource scheduling strategies can make full use of edge resources while meeting user needs. The goal of the most current work is to maximize resource utilization. Here, resource utilization is defined as the ratio of resource usage to total resources.

8.3.3.7 Multi-objective trade-off

In view of the above different optimization objectives, some studies also consider trade-offs between different objectives [43]. Typically, a trade-off between two goals, or a trade-off between three goals, is considered. For example, there is a trade-off between the two goals of minimizing latency and minimizing energy consumption. Since reducing latency requires allocating more computing resources, this will inevitably increase energy consumption. Therefore, it is necessary to balance the two conflicting goals and find the most suitable solution. Here, weight factors are generally introduced to determine the importance between different goals.

8.3.4 Optimization methods in edge computing

In order to solve different optimization problems in edge computing scenarios and achieve the established optimization goals, multiple methods can be applied. This part classifies it into mathematical optimization methods, incentive mechanism methods, and machine learning methods. The specific classification of this part is shown in Figure 8.5.

8.3.4.1 Mathematical optimization methods

Nowadays, there are various mathematical and operations research-related methods used to solve edge computing-related problems, as described below.

Convex optimization method

Optimization models designed in problems such as computation offloading, resource allocation, and edge caching are often non-convex or NP-hard problems. Usually, most studies transform non-convex problems into nearly convex or convex optimization problems and thus solve them using feasible convex optimization methods [44]. For example, Lyapunov optimization, as a stochastic optimization method, can enable real-time decision-making while maintaining sub-optimal performance. Here, the Successive Convex Approximation (SCA) method can also be used to solve non-convex optimization problems. The idea of SCA is to iteratively solve a series of convex optimization problems similar to the original non-convex problem, thereby finding the local optimal solution of the original problem [45].

In addition, many studies first decouple complex optimization problems into multiple sub-problems and then solve them separately. For example, Alternating

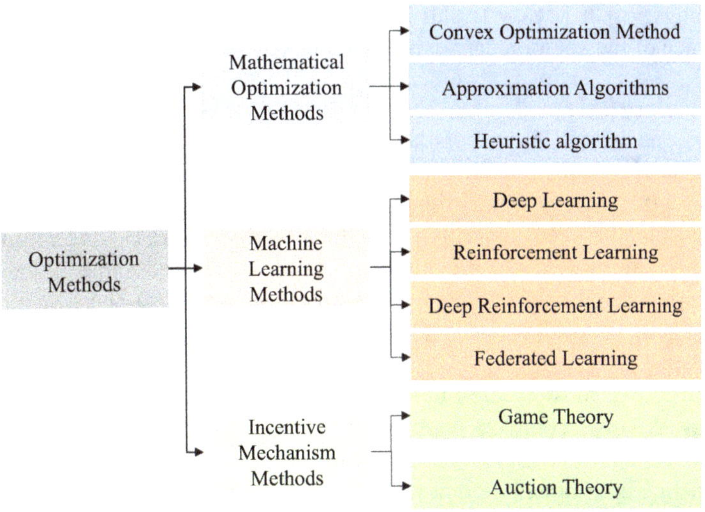

Figure 8.5 Classification of optimization methods

Direction Method of Multipliers (ADMM) is a simple method for solving decomposable convex optimization problems. Using the ADMM algorithm, the original problem can be equivalently decomposed into some solvable sub-problems, and these sub-problems can be solved in parallel [46]. Then, by coordinating the solutions to the sub-problems, the global solution to the original problem is obtained.

In general, the main technologies of convex optimization include Lyapunov technology, decomposition technology, SCA technology and ADMM technology. Technology based on convex optimization has the following advantages: (a) It is mature and widely used. (b) It can easily obtain sub-optimal optimization results. However, methods based on these techniques are often computationally complex and challenging to deal with large-scale real-world scenarios.

Approximation algorithms

In addition to traditional convex optimization methods, some studies also use various approximation algorithms to solve non-convex and NP-hard problems in edge computing [47]. In fact, the basic idea of approximation algorithms is to utilize existing approximation methods, such as relaxation, bounded, local search and dynamic programming techniques to solve established NP-hard problems. For example, in the edge-cloud collaborative resource allocation scenario, the optimization problem can be described as a multi-objective optimization problem. It can then be solved by approximation methods of k-means and mixed quadratic programming. In a multi-user edge resource allocation scenario, the scenario can be modeled and then a local search approximation algorithm can be used to solve the NP-hard problem.

Generally, approximation algorithms have the following advantages: (a) Simple, flexible and easy to implement. (b) For complex NP-hard problems, local search algorithms can also be designed. Of course, approximation algorithms also have some shortcomings: (a) It is easy to fall into local optima. (b) Due to randomness, the performance of the solution cannot be guaranteed.

Heuristic algorithm

Currently, one of the most popular methods to solve NP-hard problems is to use heuristic algorithms, including simple heuristic algorithms and meta-heuristic algorithms [48]. In edge computing research, some work utilizes simple heuristic algorithms, such as greedy algorithms, local search algorithms, etc. In addition, meta-heuristic algorithms use principles similar to bionics to abstract some biological phenomena in nature into algorithms. For example, common meta-heuristic algorithms include genetic algorithms, ant colony algorithms, particle swarm optimization, simulated annealing, etc.

In summary, most studies utilize greedy-based and genetic-based heuristic algorithms to solve complex optimization problems. However, simple heuristic algorithms are more efficient, but can easily fall into local optimal solutions. For metaheuristic algorithms, different results may be produced in different runs, causing fluctuations in calculation results and making it difficult to reuse the results. Furthermore, these parameters cannot be adjusted quickly and efficiently.

8.3.4.2 Machine learning methods

In recent years, due to the development of machine learning, advanced Artificial Intelligence (AI) technologies, such as deep learning and reinforcement learning technologies, have been applied to edge computing. In edge computing related research, when traditional mathematical methods are applied to solve, static complex optimization problems are usually solved. Here, these methods cannot make optimal decisions based on the dynamic environment. On the contrary, various machine learning methods have shown their unique advantages in complex dynamic environments in edge computing.

Deep learning

Due to its multi-layer network structure, deep learning has a stronger ability to extract advanced features from large amounts of data than traditional machine learning algorithms. Here, commonly used deep learning models include Deep Neural Networks (DNN), convolutional neural networks, recurrent neural networks, etc. This enables deep learning to autonomously learn high-level features from raw data, allowing it to efficiently perform classification and prediction tasks [49]. For example, in edge caching scenarios, based on historical cache data and content request records, deep learning methods can be used to predict the probability of future content requests. Then, based on the prediction results, the corresponding content can be cached at the edge, thereby improving the cache hit rate and system performance.

Reinforcement learning

Unlike machine learning methods that rely on static data, reinforcement learning is a method that trains models through dynamic interaction with the environment. The core idea is to receive the environmental state through the agent, and then take actions based on historical experience to maximize rewards. Since reinforcement learning is good at solving decision-making problems, recent studies have adopted reinforcement learning algorithms in decision-making for resource management, allocation, and scheduling in edge computing [50].

A typical algorithm in reinforcement learning is the Q-learning algorithm. During each iteration, the Q-learning algorithm determines the optimal action based on the current state and calculates the expected cumulative reward, called the Q-value. However, as the environment becomes more complex, the state space and action space will expand exponentially, which will lead to slower convergence and consume a lot of memory.

Deep reinforcement learning

Currently, reinforcement learning has difficulty in converging when faced with complex states and action spaces. Therefore, in order to solve this problem, various DNN in deep learning are introduced into reinforcement learning. The learning ability of DNN can solve the problem of overcomplexity of classical reinforcement learning methods. For example, combining DNN with Q-learning, the deep Q-network method is proposed, which uses DNN to approximate the Q-value. Compared with classic reinforcement learning algorithms, deep reinforcement learning has three advantages when dealing with high-complexity edge computing problems. First, it is capable of handling high dimensional and complex systems. Second, it can learn the regularity of the system environment. Finally, it is able to make optimal decisions based on current and past long-term rewards. Therefore, many deep reinforcement learning algorithms have been used to optimize control decision-making problems in edge computing scenarios [51].

In general, various deep reinforcement learning methods for edge computing have the following advantages: (1) It has strong parallel processing capabilities. (2) It has strong distributed storage and learning capabilities. (3) It has associative memory function and can fully approximate complex nonlinear relationships. Meanwhile, it also has the following shortcomings: (1) It requires a large number of training parameters. (2) It is a black box process, the learning process cannot be observed, and the output results are difficult to interpret, which affects the credibility and acceptability of the results. (3) The training time is long and it may fall into the local optimal solution or fail to achieve the learning purpose.

Federated learning

Federated learning is a machine learning method. It can be trained on multiple distributed edge devices or servers without exchanging local data samples. Here, different local users do not need to push all raw data on the central server for training, but train the model locally. Then, the model parameters are aggregated into a global model on a central server. As a distributed machine learning algorithm, federated learning not only leverages the advantages of machine learning in solving dynamic resource scheduling problems, but also protects user and data privacy [52].

Compared with traditional centralized machine learning algorithms, federated learning has the following advantages: (1) The training process is performed on distributed devices, and there is no need to upload local data to a dedicated server for centralized training. This not only protects user privacy, but also reduces the burden of data transmission. (2) Users only need to upload the training parameters of the model, and the parameters synthesized by multiple devices are fed back to the user. This can effectively reduce training time and reduce latency. But it also has the following shortcomings. (1) Training involving multiple devices requires ensuring the synchronization of training. (2) Distributed methods are more susceptible to malicious attacks.

8.3.4.3 Incentive mechanism methods

Due to individual rationality and selfishness, it is difficult for users to actively complete related computing tasks without incentives. Therefore, an incentive mechanism is needed to drive users to complete tasks. At present, incentive mechanisms have been widely studied, and a variety of incentive methods have been applied in edge computing scenarios.

Game theory

Game theory is a mathematical model based on economic theory, mainly used to solve interaction problems between rational participants [53]. It is mainly divided into cooperative games (alliance games) and non-cooperative games. The game model is mainly divided into three parts: player, action (strategy), and utility. The ultimate goal of all participants is to maximize their own interests. Generally, the game process will reach an equilibrium state, called Nash Equilibrium (NE). At this time, this indicates that all individuals participating in the game are satisfied with the current state. Meanwhile, no individual is willing to unilaterally change their decision-making. Here, the most classic model in game theory is the Stackelberg game.

The Stackelberg game divides the players into leaders and followers. The leader first gives the strategy, and the followers determine their own strategy based on the leader's strategy. Likewise, the final equilibrium state of a Stackelberg game is called a Stackelberg equilibrium [54]. For example, in a multi-edge server collaborative offloading scenario, different ES not only need to determine their own offloading strategies, but also need to determine collaborative strategies. Each edge service wants to maximize its own interests, so it is necessary to use game theory methods to find the optimal balance strategy between different ES.

In general, methods based on game theory have the following advantages: (1) Simple, flexible, and easy to implement. (2) Practical and reasonable for participants. However, it also has the following shortcomings: (1) The solution in the equilibrium state is only a solution that is satisfactory to many parties, but it is not necessarily the global optimal solution. (2) It requires continuous iteration to achieve NE.

Auction theory

The auction mechanism is also introduced from an economic perspective and then widely used in research on edge computing-related issues [55]. In a common auction scheme, entities with tasks to be processed act as bidders, and entities that provide task processing services act as sellers. A trusted entity acts as a third-party auctioneer to manage transactions and make decisions. In order to easily understand the auction

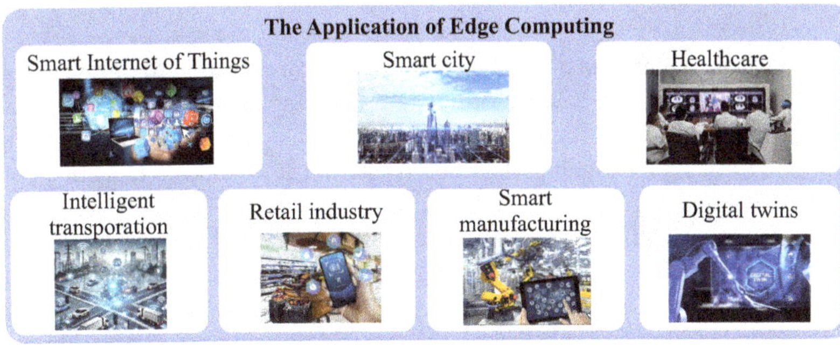

Figure 8.6 The application of edge computing

concept, an example is introduced in detail below. For example, the terminal device will first issue computing tasks and rewards for completing the tasks. Then, the edge server that can provide computing services submits a bid to the system, after analyzing the rewards that can be obtained by completing the computing tasks. Finally, the system assigns the task to the edge server with the highest bid. It should be noted that through the auction process, the entities participating in the auction is able to maximize their own interests.

In addition, reverse auction is one of the most commonly used auction methods [56,57]. Obviously, compared with the forward auction process, the reverse auction reverses this process. Here, buyers bid in a reverse auction, and sellers decide their strategies based on the corresponding bids. Reverse auctions are also widely used among platforms and participants. The main goal is to minimize platform costs and maximize participants' benefits. Reverse auctions are generally divided into two steps: selecting the winner and determining the pricing strategy. The platform selects which participants to perform the task based on the bidding, and then determines the specific bidding strategy. Moreover, some studies also distinguish between online reverse auctions and offline reverse auctions.

Similar to the game theory method, the method based on the auction mechanism has the following advantages: (1) It can realize the economic benefits of the trade-off between requests and services. (2) It can be applied to actual scenarios of edge computing. Likewise, the disadvantages are as follows: (1) Its solution is not necessarily the global optimal solution. (2) There may be additional overhead associated with a third party used to manage the auction process.

8.4 The application of edge computing

Various emerging applications are major factors in the development of edge computing. Since various applications have strict requirements on latency, energy consumption, cost, privacy, etc., edge computing plays an important role in many application scenarios, as shown in Figure 8.6.

8.4.1 Smart IoT

In smart IoT, data generated by a large number of sensors requires real-time responses. Edge computing can perform data processing near the device and reduce the time of transmission to the cloud [58]. Applying edge computing in intelligent IoT has the following advantages. The first is low latency and high real-time performance. Specifically, edge computing processes data close to IoT devices, achieving lower latency and enabling smart devices to make real-time decisions more quickly. The second is to reduce the burden on the cloud. This is because edge computing reduces the need to transmit large amounts of data to the cloud, thereby reducing the burden on cloud servers and relieving network pressure.

For example, when applied in smart homes, devices can analyze user behavior through edge computing to achieve low-latency intelligent control, such as automatic temperature and lighting adjustment. In addition, when applied in real-time monitoring of the Industrial IoT, edge computing is used to monitor equipment status in real time, predict maintenance needs, and improve production efficiency.

The Philips Hue smart lighting system is an example of application in real-world scenarios [59]. This intelligent lighting system analyzes the user's lighting needs locally on the lamp through edge computing to achieve instant lighting adjustment. In addition, practical applications include John Deere's precision agriculture solutions [60]. By deploying sensors on agricultural equipment, edge computing can be used to monitor soil conditions, meteorological conditions, and vegetation growth status in real time. This enables farmers to adjust irrigation and fertilization plans based on real-time data, improving agricultural production efficiency.

8.4.2 Smart city

In smart cities, data generated by various sensors and cameras need to be processed in real time, to support city management and improve citizens' lives [61]. Edge computing provides powerful support for real-time urban monitoring and management. By monitoring and responding to various data in real time, edge computing can accelerate the data analysis and decision-making process, thereby improving the efficiency of city operations. For example, by deploying edge devices at intersections, traffic flow data can be processed locally, enabling instant signal adjustments to reduce traffic congestion. In addition, in urban environmental monitoring, edge computing is used to analyze urban environmental data, such as air quality, trash can status, etc. This enables real-time monitoring and management of the urban environment. For example, Cisco Kinetic is a smart city management solution [62]. It realizes functions such as traffic monitoring, environmental monitoring, and infrastructure optimization through edge computing. This helps cities operate more intelligently and efficiently.

8.4.3 Healthcare

In healthcare, real-time monitoring and timely decision-making are critical to patient safety. Fortunately, edge computing can provide low-latency data processing and feedback [63]. By implementing edge computing on medical devices, real-time monitoring and analysis of patient data can be achieved. For example, real-time patient monitoring can be performed. Real-time patient data monitoring on medical devices using edge computing. Current wearable devices can analyze biological signal data in real time, such as real-time monitoring of heart rate, electrocardiogram, etc. This enables medical staff to understand the patient's condition in a timely manner and improve the real-time nature of medical services. Meanwhile, this also plays an important role in telemedicine. In particular, edge computing + 5G solutions can provide real-time remote diagnosis and treatment with low latency. In addition, edge computing reduces data transmission risks. By processing sensitive patient data on the device, the risk of transmitting data to the cloud is reduced. In specific cases, for example, the Philips Emergency Intensive Care Unit program can monitor patient data in the intensive care unit in real time through edge computing. This enables medical staff to remotely monitor and manage patients in real time, helping to improve the efficiency of medical care.

8.4.4 Intelligent transportation

In intelligent transportation systems, edge computing enables vehicles and transportation infrastructure to respond to changing traffic conditions more quickly [64]. By performing data processing on edge devices on the road, edge computing provides real-time perception and decision support for vehicles. In addition, the traffic monitoring system collects and analyzes traffic flow data in real time through edge computing, which can improve traffic management efficiency. Then, in autonomous driving, real-time decision support can be provided for vehicles. Using edge computing, vehicles can obtain surrounding environment information more quickly, which can improve the real-time nature of autonomous driving decisions and avoid special events. Lastly, in traffic monitoring and optimization, traffic flow is monitored in real time through edge nodes, and traffic lights can be adjusted according to needs to alleviate traffic congestion. The Waymo self-driving car project is a real-life example [65]. Waymo, a subsidiary of Google, uses edge computing technology to process vehicle sensor data in real time. This can support real-time decision-making of autonomous vehicles and promote the development of autonomous driving technology.

8.4.5 Retail industry

The retail industry needs to understand customer behavior in real time and provide a personalized shopping experience. The application of edge computing in the retail industry enables stores to provide a more personalized and real-time shopping experience [66]. Here, by applying edge computing to cameras and sensors in stores, retailers can analyze customer behavior in real time. They can then receive personalized product recommendations and promotions. In addition, real-time management of the supply chain is also possible. Through real-time monitoring of inventory at edge nodes, the efficiency of the supply chain can be improved. The Amazon Go unmanned store is a typical example [67]. It enables unmanned checkout and real-time shopping analysis through edge computing. Therefore, a smarter and more convenient shopping experience can be provided to customers.

8.4.6 Smart manufacturing

Smart manufacturing refers to the intelligentization of industrial operations through AI and big data technology. In smart manufacturing, industrial equipment needs to be controlled in real time based on generated data with security and privacy. Currently, the application of edge computing has become the development direction of the smart manufacturing industry [68]. It can improve system performance, ensure data security and privacy, and reduce operating costs.

With edge computing, real-time production monitoring and optimization are possible. For example, deploying edge sensors on production lines can monitor equipment status and production efficiency in real time, thereby helping manufacturers discover and solve problems promptly. In addition, the risk of production line failure can be reduced. By performing edge computing on the production site, data can be processed in a timely manner. This can reduce the risk of production line failure due to network delays. Here, Siemens' Digital Enterprise Suite is a real-world example [69]. It uses edge computing technology to achieve real-time monitoring and optimization of the manufacturing process, improving the efficiency of industrial manufacturing.

8.4.7 Digital Twins (DT)

DT refers to the modeling of physical objects or systems in virtual space using digital technology and simulation techniques. This enables real-time monitoring and prediction of the behavior of physical objects or systems. In the implementation of digital twin technology, edge computing plays a vital role. This computing mode of edge computing can greatly reduce data transmission latency, improve response speed, and ensure data security and privacy.

1. Real-time data acquisition and processing: In DT, real-time data acquisition is the basis for building virtual models. Edge computing devices are usually deployed near the data source, so they can capture and process data generated by various sensors in real time. After pre-processing, these data are uploaded to the cloud for further analysis and storage, thereby ensuring the real-time and accuracy of the data.
2. Low latency and efficient response: Digital twins require the system to respond quickly to changes in the real world. Edge computing greatly reduces the latency of data transmission by distributing computing tasks to devices at the edge of the network. This enables the system to respond to changes in the real world within milliseconds or even microseconds, making real-time control and management possible.
3. Data security and privacy protection: In DT, a large amount of sensitive data and privacy information are involved. Edge computing avoids the risk of uploading a large amount of raw data to the cloud by processing data locally. Meanwhile,

combined with advanced encryption technology and access control strategies, data security and privacy can be effectively protected.

4. Intelligent analysis and decision support: Edge computing is not only responsible for data collection and processing, but also has certain intelligent analysis capabilities. Using algorithms such as machine learning and deep learning, edge computing devices can analyze and mine data in real-time. Then valuable information is extracted to provide decision support for upper-level applications.

8.5 The technology challenges of edge computing

Along with ten years of development, edge computing has been well researched. However, with the advancement of various computing technologies, edge computing still faces many key issues. Therefore, this part will discuss several current research challenges and future research directions.

8.5.1 Security and privacy

Edge computing has demonstrated its efficient and distributed data processing capabilities. But it also faces a series of security and privacy issues, as well as corresponding technical challenges. We first discuss it from the perspective of layered architecture, and then conduct further analysis based on real-world scenarios.

8.5.1.1 The perspective of layered architecture

(1) System level: In recent years, security and privacy issues in edge computing have begun to receive attention [70]. Currently, the multi-layered architecture in edge computing makes edge systems vulnerable to malicious attacks. For example, edge nodes may experience system failures or failures caused by attacks, which may threaten the reliability and robustness of the entire edge system. Therefore, it is necessary to study the reliability of edge computing systems in terms of resource scheduling, task allocation, etc., so as to ensure safe and stable operation at the system level. Specifically, measures such as system robustness enhancement mechanisms and intrusion detection strategies can be developed.

(2) Service level: Most of the existing research on computing offloading and service provision is conducted in a safe and trusted environment by default. However, many security issues should be considered. For example, whether the offloaded edge node is trustworthy, whether users and ES trust each other, how to protect the data privacy and security of edge nodes, etc. Therefore, authentication mechanisms need to be designed for users covered by specific edge nodes. In addition, edge data centers also need to add privacy modules to improve the credibility of ES.

(3) Data level: During resource scheduling, especially during computation offloading, a large amount of users' private information will be collected or shared through collaborative methods. In most studies, data interactions between users

and ES are unconditionally trusted, thus easily accessible. However, in practical application scenarios such as smart homes and smart healthcare, these data will involve users' privacy and even business secrets. Since there is no privacy protection mechanism, it is easily leaked during transmission and processing, causing huge losses. Therefore, it is necessary to design trust mechanisms or privacy protection strategies for edges and users in the future.

Recently, Secure Access Service Edge (SASE), a security framework, has begun to be applied. It combines software-defined wide area network and zero-trust security solutions into a converged cloud delivery platform. Therefore, it can securely connect users, systems, endpoints, and remote networks to applications. SASE has four main characteristics: (1) Identity-driven: Access is granted based on the identity of users and devices. (2) Cloud-native: Both infrastructure and security solutions are cloud-delivered. (3) Support all edges: Every physical, digital, and logical edge is protected. (4) Global distribution: Users are secure no matter where they work. Overall, the main goal of the SASE architecture is to provide a seamless user experience, optimized connectivity, and comprehensive security to support the dynamic secure access needs of digital enterprises. Through SASE, enterprises can achieve higher security, flexibility, and scalability to support globally distributed users and applications, driving the digital transformation and business development of the enterprise.

8.5.1.2 The perspective of layered architecture

(1) Intelligent transportation: First, there are problems of data tampering and false information injection. Malicious attackers may tamper with road condition data or inject false signals, interfere with traffic management systems, and even cause accidents. For example, attackers hijack edge nodes and send false traffic light signals, causing vehicles to misjudge priority. In addition, the physical security of the equipment is also an issue that needs to be considered. For example, edge devices deployed on the roadside are susceptible to physical intrusion or malicious tampering, such as connecting malicious USB devices to inject viruses. Efficient data integrity verification technologies can be relied upon, such as in conjunction with blockchain tamper resistance. Moreover, a trusted execution environment can also be applied to ensure that the internal processing logic of the device is not tampered with by the outside world.

(2) Industrial Internet of Things (IIoT): In this scenario, Denial of Service (DoS) attacks may occur. Attackers may exhaust edge node resources through DoS attacks, causing equipment monitoring interruptions or production line shutdowns. For example, attackers send a large amount of false sensing data to edge devices, causing them to overload. In addition, there may be problems with malicious device tampering. For example, if edge devices in factories are hacked, they may be used to distribute malicious instructions or leak production secrets. To solve these problems, it is necessary to design anomaly detection mechanisms in resource-constrained environments, such as AI-based traffic analysis. Meanwhile, it is also necessary to study the security coordination mechanism between edge nodes to prevent single points from being compromised.

(3) Smart home: In this scenario, there will be privacy data leakage issues. Smart home devices record a large amount of user behavior and voice data, which may be stolen or abused. For example, smart speakers may leak user voice commands due to vulnerabilities and be illegally obtained by third parties. In addition, there may also be device disguise attacks. For example, attackers may disguise themselves as legitimate devices to access the home network, thereby stealing or tampering with data. In order to solve these problems, it is necessary to study the device identity authentication mechanism based on behavior patterns to prevent device disguise. Meanwhile, the use of homomorphic encryption technology can be efficiently implemented in resource-constrained edge devices.

8.5.2 Model and architecture

(1) Computing and communication model: In the model definition of basic computing tasks, processing density (in units of CPU cycles/bit) is usually used to reflect the relationship between the task data size and its required computing power. Obviously, this is a representation of a linear relationship. However, in actual scenarios, this approach is not entirely applicable due to the different processing densities of different types of tasks. Therefore, more flexible computing models need to be explored [71]. In addition, during the computation offloading process, data transmission rate is a key issue for communication resource scheduling. Current research is mainly based on Shannon's theorem, and a small part of it considers interference such as channels. In actual scenarios, terminal devices and ES live in complex environments with extremely harsh channel conditions, such as high mobility, shielding, and interference. However, for current communication models, the actual data transmission rate cannot reach the theoretical value. Therefore, it is necessary to design more targeted communication models based on real-life scenarios.

(2) Green energy: In edge computing scenarios, servers or devices consume energy to complete computing tasks. With the development trend of carbon neutrality, there is a need to achieve energy conservation and maintain longer battery life of IoT devices. Here, the use of renewable green resources to provide energy security will be a development trend. This can significantly reduce carbon emissions and environmental pollution. In addition, devices capable of energy harvesting could also be considered in the future, thereby promoting sustainable development [72].

(3) Heterogeneous architecture: The current edge computing architecture is mainly divided into three layers, including the end layer, edge layer, and cloud layer. Then, based on this architecture, optimization problems in numerous edge computing scenarios were studied [73]. However, the integration of Space-Air-Ground Integrated Network (SAGIN) is the future development trend. Under the heterogeneous architecture of space and ground, SAGIN combined with edge computing can provide richer services. However, more types of heterogeneous nodes (end devices, ES, drones, and satellites) make resource scheduling and management complicated. In addition, this scenario is more

restricted in terms of time and space, thus facing many challenges. In the future, more effective resource management and scheduling methods need to be studied.

8.5.3 Dynamic

Mobility is an important challenging feature of edge computing [74]. Especially for vehicles, the dynamic connection of the network and the service connection between different sub-areas are issues that need to be faced. Frequent movement of vehicles has a significant impact on task offloading and caching decisions. The offloading decision and caching decision at the current moment may not be applicable to the user at the next moment, or even if the user has moved out of the service range of the current edge node. In addition, moving vehicles also have an impact on communication stability. Therefore, it is necessary to design a mobility management strategy to enable vehicles to access ES uninterruptedly, thereby improving service stability. Then, through vehicle trajectory prediction, targeted deployment decisions can be made in advance, thereby improving its QoS.

8.5.4 Development opportunity

With the development of emerging technologies such as the Metaverse and Generative AI, it has brought opportunities for the development of edge computing.

(1) Further development of edge intelligence: With the continuous advancement of AI and machine learning technology, edge devices will become more intelligent. Improvements in edge intelligence will allow devices to better understand, adapt, and respond to their surroundings, allowing higher levels of autonomous decision-making and behavior [75].
(2) Quantum edge computing: The development of quantum computing is expected to introduce new computing models and algorithms in the field of edge computing. Quantum edge computing promises to provide more powerful computing capabilities, especially when large-scale and complex problems need to be processed [76].
(3) Deep integration of edge computing and 5G/6G: With the comprehensive construction of 5G networks, edge computing and 5G will be more deeply integrated. Edge computing can better utilize the high bandwidth and low latency of 5G to promote the development of more application scenarios, such as AR, VR, and cloud gaming [77].
(4) Multi-modal sensing of smart edge devices: Future edge devices may integrate more sensors and multi-modal sensing technologies, such as vision, hearing, touch, etc. This enables a more comprehensive perception and understanding of the surrounding environment [78].
(5) Integration of the Metaverse and edge computing: The Metaverse is a digital virtual world that is interconnected with the real world. By combining the Metaverse with edge computing, richer AR and VR experiences can be

achieved. It enables edge devices to perceive, understand and respond to the virtual world more intelligently [79].

(6) Synergy between generative AI and edge computing: Generative AI can generate realistic images, sounds, text, and other content by learning data distribution. Edge computing provides lower latency and more efficient inference capabilities for generative AI. This makes it possible to deploy generative AI applications on edge nodes such as mobile devices and smart cameras. This will promote more innovative application scenarios, such as smart cameras, real-time voice translation, etc [80].

8.6 Conclusion

This chapter provided a detailed introduction to edge computing. First, the development history of edge computing is introduced, and the relevant architecture of edge computing is explained. Then, the basic optimization models and optimization problems in edge computing are introduced. Meanwhile, various optimization methods applied to edge computing are also discussed. Furthermore, the application of edge computing in various real-world scenarios is also introduced. Finally, existing challenges and future research directions are discussed.

References

[1] Wang Z, Cao Y, Jiang K, *et al.* When crowdsensing meets smart cities: A comprehensive survey and new perspectives. IEEE Communications Surveys & Tutorials. 2025;27(2):1101–1151.

[2] Xing L. Reliability in Internet of Things: Current status and future perspectives. IEEE Internet of Things Journal. 2020;7(8):6704–6721.

[3] Abbas N, Zhang Y, Taherkordi A, *et al.* Mobile edge computing: A survey. IEEE Internet of Things Journal. 2017;5(1):450–465.

[4] Luo Q, Hu S, Li C, *et al.* Resource scheduling in edge computing: A survey. IEEE Communications Surveys & Tutorials. 2021;23(4):2131–2165.

[5] He S, Shi K, Liu C, *et al.* Collaborative sensing in internet of things: A comprehensive survey. IEEE Communications Surveys & Tutorials. 2022;24(3):1435–1474.

[6] Zhang Y, Lan X, Ren J, *et al.* Efficient computing resource sharing for mobile edge-cloud computing networks. IEEE/ACM Transactions on Networking. 2020;28(3):1227–1240.

[7] Cao K, Hu S, Shi Y, *et al.* A survey on edge and edge-cloud computing assisted cyber-physical systems. IEEE Transactions on Industrial Informatics. 2021;17(11):7806–7819.

[8] Babar M, Khan MS, Ali F, *et al.* Cloudlet computing: recent advances, taxonomy, and challenges. IEEE Access. 2021;9:29609–29622.

[9] Costa B, Bachiega Jr J, De Carvalho LR, *et al.* Orchestration in fog computing: A comprehensive survey. ACM Computing Surveys (CSUR). 2022;55(2): 1–34.

[10] Siriwardhana Y, Porambage P, Liyanage M, *et al.* A survey on mobile augmented reality with 5G mobile edge computing: Architectures, applications, and technical aspects. IEEE Communications Surveys & Tutorials. 2021;23(2):1160–1192.

[11] Ali B, Gregory MA, and Li S. Multi-access edge computing architecture, data security and privacy: A review. IEEE Access. 2021;9:18706–18721.

[12] Cao K, Weng J, and Li K. Reliability-driven end–end–edge collaboration for energy minimization in large-scale cyber-physical systems. IEEE Transactions on Reliability. 2024;73(1):230–244.

[13] Long S, Zhang Y, Deng Q, *et al.* An efficient task offloading approach based on multi-objective evolutionary algorithm in cloud-edge collaborative environment. IEEE Transactions on Network Science and Engineering. 2022;10(2):645–657.

[14] Qi J, Zhang H, Li X, *et al.* Edge-edge collaboration based micro-service deployment in edge computing networks. In: 2023 IEEE Wireless Communications and Networking Conference (WCNC). IEEE; 2023. p. 1–6.

[15] Zeng F, Zhang K, Wu L, *et al.* Efficient caching in vehicular edge computing based on edge-cloud collaboration. IEEE Transactions on Vehicular Technology. 2022;72(2):2468–2481.

[16] Mao Y, You C, Zhang J, *et al.* A survey on mobile edge computing: The communication perspective. IEEE Communications Surveys & Tutorials. 2017;19(4):2322–2358.

[17] Liu Y, He Q, Zheng D, *et al.* Data caching optimization in the edge computing environment. IEEE Transactions on Services Computing. 2020;15(4): 2074–2085.

[18] Naouri A, Wu H, Nouri NA, *et al.* A novel framework for mobile-edge computing by optimizing task offloading. IEEE Internet of Things Journal. 2021;8(16):13065–13076.

[19] Sun Z, Sun G, Liu Y, *et al.* BARGAIN-MATCH: A game theoretical approach for resource allocation and task offloading in vehicular edge computing networks. IEEE Transactions on Mobile Computing. 2023;23(2):1655–1673.

[20] Mukherjee M, Kumar V, Kumar S, *et al.* Computation offloading strategy in heterogeneous fog computing with energy and delay constraints. In: ICC 2020–2020 IEEE International Conference on Communications (ICC). IEEE; 2020. p. 1–5.

[21] Liu F, Huang J, and Wang X. Joint task offloading and resource allocation for device-edge-cloud collaboration with subtask dependencies. IEEE Transactions on Cloud Computing. 2023;11(3):3027–3039.

[22] Du M, Wang Y, Ye K, *et al.* Algorithmics of cost-driven computation offloading in the edge-cloud environment. IEEE Transactions on Computers. 2020;69(10):1519–1532.

[23] Wang T, Liang Y, Zhang Y, *et al.* An intelligent dynamic offloading from cloud to edge for smart IoT systems with big data. IEEE Transactions on Network Science and Engineering. 2020;7(4):2598–2607.

[24] Alameddine HA, Sharafeddine S, Sebbah S, *et al.* Dynamic task offloading and scheduling for low-latency IoT services in multi-access edge computing. IEEE Journal on Selected Areas in Communications. 2019;37(3):668–682.

[25] Ko H and Pack S. Distributed device-to-device offloading system: Design and performance optimization. IEEE Transactions on Mobile Computing. 2020;20(10):2949–2960.

[26] Chen G, Wu Q, Liu R, *et al.* IRS aided MEC systems with binary offloading: A unified framework for dynamic IRS beamforming. IEEE Journal on Selected Areas in Communications. 2022;41(2):349–365.

[27] Kuang Z, Li L, Gao J, *et al.* Partial offloading scheduling and power allocation for mobile edge computing systems. IEEE Internet of Things Journal. 2019;6(4):6774–6785.

[28] Xiong X, Zheng K, Lei L, *et al.* Resource allocation based on deep reinforcement learning in IoT edge computing. IEEE Journal on Selected Areas in Communications. 2020;38(6):1133–1146.

[29] Saleem U, Liu Y, Jangsher S, *et al.* Mobility-aware joint task scheduling and resource allocation for cooperative mobile edge computing. IEEE Transactions on Wireless Communications. 2020;20(1):360–374.

[30] Liu X, Yu J, Wang J, *et al.* Resource allocation with edge computing in IoT networks via machine learning. IEEE Internet of Things Journal. 2020;7(4):3415–3426.

[31] Wang L and Zhang G. Joint service caching, resource allocation and computation offloading in three-tier cooperative mobile edge computing system. IEEE Transactions on Network Science and Engineering. 2023;10(6):3343–3353.

[32] Wang S, Chen M, Liu X, *et al.* A machine learning approach for task and resource allocation in mobile-edge computing-based networks. IEEE Internet of Things Journal. 2020;8(3):1358–1372.

[33] Zhang X, Li Z, Lai C, *et al.* Joint edge server placement and service placement in mobile-edge computing. IEEE Internet of Things Journal. 2021;9(13):11261–11274.

[34] Song C, Xu W, Wu T, *et al.* QoE-driven edge caching in vehicle networks based on deep reinforcement learning. IEEE Transactions on Vehicular Technology. 2021;70(6):5286–5295.

[35] Kim M, Cho H, Cui Y, *et al.* Joint service caching and computing resource allocation for edge computing-enabled networks. IEEE Transactions on Wireless Communications. 2023;22(12):9029–9044.

[36] Ma X, Zhou A, Zhang S, *et al.* Cooperative service caching and workload scheduling in mobile edge computing. In: IEEE INFOCOM 2020-IEEE Conference on Computer Communications. IEEE; 2020. p. 2076–2085.

[37] Bai T, Pan C, Deng Y, *et al.* Latency minimization for intelligent reflecting surface aided mobile edge computing. IEEE Journal on Selected Areas in Communications. 2020;38(11):2666–2682.

[38] Ji J, Zhu K, Yi C, *et al.* Energy consumption minimization in UAV-assisted mobile-edge computing systems: Joint resource allocation and trajectory design. IEEE Internet of Things Journal. 2020;8(10):8570–8584.
[39] Zhou H, Wang Z, Zheng H, *et al.* Cost minimization-oriented computation offloading and service caching in mobile cloud-edge computing: An A3C-based approach. IEEE Transactions on Network Science and Engineering. 2023;10(3):1326–1338.
[40] Zhou H, Wang Z, Cheng N, *et al.* Stackelberg-game-based computation offloading method in cloud–edge computing networks. IEEE Internet of Things Journal. 2022;9(17):16510–16520.
[41] Yuan H and Zhou M. Profit-maximized collaborative computation offloading and resource allocation in distributed cloud and edge computing systems. IEEE Transactions on Automation Science and Engineering. 2020;18(3):1277–1287.
[42] Sharif Z, Jung LT, Razzak I, *et al.* Adaptive and priority-based resource allocation for efficient resources utilization in mobile-edge computing. IEEE Internet of Things Journal. 2021;10(4):3079–3093.
[43] Bozorgchenani A, Mashhadi F, Tarchi D, *et al.* Multi-objective computation sharing in energy and delay constrained mobile edge computing environments. IEEE Transactions on Mobile Computing. 2020;20(10):2992–3005.
[44] Zhan C, Hu H, Sui X, *et al.* Completion time and energy optimization in the UAV-enabled mobile-edge computing system. IEEE Internet of Things Journal. 2020;7(8):7808–7822.
[45] Yu Z and Fan G. Joint differential evolution and successive convex approximation in UAV-enabled mobile edge computing. IEEE Access. 2022;10:57413–57426.
[46] Zhou Z, Feng J, Chang Z, *et al.* Energy-efficient edge computing service provisioning for vehicular networks: A consensus ADMM approach. IEEE Transactions on Vehicular Technology. 2019;68(5):5087–5099.
[47] Bhatta D and Mashayekhy L. A bifactor approximation algorithm for cloudlet placement in edge computing. IEEE Transactions on Parallel and Distributed Systems. 2021;33(8):1787–1798.
[48] Mei J, Tong Z, Li K, *et al.* Energy-efficient heuristic computation offloading with delay constraints in mobile edge computing. IEEE Transactions on Services Computing. 2023;16(6):4404–4417.
[49] Muhammad G and Hossain MS. Emotion recognition for cognitive edge computing using deep learning. IEEE Internet of Things Journal. 2021;8(23):16894–16901.
[50] Xiao L, Lu X, Xu T, *et al.* Reinforcement learning-based mobile offloading for edge computing against jamming and interference. IEEE Transactions on communications. 2020;68(10):6114–6126.
[51] Zhou H, Jiang K, Liu X, *et al.* Deep reinforcement learning for energy-efficient computation offloading in mobile-edge computing. IEEE Internet of Things Journal. 2021;9(2):1517–1530.

[52] Mills J, Hu J, and Min G. Multi-task federated learning for personalised deep neural networks in edge computing. IEEE Transactions on Parallel and Distributed Systems. 2021;33(3):630–641.

[53] Ning Z, Dong P, Wang X, *et al.* Mobile edge computing enabled 5G health monitoring for Internet of medical things: A decentralized game theoretic approach. IEEE Journal on Selected Areas in Communications. 2020;39(2):463–478.

[54] Zhou H, Wang Z, Min G, *et al.* UAV-aided computation offloading in mobile-edge computing networks: A Stackelberg game approach. IEEE Internet of Things Journal. 2022;10(8):6622–6633.

[55] Qiu H, Zhu K, Luong NC, *et al.* Applications of auction and mechanism design in edge computing: A survey. IEEE Transactions on Cognitive Communications and Networking. 2022;8(2):1034–1058.

[56] Zhou H, Wu T, Chen X, *et al.* Reverse auction-based computation offloading and resource allocation in mobile cloud-edge computing. IEEE Transactions on Mobile Computing. 2022;22(10):6144–6159.

[57] Wang Z, Cao Y, Zhou H, *et al.* Fairness-aware two-stage hybrid sensing method in vehicular crowdsensing. IEEE Transactions on Mobile Computing. 2024;23(12):11971–11988.

[58] Gong C, Lin F, Gong X, *et al.* Intelligent cooperative edge computing in internet of things. IEEE Internet of Things Journal. 2020;7(10):9372–9382.

[59] Sypalova A, Krivobok L, and Tyschuk Y. Lighting control module in the "smart home" system. 2021.

[60] Yang C. Remote sensing and precision agriculture technologies for crop disease detection and management with a practical application example. Engineering. 2020;6(5):528–532.

[61] Khan LU, Yaqoob I, Tran NH, *et al.* Edge-computing-enabled smart cities: A comprehensive survey. IEEE Internet of Things Journal. 2020;7(10):10200–10232.

[62] Haron H, and binti Zulkanain NNA. Managing information in the smart city: A proposed framework. Journal of Information & Knowledge Management. 2019;9(2).

[63] Li J, Cai J, Khan F, *et al.* A secured framework for SDN-based edge computing in IoT-enabled healthcare system. IEEE Access. 2020;8:135479–135490.

[64] Arthurs P, Gillam L, Krause P, *et al.* A taxonomy and survey of edge cloud computing for intelligent transportation systems and connected vehicles. IEEE Transactions on Intelligent Transportation Systems. 2021;23(7):6206–6221.

[65] Manikandan T, Jayashwanth J, Harish S, *et al.* Self driving car. International Journal of Psychosocial Rehabilitation. 2020;24(5):380–388.

[66] Zhang K, Leng S, He Y, *et al.* Mobile edge computing and networking for green and low-latency Internet of Things. IEEE Communications Magazine. 2018;56(5):39–45.

[67] Hamidi SR, Yusof MAM, Shuhidan SM, *et al.* IR4. 0: unmanned store apps. Indonesian Journal of Electrical Engineering and Computer Science. 2020;17(3):1540–1547.

[68] Lin CC, Deng DJ, Chih YL, *et al.* Smart manufacturing scheduling with edge computing using multiclass deep Q network. IEEE Transactions on Industrial Informatics. 2019;15(7):4276–4284.

[69] Buchta ST. Digital Enterprise Suite for Electronics Industry. Silicon Valley, i4.0 Today; 2018.

[70] Ranaweera P, Jurcut AD, and Liyanage M. Survey on multi-access edge computing security and privacy. IEEE Communications Surveys & Tutorials. 2021;23(2):1078–1124.

[71] Qiu T, Chi J, Zhou X, *et al.* Edge computing in industrial internet of things: Architecture, advances and challenges. IEEE Communications Surveys & Tutorials. 2020;22(4):2462–2488.

[72] Jiang C, Fan T, Gao H, *et al.* Energy aware edge computing: A survey. Computer Communications. 2020;151:556–580.

[73] Zhang Y, Di B, Wang P, *et al.* HetMEC: Heterogeneous multi-layer mobile edge computing in the 6 G era. IEEE Transactions on Vehicular Technology. 2020;69(4):4388–4400.

[74] Ning Z, Dong P, Wang X, *et al.* Distributed and dynamic service placement in pervasive edge computing networks. IEEE Transactions on Parallel and Distributed Systems. 2020;32(6):1277–1292.

[75] Liu Y, Peng M, Shou G, *et al.* Toward edge intelligence: Multiaccess edge computing for 5G and Internet of Things. IEEE Internet of Things Journal. 2020;7(8):6722–6747.

[76] Lin P, Song Q, Wang D, *et al.* Resource management for pervasive-edge-computing-assisted wireless VR streaming in industrial Internet of Things. IEEE Transactions on Industrial Informatics. 2021;17(11):7607–7617.

[77] Ji B, Wang Y, Song K, *et al.* A survey of computational intelligence for 6G: Key technologies, applications and trends. IEEE Transactions on Industrial Informatics. 2021;17(10):7145–7154.

[78] Ren C, Gong C, and Liu L. Task-oriented multimodal communication based on cloud–edge–UAV collaboration. IEEE Internet of Things Journal. 2024;11(1):125–136.

[79] Xu M, Ng WC, Lim WYB, *et al.* A full dive into realizing the edge-enabled metaverse: Visions, enabling technologies, and challenges. IEEE Communications Surveys & Tutorials. 2022;25(1):656–700.

[80] Xu M, Du H, Niyato D, *et al.* Unleashing the power of edge-cloud generative AI in mobile networks: A survey of AIGC services. IEEE Communications Surveys & Tutorials. 2024;26(2):1127–1170.

Chapter 9

Internet of Things and CPS

Jiaxin Hou[1], Haotian Wang[1], Yu'ang Zhang[1] and Yue Cao[1]

9.1 The basic concept of Internet of Things (IoT)

The IoT technology is a broad and profound concept that has witnessed tremendous progress [1] since its inception by American scientist Kevin Ashton in the 1990s. IoT technology harnesses the power of the network to tightly interconnect various physical devices, sensors, and other equipment, enabling them to communicate seamlessly with each other. By leveraging information-sensing devices such as Radio-Frequency Identification (RFID) [2], infrared sensors, global positioning systems, laser scanners, core technologies including wireless communication technologies and cloud computing [3], IoT technology achieves interconnection between objects, empowering these devices and items with human-like capabilities of perception, recognition, location, tracking, monitoring, and management.

In essence, IoT constructs a vast network where not only computers and smartphones but also a myriad of devices, objects, and even entire environments are capable of intelligent identification [1], communication, and interaction through the internet. The core of this concept lies in seamlessly integrating various entities from the physical world into the digital realm, endowing them with unprecedented intelligent capabilities.

The application scope of IoT is extremely broad, encompassing various fields such as smart homes, smart cities, industrial automation, intelligent transportation, healthcare, agricultural monitoring, etc. In smart homes, IoT technology enables electrical appliances like lights, air conditioners, televisions, and others to connect to the internet [4], allowing for remote control and fine-tuned adjustment through smartphones or other smart devices. This significantly enhances the convenience and comfort of daily living. In the realm of smart cities [5], IoT technology enables the gathering and analysis of extensive data, aiding city administrators in more efficient planning and management of urban resources, ultimately enhancing operational effectiveness and safety within the city.

[1]The School of Cyber Science and Engineering, Wuhan University, China

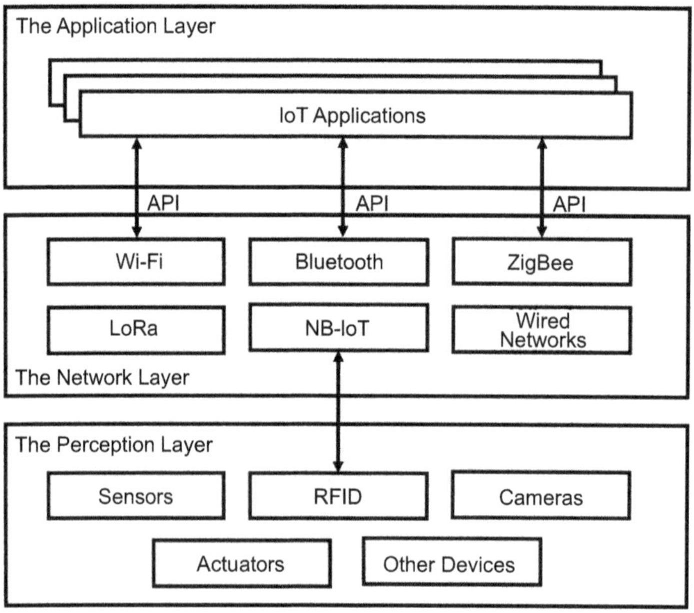

Figure 9.1 Architecture of IoT

9.2 The architecture of IoT

The fundamental architecture of IoT constitutes a multi-layered system designed to achieve seamless integration and interaction between the physical and digital worlds. This framework is typically divided into three basic layers: the perception layer, the network layer, and the application layer [6]. The basic architecture of IoT is illustrated in Figure 9.1.

- The perception layer, as the bottommost tier of the IoT architecture, serves as the sensory organ of IoT, responsible for gathering data from the physical world. This layer encompasses various sensors such as light sensors, sound sensors, motion sensors, RFID tags, cameras, actuators, and other devices. These devices can perceive environmental parameters, monitor object states, identify identity information, and convert these raw data into digital signals, laying the foundation for subsequent processing.
- The network layer, serving as a bridge between the perception layer and the application layer, is responsible for data transmission and communication. Utilizing wireless communication technologies such as Wi-Fi, Bluetooth, ZigBee, LoRa [7], NB-IoT [8], or wired networks, the network layer ensures secure and reliable data transmission among IoT devices, as well as between devices and the cloud. Furthermore, the network layer provides functionalities such as data routing, protocol conversion, and network security, supporting the connectivity of large-scale devices and complex data interactions.

- The application layer, situated at the topmost tier of the IoT architecture, directly interfaces with users and industry applications [9]. Within this layer, utilizing the data and services provided by the network layer, various IoT applications are developed, such as smart home control, industrial remote control, intelligent traffic dispatching, health monitoring management, etc. Through user-friendly interfaces and extensive functionalities, the application layer seamlessly integrates IoT technology with actual business needs, offering unprecedented convenience and intelligent experiences to users and industries alike.

The IoT achieves interconnectivity among things through its fundamental framework comprising three layers: the perception layer, network layer, and application layer. Utilizing devices within the perception layer, it collects environmental data. The network layer then retrieves and processes these data captured by the perception layer. Based on the services provided by the network layer, the application layer enables the development of various IoT applications, thereby realizing a profound integration and interaction between the physical and digital worlds [10]. This framework provides a robust foundation for driving the intelligent development of society and the economy.

The basic architecture of IoT possesses the following four key characteristics:

- **Security and privacy protection**

The layered architecture aids in isolating potential security risks by dividing the IoT system into distinct layers. Each layer possesses its unique security requirements and protection measures, thereby mitigating cross-layer security threats. Additionally, more granular security policies can be formulated tailored to the characteristics of each layer. For instance, at the perception layer, security authentication and access control for devices can be strengthened. At the network layer, data encryption and transmission security strategies can be implemented. At the application layer, management of data access permissions and security audits can be enhanced.

- **Scalability**

The layered architecture divides the IoT system into multiple relatively independent modules, each with its specific functions and responsibilities. This modular design renders the system more flexible, allowing for the addition, deletion, or replacement of modules as needed without affecting the normal operation of other modules. As the network infrastructure evolves, with the continuous growth of IoT devices and expanding business requirements, the system necessitates robust scalability. The layered architecture enables the system to effortlessly accommodate new devices, services, and functions without the need for extensive reconfiguration of the entire system.

- **Device interoperability**

The layered architecture facilitates communication among IoT devices from different vendors and platforms by defining clear layers and interfaces that adhere to unified standards and protocols. This helps break down barriers between devices, enabling cross-platform and cross-manufacturer interoperability. Within the layered architecture, integration efforts primarily focus on the lower layers, while the application layer is more concerned with the implementation of business logic. This separation clarifies and streamlines the integration process, reducing the complexity and cost of cross-platform integration.

- **Ease of integration and compatibility**

The open and compatible design of the IoT architecture seamlessly integrates crucial business systems such as Enterprise Resource Planning (ERP), Customer Relationship Management (CRM), and Supervisory Control and Data Acquisition (SCADA). The design also ensures wide compatibility with various cloud services. As a result, it establishes a freely flowing data ecosystem. This integration and compatibility capability significantly facilitates cross-platform, cross-domain data sharing and real-time exchange, enhancing the overall system efficiency. Furthermore, it imparts unparalleled flexibility to enterprises, enabling them to swiftly respond to market changes, optimize operational processes, and drive business innovation and growth.

Based on the aforementioned characteristics, the layered architecture has a profound impact on IoT compatibility. By fostering standardization and compatibility, enhancing system flexibility and scalability, supporting a diverse range of devices, platforms, driving technological innovation and industrial upgrading, the layered architecture provides robust support for the development and application of IoT systems.

9.3 Enabling technologies of IoT

The enabling technologies of IoT mainly refer to the core technologies that support the operation of IoT systems and devices, through which IoT can digitize everything in the real world and connect them to realize the interconnection of everything [11]. Its key technologies include perception layer technology, network communication technology, IoT protocols, data processing and intelligent analysis, and security and privacy protection.

9.3.1 Perception layer technology

The perception layer, as the first layer in the entire IoT system, has the primary task of detecting the presence of objects and collecting relevant information. This mainly includes Wireless Sensor Networks (WSNs), RFID, and Global Navigation Satellite System (GNSS). WSNs comprise a large number of sensor nodes that typically have data acquisition, data processing, and wireless communication functions. These nodes can be deployed in various environments and scenarios to collect data such as temperature, humidity, light, pressure, and other environmental information. This data can be analyzed and used by other devices or systems, to achieve automation and intelligence.

RFID technology utilizes radio waves to identify and track objects with RFID tags, making it suitable for scenarios such as inventory management, logistics tracking, and identity verification. RFID systems consist of tags, readers, and middleware or software. GNSS refers to all satellite navigation systems that provide global positioning services, including the U.S. GPS, Russia's GLONASS, Europe's Galileo, and China's BeiDou system [12]. These systems can be employed in various applications, such as automation and intelligence. Compared to GPS, GNSS offers broader coverage and higher positioning accuracy, particularly in areas where GPS signals may be obstructed, such as urban canyons or mountainous regions.

9.3.1.1 WSNs

WSNs are self-organized network systems composed of a large number of distributed wireless sensor nodes [13]. These nodes can monitor and sense various information about the environment or specific objects in real time, process this information, and transmit it through wireless communication. WSNs have characteristics such as self-organization, low power consumption, and high reliability. They are widely used in many fields, including environmental monitoring, intelligent agriculture, industrial automation, health monitoring, smart homes, and smart cities [14].

The schematic diagram of the wireless sensor network is shown in Figure 9.2 and includes three major parts: the sensor network composed of numerous sensor nodes, the aggregation node, and the management node. The core task of the sensor node is to monitor and control the state of the environment. The aggregation node serves as a bridge between the sensor network and the data management center, responsible for integrated data processing and protocol conversion. In contrast, the management node is responsible for the comprehensive management of the sensor network and the execution of control instructions.

WSNs are capable of covering a wide area, which necessitates that they be highly adaptive to cope with hardware and software failures, as well as environmental changes. These networks are also self-maintaining, monitoring their own state, adapting to changes in the environment, and reconfiguring network resources when necessary. WSNs tend to be data-centric, focusing primarily on data collection. Each node in WSNs can act as a data relay station, requiring the networks to effectively manage dynamic connections and disconnections between nodes, along with the resulting topology changes, to ensure effective communication.

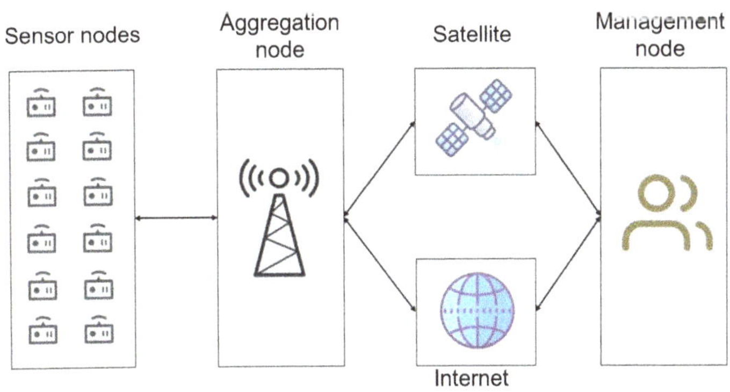

Figure 9.2 WSNs illustration

9.3.1.2 RFID

Wireless radio frequency identification technology, known as RFID, is an advanced automatic diagnosis technology. It enables contactless information interaction through radio waves and allows for remote read-write operations on electronic labels or radio frequency cards. This technology makes recognizing and exchanging data with target objects highly efficient and convenient, eliminating the need for physical contact.

The core working principle of RFID technology is illustrated in Figure 9.3. When an electronic tag enters the reader's range, it captures the radio frequency signal emitted by the reader. This signal excites the inductive current within the tag, providing the energy needed for the tag to transmit the product information stored on its chip as a wireless signal [15]. In some cases, tags may also actively transmit signals at a specific frequency. The reader receives these signals, decodes them, and then transmits the decoded data to a centralized information system for further processing.

The function of a reader is not limited to reading as it can also perform write operations based on its design and technology, acting as the information control and data processing center of the RFID system. A complete reader typically includes a coupling module, transceiver module, control module, and interface unit. Communication between the reader and the tag is usually half-duplex, meaning the reader provides energy and synchronization signals while facilitating data exchange with the tag. In actual deployments, technologies such as Ethernet or Wireless Local Area Networks (WLAN) enable real-time collection, processing, and long-distance transmission of identification information, facilitating the intelligent management and tracking of objects.

At the same time, RFID technology faces a series of security challenges, such as the proliferation of counterfeit products. To address this issue, a compact RFID system has been proposed. This system integrates a multilayer anti-counterfeiting tag with holographic components for enhanced security applications [16].

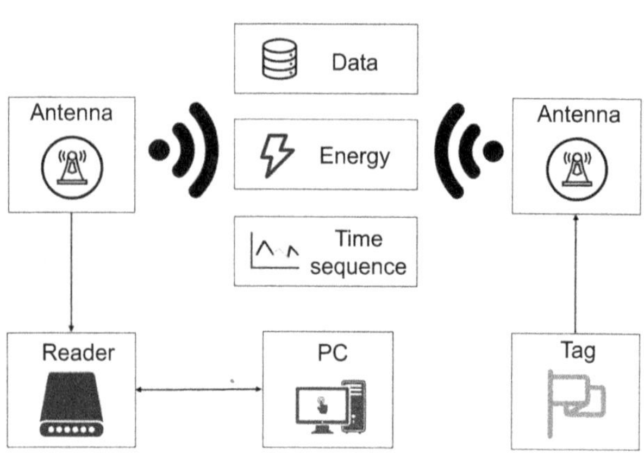

Figure 9.3 RFID working principle

9.3.1.3 GNSS

GNSS is a unified term that encompasses the BeiDou Navigation System, GPS, GLONASS, and various individual satellite navigation and positioning systems from other countries. It can also refer to a larger system comprising multiple satellite navigation and positioning systems. The integration of GNSS with IoT provides precise positioning and navigation capabilities for smart devices, which is essential for enabling extensive connectivity and smart management of IoT devices.

With advancements in GNSS technology, an increasing number of GNSS satellites are now capable of delivering excellent performance and capabilities [17]. GNSS technology is an important source of information for the perception layer of IoT. It provides global positioning services by receiving signals from Earth-orbiting satellites. Furthermore, improvements in GNSS technology have enabled more accurate spatio-temporal localization services for IoT devices. For instance, positioning accuracy can be significantly enhanced using Real-time Differential GPS (RTDGPS) techniques, such as Real-Time Kinematic (RTK) measurement, which is particularly important for applications requiring high-precision positioning, such as self-driving cars.

9.3.2 Network communication technology

Network communication technologies for IoT are key to interconnecting devices. They ensure the efficient functioning of the IoT ecosystem through data collection, transmission, processing, and analysis [18]. This chapter will introduce the primary network technologies used in IoT, including cellular and satellite networks. Cellular networks offer extensive coverage and high-speed data transmission capabilities, making them suitable for scenarios with mobility and large bandwidth requirements. In contrast, satellite networks provide seamless global coverage and ensure highly reliable communication services.

9.3.2.1 Cellular network

Cellular network technology is a key infrastructure for enabling wireless communications. It provides services by dividing a geographic area into multiple cells, each served by a station as shown in Figure 9.4. These base stations overlap each other geographically and resemble honeycombs, hence the name. Cellular networks have evolved from the first generation (1G) to the upcoming sixth generation (6G). From analog voice communication in 1G to high-speed data transmission in 5G, cellular network technology has continuously adapted to support the growth of the mobile Internet and IoT.

The core of cellular networks includes various access technologies, such as Frequency Division Multiple Access (FDMA), Time Division Multiple Access (TDMA), and Code Division Multiple Access (CDMA), as well as modulation and demodulation technologies like Orthogonal Frequency Division Multiplexing (OFDM). In the context of IoT, applications for cellular networks encompass scenarios such as remote monitoring, mobility tracking, and smart cities, enabling devices to transmit data remotely and interconnect. As 5G technology advances, cellular networks

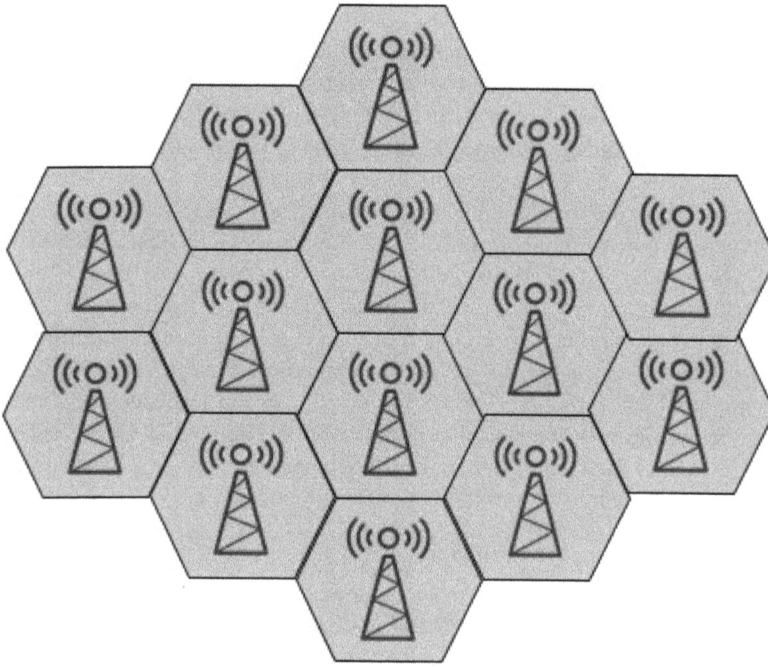

Figure 9.4 Cellular network

are expected to provide wider coverage, higher speeds, and lower latency, further expanding the scope and effectiveness of IoT applications.

- 1G marked the beginning of mobile communications with a predominantly analog signal that provided basic voice communication capabilities [19].
- 2G enabled the transition from analog to digital signals, introduced the Global System for Mobile Communications (GSM) standard and data services, increased speeds to 64 Kbps, and supported Short Message Service (SMS) and basic Multimedia Message Service (MMS) for the first time [20].
- 3G dramatically increased data transfer speeds for mobile internet, reaching up to 384 Kbps or more. It introduced mobile video, mobile gaming, and audio on demand [21], promoting the development of smartphones as multimedia devices.
- 4G technology heralded the mobile broadband era with speeds exceeding 100 Mbps, characterized by high capacity and low latency [22]. This enabled fast internet access through Long-Term Evolution (LTE) technology and facilitated the development of digital ecosystems, streaming services, and cloud applications.
- 5G will unlock multi-gigabit speeds and single-millisecond latency to support mission-critical applications such as autonomous driving or smart manufacturing, dramatically advancing the IoT [23]. Specifically, the high speed, low latency, and dense connectivity of 5G networks provide more powerful and

flexible connectivity for IoT devices. 5G not only supports massive device connectivity but also enables real-time monitoring and management through its low-latency characteristics.
- 6G is the next generation of wireless communication technology after 5G and is expected to be available around 2030 [24]. It aims to provide higher data transmission rates, lower latency, wider connectivity range, and higher reliability than 5G to support various applications in the future smart society.

From Table 9.1, it is evident that 5G offers significant advantages over previous generations of mobile networks regarding data rate, latency, and bandwidth coverage–key factors in supporting and facilitating the development of IoT. Additionally, 5G's high connection density enables large-scale deployment of IoT devices. Through network slicing, 5G can provide customized network environments for various IoT applications while ensuring quality of service.

9.3.2.2 Satellite network

A satellite network is a communications system that uses artificial satellites orbiting the Earth as relay stations for data transmission, enabling communication links between various locations on the planet. This type of network offers extensive coverage, making it particularly suitable for remote areas, oceans, and airspace that are difficult to reach with terrestrial networks, thereby providing seamless communication services worldwide. Satellites are classified into three main types based on the altitude of their operational orbits: Geostationary Earth Orbit (GEO), Medium Earth Orbit (MEO), and Low Earth Orbit (LEO). LEO satellites [25] have garnered special attention because they can deliver data transmission rates comparable to those of fiber-optic networks, with very low latency, making them ideal for modern high-speed Internet and IoT applications.

The principle of satellite communications is illustrated in Figure 9.5. When a user requests access to the Internet, the data first departs from a data center, which serves as the staging area for Internet content and resources. The data then flows through the core network, the backbone of the Internet responsible for high-speed

Table 9.1 1G–5G comparison

Cellular networks	Transmission rate	Latency	Primary frequency bands	Applications
1G	10 Kbps	High	800 MHz–900 MHz	Voice
2G	10–100 Kbps	Medium	800 MHz–900 MHz	Voice/SMS/ Basic data
3G	384 Kbps–2 Mbps	Lower	450 MHz–6 GHz	Mobile Internet/ Video Call
4G	100 Mbps–1 Gbps	Low	450 MHz–6 GHz	HD video/massive data services
5G	10 Gbps (theoretically)	Very low	410 MHz–6 GHz and 24–52 GHz	IoT/autonomous Driving/VR/AR

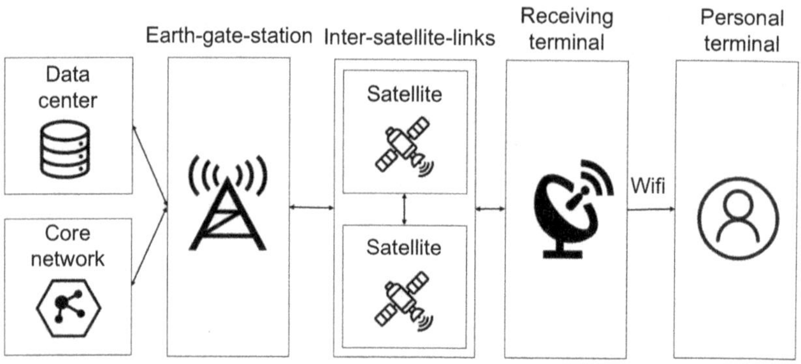

Figure 9.5 Principles of satellite communication

transmission and routing. Next, the data reaches the ground station, also known as the earth gate station, which acts as the terrestrial interface for satellite communications and is responsible for uplinking the data to the satellite [26]. Since data centers cannot be established in space, the ground station plays a crucial intermediary role.

The data is sent via the ground station's uplink to the communication satellite, which functions as a relay node, receiving and forwarding the data. In a satellite network, data transmission between different satellites may be facilitated through inter-satellite links to ensure the data reaches the appropriate satellite covering the target area.

When the data arrives at the communication satellite above the user's location, the satellite downlinks it to the user's receiving terminal. This terminal may be a satellite communications device installed on a vehicle, airplane, or ship. Finally, the receiving terminal converts the data into a wireless signal via Wi-Fi, allowing the user to access the Internet using a smartphone or other mobile device.

9.3.3 IoT protocols

The rapid growth of the IoT has led to the development of a wide range of communication protocols to meet various device and deployment requirements. With the significant increase in the number and scope of connected devices, the number of IoT connections is expected to surpass the number of non-IoT online connections for the first time in 2020. Current IoT protocols include Advanced Message Queuing Protocol (AMQP), Cellular Network, Constrained Application Protocol (CoAP), Data Distribution Service (DDS), Long Range Wide Area Network (LoRa/LoRaWAN), Extensible Messaging and Presence Protocol (XMPP), Message Queuing Telemetry Transport (MQTT), and Lightweight Machine-to-Machine (LwM2M). Each of these protocols is suitable for different scenarios, such as proximity communication, low-power devices, high-speed data transfer, or long-distance communication.

Not every IoT communication protocol is suitable for all deployment scenarios or devices. Many requirements such as power and security need to be considered before choosing a protocol to ensure that data is transmitted efficiently and securely through the IoT ecosystem. As the number of IoT devices continues to grow, with connections expected to reach 30.9 billion by 2025, these protocols will play a crucial role in supporting this growth. A description of some commonly used IoT protocols and their networking models follows.

9.3.3.1 MQTT

MQTT is a lightweight messaging protocol based on a publish/subscribe model. It is simple in design, easy to implement, and well-suited for use in low-bandwidth, high-latency, or unreliable network environments. Among the protocols mentioned above, it is the most commonly used [27]. Next, MQTT will be introduced in terms of its features and networking patterns.

Advantages:
Lightweight publish/subscribe messaging protocol: The publish/subscribe model of the protocol improves the flexibility and scalability of communication. It allows devices to publish messages to specific topics, while other devices can subscribe to those topics to receive related messages.

Designed for high-latency or unreliable network environments: Tailored for low-bandwidth, high-latency, or unreliable network conditions, it facilitates efficient data exchange between devices with minimal communication overhead.

One-to-many message distribution: MQTT's one-to-many message delivery mechanism is ideal for scenarios where messages need to be broadcast to multiple recipients. For example, when a sensor detects an anomaly, it can send a warning message to all clients in the monitoring system. This mechanism improves message delivery efficiency by allowing the MQTT agent to handle distribution, rather than the publisher sending messages to each subscriber individually. It also alleviates the publisher's burden, as it does not need to track available subscribers and can focus solely on message distribution.

Disadvantages:
MQTT is based on a publish/subscribe model and does not support broadcast messages, which limits its use in certain scenarios that require broadcast communication. Additionally, MQTT does not support push notifications. Therefore, if there is a requirement to actively push messages from the client to the server, it may be necessary to combine it with other protocols or mechanisms.

Networking patterns:
MQTT typically operates on a client–server model, where an MQTT client connects to an MQTT server to publish or subscribe to topics. The MQTT network pattern is shown in Figure 9.6. In MQTT, the device acts as a client that publishes messages to the server, which other devices can subscribe to. The server is responsible for distributing these messages.

9.3.3.2 CoAP

Advantages:
Web transport protocol designed for small devices: CoAP is a communication solution tailored for resource-constrained devices in the IoT. These small devices

Figure 9.6 MQTT networking patterns

often have limited computing power, memory, battery life, and network bandwidth. CoAP adapts the Hypertext Transfer Protocol (HTTP) to better suit constrained environments by simplifying its core concepts. It maintains the ease of use and flexibility characteristic of web protocols.

Based on the REST model for resource-constrained devices and networks: CoAP is based on the concept of resources, where each resource can be identified and accessed by a unique Uniform Resource Identifier (URI). This architectural style of the REST model allows CoAP to operate in a distributed and decentralized manner, making it ideal for dynamic and highly scalable IoT environments.

Support for basic web operations (GET, POST, PUT, DELETE): These operations enable CoAP to facilitate simple management and interaction of resources without the overhead of complex protocols. Since IoT devices often need to perform straightforward tasks, such as reading sensor data or controlling device status, these features of CoAP make it particularly suitable for implementing these functions.

Disadvantages:
Since the CoAP protocol is based on User Datagram Protocol (UDP) and has no built-in retransmission mechanism, there may be problems such as packet loss or retransmission during transmission. In addition, as more and more devices join IoT, the existing CoAP architecture may not be able to control congestion effectively. For example, when CoAP is applied to remotely control sensor devices, the load on the server increases with the increase of sensor devices [28]. Although new protocols have emerged to mitigate congestion, there are still real-time and compatibility challenges.

Networking patterns: CoAP is based on a client–server architecture, but it also supports resource discovery and multicast communication, enabling devices to function as servers. The CoAP network pattern is shown in Figure 9.7. Clients can send GET (retrieves data), POST (submits new data), PUT (updates existing data), and DELETE (removes data) requests to the server.

9.3.3.3 WebSocket

Advantages:
Full-duplex communication: WebSocket enables real-time, two-way interaction between clients and servers. WebSocket differs from the traditional HTTP request-response model. It establishes a persistent connection. This connection allows data

Figure 9.7 CoAP networking patterns

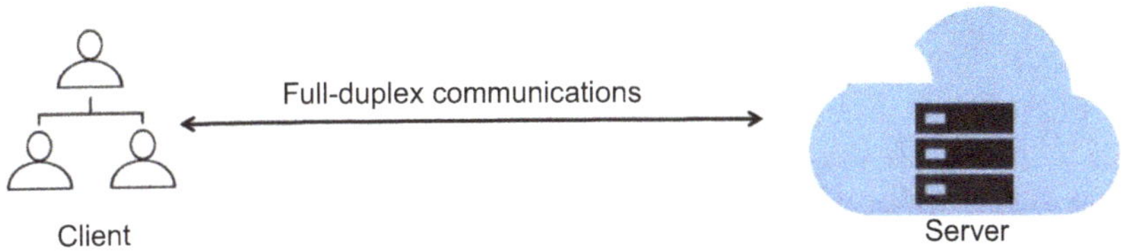

Figure 9.8 WebSocket networking patterns

to be sent and received at any time. There is no need to re-establish the connection for each communication.

WebSocket allows the server to actively send information to the client: This persistent connection enables the server to respond to the client's requests. Additionally, it allows the server to actively push messages at appropriate times. This capability is crucial in areas such as industrial automation. For instance, in real-time sensor data transmission, the server can collect and transmit data from sensors instantaneously. In smart home applications, the server can send and receive instructions in real time to control smart devices within the home.

Security: WebSocket can be encrypted via Transport Layer Security Protocol (TLS) to ensure secure data transmission. In addition, WebSocket supports cross-origin communication, but requires the server to be configured with a Cross-Origin Resource Sharing (CORS) policy to prevent malicious sites from accessing sensitive data through a WebSocket connection. WebSocket offers basic security mechanisms to safeguard communication; however, implementing a fully secure WebSocket solution requires careful consideration of several factors, including encryption protocols, authentication methods, and more.

Networking patterns:
The WebSocket protocol is based on Transmission Control Protocol (TCP) and begins with an HTTP handshake, which is then upgraded to a WebSocket connection, enabling two-way communication. The WebSocket network pattern is shown in Figure 9.8. WebSocket establishes a persistent, full-duplex communication channel that enables real-time, two-way communication between the server and client.

9.3.4 Data processing and intelligent analysis

This section will introduce data processing and intelligent analysis in IoT from three aspects: cloud computing, edge computing, and artificial intelligence Internet of Things (AIoT).

9.3.4.1 Cloud computing

Cloud computing is a service model that provides on-demand access to computing resources, such as servers, storage, databases, networks, software, and analytics. These resources are typically managed by third-party service providers and delivered to users via the Internet. This model allows users to access and utilize these resources without needing to manage the underlying infrastructure directly [29].

In today's era of rapid advancements in computer technology, hardware is indispensable, and its maintenance and management are equally important. The on-demand and pay-as-you-go model of cloud computing can save users significant trouble. Additionally, cloud computing offers flexible computing resources that can automatically adjust based on user needs, providing elastic scaling capabilities. Users can utilize and pay for computing resources according to their actual requirements, thereby avoiding resource waste.

Cloud computing is generally categorized into four service models: Infrastructure as a Service (IaaS), Platform as a Service (PaaS), Software as a Service (SaaS), and serverless computing. For more details, see Table 9.2.

Characteristics of cloud computing:

- **On-demand self-service**

Users can obtain and configure resources at any time according to their needs without manual intervention.

- **Wide network access**

Services can be accessed globally through the network using various devices, such as mobile phones, tablets, laptops, and workstations.

- **Resource pooling**

The provider's computing resources are centrally managed to create a resource pool that offers services to multiple users in a multi-tenant environment.

Table 9.2 Cloud computing service model

Service	Details
IaaS	Providing virtualized computing resources
PaaS	Provides a platform for application development and deployment, including operating systems, databases, and development tools
SaaS	By providing applications through the Internet, users can use them directly without installation and maintenance
FaaS	Offload all backend infrastructure management tasks (including configuration, scaling, scheduling, and patching) to the cloud provider

- **Rapid elasticity**

Resources can be quickly expanded or contracted in response to changes in demand.

9.3.4.2 Edge computing

Edge computing, also known as distributed cloud computing, fog computing, or the fourth-generation data center, refers to the practice of collecting and analyzing data on local devices and networks near the point of data generation. This approach contrasts with cloud computing, which involves transmitting data to a centralized cloud for processing [30]. A schematic diagram of edge computing is shown in Figure 9.9.

As more smart devices connect to the Internet, the volume of data is growing explosively. Transmitting all data to the cloud for processing presents significant challenges for network traffic control, bandwidth, and cloud storage capabilities. In certain hard real-time scenarios, minimizing time delays is crucial, and this is where edge computing becomes essential. By placing data analysis functions closer to the application environment—such as at terminals or gateways – edge computing helps ensure critical requirements like real-time processing are met.

Characteristics of edge computing

- **Distributed and low latency**

Edge computing minimizes the transmission distance of data by processing it on devices located at the edge of the network. This approach reduces latency and enhances the speed and efficiency of data processing.

- **High efficiency**

Edge computing enables data to be processed at nodes closer to users, ensuring more efficient data handling.

- **Reduced traffic pressure**

By performing basic data processing at edge nodes before transmitting to the cloud, edge computing can accelerate device response times and decrease the volume of data traffic sent from devices to the cloud.

9.3.4.3 AIoT

With the rapid development of IoT, data processing and intelligent analysis have become crucial for realizing its potential. As the scale and complexity of data continue

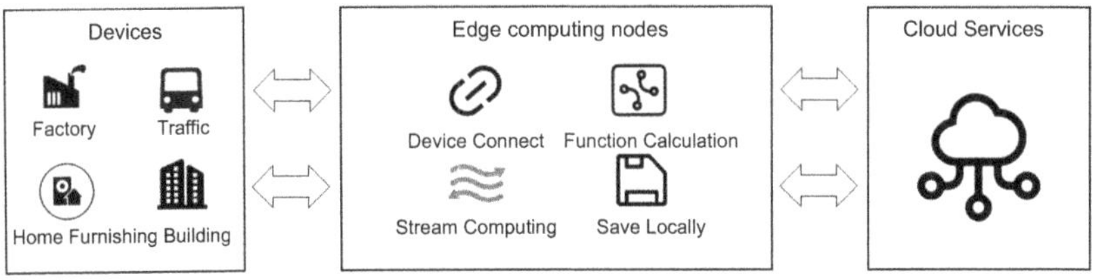

Figure 9.9 Illustration of edge computing

to grow, traditional data processing methods are increasingly inadequate for meeting the demands of real-time accuracy. Consequently, the integration of Artificial Intelligence (AI) technology into IoT has led to the emergence of AIoT, which not only processes and analyzes vast amounts of data but also extracts valuable information to support decision-making.

AIoT employs algorithms such as machine learning and deep learning to perceive, learn, and reason about the collected data, enabling the understanding of complex environments and, in some cases, autonomous decision-making. Deep learning, in particular, has endowed IoT with powerful data processing and intelligent analysis capabilities. Typical network models in deep learning, including Convolutional Neural Networks (CNNs) and Recurrent Neural Networks (RNNs), can effectively handle and analyze large volumes of data from IoT devices and sensors, facilitating intelligent decision-making and automated control. Given these advantages, AIoT systems have demonstrated significant application potential across various fields, including smart homes, smart cities, and industrial automation [31].

Deep learning plays an important role in the following aspects:

- **Data processing**

Deep learning can process a vast amount of heterogeneous data collected by IoT systems, including time series data, images, videos, and sensor data. By utilizing deep learning tools, these diverse types of data can be converted into suitable formats and input into the network model for analysis.

- **Pattern recognition**

Through deep learning, IoT systems can intelligently identify various data types, such as videos, images, and voice, enabling automated monitoring and recognition tasks.

- **Prediction and decision-making**

Deep learning models can be trained on historical data to predict the future state of devices, providing valuable support for decision-making.

- **Security protection**

Deep learning enhances the security of IoT systems by detecting abnormal behavior and identifying potential security threats.

9.3.5 Security issues and defense

At present, with the rapid development of the IoT, various IoT devices have emerged in everyday life, including those used in smart homes, smart cities, and industrial applications. The data generated in these areas often pertains to individuals' privacy, and any leakage of this data or attacks on related IoT devices can have serious consequences. Therefore, ensuring the security of the IoT is of paramount importance. This section will introduce the security issues and defense technologies that exist in each layer of the IoT.

9.3.5.1 Security issues in the perception layer

The perception layer of IoT is the lowest layer in the entire IoT architecture. It is in direct contact with physical devices and environment. Therefore, security issues in this layer should be taken seriously. The main security issues faced by this layer include the following sections [32].

- **Node capture**

Nodes present at the network gateway are more vulnerable to attack, which may lead to the leakage of important information, thus jeopardizing the security of the entire network [33]. There are a series of methods to solve the node capture problem in the perception layer of the IoT:

Securing Nodes in Perception Layer (SNPL) scheme: A scheme has been proposed to ensure data authenticity from sources and to distinguish authentic nodes from malicious ones [34].

Security properties: Solutions often focus on security properties such as authentication, confidentiality, integrity, freshness, availability, communication security, non-repudiation, and access control.

Machine learning algorithms: Machine learning algorithms, such as the K-Nearest Neighbor (KNN) algorithm, have been found to detect malware with excellent accuracy and can be used to defend against IoT threats [35].

- **Fake node and malicious data**

Fake nodes refer to malicious devices introduced into the network by attackers or existing devices that have been physically compromised to inject false sensor data. These nodes might join botnets to participate in large-scale distributed attacks or recruit additional nodes.

Malicious data injection involves attackers tampering with devices to inject erroneous sensor data or using Man-in-the-Middle (MITM) attacks to modify IoT device data. Additionally, malicious data is introduced into the system due to faulty equipment or degraded communication channels. These erroneous measurements are usually detected based on statistical analysis, but these detection mechanisms can be bypassed by attackers causing correlated errors in the measurements [36].

The above issues of fake nodes and malicious data can be solved using techniques such as device attestation, data integrity verification, zero watermarking [37], Intrusion Detection System (IDS), etc.

- **Denial of Service (DoS) attack**

DoS attacks in the perception layer of IoT pose a significant threat by overwhelming devices with excessive traffic or sending invalid data, rendering them unavailable to legitimate users [38].

- **Replay attack**

Attackers may cause serious issues in critical information such as control commands by capturing and retransmitting previous data exchanges, regardless of whether the data is encrypted and/or integrity protected [39]. Here are some possible countermeasures against replay attacks [40]:

Use session key: Combine security measures such as session key, timestamp, and unique password to prevent replay attacks.

Timestamp and uniqueness verification: By including timestamps and unique identifiers in data transmission, replay attacks can be detected and prevented because replayed packets will have expired timestamps or duplicate unique identifiers.

Encryption method: Using encryption technology to protect the integrity and confidentiality of data. Even if the data is replayed, it cannot be exploited by unauthorized users.

9.3.5.2 Security issues in the network layer

The network layer plays a crucial role in IoT architecture, responsible for communication and data transmission between devices. Dealing with security issues in the network layer is crucial. The main security issues faced by this layer include following sections.

- **Heterogeneity**

Due to the use of different technologies and protocols by IoT devices, there are differences in their security performance, which increases the risk of network attacks. For example, devices may use default passwords or weak authentication mechanisms, making it easier for hackers to gain access. Here are several solutions provided:

Enhanced authentication and authorization: IoT devices use strong authentication mechanisms such as Two Factor Authentication (2FA) and Context Aware Authentication (CAA).

Use strong encryption and secure protocols: Use the strongest possible encryption, such as IPsec or TLS/Secure Socket Layer (SSL).

- **Scalability issues**

Scalability is a key challenge at the network layer, especially with a significant increase in the number of devices. IoT networks require managing a large number of devices that may join or leave the network at any time [41]. This increases the complexity of network management. Here are two solutions provided:

Lightweight protocols and standards: In order to overcome the resource limitations of IoT devices, the network layer uses lightweight protocols and standards such as IPv6 over Low-Power Wireless Personal Area Networks (6LoWPAN) and Routing Protocol for Low-Power and Lossy Networks (RPL) [42].

Resource management: IoT devices are limited by resources such as low power consumption, limited memory, and processing power. Effective resource management is crucial for the scalability of a network.

9.3.5.3 Security issues in the application layer

The application layer requires varied security standards based on the specific needs of each application, which complicates the task of securing the application. Some of the challenges in this area include addressing security and privacy issues at this layer.

- **Mutual authentication issues**

Mutual authentication, also known as two-way authentication, is a security process where both the client and the server must authenticate each other before communication occurs. In IoT, this process is crucial to prevent unauthorized devices from accessing the network or communicating with other devices.

Mutual authentication issues can be achieved using a lightweight routing scheme that ensures the integrity, authenticity, and confidentiality of information in IoT networks [43].

- **Key privacy issues**

Key privacy issues involve unauthorized data collection and potential breaches due to weaknesses in encryption and authentication protocols. These concerns can compromise the confidentiality and integrity of user data within IoT systems, risking sensitive information being exploited by attackers.

To address key privacy concerns, the proposed IoT framework leverages its multi-layered security monitoring capabilities, incorporating both supervised and unsupervised learning techniques [44], to effectively address key privacy issues within IoT systems, safeguarding the confidentiality and integrity of user data.

- **Data management issues**

Data management issues relate to the challenges of securely and efficiently handling, storing, and analyzing the vast amounts of data generated by IoT devices, ensuring data integrity, confidentiality, and availability, while also addressing potential privacy concerns and ensuring compliance with relevant regulations.

There are various effective methods to address data management issues, such as data integration and standardization, and data quality management [45]. Data integration and standardization involves developing mechanisms and tools that capture data from various IoT sources and ensure its consistent format and quality. Data quality management, on the other hand, discusses techniques aimed at improving data accuracy, completeness, consistency, and timeliness.

9.4 Use cases of IoT and CPS

Cyber-Physical Systems (CPS) is a multidimensional complex system that integrates computation, network, and physical environment. It realizes real-time perception, dynamic control, and information service of the physical world through the organic integration of computation, communication, and control technologies. The core of CPS lies in the close integration of the physical system with the information system, so that the physical equipment can be equipped with the functions of computation, communication, precise control, remote coordination, and autonomy. Conceptually, there is not much difference between CPS and IoT, but CPS focuses more on applications in industrial settings.

9.4.1 Smart agriculture

Smart agriculture is the combination of traditional agriculture and IoT technology to realize automated and intelligent agricultural production and management [46]. Specifically, smart agriculture can realize the functions of agricultural environment monitoring, remote control, and intelligent warning as shown in Figure 9.10.

- **Environmental monitoring**

Various different sensors are located in the agricultural environment, including temperature sensors and humidity sensors. These sensors transmit real-time data information to the cloud platform. They sense parameters such as air temperature, air humidity, light intensity, and plant nutrient content in the environment. The cloud platform summarizes and stores the data sent by all the sensor nodes, realizes the collection of data from all the test points in the agricultural environment, and presents them to the user in the form of visualized charts or curves.

- **Remote control**

After acquiring the data in the environment, the data can be analyzed and processed to realize automatic control of the agricultural park such as automatic irrigation, automatic cooling, automatic fertilizer application, automatic spraying, and so on. Taking automatic irrigation as an example, when the soil moisture in a certain area is detected

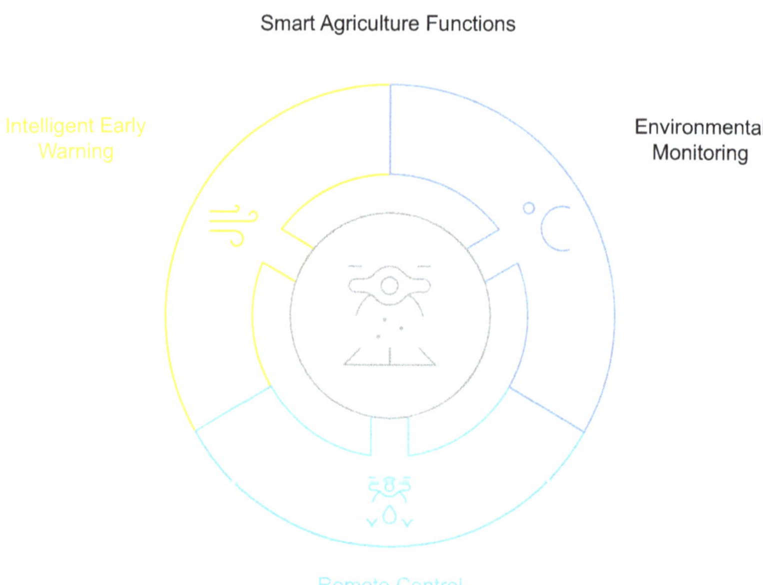

Figure 9.10 Technologies in smart agriculture

to be below a certain threshold, the surrounding irrigation devices will automatically irrigate the dry area and stop irrigating when the soil moisture content tends to normalize.

- **Intelligent early warning**

Intelligent early warning involves real-time monitoring and analysis of various parameters in the agricultural production process. Its purpose is to prevent and mitigate possible agricultural production risks. Early warnings include the following: crop pest and disease monitoring and warning, agro-meteorological warning, crop growth monitoring, and agricultural disaster warning.

Crop pest and disease monitoring and early warning systems are designed to track crop growth conditions and detect the presence of pests and diseases in real time. This is achieved through sensors and cameras installed in the farmland. These devices utilize image recognition and machine learning algorithms to analyze the data they collect. The agro-meteorological early warning system predicts the impact of extreme weather on crop growth by combining data from weather stations with farmland environmental monitoring information. Based on these predictions, early warnings are issued to assist farmers in taking timely measures to minimize losses. Crop growth monitoring and early warning is the use of remote sensing technology and field monitoring equipment, real-time monitoring of crop growth, predicting crop growth trends, and early warning of growth anomalies. The agricultural disaster early warning combines Geographic Information System (GIS) and GPS technology to monitor and predict agricultural disasters such as floods, droughts, fires, locust plagues, and issue timely warnings to reduce disaster losses.

9.4.2 Smart city

With the continuous increase of urban population, there is a consequent growth of traffic pressure and environmental problems, which is alleviated to a certain extent by the emergence of smart cities [47]. Smart city is a combination of IoT, AI technology, and the management of the city, so as to enhance the efficiency of urban management, improve the quality of life of residents, and promote economic development. The application scenarios of smart cities mainly include: intelligent transportation, intelligent environmental protection, smart community, etc as shown in Figure 9.11.

- **Intelligent transportation**

With the growth of urban population, traffic congestion has become a major challenge for city managers. The application of IoT in smart city, through real-time data collection and big data analysis, helps cities to optimize traffic flow and improve the efficiency of city operation. For example, sensors are strategically placed in various locations including traffic signals, vehicles, and roadsides to gather real-time traffic flow information. After the data is transmitted to the cloud, the system is able to intelligently adjust the timing of signals according to real-time traffic conditions to optimize traffic flow. At the same time, citizens can also view real-time road conditions and choose the best travel routes through mobile applications.

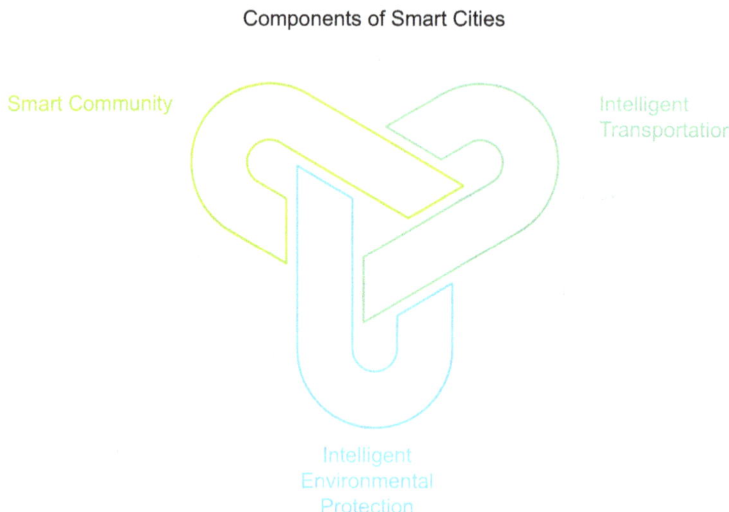

Figure 9.11 Components of smart cities

- **Intelligent environmental protection**

Intelligent environmental protection is a new environmental protection model that utilizes modern technologies such as IoT to detect, manage, and protect the environment. It improves the efficiency and effectiveness of environmental management and decision-making by realizing comprehensive sensing of environmental information, high-speed transmission of data, intelligent processing of information, and intelligent services. It provides a variety of intelligent solutions for the construction of ecological civilization in cities, including pollution prevention, ecological environment monitoring, and atmospheric environment supervision.

In pollution prevention, it monitors data on pollution generation, pollution control process and pollution discharge. This ensures that pollutant discharges are rationalized and enables accurate monitoring of pollution discharges. In terms of ecological environment monitoring, a network is established for comprehensive monitoring. This network enables the integration of monitoring and supervision, allowing for the timely identification and addressing of significant environmental issues. In terms of atmospheric environment monitoring, it mainly monitors industrial pollutant gases, restaurant fume gases, motor vehicle exhaust, and harmful gases. After collecting this data, the system analyzes it to generate corresponding early warnings.

- **Smart community**

Smart community is the use of 5G, IoT, and other technologies to provide community residents with a safe, comfortable, and convenient community life. Smart community solutions usually involve multiple aspects, including infrastructure development, smart system integration, and safety and security.

In terms of infrastructure construction, it is crucial to ensure high-speed network connections in the community. These connections include fiber-optic broadband and 5G networks, which support the operation of various smart devices and systems. Additionally, it is necessary to deploy smart terminal devices in the community. Examples of these devices are smart access control, smart lighting, and smart parking systems. In terms of smart system integration, various devices and systems in the community are connected through IoT technology to realize data collection and remote control. It also builds a cloud computing platform for data storage, processing and analysis to provide intelligent decision-making support. In terms of safety and security, a video surveillance system is deployed for security monitoring and emergency response in the community. In addition, sensors and AI technologies are used to monitor suspicious behavior and provide timely warnings.

9.4.3 Smart home

Smart home is a product of the mutual integration of IoT, AI, and other technologies in the home scene [48]. Specifically, it collects various types of data in the home environment by deploying a large number of sensor nodes in the home environment and stores these data in the cloud platform. Meanwhile, the smart home system can analyze various types of data, including locating, generating, regulating, and predicting, through AI technologies such as deep learning and Large Language Model (LLM). Next, the service areas of smart home will be introduced from the following three aspects: home service intelligence, home safety and security, and family member care.

- **Home service intelligence**

In terms of home service intelligence, smart home makes our life more convenient, and its application carriers include smart locks, smart cameras, sweeping robots, etc., as shown in Figure 9.12. Home service intelligence is mainly embodied in intelligent lighting, intelligent control, intelligent cleaning, intelligent audio and video. In terms of intelligent lighting, the lights in the home environment can be controlled by sound. In terms of intelligent control, for example, some voice-controlled home appliances and smart door locks use perception algorithms such as face recognition, making home life more convenient and intelligent. In intelligent cleaning, for example, sweeping robots combine navigation planning algorithms and multi-dimensional perception algorithms, greatly saving our time. In terms of smart audio and video, for example, smart speakers use audio AI algorithms, improving audio quality while facilitating ease of use.

- **Home safety and security**

Smart home not only makes our life more convenient, but also protects our property safety and personal safety to a certain extent. The sensors in the smart home environment can detect harmful gases in the home environment and give warnings, which can effectively ensure our physical health. It can make intelligent decisions when a fire is detected, initiate protective measures, and give timely alarms.

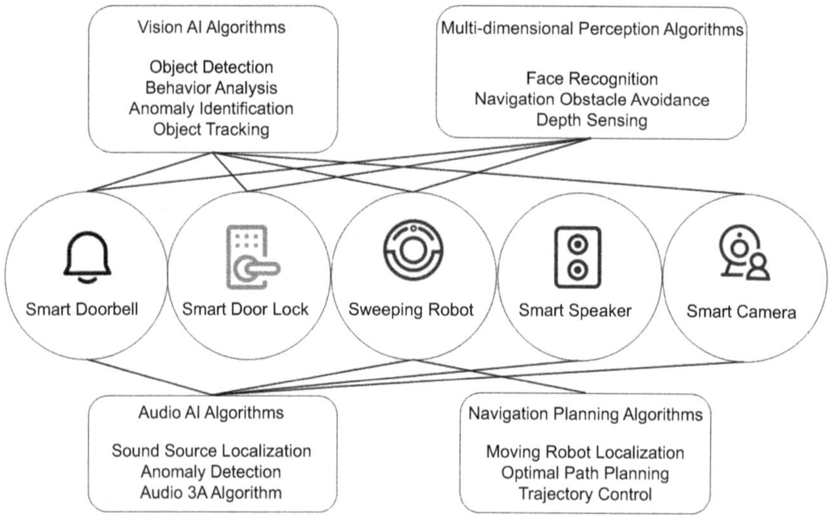

Figure 9.12 Smart home application carriers and related technologies

- **Family member care**

The smart home also includes intelligent care for family members, which is mainly reflected in the companionship of children's growth, care for the elderly living alone, and daily care for pets. In terms of child care, audio AI technology and IoT technology are combined to clone the voice of the child's mother. This cloned voice is then deployed on toys, enabling conversational communication with the child and helping to reduce the mother's stress. In pet care, through visual AI, automation, and other technologies, it realizes the automatic replenishment of pet food.

9.4.4 Intelligent manufacturing

Intelligent manufacturing is an advanced production mode deeply integrated with the new generation of information technology and advanced manufacturing technology [49]. It permeates every aspect of manufacturing activities, including design, production, and management and is characterized by its capabilities of self-perception, autonomous decision-making, adaptive behavior, and continuous self-learning. The goal of intelligent manufacturing is to enhance the quality, efficiency, and core competitiveness of the manufacturing industry. As the core application of CPS, CPS plays a pivotal role in intelligent manufacturing. It integrates computing, communication, and control technologies to achieve seamless connection between the physical and digital worlds. Figure 9.13 shows several parts of intelligent manufacturing.

- **Production process control**

CPS has the ability to monitor various production process parameters in real-time, including temperature, pressure, and flow rate. It employs algorithm models to ensure accurate control of the production process. The real-time capability and precision

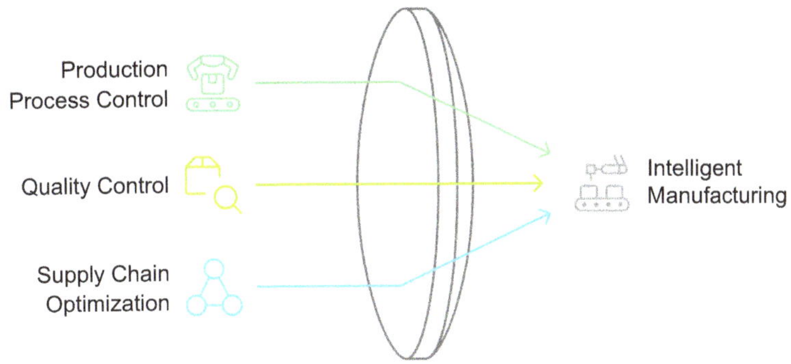

Figure 9.13 Intelligent manufacturing

make the production process more stable. This reduces human intervention and errors, while improving production efficiency and quality.

- **Quality control**

By monitoring product quality data in real-time, CPS can promptly detect quality issues during the production process. It can automatically adjust production parameters or trigger alerts. These actions ensure the consistency and stability of product quality. Additionally, CPS can utilize big data analytics to conduct in-depth exploration and analysis of product quality data. This provides robust support for quality improvement.

- **Supply chain optimization**

CPS can also be applied to supply chain optimization. By integrating IoT technology and big data analytics, CPS enables comprehensive monitoring and optimization of the supply chain. This supply chain management capability helps enterprises improve supply chain efficiency, reduce inventory costs, and enhance customer satisfaction.

The application of CPS in intelligent manufacturing is both extensive and profound. It not only enhances production efficiency and quality, but also reduces production costs and energy consumption. This brings significant economic and social benefits to enterprises. Furthermore, based on intelligent manufacturing, it drives the development of other CPS applications. With the continuous development and improvement of technology, CPS will play an increasingly important role in the field of intelligent manufacturing.

9.4.5 Smart grid

Currently, smart grids have already demonstrated the typical characteristics of CPS. The communication network component in their architecture is crucial for realizing the various functions of smart grids [50]. Smart grids encompass a variety of power generation equipment, transmission networks, electricity consumption devices, and energy storage devices. By integrating modern sensing technologies, networking technologies, communication technologies, computing technologies, automation,

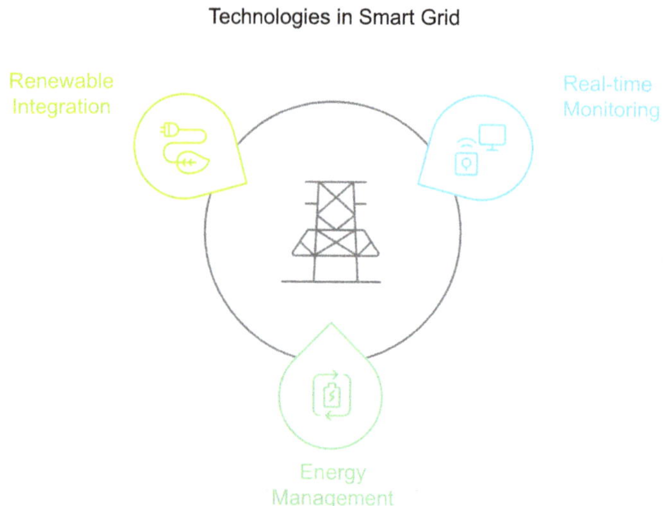

Figure 9.14 Technologies in smart grid

and intelligent control technologies, they form a fully automated power supply network. Figure 9.14 shows the relevant technologies of smart grid.

- **Real-time monitoring**

Through sensor networks and communication networks, CPS conducts real-time monitoring of the status of various nodes in the smart grid. It mainly monitors parameters such as voltage, current, and power. Based on real-time monitoring data, CPS can predict potential issues in the grid, such as overload and voltage fluctuations. It can take proactive measures in advance, such as adjusting power generation capacity and switching transmission lines. These actions ensure the stable operation of the grid.

- **Energy management**

CPS is capable of integrating data from various energy production enterprises and consumers, enabling intelligent energy management. By analyzing historical and real-time data, CPS can optimize the allocation and utilization of energy. It can improve energy efficiency and reduce energy costs.

- **Renewable energy integration**

IoT enables the deployment of sensors in renewable energy equipment such as solar panels, wind turbines, and hydropower stations, allowing for real-time monitoring of energy production, storage, transmission, and consumption. This provides seamless technology for the supervision and utilization of renewable energy. Additionally, through smart grid technology, intermittent energy sources such as wind and solar power can be better managed and dispatched, ensuring a stable supply of these energy sources and reducing energy waste caused by mismatches between supply and demand.

CPS enables efficient dynamic management of grid resources, promoting the efficient application of electricity through intelligent means and significantly reducing power loss due to improper management. At the same time, by leveraging IoT to deploy sensors in renewable energy equipment, it achieves seamless integration of energy sources, thereby substantially enhancing the utilization rate of renewable resources.

9.5 Conclusion

IoT stands as a pivotal element in information technology today, with its origins and evolution deeply embedded in the swift progression of information technology and the pervasive use of the internet. With the continuous maturation of technologies such as sensors and embedded systems, the concept of IoT has gradually transitioned from theory to practice, becoming a bridge connecting the physical world with the digital world. By connecting various smart devices, systems, and applications through the internet, IoT enables intelligent identification, location tracking, monitoring, and management of information. This significantly expands the boundaries and application scope of the internet.

However, as IoT technology continues to advance, its security issues have gradually come to the forefront. The number of IoT devices is constantly increasing, with a wide variety of types, and they are often deployed in open environments, which attracts numerous attacks from hackers and malicious software. These attacks not only lead to the leakage of personal privacy but also pose significant threats to society and even national security. In order to address these increasingly severe challenges, we must adopt effective defensive measures.

In the future, IoT will profoundly transform people's lifestyles and modes of production in unprecedented ways. By deeply integrating with cutting-edge technologies such as sensors, AI, cloud computing, and big data, IoT will realize a smart world where everything is interconnected. Additionally, IoT and CPS will drive the transformation and upgrading of traditional industries, promoting the development of emerging sectors such as smart agriculture, smart city, and intelligent manufacturing and injecting new vitality into global economic development.

References

[1] Madakam S, Ramaswamy R, and Tripathi S. Internet of Things (IoT): A Literature Review. Journal of Computer and Communications. 2015;3(3): 164–173.

[2] Manara G. A Review of RFID Sensors, the New Frontier of Internet of Things. Sensors. 2021;21.

[3] Sunyaev A. Internet Computing: Principles of Distributed Systems and Emerging Internet-Based Technologies. Internet Computing. 2020.

[4] Ramson SRJ, Vishnu S, and Shanmugam M. Applications of Internet of Things (IoT) – An Overview. In: 2020 5th International Conference on Devices, Circuits and Systems (ICDCS); 2020. p. 92–95.

[5] Kirimtat A, Krejcar O, Kertesz A, *et al.* Future Trends and Current State of Smart City Concepts: A Survey. IEEE Access. 2020;8:86448–86467.

[6] Sobin CC. A Survey on Architecture, Protocols and Challenges in IoT. Wireless Personal Communications. 2020;112(4).

[7] Ali AI, Partal SZ, Kepke S, *et al.* ZigBee and LoRa Based Wireless Sensors for Smart Environment and IoT Applications. In: 2019 1st Global Power, Energy and Communication Conference (GPECOM); 2019. p. 19–23.

[8] Ratasuk R, Vejlgaard B, Mangalvedhe N, *et al.* NB-IoT System for M2M Communication. In: 2016 IEEE Wireless Communications and Networking Conference; 2016. p. 1–5.

[9] Khan M. Challenges Facing the Application of IoT in Medicine and Healthcare. International Journal of Computations, Information and Manufacturing (IJCIM). 2021;12:1.

[10] Lakhwani K, Gianey H, Agarwal N, *et al.* Development of IoT for Smart Agriculture a Review. In: Rathore VS, Worring M, Mishra DK, *et al.*, editors. Emerging Trends in Expert Applications and Security. Singapore: Springer Singapore; 2019. p. 425–432.

[11] Reddy B. Unleashing the Power of the Internet of Things: Enabling Technologies, Protocols, and Applications for a Connected World. In: 2023 3rd International Conference on Advancement in Electronics & Communication Engineering (AECE); 2023. p. 739–743.

[12] Ferrara NG, Nurmi J, and Lohan ES. Multi-GNSS analysis based on full constellations simulated data. In: 2016 International Conference on Localization and GNSS (ICL-GNSS); 2016. p. 1–6.

[13] Sehrawat D and Gill NS. Smart Sensors: Analysis of Different Types of IoT Sensors. In: 2019 3rd International Conference on Trends in Electronics and Informatics (ICOEI); 2019. p. 523–528.

[14] Jovanovska EM and Davcev D. No pollution Smart City Sightseeing Based on WSN Monitoring System. In: 2020 Sixth International Conference on Mobile And Secure Services (MobiSecServ); 2020. p. 1–6.

[15] Yousuf Y and Potdar V. A Survey of RFID Authentication Protocols. In: 22nd International Conference on Advanced Information Networking and Applications – Workshops (AINA workshops 2008); 2008. p. 1346–1350.

[16] Pârvulescu C, Aldrigo M, Tomescu R, *et al.* Multilayer Anti-Counterfeiting Tag with Holographic Elements Integrated into a Compact RFID System. In: 2023 IEEE 13th International Conference on RFID Technology and Applications (RFID-TA); 2023. p. 107–110.

[17] Wang JJH. Antennas for Global Navigation Satellite System (GNSS). Proceedings of the IEEE. 2012;100(7):2349–2355.

[18] Kameda S, Oguma H, Izuka N, *et al.* Proposal of Heterogeneous Wireless Communication Network with Soft Handover in Application Layer: Feasibility Study Based on Field Trial Results. In: 2011 6th International ICST

Conference on Cognitive Radio Oriented Wireless Networks and Communications (CROWNCOM); 2011. p. 211–215.
[19] Agrawal J, Patel R, Mor DP, *et al.* Evolution of Mobile Communication Network: From 1G to 4G. International Journal of Multidisciplinary and Current Research. 2015;3. Available from: https://api.semanticscholar.org/CorpusID:65104118.
[20] Jiang W and Han B. In: Evolution to Second-Generation (2G) Mobile Cellular Communications. Cham: Springer Nature Switzerland; 2024. p. 23–36. Available from: https://doi.org/10.1007/978-3-031-57820-5_3.
[21] JunWu X and JunLing L. Develop Mobile Application with J2ME for 3G Networks. In: 2010 Second International Workshop on Education Technology and Computer Science. vol. 1; 2010. p. 770–773.
[22] He L and Zhao C. 4G Technology Promote Mobile Learning for New Development. In: 2008 International Symposium on Knowledge Acquisition and Modeling; 2008. p. 486–490.
[23] Varotto M, Valentin S, and Tomasin S. Detecting 5G Signal Jammers Using Spectrograms with Supervised and Unsupervised Learning. In: 2024 IEEE International Conference on Communications Workshops (ICC Workshops); 2024. p. 767–772.
[24] Yrjölä S, Matinmikko-Blue M, and Ahokangas P. Developing 6G Visions with Stakeholder Analysis of 6G Ecosystem. In: 2023 Joint European Conference on Networks and Communications & 6G Summit (EuCNC/6G Summit); 2023. p. 705–710.
[25] Wang D, Sun C, Liu L, *et al.* 5G Integrated Radio Transmission Scheme for Low Earth Orbit Satellite Access Network. In: 2022 IEEE 22nd International Conference on Communication Technology (ICCT); 2022. p. 1417–1420.
[26] Rasila T and Ojala A. In: Ojala A, Baber WW, editors. National Regulation of Satellite Ground Stations: A Global Comparison. Singapore: Springer Nature Singapore; 2024. p. 195–217. Available from: https://doi.org/10.1007/978-981-97-3430-6_8.
[27] Phuc BH, Van Quang P, Linh NQ, *et al.* Dynamic Threading to Improve Embedded Software Performance in IoT Devices Using MQTT Protocol. In: 2018 International Conference on Advanced Technologies for Communications (ATC); 2018. p. 321–325.
[28] Choi DK, Jung JH, and Koh SJ. Enhanced Cluster-based CoAP in Internet-of-Things Networks. In: 2018 International Conference on Information Networking (ICOIN); 2018. p. 652–656.
[29] Linthicum DS. Connecting Fog and Cloud Computing. IEEE Cloud Computing. 2017;4(2):18–20.
[30] Song Y, Yau SS, Yu R, *et al.* An Approach to QoS-based Task Distribution in Edge Computing Networks for IoT Applications. In: 2017 IEEE International Conference on Edge Computing (EDGE); 2017. p. 32–39.
[31] Zhang J and Tao D. Empowering Things With Intelligence: A Survey of the Progress, Challenges, and Opportunities in Artificial Intelligence of Things. IEEE Internet of Things Journal. 2021;8(10):7789–7817.

[32] Tewari A and Gupta BB. Security, Privacy and Trust of Different Layers in Internet-of-Things (IoTs) Framework. Future Generation Computer Systems. 2020;108:909–920. Available from: https://www.sciencedirect.com/science/article/pii/S0167739X17321003.

[33] Tahir R and McDonald-Maier K. Improving Resilience Against Node Capture Attacks in Wireless Sensor Networks Using ICmetrics. In: 2012 Third International Conference on Emerging Security Technologies; 2012. p. 127–130.

[34] Fan Y, Zhao G, Li KC, *et al.* SNPL: One Scheme of Securing Nodes in IoT Perception Layer. Sensors. 2020;20(4). Available from: https://www.mdpi.com/1424-8220/20/4/1090.

[35] Altulaihan E, Almaiah MA, and Aljughaiman A. Cybersecurity Threats, Countermeasures and Mitigation Techniques on the IoT: Future Research Directions. Electronics. 2022;11(20). Available from: https://www.mdpi.com/2079-9292/11/20/3330.

[36] Makhdoom I, Abolhasan M, Franklin D, *et al.* Detecting Compromised IoT Devices: Existing Techniques, Challenges, and a Way Forward. Computers & Security. 2023;132:103384. Available from: https://www.sciencedirect.com/science/article/pii/S0167404823002948.

[37] Faraj O, Megías D, and Garcia-Alfaro J. ZIRCON: Zero-Watermarking-Based Approach for Data Integrity and Secure Provenance in IoT Networks. Journal of Information Security and Applications. 2024;85:103840. Available from: https://www.sciencedirect.com/science/article/pii/S221421262400142X.

[38] Bukhowah R, Aljughaiman A, and Rahman MMH. Detection of DoS Attacks for IoT in Information-Centric Networks Using Machine Learning: Opportunities, Challenges, and Future Research Directions. Electronics. 2024;13(6). Available from: https://www.mdpi.com/2079-9292/13/6/1031.

[39] Wu CK. IoT Perception Layer Security. Singapore: Springer Singapore; 2021. p. 95–106. Available from: https://doi.org/10.1007/978-981-16-1372-2_6.

[40] Almarri S and Aljughaiman A. Blockchain Technology for IoT Security and Trust: A Comprehensive SLR. Sustainability. 2024;16(23). Available from: https://www.mdpi.com/2071-1050/16/23/10177.

[41] Musaddiq A, Olsson T, and Ahlgren F. Reinforcement-Learning-Based Routing and Resource Management for Internet of Things Environments: Theoretical Perspective and Challenges. Sensors. 2023;23(19). Available from: https://www.mdpi.com/1424-8220/23/19/8263.

[42] Sharma R, Pandey N, and Khatri SK. Analysis of IoT Security at Network Layer. In: 2017 6th International Conference on Reliability, Infocom Technologies and Optimization (Trends and Future Directions) (ICRITO); 2017. p. 585–590.

[43] Adil M, Jan MA, Mastorakis S, *et al.* Hash-MAC-DSDV: Mutual Authentication for Intelligent IoT-Based Cyber–Physical Systems. IEEE Internet of Things Journal. 2022;9(22):22173–22183.

[44] Wan Y, Xu K, Xue G, *et al.* IoTArgos: A Multi-Layer Security Monitoring System for Internet-of-Things in Smart Homes. In: IEEE INFOCOM 2020 – IEEE Conference on Computer Communications; 2020. p. 874–883.

[45] Diène B, Rodrigues JJPC, Diallo O, *et al.* Data Management Techniques for Internet of Things. Mechanical Systems and Signal Processing. 2020;138:106564. Available from: https://www.sciencedirect.com/science/article/pii/S088832701930785X.

[46] Zhang Z, Chen H, Liu L, *et al.* Smart Agriculture System Based on HarmonyOS. In: 2023 7th International Conference on Electrical, Mechanical and Computer Engineering (ICEMCE); 2023. p. 214–217.

[47] Cui Q, Kan H, Zhao J, *et al.* Current Status of Smart City Researches in China Using the Co-Word Analysis Method. In: 4th International Conference on Smart and Sustainable City (ICSSC 2017); 2017. p. 1–6.

[48] Yoon Jj. The Case Study of Smart Home in LH. In: 2019 IEEE Transportation Electrification Conference and Expo, Asia-Pacific (ITEC Asia-Pacific); 2019. p. 1–4.

[49] Ji Z, Yanhong Z, Wang B, *et al.* Human–Cyber–Physical Systems (HCPSs) in the Context of New-Generation Intelligent Manufacturing. Engineering. 2019.

[50] Yu X and Xue Y. Smart Grids: A Cyber–Physical Systems Perspective. Proceedings of the IEEE. 2016;104(5):1058–1070.

Chapter 10
Intelligent transportation system

Yujie Song[1], Junqiao Gao[1], Yue Cao[1] and Bo Zhao[1]

This chapter introduces the development of intelligent transportation system, pre-sentative characteristics, architecture, advantages and disadvantages, technologies, security, and applications.

10.1 Introduction

Intelligent Transportation System (ITS) is a holistic system employed in the whole transportation management system, including information, communication, sensing, electronic control, Artificial Intelligence (AI), and computer technologies [1]. ITS provides comprehensive, real-time, accurate, efficient transportation and management capabilities to service citizens and operate the city efficiently, such as traffic control [2,3], disaster management [4,5], and driver monitoring [6,7]. The development of ITS is divided into three parts with the view of technologies as shown in Figure 10.1.

- The development stage of traditional ITS with electronation and informatization.
- The development stage of novel generation ITS with networking and cooperation.
- The development stage of advanced generation ITS with digital intelligence and automation [8].

The development of traditional ITS with electronation and informatization builds the architecture of ITS, forming the complete technical framework (1970–2005). In the 1970s and 1980s, as urbanization continued to increase, traffic congestion became a major enemy affecting travel. Meanwhile, with the rapid extension of highways and the increasing speed of vehicles, it has become inevitable to strengthen the safety monitoring and management of numerous vehicles. Furthermore, in the 1990s, the US spread two landmark bills for ITS development, namely the Intermodal Surface Transportation Efficiency Act (ISTEA) and the Transportation Equity Act for the 21st Century (TEA-21) [9,10], respectively. Specifically, in the ISTEA, the research and implementation of ITS have piggybacked the central project of traffic construction policy with the financial support of the United States Department of Transportation

[1]School of Cyber Science and Engineering, Wuhan University, China

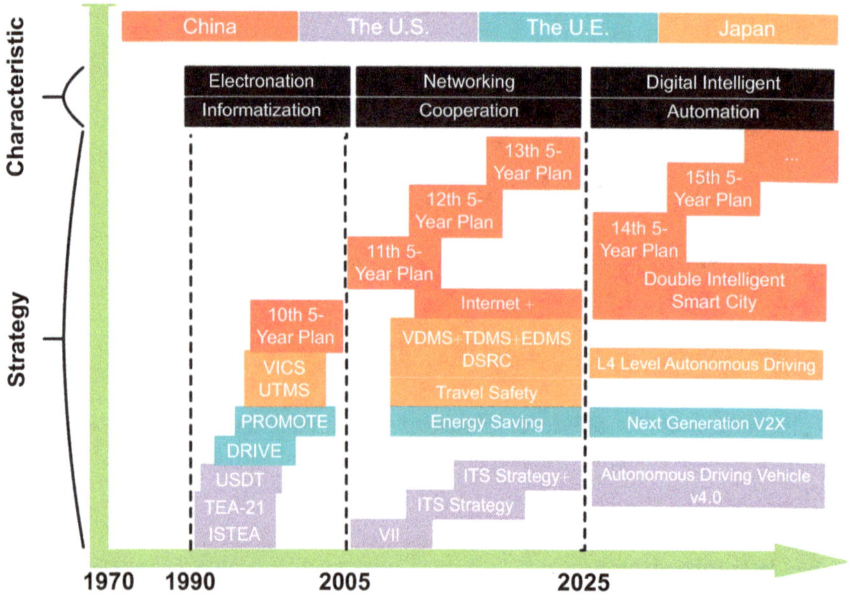

Figure 10.1 The development of ITS

(USDT) [11]. During the ISTEA implementation period, the USDT organizes various ITS projects including ITS technology development and operational testing. To integrate the ITS with traffic arrangement and improve the cross-area cooperation of private resources, TEA-21 focuses on the infrastructure and integration of ITS, such as the development of key standards, the consistency of architecture, and standards of ITS.

Furthermore, the United Europe (UE) proposed several bills to address road safety and traffic management problems, e.g., the Dedicated Road Infrastructure for Vehicle Safety in Europe (DRIVE) [12], PROgram for MObility in Transportation in Europe (PROMOTE) [13]. Japan proposed the Universal Traffic Management System (UTMS) and Vehicle Information and Communication System (VICS) [14,15]. Specifically, DRIVE provides navigation, event detection, traffic control, requirement management, and multimodal transportation. Based on the above bill, PROMOTE focuses on vehicle–road communication, collision avoidance, Electronic Toll Collection (ETC), and traffic data sharing. To explore the integration of vehicle and information systems, UTMS with several digital systems has been researched and implemented in Japan, e.g., the integrated traffic control system, advanced mobile information system, mobile operation control system, dynamic route guidance system, and public transportation priority system. Japan employed the VICS as the national ITS development strategy to improve the efficiency of navigation systems, traffic optimization and management, emergency vehicle rescue, etc.

Moreover, the ITS framework with various standards of China establishes the foundation of ITS development and illustrates its development directions. During the 10th 5-year plan period (2000–2005), 12 key technologies supported projects for ITS have established to explore the basic theoretical research, road construction framework, and conception of smart roads, including in-vehicle information devices, traffic information collection, Dedicated Short Range Communication (DSRC) [16], vehicle safety assistance, and traffic shared information platform. Thanks to the mushroom technology of internet and development of communication technologies, the requirement of ITS can be satisfied.

The development stage of novel generation ITS with networking and cooperation expands the connotation and application of ITS (2005–2025), integrating novel technologies, formats, and models, e.g., cloud computing, Internet of Things (IoTs), big data, and AI. The US promotes the Vehicle-Infrastructure Integration [17] to develop the vehicle–road cooperation system based on the Vehicle-to-Vehicle (V2V) and Vehicle-to-Infrastructure (V2I) communications [18]. In 2010, the ITS strategy project (2010–2014) was proposed by the US government to continually improve research on V2V/V2I communication and vehicle safety assistance system, etc. In 2020, the new generation ITS strategy (2020–2025) illustrates the importance and requirements of ITS implementation to construct a systemic and complete travel service system. It focuses on energetic management technologies, cyber security, data access and exchange, autonomous driving, and accelerated ITS deployment.

Furthermore, Japan has changed the focus from traditional content (e.g., navigation system, traffic optimization and management, etc.) to improvements in travel safety, traffic fluidity, environment protection, and Quality of Experience (QoE). ITS collects and processes traffic data and directly provides service information to citizens with visualization. Several projects are promoted to perceive and construct a digital environment, such as DSRC, advanced safety vehicles, and driving safety support systems. Meanwhile, the ITS world congress indicates that the ITS development and proposes several subjects, development directions, and key techniques, e.g., vehicle data management system, traffic data management system, energy data management system, and mobility as a service [19]. The green-intelligent transportation mode has received more sights. Digital twins, intelligent vehicles and infrastructure, and vehicle–road cooperation become major topics for future ITS development.

Moreover, intelligent transportation has entered the stages of innovation and development since 2015 in China. Specifically, the model with Internet+, transportation cooperation service, big data, AI, and autonomous driving focuses on improving the efficiency of digitalization system for ITS. Thanks to massive sensors and mobile terminals, the perceived data is utilized to establish the relationship among the above subjects to integrate perceiving, communication, and computing. Then, a series of outlines is proposed to construct a holistic system with AI, networking, data, offloading, and management until 2035, e.g., the outline of building a strong country in transportation, traffic development planning, national stereoscopic traffic architecture, etc.

The development stage of advanced generation ITS with digital intelligence and automation provides digital intelligent, virtual-real synthesis, and high-performance automation services (2025+), updating the concept and model of ITS, so-called, double intelligence. Vehicles with L4-level autonomous driving services support ubiquitous connectivity in Japan. The UE has proposed the technical route to support the implementation of next-generation Vehicle-to-Everything (V2X) and achieve commercial deployment of unmanned driving in 2030. The US has proposed a project about autonomous driving vehicles v4.0 to improve the implementation of ITS applications. In China, various cities have built test driving and operating areas, and the department of transportation has invested a series of projects about autonomous driving and intelligent shipping.

Furthermore, the changes in transportation system elements and system operations reflect important trends in the future ITS, including the holographic transportation, digital transportation, robustness transportation, green transportation, and autonomous transportation.

- **Holographic transportation:** the massive heterogeneous devices (e.g., mobile terminals, in-vehicle devices, machine vision, embedded sensors) and networks (e.g., infrastructure networks, core networks, and IoVs) will establish a multiple dimensional and spatial–temporal traffic system, realizing dynamic perception and real-time interaction of pedestrians–vehicles–roads, environment, dynamic management optimization, and intelligent services.
- **Digital transportation:** the digital-twins system, building information modeling, and high-definition map are built based on traffic perceiving, real-time data analysis, and intelligent decision-making, to improve the traffic resource allocation and QoE of users.
- **Robustness transportation:** traffic resources can be optimized and efficiently allocated through reservation and sharing, to cope with traffic requirements. Furthermore, traffic infrastructures can predict and adapt to the changing external environment based on dynamic sensing, providing fined data for traffic resources management.
- **Green transportation:** the structure of transportation energy consumption is changed to pursue the goal of zero emissions, promote ecological construction, and operate transportation infrastructure.
- **Autonomous transportation:** it is an intelligent and complex traffic system with autonomous perception, learning, decision-making, response, etc.

In conclusion, the evolution of ITS is demand-driven and technology-driven for complex systems and technology iterations. Each generation of ITS (traditional ITS, novel ITS, and advanced generation ITS) does not represent a subversion of preceding systems, but the inheritance and innovation of the existing development aimed at enhancement.

10.2 The presentative characteristics of ITS development stages

The presentative characteristics of ITS development stages consist of (1) electronation and information, (2) networking and cooperation, and (3) digital intelligence and automation.

10.2.1 Electronation and informatization

The traditional ITS is called ITS-1.0. Its major supporting technology is the service-oriented electronic information technology. The electronation and information technologies are key words of ITS-1.0, and its contents are listed as follows:

- **The widespread application of electronic communication and computer information technologies.** In the early development of ITS in the US, Europe, Japan, etc., the application of advanced electronics and communication technology in the field of transportation was the pioneer. Furthermore, the construction of single electronic communication, other technical products, and transportation application systems are the main research and development contents.
- **The major foundation is information technology-driven traffic informatization.** The basic process of constructing ITS involves the perception, processing, and service of traffic information. Furthermore, the business-oriented informatization technology system is the key development item, including the intelligent traffic management system, intelligent security system, and intelligent traffic information service system.
- **The framework structure of ITS is constructed based on system engineering methods.** In the process, drawing on the ideas of software engineering, a logical framework with functional processing and information flow analysis as the main contents, and a physical framework based on concrete implementation are necessary to achieve service objects.

10.2.2 Networking and cooperation

The next-generation ITS is called ITS-2.0. The novel information-oriented technology paradigm is proposed to improve disadvantages of ITS-1.0 and promote the shift from a people-oriented to a data-oriented model, including big data, mobile internet, big data, and cloud computing. Its contents are listed as follows:

- **Traffic element interconnection and holographic traffic awareness.** Novel monitoring devices (e.g., high-definition video devices) have changed the paradigm of traffic information collection, i.e., instead of detecting traffic flow data in the past, multi-dimensional indicators (e.g., traffic status, vehicle status, traffic environment, personalized information, and dynamic information on infrastructure status) are now fully perceived. The above data can be utilized to construct a whole digital world and provide a high probability of full spatial–temporal traffic perception.
- **Vehicles and Roadside Units (RSUs) are integrated to implement vehicle–road cooperation.** In this mode, the real-time perception and interaction of vehicle–road information enable more efficient and safe traffic operation and management for user travel.
- **Informatization infrastructure and digital transportation development.** Various information technology infrastructures [e.g., 5 Generation (5G), IoTs, cloud computing, edge computing] promote the integration of physical devices

and digital technologies. This integration drives the digitalization process and provides hardware/software support for autonomous decision-making.

- **The integration application of big data and AI in ITS.** The traffic big data has become an important resource for ITS by the perceiving, processing, and storing technologies. Various information technologies are utilized to refine those data, e.g., cloud computing, offloading, and AI. Therefore, data-driven technologies improve the intelligent traffic operation and control with precise services, thanks to the feature mining and utilization of numerous data.
- **Green ecology and multi-modal synergy have become the necessary path for ITS development.** As ecological environmental protection is focused by citizens, the ecological and green intelligent travel has emerged as one of the characteristics of ITS. The cooperation of people–vehicle–road and transportation modes become the major topics of ITS system application.
- **A novel model of intelligent travel.** Based on the implement of online taxi, reservation travel, and shared travel, the novel model of intelligent travel is employed to improve the QoE of users.

10.2.3 Digital intelligence and automation

In ITS-3.0, the intelligent mobile Internet based on people–vehicle–road–environment forms a holistic traffic information network. To operate this network, various advanced technologies focus on improving travel safety, personalization, refinement, and intelligence, such as the dynamic scheduling and control optimization of requirements of transportation systems, and collaborative operation of multi-modal transportation networks.

- **Digital wisdom.** Digital wisdom is the synthesis of intelligent technologies and digitalization, which is an important trend in the development of digital transformation. The future transportation informatization is the comprehensive, full-coverage, and End-to-End (E2E) traffic digitalization in the framework of people–vehicle–roads cooperation.
- **Organization.** The popularity of intelligent networking vehicles, the establishment of vehicle–road cooperation systems, and the commercialization of autonomous driving technology have led to significant changes in the operation mechanism and organization of transportation systems.
- **Automation.** The next-generation ITS characterized by digital intelligence and automation begins to advance the development of autonomous transportation systems and enhances the foundation for self-organized operation and autonomous services. Furthermore, the integration of smart highway, smart shipping, smart civil aviation, smart railroad, and smart city constitutes a new efficient, safe, intelligent, and autonomous transportation system.

The different focus of ITS development between various countries is shown in Table 10.1. The focus of various countries is different according to the requirements of their development targets. First, China focuses on interdisciplinary transportation technologies, including stereo transportation networks, multi-modal integration, and advanced intelligent management. Second, in the US, the implementation of ITS

Table 10.1 The detail of representative development direction and focus in different countries

Country	Representative development direction	Focus
China	(1) Stereo transportation network (2) Multi-modal integration (3) Advanced intelligent management	Interdisciplinary
The US	(1) Implement of its applications (2) Data sharing and network security (3) Communication technology	Technology innovation
The UE	(1) Service-orient and energy-saving (2) Intelligent, ecological, and safety travel	Energy and efficiency
Japan	(1) ETC, vehicle–road cooperation, navigation (2) In-vehicle device service	In-vehicle service

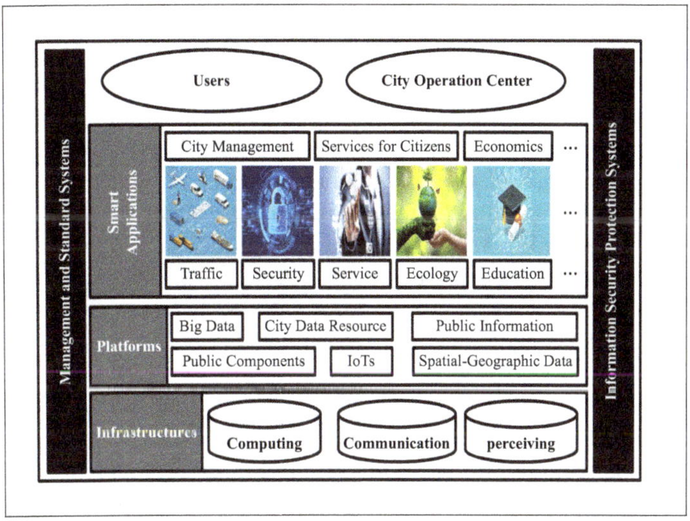

Figure 10.2 The architecture of ITS

applications, data sharing, networking security, and communication technologies are improved to innovate ITS technologies. Third, the UE focuses on saving energy based on service-orient applications and intelligent technologies, to provide efficient, intelligent, ecological, and safe travel. Finally, Japan expands the in-vehicle devices services to provide the in-vehicle services, e.g., ETC, navigation, etc.

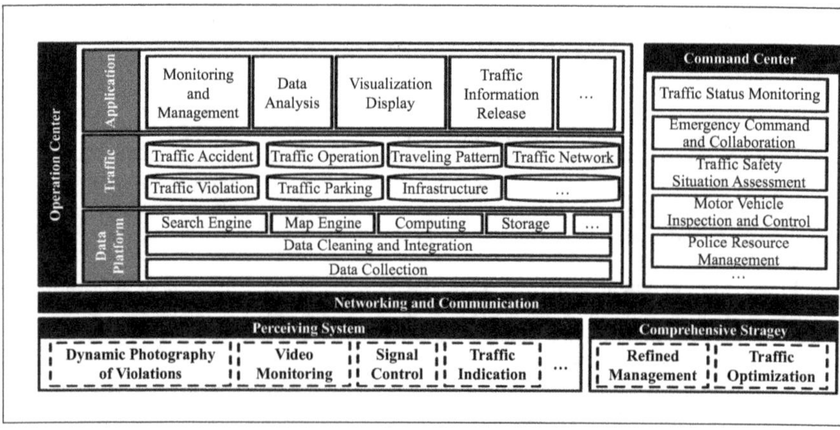

Figure 10.3 The traffic management and standard system

10.3 The architecture of ITS

10.3.1 Overall architecture

The overall architecture of ITS is shown in Figure 10.2. ITS plays a significant role in constructing a digital city by sharing basic information and building a perceiving system. Specifically, events, spatial-geographic data, and parking lots belong to basic information. A perceiving system consists of communication, computer security, and engine technologies.

Furthermore, transportation construction is divided into intelligence command centers, transportation platforms, perceiving systems, cloud storage systems, and optical transmission links. As an example of a perceiving system, cameras photograph various photos to grasp the people who run a red light or park violation. Those photos are refined (i.e., something after processing has higher quality) and uploaded to a traffic department and will be shared with other complementary systems, such as a big data platform.

The traffic management and standard systems are shown in Figure 10.3. The cloud computing, big data, and other informatization technologies are integrated into ITS, sharing data between departments, monitoring traffic status, and scheduling elements in ITS. Moreover, the functions and roles of transportation infrastructure are fully utilized to provide an effective guarantee for the operational efficiency and management improvement of ITS.

10.3.2 Perceiving system

The perceiving system is utilized to perceive traffic environments in a city, including dynamic photography of violations, video monitoring, signal control, traffic indication, etc. Based on sensors employed in the above applications, ITS can perceive the changes in traffic environments and collect data to analyze for intelligent traffic decision-making.

10.3.3 Comprehensive strategy

The comprehensive strategy focuses on refining the models of managements and optimizing the traffic organization to improve the universality of management strategies in various scenario of ITS. Specifically, the fine-tuning management provides customized strategy services for administrators, such as infrastructure development for multi-scenarios, road construction projects, etc. Then, the optimization of traffic organization is responsible for improving the efficiency of traffic operation and optimizing the allocation of traffic resources.

10.3.4 Networking and communication

Networking and communication technologies are an integral step in the data transmission process to enable edge-cloud data transmission. A novel networking technology can reduce the computing overhead, computing time, and network overhead to provide high stable quality of networks, such as 5G/6G, space-ground integrated information networks, etc. Meanwhile, novel communication technology provides ultra-low E2E latency between sender and receiver, such as beamforming, channel evaluation, data allocation, etc.

10.3.5 Operation center

The operation center consists of data platforms, traffic, and applications. Specifically, based on the perceived data from edge devices, data platform collects, cleans, and integrates data by various engines, e.g., search engine, map engine, etc. The refined data is utilized to support information and satisfy the requirements of ITS applications. Furthermore, data can be classified into various categories according to application scenarios, such as traffic accidents, parking, violations, networking, etc. Moreover, ITS applications provide services by searching and processing data according to specific scenarios or requirements of users, including monitoring, regional data analysis, traffic information release, etc.

10.3.6 Command center

The command center focuses on monitoring traffic status, managing traffic signal lights, responding to special events, scheduling police, etc. Its responsibility is to rapidly restore the traffic environment when an emergency occurs.

10.4 The advantages and disadvantages in ITS

10.4.1 Advantages

10.4.1.1 Precise visibility

Ubiquitous sensors perceive traffic data to monitor the real-time change in traffic status. The collected data is filtered, processed, and integrated to construct data features, i.e., refining the process of data. Furthermore, the refined data is classified into various databases according to the different application scenarios. To improve the QoE of users, the corresponding data is utilized to train models and predict the traffic status according to the requirement of applications.

10.4.1.2 High security

Security is a hot topic in every domain, especially in ITS. On the one hand, ITS provides multi-dimensional data to assist in driving accident avoidance. According to the supplement of real-time data, pedestrians can receive messages about abnormal vehicles and their trajectories to perform emergency avoidance. On the other hand, to reduce potential accidents caused by distracted drivers, ITS monitors the driver's status concerning mood, fatigue, and whether interferences are present based on the techniques of emotion analysis and fatigue detection. Then, ITS provides various autonomous services for drivers to avoid maloperations, such as autonomous driving, auxiliary driving, autonomous parking, etc.

10.4.1.3 Easy management

The management system in ITS is utilized to monitor operations and track maintenance, increasing the capability of traffic awareness and control. Perceiving data reflects the change of traffic status, and comprehensive strategies support partially automatic decision-making according to the perceiving data. Furthermore, the command center provides several data and instruction services, such as traffic status monitoring, emergency command and collaboration, traffic safety situation assessment, motor vehicle inspection and control, police resource management, etc.

10.4.1.4 High efficiency

According to data-driven and decision-making systems, ITS improves the travel QoE of users by dynamically optimizing travel paths and arranging travel time. Compared with the last generation ITS, the data collection mode provides massive data support for ITS, and achieves high data utilization by data reorganization and modeling. Then, the real-time perceived data can be utilized to predict traffic status changes and improve traffic operation efficiency.

10.4.1.5 Low cost

Thanks to the data support and intelligent decision-making, ITS drives green travel in collaboration with all aspects of technologies (e.g., intelligent battery change and charging, platoon arrangement, and intelligent communication) and supports affordable public travel to reduce energy consumption and accidents. For instance, the data-driven charging application plans the path for electric vehicles to charging stations, which can reduce the waiting time in a queue and the energy consumption of electric vehicles.

10.4.2 Disadvantages

10.4.2.1 Deployment and replenishment of sensors

Various sensors with different interfaces, installation, and networking requirements are hardly deployed within a limited space, such as alleyway, lane, tunnel, etc.

Furthermore, where to deploy sensors to alleviate interference, increase data transmission efficiency, and reduce costs is a challenge. Then, unexpected errors and abnormalities often appear when the equipment is running. Locating and maintaining damaged devices will consume a lot of human and material resources costs. Moreover, sensor monitoring and performance optimization systems require considerable financial support. To facilitate people to manage massive heterogenous sensors, the virtualization and intelligence of heterogeneous devices needs further development.

10.4.2.2 User privacy and security

In the process of On-Board Unit (OBU) device operation, user privacy data needs to be collected and transmitted in real time. Specifically, the above process involves different flow links and operation types, such as collection, transmission, storage, query, and modification of user privacy data. These operations are highly likely to cause data leakage, affecting users' personal safety and driving safety. Furthermore, a variety of attacks will violate user privacy (e.g., name, location, financial, social relationship, personal identity number) because the heterogenous devices have different potential security issues. Therefore, user privacy needs to be further protected during the process data transmission and storage.

10.4.3 Challenges

Based on data filtering and processing technologies, valuable information can be mined and utilized in the decision-making system in ITS. However, besides secure transmission and data sharing, ITS encounters a variety of challenges, i.e., non-uniform industry standards, inadequate infrastructures, poor data quality, privacy leakage risk, data risk, data storage security, inadequate financial, and cross-domain technology.

10.4.3.1 Untimely data sharing

The lack of effective data communication and sharing among departments and platforms is one of the challenges. Specifically, the existence of serious data transmission barriers leads to the fragmented distribution of traffic data, low data utilization, and difficulty in data synchronization within an ultra-low latency, which seriously restricts the accessibility, real-time and reliability of traffic data sharing. Furthermore, the information systems of each department are independent of each other, and the data standards and formats are different, resulting in limited perception and collection of traffic data. It is difficult to improve the utility of data since the potential value of data lacks performance mining.

10.4.3.2 Non-uniform industry standards

In terms of implementing ITS projects, there is no unified industry standard in different countries and regions, causing different versions of ITS to be relatively independent. Specifically, various sensors produced by different manufacturers do not have uniform standard interfaces, thus mismatched interfaces cannot deliver data between heterogeneous systems. Then, the different data types cannot be processed by a special model with different versions, causing data redundancy and computing resource abuse for data processing.

10.4.3.3 Inadequate infrastructures

As ITS without robustness becomes more integrated and complex, its stability is challenging. A massive number of servers and devices generate data in inconsistent formats, including signal lights, RSUs, cameras, and routers. Furthermore, ITS is characterized by complex processes, numerous business systems, and heterogeneous clients, thus rendering non-normalized data difficult to deconstruct and utilize. With the system scale expansion, the number of devices increases and equipment failures grow. Then, faulty devices will affect the stability and reliability of data transmission in ITS.

10.4.3.4 Poor data quality

Data quality mainly refers to the authenticity or credibility of the data, which can be divided into two levels: (1) data provenance and (2) data distortion. Specifically, data mainly derives from devices such as sensors and surveillance equipment. Massive data generated by those devices makes it difficult to mine valid information. The large amount of invalid information may degrade data quality. Furthermore, various interference factors are existed in the process of data collection and transmission (e.g., channel interference, noise, etc.), which leads to a reduction in the data reliability.

10.4.3.5 Privacy leakage risk

User terminals generate a large amount of privacy sensitive personal data, e.g., personal name, financial, Identity, phone number, etc. However, in the process of data transmission and processing, data is at risk of leakage. If these leaked data are utilized illegally, it will cause significant consequences and even threaten personal life and property. Moreover, due to the huge amount of data, individual applications do not have clear standards to regulate the ownership and usage of sensitive data and do not even consider the personal privacy.

10.4.3.6 Inadequate financial

The lack of top-level design and funding budget for related intelligent transportation functions has resulted in a small scale of investment in ITS construction, affecting the overall planning and unified promotion of intelligent transportation construction. Furthermore, due to the lack of sufficient funds as a guarantee, it is difficult to achieve breakthroughs in the research and development of emerging technologies, such as artificial intelligence, blockchain, and intelligent networked vehicle–road cooperation.

10.4.3.7 Cross-domain technology

ITS as a holistic system consists of data perceiving, communication, processing, application, security, and other modules, involving physical, data link, network, transport, and application layers. For instance, the cross-domain/layer data flow control technology empowers multi-layer data collaborative transfer capability with inter-layer data perceiving and feedback. However, the feedback mechanism lacks efficiency and fails to satisfy the requirement of ultra-low latency applications, thus the inefficiency of cross-layer data transmission limits the decision-making capability of ITS to address the problem of real-time tasks.

10.5 Technologies in ITS

The technology in ITS is divided into the following five parts according to the architecture of ITS, i.e., (1) perceiving with sensors, (2) data processing, (3) networking and communication, (4) decision-making, and (5) operation and management.

10.5.1 Perceiving with sensors

Numerous sensors with perceiving capabilities are employed to be aware of the changes in the traffic environment, such as traffic lanes, data flows, accidents, events, violations, etc. Based on various types of sensors, different types of data are generated to reflect the traffic status in various ways, such as video, image, sound, radar, mobile terminal, OBU, etc. Furthermore, different perceiving technologies provide several ways to construct the multi-modal traffic model, including visual recognition technology, ultrasonic sensor technology, wireless communication technology, high-definition maps, and LiDaR technology.

10.5.1.1 Video and image

Videos and images are obtained by cameras and utilized to recognize objects and boundaries, such as vehicles, pedestrians, roads, traffic signals, etc. Those data work as input information to support decision-making. Based on this, the processed video and image data is significant for autonomous driving by integrating several new generation technologies, such as signal processing, image processing, AI, and edge computing. Several representative works are elaborated as follows.

The work [20] proposed a smart IoT-enabled deep learning system to detect E2E 3D objects for autonomous driving based on YOLOv3. The IoT-enabled system first perceives 2D objects and then constructs 3D objects, considering the point cloud, RGB image, and bounding box. Geiger *et al.* [21] proposed a data perceiving device (e.g., video cameras, laser scanners, localization systems) to collect the information of traffic entities and constructed the multi-sensor data set (namely, KITTI). KITTI is utilized to track and detect objects thanks to the perceiving data of various sensors, i.e., synchronized radio cameras, and LiDaR sensors. The work [22] proposed a subsystem to detect pedestrians in crosswalks based on the deep neural network. Real-time perceived images are decoded to construct the LiDaR point cloud based on a Convolutional Neural Network (CNN). The work [23] focused on identifying traffic signals based on a scoring support vector machine model. Multi-dimensional indicators are considered to process images, including traffic sign color, color gradient, and shape of traffic sign.

10.5.1.2 Radar

Radars can be divided into three categories, i.e., LiDaR, millimeter wave radar, and ultrasonic radar. They utilize the phenomenon of reflection or scattering of electromagnetic waves by targets to detect, locate, track, and identify targets. Radar technologies are employed on vehicles, shipboards, air boards, starboards, and so on.

Numerous works utilize radar technologies to perceive data for upper-layer applications. The work [24] proposed a collaborative fusion method to balance vehicle detection accuracy and computational efficiency. To alleviate the backlog of user data generated by numerous radars, an Orthogonal Frequency Division Multiple Access (OFDMA) method was proposed to support massive user communications in [25]. Similarly, the work [26] focused on designing cache placement and delivery strategies based on OFDMA in the cache-enabled heterogeneous cellular network. A novel proactive fairness and transmission-aware cache placement method was proposed to minimize latency. In cognitive radio enabled Vehicular Ad-hoc Networks (VANETs), the work [27] proposed a joint radar perceiving and data transmission framework, to address the problem about sensing-throughput trade-off.

10.5.2 Data processing

Data processing technologies consist of identification, extraction, data cleaning, reconstruction, and integration technologies. First, based on the perceived data, identification and extraction technologies recognize and transform data into a uniform type to facilitate analysis. Second, to seek the data with crucial information and unlock data value, the noise signal and data need to be filtered out by data cleaning technologies. Third, reconstruction and integration technologies are utilized to improve the utility of data based on the refined data and construct integrated multi-dimensional features of data.

10.5.2.1 Identification and extraction

Identification and extraction technologies filter the worthy data according to the requirements of applications to improve data quality. Specifically, the work [28] proposed a novel autonomous extraction system based on RGB images to seek the semi-transparent motion-blurred hand, including alpha matte prediction and foreground prediction with encoder–decoder networks. The above system can address the unclear image with residual shadow. Furthermore, the work [29] proposed a CNN-based three-channel prediction scheme, it extracts and processes a single RGB image to predict the foreground alpha matte based on a deep CNN. An extraction model [30] was proposed to seek the major lines from a 2D image based on the Sobel highlights. This model extracts cursive lines with a larger curvature and maintains the continuity of lines without sensitive edge thresholding.

10.5.2.2 Data cleaning

Data cleaning is an important tool to improve data quality and reduce the size of data. It detects and eliminates quality issues, such as errors and inconsistencies in data. Data will be evaluated and transformed after data analysis to ensure the weight of multi-dimensional data and refine data. Then, according to the requirements of users, various types of data are picked to form data sets to support the upper-layer applications.

Based on a frequency-domain signal model, a second-order transient-extraction transform [31] was proposed to normalize a non-stationary signal, considering the second-order delay, Time Frequency (TF), and energy-concentrated TF representation. To overcome the challenge that how to clean data noise with machine learning, the work [32] proposed a federated data cleaning protocol to protect data privacy in edge intelligence scenarios. Due to massive data generated by numerous user terminals in edge regions, those data processed by cloud centers will waste communication and computing resources, thus an angle-based data cleaning method [33] was proposed to analyze and process data in edge regions to reduce the network overhead and save computing resources.

10.5.2.3 Reconstruction and integration

According to various indicators (e.g., data type, generated time, location, importance, contents, etc.), reconstruction and integration technologies are designed to reduce the redundancy of data, communication cost, and energy consumption. Various reconstruction and integration methods consist of direct transmission models and multi-hop transmission models.

Direct transmission model: As shown in Figure 10.4, sensors directly transmit data to the aggregation node (a sensor), where the aggregation node centrally processes the received data. However, data transmission over long distances is easily affected by noise, causing more code errors and reducing the data quality.

Multi-hop transmission model: As shown in Figure 10.5, sensors transmit data to neighbor nodes based on an energy utility function. Specifically, some sensors work as intermediate nodes (i.e., N1, N2, N3, N4, N5) to relay data similar to the delay-tolerant network, to reduce the energy consumption of sensors. However, the intermediate node becomes the bottleneck when it has received massive data that exceeds its process capability.

Previous works focus on random mechanisms and AI-based methods, such as (1) weighted average mechanism [34], Kalman filter mechanism [35], Bayesian estimation mechanism [36], Dempster-Shafer (D-S) evidence inference mechanism [37], (2) fuzzy logic method [38], and neural networks [39].

Random mechanism: The work [34] proposed a weighted average method based on Fourier coefficients ratio and bilateral correction to resist noise. It utilizes the correction principle to respond to the changes in the initial phase, frequency deviation, and signal-to-noise ratio. To integrate data sets collected at different speeds in the same stage, an extensive performance comparison model is proposed in [35], combining the data of accelerometers and gyroscopes. The work [36] proposed a novel data integration model without the intervention of point spread function based on a Bayesian framework to integrate hyperspectral and multispectral images. According to the D-S evidence theory, the work [37] focused on integrating sensory information of heterogeneous sensors to monitor buildings in real-time by detecting the occupancy in a room from various ambient sources, e.g., humidity, CO_2, temperature, etc.

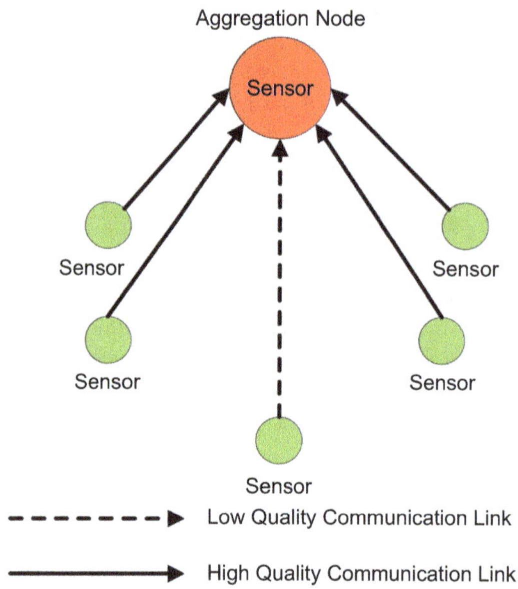

Figure 10.4 Direct transmission model

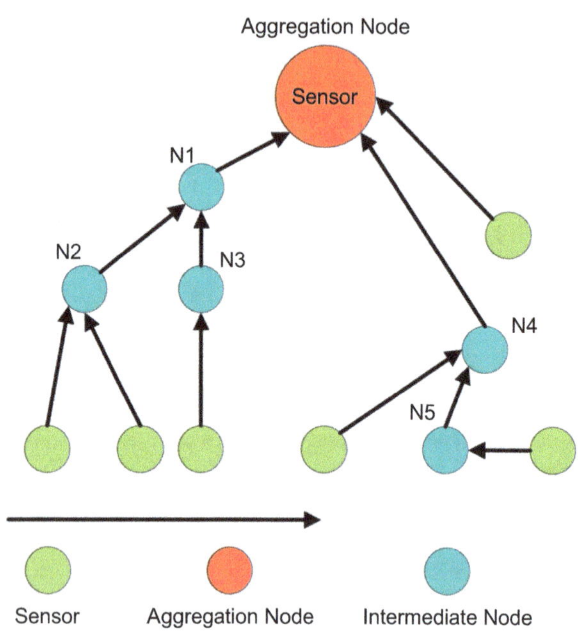

Figure 10.5 Multi-hop transmission model

AI-based method: To address the double-stage variant uncertainty problem, the work [38] proposed an adaptive integration method for multi-sensor odometry based on a fuzzy inference system. To avoid widespread traffic congestion, ST-ChebNet [39] was proposed to predict traffic flows based on the Chebyshev graph neural network with the spatial–temporal view.

10.5.3 Networking and communication

To improve the data quality and efficiency of data transmission, networking and communication technologies focus on networking mode and 5G Next Generation Core (5G NGC) [40], including the channel estimation, Software-Defined Network, network slicing, Mobile Edge Computing (MEC), and network function reconstructions.

10.5.3.1 Network mode

According to the connected objects, networking modes can be divided into two categories, i.e., Non-Stand Alone (NSA) and Stand Alone (SA).

NSA: As shown in Figure 10.6, user terminals are connected to both Long Term Evolution (LTE) and New Radio (NR) wireless access modes [41]. Based on the 4G Core Network (CN), numerous novel 5G infrastructures are deployed to server users and 5G applications by improving 4G CN. Furthermore, thanks to the basic network devices and services (i.e., 4G), NSA has the advantages of low cost, quick deployment, and rapid advancement of 5G network coverage.

SA: As shown in Figure 10.7, 4G user terminals connect to 4G infrastructures based on the LTE-based access mode, and 5G user terminals only establish connectivities with 5G infrastructures by NR-based wireless access mode. Furthermore, the SA model requires a longer time to advance the network, because the 5G infrastructure is

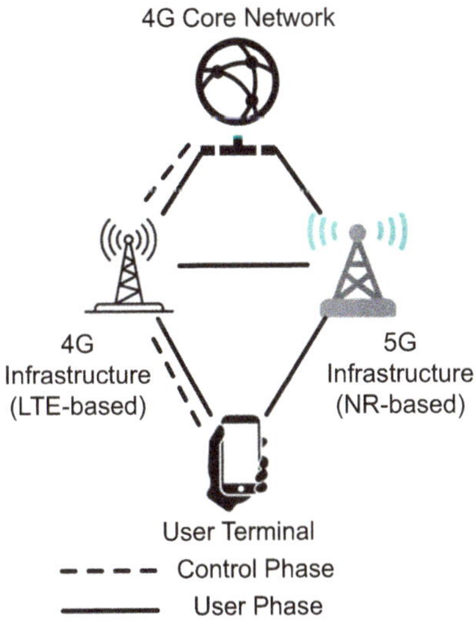

Figure 10.6 An example of NSA

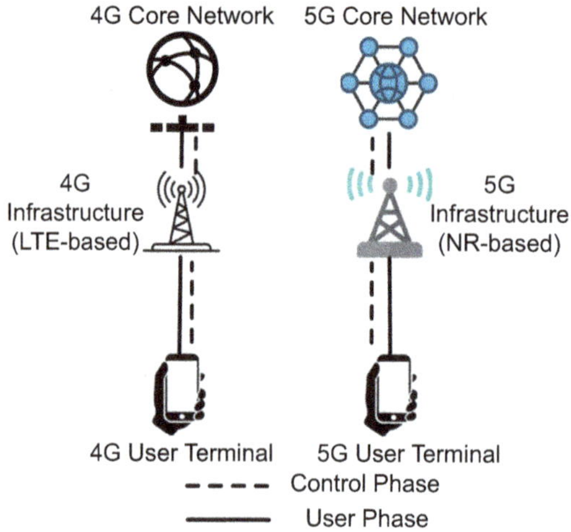

Figure 10.7 An example of SA

no longer connected to the 4G network. Specifically, 5G infrastructures establish connectivities with each other, and 5G CN needs to be developed from scratch. Moreover, all 5G applications are supported to leverage the ultra-low latency and high quality of services of the SA model.

10.5.3.2 5G NGC

5G NGC has four technical characteristics, i.e., (1) control-carrier separation, (2) MEC, (3) Network Function Virtualization (NFV), and (4) network slicing [42–45].

Control-carrier separation: It separates the user phase from the control phase, i.e., the data flow is separated from the control command flow. Operators can manage and upgrade software at any time to dynamically adjust network resource allocation and optimize data transmission efficiency. The above process is transparent to users to improve their QoE.

MEC: It effectively integrates wireless network and Internet technologies together. Specifically, wireless networks employ various additional functions (e.g., computing, storage, processing, etc.) and construct an open platform to implant applications. Furthermore, based on the information interactions between wireless networks and service servers through wireless application programming interfaces, MEC integrates wireless network and service servers to build intelligent base stations.

NFV: It represents that various virtualization technologies are utilized to realize network functions. The goal of NFV is to replace the private, dedicated, and closed network units of communication networks by implementing a unified common hardware and software platform. Furthermore, Figure 10.8 depicts the changes from a traditional network architecture to a novel network architecture (NFV-based unified virtualization platform). This novel platform provides several virtualization functions to optimize and allocate the computing, storage, and communication resources for better performance.

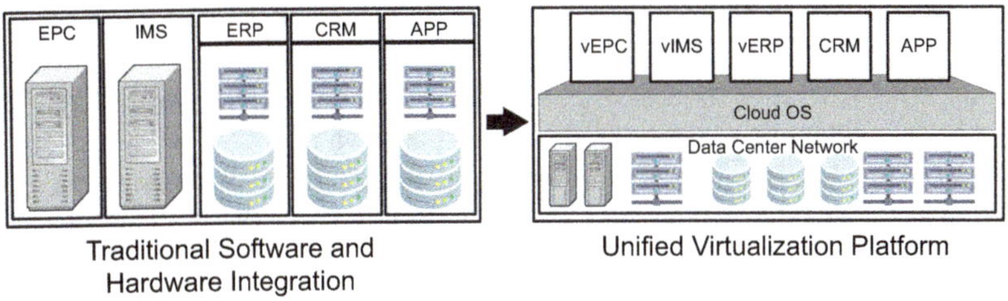

Figure 10.8 The evolution of network architectures

Network slicing: It is a virtual cut of network resources to provide customized services and complete E2E connectivity for users. Network slicing allows users to run their private mobile network without owning any hardware. Furthermore, network slicing is achieved through NFV, and all network functions can also be divided into different slices.

10.5.4 Operation and management

Thanks to various novel data-driven technologies and high-performance devices (e.g., big data, AI, cloud-edge cooperation, OBU, high-definition camera, etc.), operation and management platforms in ITS provide intelligent decision-making services according to various scenarios [46]. Based on the perceived data from numerous devices, the automated monitoring and management system provides visualization services for managers, including comprehensive situation monitoring, traffic status monitoring, electronic police system, signal control system, intelligent bus system, and emergency event monitoring.

10.6 Information security in ITS

The common security problems in ITS consist of communication security, terminal security, and cloud security.

10.6.1 Communication security

The 5G technology provides massive connectivity, high throughput, and ultra-low latency services thanks to numerous connectivities among network entities. However, massive communication security problems are explored with the development of novel communication models and network architectures [47], e.g., data tampering, link deletion, malicious packet loss, unauthorized access, etc.

To protect the communication security in ITS, numerous works focus on constructing confidentiality, integrity, availability, and controllability of communication. The work [48] investigated the physical layer security in 5G wireless networks, including the security coding, massive multiple-input multiple-output, heterogeneous networks, and millimeter wave communications. The randomness of channels is utilized to protect data transmission security in [48]. To improve the efficiency and compatibility with novel network designs, the work [49] proposed a two-stage network traffic anomaly detection mechanism based on 5G network architectures, including dimensionality reduction and traffic anomaly detection with deep neural networks. To implement of autonomous driving based on 5G-V2X, the work [50] proposed a novel architecture with network slicing and analyzed security requirements according to service types. The work [51] proposed to solve the gradient disappearance problem by modifying a loss function, providing an access control mechanism based on the risk prediction.

10.6.2 Terminal security

10.6.2.1 RSU security

The risks exposure of RSU mainly consists of wireless interface risks, device vulnerability risks, and maintenance risks. First, wireless interfaces, which is a mandatory route for data transmission, are a major focus of attackers and are vulnerable to the following risks such as fake terminal risk, pseudo base station risk, data eavesdropping risk, and data tampering risk [52]. Second, physical devices have inherent security vulnerabilities due to lapses in logic and generation processes. Third, human factors and natural weather affect the normal operation of RSU, i.e., maintenance risks.

10.6.2.2 In-vehicle security

In-vehicle security involves a wide range of elements, such as physical interface risk [53], wireless interface risk [54], access control risk [55], permission abuse risk [56], application risk [57], system vulnerabilities exposure risk [58], etc. Specifically, attackers compromise and take control of in-vehicle terminals, by exposing physical access interfaces to implant faulty hardware or upgrade malicious programs. Furthermore, the attacker spoofs, compromises, and controls vehicle terminals through wireless access (e.g., user to network interface, proximity communication, and bluetooth).

10.6.3 Cloud security

The business applications of cloud-based intelligent transportation information system face major security risks [59], e.g., the reliability, unclear security boundaries, malicious users, fake business servers, unauthorized access, and data security. Furthermore, the risks faced by edge cloud computing consist of insecure communication protocols, data vulnerability to corruption, insufficient privacy data protection, insecure systems, components, insufficient identity, credential and access management, account information vulnerability to hijacking, insecure interfaces, and vulnerability to launching distributed denial-of-service attacks [60].

10.7 Application in ITS

10.7.1 Smart bus

Based on the perceived traffic data, the smart bus is oriented to serve the transportation management department and build a visualized public transportation scheduling platform. This platform provides bus monitoring, operation regulation, decision-making, and scheduling services, thus reducing the cost of operating buses. Furthermore, the effectiveness of public transportation services is improved through an intelligent way, such as AI-assisted data mining and high-dimensional data integration.

10.7.2 Smart parking

Smart parking is concerned with information service demand and resource regulation to integrate the resource of parking information and provide intelligent navigation services. It improves the utility of parking resources and decreases parking costs.

10.7.3 Smart hub

Smart hubs construct the multi-dimensional perceiving and comprehensive interconnection system based on urban hub infrastructures, to provide efficient operation, safe operation, quality service, and multi-party collaborative wizard services.

10.7.4 Vehicle supervision

To avoid traffic accidents, vehicle supervision can realize the status monitoring of specified types of vehicles and personnel (such as truck driver fatigue monitoring, truck status detection, etc.) through the support of satellite positioning, vehicle video monitoring, and wireless communication technologies.

10.7.5 Road digital perceiving

Based on the road network monitoring and surveillance system, traffic statuses and road events are monitored thanks to the real-time perceiving infrastructures. The digital perceiving system consists of road facilities monitoring, traffic status monitoring, and highway meteorological environment monitoring.

10.7.6 Road smart maintenance

The road smart maintenance system is a comprehensive inspection information management system based on network and Geographic Information System (GIS), which mainly completes the tracking, supervision, information receiving, processing, and feedback of maintenance inspection situation. The maintenance system not only provides complete reports and data processing results, but also basic functions of web GIS system, which can be directly accessed and operated by web browser.

10.8 Conclusion

This chapter first introduced ITS and its development, including the definition of ITS and three development stages. Furthermore, according to the requirements of traffic informatization, the presentative characteristic of ITS development was proposed to illustrate the focus in different stages. Then, the architecture of ITS was divided into five parts, i.e., (1) perceiving system, (2) comprehensive strategy, (3) networking and communication, (4) operation center, and (5) command center. Based on the above division, the advantages, disadvantages, and challenges were listed to illustrate the development direction of ITS. Moreover, to capture recent advances in ITS, its technologies were introduced, including perceiving, data processing, networking, communication, operation, and management. To address the security problems in ITS, several aspects of security are investigated, such as communication security, terminal security, and cloud security. Finally, various applications were introduced.

References

[1] Smith BL and Demetsky MJ. Traffic flow forecasting: Comparison of modeling approaches. Journal of Transportation Engineering. 1997;123(4): 261–266.

[2] Hou Z, Xu JX, and Zhong H. Freeway traffic control using iterative learning control-based ramp metering and speed signaling. IEEE Transactions on Vehicular Technology. 2007;56(2):466–477.

[3] Jin J, Guo H, Xu J, *et al.* An end-to-end recommendation system for urban traffic controls and management under a parallel learning framework. IEEE Transactions on Intelligent Transportation Systems. 2020;22(3):1616–1626.

[4] Chandana S and Leung H. A system of systems approach to disaster management. IEEE Communications Magazine. 2010;48(3):138–145.

[5] George SM, Zhou W, Chenji H, *et al.* DistressNet: A wireless ad hoc and sensor network architecture for situation management in disaster response. IEEE Communications Magazine. 2010;48(3):128–136.

[6] Baccour MH, Driewer F, Schäck T, *et al.* Comparative analysis of vehicle-based and driver-based features for driver drowsiness monitoring by support vector machines. IEEE Transactions on Intelligent Transportation Systems. 2022;23(12):23164–23178.

[7] Chen LW and Chen HM. Driver behavior monitoring and warning with dangerous driving detection based on the internet of vehicles. IEEE Transactions on Intelligent Transportation Systems. 2020;22(11):7232–7241.

[8] Liao S, Wu J, Bashir AK, *et al.* Digital twin consensus for blockchain-enabled intelligent transportation systems in smart cities. IEEE Transactions on Intelligent Transportation Systems. 2022;23(11):22619–22629.

[9] Lyons WM. Policy innovations of the US intermodal surface transportation efficiency act and clean air act amendments. Transportation. 1995;22: 217–240.

[10] Bulger T and Crane S. Transportation Equity Act for the 21st century (TEA 21). TDM Review. 1998;6(3):1–4.
[11] Wang Sy and Shen HW. Incipient sediment motion and riprap design. Journal of Hydraulic Engineering. 1985;111(3):520–538.
[12] Libbrecht R. Dedicated road infrastructure for vehicle safety in Europe (drive). In: Conference on Metros at the 1992 European Horizon (1989: Brussels Belgium). Metros at the 1993 European Horizon; 1989.
[13] Brusaglino G. Safe and effective mobility in Europe-the contribution of the PROMETHEUS programme. In: IEE Colloquium on Prometheus and Drive. IET; 1992. p. 1.
[14] Aoyama KI. Universal traffic management system (UTMS) in Japan. In: Proceedings of VNIS'94-1994 Vehicle Navigation and Information Systems Conference. IEEE; 1994. p. 619–622.
[15] Yamamoto T, Onosato M, and Ogiso K. Vehicle information and communication system (VICS) information services via FM radio multiplex. In: Intelligent Transportation: Realizing the Future. Abstracts of the Third World Congress on Intelligent Transport SystemsITS America; 1996. .
[16] Qi W, Landfeldt B, Song Q, *et al.* Traffic differentiated clustering routing in DSRC and C-V2X hybrid vehicular networks. IEEE Transactions on Vehicular Technology. 2020;69(7):7723–7734.
[17] Ma Y, Chowdhury M, Sadek A, *et al.* Real-time highway traffic condition assessment framework using vehicle–infrastructure integration (VII) with artificial intelligence (AI). IEEE Transactions on Intelligent Transportation Systems. 2009;10(4):615–627.
[18] Song Y, Jiang K, Cao Y, *et al.* STALB: A spatio-temporal domain autonomous load balancing routing protocol. IEEE Transactions on Network and Service Management. 2022;20(1):73–87.
[19] Wong YZ, Hensher DA, and Mulley C. Mobility as a service (MaaS): Charting a future context. Transportation Research Part A: Policy and Practice. 2020;131:5–19.
[20] Ahmed I, Jeon G, and Chehri A. A smart IoT enabled end-to-end 3D object detection system for autonomous vehicles. IEEE Transactions on Intelligent Transportation Systems. 2022;24(11):13078–13087.
[21] Geiger A, Lenz P, and Urtasun R. Are we ready for autonomous driving? The KITTI vision benchmark suite. In: 2012 IEEE Conference on Computer Vision and Pattern Recognition. IEEE; 2012. p. 3354–3361.
[22] Guidolini R, Scart LG, Jesus LF, *et al.* Handling pedestrians in crosswalks using deep neural networks in the IARA autonomous car. In: 2018 International Joint Conference on Neural Networks (IJCNN). IEEE; 2018. p. 1–8.
[23] Tian B, Chen R, Yao Y, *et al.* Robust traffic sign detection in complex road environments. In: 2016 IEEE International Conference on Vehicular Electronics and Safety (ICVES). IEEE; 2016. p. 1–5.
[24] Wang X, Xu L, Sun H, *et al.* On-road vehicle detection and tracking using MMW radar and monovision fusion. IEEE Transactions on Intelligent Transportation Systems. 2016;17(7):2075–2084.

[25] Yang H, Wei Z, Feng Z, *et al.* Queue-aware dynamic resource allocation for the joint communication-radar system. IEEE Transactions on Vehicular Technology. 2020;70(1):754–767.

[26] Rezvani S, Mokari N, Javan MR, *et al.* Fairness and transmission-aware caching and delivery policies in OFDMA-based HetNets. IEEE Transactions on Mobile Computing. 2019;19(2):331–346.

[27] Huang S, Jiang N, Gao Y, *et al.* Radar sensing-throughput tradeoff for radar assisted cognitive radio enabled vehicular ad-hoc networks. IEEE Transactions on Vehicular Technology. 2020;69(7):7483–7492.

[28] Zhao X and Wu Y. Automatically extract semi-transparent motion-blurred hand from a single image. IEEE Signal Processing Letters. 2019;26(11):1598–1602.

[29] Zhang Y, Gong L, Fan L, *et al.* A late fusion cnn for digital matting. In: Proceedings of the IEEE/CVF Conference on Computer Vision and Pattern Recognition; 2019. p. 7469–7478.

[30] Kim J and Lee S. Extracting major lines by recruiting zero-threshold canny edge links along sobel highlights. IEEE Signal Processing Letters. 2015;22(10):1689–1692.

[31] He Z, Tu X, Bao W, *et al.* Second-order transient-extracting transform with application to time-frequency filtering. IEEE Transactions on Instrumentation and Measurement. 2019;69(8):5428–5437.

[32] Ma L, Pei Q, Zhou L, *et al.* Federated data cleaning: Collaborative and privacy-preserving data cleaning for edge intelligence. IEEE Internet of Things Journal. 2020;8(8):6757–6770.

[33] Wang T, Ke H, Zheng X, *et al.* Big data cleaning based on mobile edge computing in industrial sensor-cloud. IEEE Transactions on Industrial Informatics. 2019;16(2):1321–1329.

[34] Shao CL, Xu KJ, Shu ZP, *et al.* A frequency correcting method combining bilateral correction with weighted average for vortex flow sensor signal. IEEE Transactions on Instrumentation and Measurement. 2017;66(10):2711–2724.

[35] Erdem AT and Ercan AÖ. Fusing inertial sensor data in an extended Kalman filter for 3D camera tracking. IEEE Transactions on Image Processing. 2014;24(2):538–548.

[36] Lin B, Tao X, Xu M, *et al.* Bayesian hyperspectral and multispectral image fusions via double matrix factorization. IEEE Transactions on Geoscience and Remote Sensing. 2017;55(10):5666–5678.

[37] Nesa N and Banerjee I. IoT-based sensor data fusion for occupancy sensing using Dempster—Shafer evidence theory for smart buildings. IEEE Internet of Things Journal. 2017;4(5):1563–1570.

[38] Zhu J, Tang Y, Shao X, *et al.* Multisensor fusion using fuzzy inference system for a visual-IMU-wheel odometry. IEEE Transactions on Instrumentation and Measurement. 2021;70:1–16.

[39] Yan B, Wang G, Yu J, *et al.* Spatial–temporal Chebyshev graph neural network for traffic flow prediction in IoT-based ITS. IEEE Internet of Things Journal. 2021;9(12):9266–9279.

[40] Liu Y, Wang CX, Huang J, *et al.* Novel 3-D nonstationary mmWave massive MIMO channel models for 5G high-speed train wireless communications. IEEE Transactions on Vehicular Technology. 2018;68(3):2077–2086.
[41] Saatchi NS, Yang HC, and Liang YC. Novel adaptive transmission scheme for effective URLLC support in 5G NR: A model-based reinforcement learning solution. IEEE Wireless Communications Letters. 2022;12(1):109–113.
[42] Wu T, Yin X, Zhang L, *et al.* Measurement-based channel characterization for 5G downlink based on passive sounding in sub-6 GHz 5G commercial networks. IEEE Transactions on Wireless Communications. 2021;20(5): 3225–3239.
[43] Ding Z, Xu D, Schober R, *et al.* Hybrid NOMA offloading in multi-user MEC networks. IEEE Transactions on Wireless Communications. 2022;21(7):5377–5391.
[44] Xu Z, Liang W, Huang M, *et al.* Efficient NFV-enabled multicasting in SDNs. IEEE Transactions on Communications. 2018;67(3):2052–2070.
[45] Chahbar M, Diaz G, Dandoush A, *et al.* A comprehensive survey on the E2E 5G network slicing model. IEEE Transactions on Network and Service Management. 2020;18(1):49–62.
[46] Ferreira D, Reis AB, Senna C, *et al.* A forecasting approach to improve control and management for 5G networks. IEEE Transactions on Network and Service Management. 2021;18(2):1817–1831.
[47] Carvalho GH, Woungang I, Anpalagan A, *et al.* Optimal security risk management mechanism for the 5G cloudified infrastructure. IEEE Transactions on Network and Service Management. 2021;18(2):1260–1274.
[48] Wu Y, Khisti A, Xiao C, *et al.* A survey of physical layer security techniques for 5G wireless networks and challenges ahead. IEEE Journal on Selected Areas in Communications. 2018;36(4):679–695.
[49] Sood K, Nosouhi MR, Nguyen DDN, *et al.* Intrusion detection scheme with dimensionality reduction in next generation networks. IEEE Transactions on Information Forensics and Security. 2023;18:965–979.
[50] Mun H, Seo M, and Lee DH. Secure privacy-preserving V2V communication in 5G-V2X supporting network slicing. IEEE Transactions on Intelligent Transportation Systems. 2021;23(9):14439–14455.
[51] He Y, Kong M, Du C, *et al.* Communication security analysis of intelligent transportation system using 5G Internet of Things from the perspective of big data. IEEE Transactions on Intelligent Transportation Systems. 2022;24(2):2199–2207.
[52] Farhat J, Brante G, Souza RD, *et al.* On the secure spectral efficiency of URLLC with randomly located colluding eavesdroppers. IEEE Internet of Things Journal. 2021;8(19):14672–14682.
[53] Li M, Yang X, Khan F, *et al.* Improving physical layer security in vehicles and pedestrians networks with ambient backscatter communication. IEEE Transactions on Intelligent Transportation Systems. 2022;23(7):9380–9390.
[54] Xie G, Yang LT, Liu Y, *et al.* Security enhancement for real-time independent in-vehicle CAN-FD messages in vehicular networks. IEEE Transactions on Vehicular Technology. 2021;70(6):5244–5253.

[55] Yu D, Hsu RH, Lee J, *et al.* EC-SVC: Secure CAN bus in-vehicle communications with fine-grained access control based on edge computing. IEEE Transactions on Information Forensics and Security. 2022;17:1388–1403.
[56] Wang Q, Gao D, Foh CH, *et al.* Decentralized CRL management for vehicular networks with permissioned blockchain. IEEE Transactions on Vehicular Technology. 2022;71(11):11408–11420.
[57] Xie G, Yang LT, Wu W, *et al.* Security enhancement for real-time parallel in-vehicle applications by CAN FD message authentication. IEEE Transactions on Intelligent Transportation Systems. 2020;22(8):5038–5049.
[58] Duan X, Yan H, Tian D, *et al.* In-vehicle CAN bus tampering attacks detection for connected and autonomous vehicles using an improved isolation forest method. IEEE Transactions on Intelligent Transportation Systems. 2021;24(2):2122–2134.
[59] Qiang W, Chunming W, Xincheng Y, *et al.* Intrinsic security and self-adaptive cooperative protection enabling cloud native network slicing. IEEE Transactions on Network and Service Management. 2021;18(2):1287–1304.
[60] Dbouk T, Mourad A, Otrok H, *et al.* A novel ad-hoc mobile edge cloud offering security services through intelligent resource-aware offloading. IEEE Transactions on Network and Service Management. 2019;16(4):1665–1680.

Chapter 11
Multimedia networks

Zixuan Li[1], Haotian Wang[1] and Yue Cao[1]

This chapter includes multimedia networking applications (audio and video nature, multimedia networking application types, and problems faced in application development), emerging technologies for streaming stored video (DASH, RTP, and SIP), Streaming Stored Video (overview, UDP, TCP, emerging trends and impact of Web 3.0), Voice-over-IP (basic concept, VoIP principles and architecture, fixed playback delay and evolution), network support for multimedia (three network layer approaches, three important regulatory principles, and multi-cloud networking for multimedia applications).

11.1 Multimedia networks

11.1.1 Multimedia networking applications

High-speed network technology has improved the environment to drive the development of multimedia network applications and systems. Examples include video phones, multimedia conference systems, multimedia email systems, IP phones, etc. [1]. Simultaneously, multimedia network applications require advanced computer network technology, data storage technology, and distributed processing technology, driving progress in these areas [2].

A multimedia network is a specialized computer system tailored for the effective transmission, reception, and management of a wide range of multimedia data, including but not limited to text, audio, and video. These networks prioritize high bandwidth and low latency to deliver real-time, seamless multimedia content. They are well-suited for applications like video conferencing, online streaming, multimedia messaging, and other interactive multimedia services. Various multimedia services require tailored protocols for practical functionality, such as Voice-over-IP (VoIP) for voice communication and streaming protocols for video and audio.

11.1.2 Audio and video nature

- **Audio**

The fundamental analog audio coding technique is Pulse Code Modulation (PCM) [3]. It begins by constantly sampling the analog audio signal at 8,000 samples per

[1] School of Cyber Science and Engineering, Wuhan University, China

second. Each arbitrary natural number is rounded to a finite value. This process is called quantization, and the limit is usually a power of 2. For example, there are typically 256 quantized values.

A fixed number of bits represents each quantization value. For instance, if there are 256 quantization values, each value is represented by 1 byte. The bit representations of all samples are cascaded together to form a digital representation of a signal. If an analog signal is sampled at 8,000 samples per second and each sample is quantized to 8 bits, then the generated digital signal has a rate of 64,000 bits per second [4].

The digital signal is converted to analog when played through a speaker. However, the decoded analog signal only approximates the original signal. This can result in significant degradation of sound quality [5]. As shown in Figure 11.1, high-frequency sounds may be lost in a decoded signal. By increasing the sample rate and number of quantization values, the signal can better approximate the initial analog signal [6]. Thus, the quality and bit rate of decoded signals must be balanced with the storage space of digital signals.

PCM-encoded voice and music are rarely used on the Internet [7]. As with video, compression techniques reduce the bit rate of stream. Human speech can be compressed to less than 10 kbps and still be intelligible [8]. MPEG1 Layer 3, also known as MP3, is a popular compression technique for approaching CD-quality stereo music. MP3 encoders can compress to various rates, with 128 kbps being the most commonly used one that does not produce significant sound distortion. Advanced Audio Coding (AAC), which is related to MP3, has gained popularity among Apple users. As with video, it can generate multiple versions of a pre-recorded audio stream at different bit rates.

- **Video**

The most remarkable feature of video is its high bit rate [9]. Typically, Internet video transmission rates come in two categories: low-quality video conferences generally

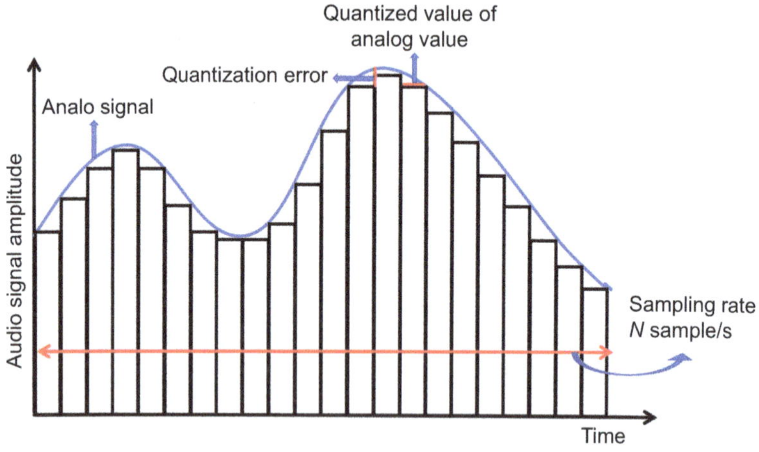

Figure 11.1 The relationship between time and audio amplitude

are around 100 kbps, while high-resolution movie streams can reach up to 3 Mbps. This section briefly describes three users, each using a separate Internet application.

- The first user, Frank, intended to post photos to his Chinese "Youku" application quickly. Viewers can download and share videos from sites like YouTube. Frank takes photos for every 10 s, each photo being around 200 KB in size (1 KB = 8000 bits). His photos were uploaded to his friend's Facebook page.
- The second user, Martha, is streaming music from the Internet to her smartphone. She listens to several MP3 songs in succession, all encoded at 128 kbps. The third user, Victor, is watching a video encoded at 2 Mbps.
- Finally, it is worth noting that, with three users concurrently streaming video, the maximum bandwidth usage is achieved during a session of 4000 s. In comparison, the bit rate used for streaming video is ten times higher than the bit rate used for streaming music or Facebook. Hence, while designing network video applications, the high bit rate requirements of video should be the top priority.

Another essential characteristic of video is that it can be compressed [10]. Thus, there is a trade-off between video quality and bit rate. The video is a sequence of images displayed constantly, such as 24 or 30 images per second. An uncompressed, digitally encoded image consists of an array of pixels, each encoded with a certain number of bits to represent brightness and color. There are two types of redundancy in video, both of which can be used for video compression. The spatial redundancy is the internal redundancy of a given image. Intuitively, an image mainly consisting of blanks has a high degree of redundancy and can be effectively compressed without significantly degrading image quality. The time-domain redundancy reflects the degree of repetition between an image and a subsequent image. For example, if the frame and following pictures are identical, there is no reason to encode the following photos. Instead, indicating directly that the subsequent images are similar during the encoding process is more efficient. Today, off-the-shelf compression algorithms can compress video to any desired base bit rate. The higher the bit rate, the better the image quality and the better the overall visual experience for the user.

11.1.3 Multimedia networking application types

Multimedia network application types fall into three categories: churned stored audio/video, conversational IP voice/video, and live audio/video streaming.

- **Streaming storage for audio and video**

- Streaming: In the streaming storage video application, the video usually starts playing a few seconds after the client receives a file from server. This means that while the client begins playout from one video location, it simultaneously receives subsequent portions of that video from server. This technology, known as streaming, avoids downloading the entire video before starting playback.
- Interaction: Because the media is pre-recorded, the user can pause, reconfigure forward, reconfigure, rewind, fast forward, etc., for multimedia content. The acceptable response time should be less than a few seconds, starting from when

the customer makes the request until the operation result is displayed on the client side.
- Continuous playout: Once the video starts playing, it should proceed according to the initially recorded timing. Therefore, data must be received from the server in time to play on the client side. Otherwise, the user experiences video frame stalls (when the client waits for delayed frames) or frame skips (when the client misses delayed frames).

The most critical performance measure for streaming video is the average throughput [11]. The network throughput must meet or exceed the streaming video bit rate to ensure uninterrupted video playback. Caching and pre-fetching allow continuous playout even when throughput fluctuates, as long as the average throughput (averaged over the 5–10 s interval) remains above the video rate.

For many streaming video applications, pre-recorded video is stored and streamed from a Content Delivery Network (CDN) [12] rather than a single data center. There are also many P2P video streaming applications where video is stored on user hosts (peers), and different blocks of video arrive from other peers that may be distributed globally. Special attention is given to client caching, pre-fetching, adaptation quality to available bandwidth, and CDN distribution for streaming video over the Internet.

- **Conversational voice/video-over-IP**

From a user's perspective, real-time voice conversations are commonly referred to as Internet telephony. This is because they bear a resemblance to traditional circuit switched telephone services. It is also often referred to as VoIP [13]. The conversational video is similar, except that it includes the participant's voice and video. Most voice and video-conversational systems allow users to generate conferences with three or more participants. Nowadays, conversational voice and video have become ubiquitous on the Internet, with companies such as Skype, QQ, and Google Talk claiming hundreds of millions of daily users. When it comes to audio and video sessions, factors such as time constraints and packet loss become critical.

- Timing considerations: Timing considerations are crucial because audio and video applications are sensitive to latency [14]. In sessions with two or more speakers, the delay between when one user speaks and when the other hears it should be under a few hundred milliseconds. Latencies below 150 ms are imperceptible to humans, while latencies between 150 and 400 ms are acceptable for voice. In comparison, a latency of more than 400 ms can make a voice session frustrating, if not completely incomprehensible.
- Tolerance of packet loss: Conversational multimedia apps can handle packet loss, which means occasional failures only slightly affect audio/video playout and are usually concealed. These latency-sensitive but packet loss-tolerant characteristics differ from those of elastic data applications (e.g., web browsing, email, social networking, and remote registration). For these resilient applications, long latency is annoying but not particularly detrimental, yet the completeness and integrity of transmitted data are of primary importance. Adaptive

playout, forward error correction, and error masking are employed to effectively mitigate network-introduced packet loss and latency, receiving special attention throughout the paper.

- **Streaming live audio/video**

The third category of applications is similar to traditional radio broadcasting and television, except that it is transmitted over the Internet [15]. These applications allow users to receive live radio broadcasts and television transmissions anywhere. Today, there are thousands of radio and television stations around the world broadcasting content over the Internet.

Like radio, the Live platform delivers audio and video programs to multiple customers simultaneously. Nowadays, such applications are usually implemented with CDNs. Due to the live nature of event, although the time constraints are more relaxed than with voice conversations, latency can still be a concern. The maximum acceptable delay between choosing a live transmission and playout is 10 s. Many technologies used for streaming live media (such as initial cache latency, adaptive bandwidth usage, and CDN distribution) are similar to those used for streaming storage media.

11.1.4 Problems faced in application development

The Internet provides two types of services for all applications: reliable connection-oriented service and unreliable connectionless service. The service provided using Transfer Control Protocol (TCP) protocol is reliable. Reliable TCP services ensure mutual transmission between data packets with relatively low demands for packet latency, and thus the delay requirement for data packets is low. Additionally, the User Datagram Protocol (UDP) service is unreliable, as it does not guarantee packet delivery or fulfill application requirements. For example, voice and video streaming media typically opt for UDP because they are more sensitive to low latency, and the loss of some data packets has a relatively minor impact on the user experience. However, the services provided by the Internet treat all data packets equally, with no prioritization in router queues for packages, such as voice packets with high latency requirements and television packets. In other words, every data packet on the Internet has to wait in line.

Developing a successful multimedia network application is challenging due to the lack of guarantee on packet size and time delay. To date, multimedia applications on the Internet have achieved significant but limited success. For instance, Interactive voice streaming with delays of a few seconds is a common feature on the Internet. However, when it passes through congested links, the latency and loss of sound can make it unacceptable. Even in continental areas, sound quality is significantly degraded by the congestion that occurs at peak times.

In summary, the current multimedia network applications should focus on solving the following problems: (i) increasing network bandwidth, (ii) reducing latency, and (iii) reducing jitter.

11.2 Streaming stored video

11.2.1 Streaming storage video overview

For streaming video applications, pre-recorded videos are placed on servers, and users send requests to these servers to watch these videos on demand [16]. Users can watch the video from start to finish without pausing. They may interact with the video by pausing and redirecting to the back or front shots. Streaming video systems can be divided into three types: UDP streaming, HTTP streaming, and adaptive HTTP streaming. While all three are in practice, most of today's systems apply HTTP streaming and adaptive HTTP streaming.

The commonality among all three video streaming formats is the widespread use of client-side buffering [3]. This buffering helps to mitigate the effects of end-to-end latency in available bandwidth between the server and the client. For streaming video (stored and live), users typically tolerate a few seconds of delay from the request to play a specific video to play the media content. As depicted in Figure 11.2, the client can buffer the incoming video in the application cache before playing it. Once the client has built up a few seconds of "buffered but unplayed" video, the client can start the video playout.

In summary, client buffering has two crucial advantages. First, client buffering can absorb fluctuations in server-to-client latency. That means if a particular portion of video data experiences a delay, it will not be noticed until after the "received but not yet played" video is exhausted. Second, if the server-to-client bandwidth temporarily decreases below the video consumption rate, the user can continue to enjoy uninterrupted playback as long as the client application buffer has not been fully consumed.

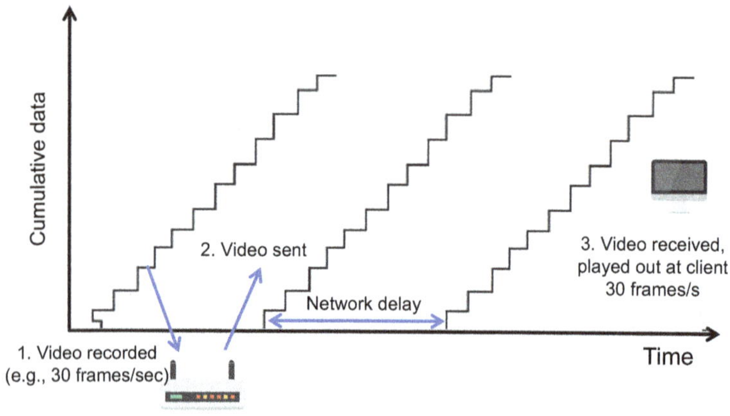

Figure 11.2 Cumulative data versus time

11.2.2 The need for streaming storage video

For streaming video, the principle is similar to requesting a standard web page. However, since the file size of streaming video is very large, it cannot be transferred in a few seconds. Furthermore, streaming videos require a seamless user experience without any buffering issues, meaning they should not be affected by fluctuations in network conditions. Therefore, the challenge of streaming stored videos is to avoid client-side buffering when the transmission rate is higher than the playback rate while also preventing network interruptions. Here, both the client's and server's perspectives are concerned.

- **Client: caching**

The technology used on the client side is mainly client caching. It is important to buffer a portion of data first before observing, especially with potentially unstable network conditions. This way, ample buffering time is provided for waiting until network performance improves, even if the current network condition is not ideal, as network fluctuations are usually temporary. This technique can be found in many audio and video applications.

A TCP connection is re-established when a client repositions, specifying a new starting point. Video chunks are assigned sequence numbers, and the server sends requested video chunks to the client from a specified starting time onwards. The video can be watched continuously if the average network throughput exceeds the playback. The video quality can be adjusted based on the current network speed, ensuring uninterrupted playback. This process, known as adaptive HTTP streaming, requires the server to have prepared various quality versions of video [17]. Switching can be done manually or automatically by the client. When the client switches, it re-establishes the HTTP connection with the video using the specified serial number in the designated block, allowing users to watch the video at their chosen resolution.

When the client receives the video, it can be stored in the application cache instead of being played immediately. Once the client has built up a few seconds of "cached but unplayed" video reserves, the client can begin video playback. This client caching has two essential advantages. First, the client cache can absorb fluctuations in server-to-client latency. Second, if the server-to-client bandwidth briefly drops below the video consumption rate, continuous playback remains possible as long as the client application cache is not fully depleted.

- **Servers: content delivery networks**

Even if the network throughput and playback speed are satisfactory, the user might need help playing videos smoothly if the server faces issues with its delivery speed. For instance, if a server is installed on a single machine with a network bandwidth of 100 Mbps, and 10,000 users attempt to watch videos simultaneously, the available bandwidth for each video is only 0.01 Mbps. This limited bandwidth can cause playback failures and disrupt the user experience.

The solution is to set up eight large data centers, each distributed in different locations worldwide, with about 100,000 machines in one center [18]. Then, 30 medium-sized clusters are established, each with 100–500 servers. Subsequently, several hundred small clusters are established, each with ten servers. Different servers are responsible for different content. This way, the traffic is distributed among the clusters, while each user can still connect to the nearest server, reducing latency and packet loss.

The key lies in the cluster selection strategy of CDN servers, that is, who should respond to a user's request. The key point is that the content provided on each CDN server may vary, and it is infeasible for a single server to accommodate the vast number of videos found on YouTube. Therefore, DNS servers typically match the nearest CDN server, or the one with the least latency and resource demands. Each company may adopt a different CDN cluster selection strategy, which is related to many other factors, such as the structure of their CDN and their clients.

11.2.3 Streaming multimedia: UDP

UDP streams typically use a tiny client-side cache. With UDP streaming, the server records video blocks steadily over UDP, transmitting the video at a rate that matches the client's video consumption rate [19]. For example, if the video consumption rate is 2 Mbps and each UDP packet carries 8000 bits of video, the server will send a UDP packet to its socket every (8000 bits)/(2 Mbps) = 4 ms. Because UDP does not employ a congestion control mechanism, the server can push the packet into the network at the video consumption rate, unrestricted by TCP rate control. Before passing the video block to UDP, the server encapsulates the video block in a transport packet specifically designed to carry audio and video, using RTP (Real-Time Transport Protocol) or some similar (possibly proprietary) scheme.

The UDP stream has a unique characteristic where, apart from the server-to-client video stream, a distinct control connection is also established between the two. This connection is used for the client to send commands related to changes in session status, such as pausing, restarting, relocating, and more. This control connection is similar to File Transfer Protocol (FTP) control connection in many ways. Although UDP streaming has been used in several open-source systems and proprietary products, it has three significant shortcomings.

- First, constant-rate UDP streaming cannot guarantee uninterrupted playback, as the bandwidth between the server and control is unpredictable. For example, consider this scenario: the video transmission rate is 1 Mbps, and the bandwidth from the server to the client usually exceeds 1 Mbps. However, for every few minutes, it briefly drops below 1 Mbps. In such a scenario, a UDP streaming system that delivers video at a constant rate of 1 Mbps via RTP/UDP can lead to a suboptimal user experience. This is because when the available bandwidth drops below 1 Mbps, buffering or frame-dropping issues may arise.
- Another disadvantage of using UDP streaming is that it necessitates a media control server, such as an Real-Time Streaming Protocol (RTSP) server, to manage client-to-server interaction requests and keep track of client status for each ongoing session. This includes information such as where the client is playing in the video, whether the video is paused or playing, and so on. This adds to the overall cost and complexity of deploying a large-scale, on-demand video system.

- A third drawback is that many firewalls are configured to block UDP traffic, preventing users behind these firewalls from receiving UDP video.

11.2.4 Streaming multimedia: HTTP

In a HTTP stream, video is stored directly on the HTTP server as a regular file with a specific Uniform Resource Locator (URL). Whenever a client demands to watch a video, a TCP connection is instantly established between the client and server. In the meantime, an HTTP GET request is sent to the corresponding URL. The server then sends the video file in an HTTP response message as quickly as possible, at the fastest rate allowed by TCP congestion control and flow control. On the client side, bytes are collected in a client application cache. The client application begins playback once the number of bytes in the cache exceeds a predetermined threshold. Specifically, it periodically grabs video frames from the client application cache, decompresses them, and displays them on the user's screen.

The use of HTTP over TCP also eases the passage of video through firewalls and NATs, often configured to block UDP traffic but permit the majority of HTTP traffic [20]. HTTP streaming eliminates the inconvenience associated with the need for media control servers (such as RTSP servers), reducing the cost of large-scale deployments over the Internet. Because of all these advantages, most of today's streaming video applications use HTTP streaming (over TCP) as their underlying streaming protocol.

Pre-fetch video: As mentioned above, client-side caching can mitigate the effects of varying end-to-end latency and varying available bandwidth. The server delivers at the rate of playing the video. However, with streaming stored video, the client can attempt to download the video at a rate higher than the consumption rate, thus pre-fetching the video frames that will be consumed in the future. This pre-fetched video is stored in the client application cache. Such pre-fetching naturally occurs in TCP streams, as the TCP congestion avoidance mechanism strives to fully utilize all available bandwidth between the server and client.

If a user is watching a video at 1 Mbps, yet the speed of network transmitting the video from the server to the client is always 1.5 Mbps, then the playback latency will be very low. Users can accumulate 500 KB of video buffer data per second. In this way, if the customer later receives data at a rate of less than 1 Mbps for a short period, the customer can continue to provide continuous playback due to the reserves in its cache.

Client application cache and TCP cache: As shown in Figure 11.3, on the server side, the white part of video file has been sent through the socket of server, while the black part is the part left to be sent. After transferring data through the socket gate, the server immediately stops sending additional bytes from the video file to the socket until the bytes in the TCP send buffer are transmitted to the Internet, as the send buffer is full. On the client side, the client application (media player) reads the bytes from the TCP receive cache (via its client socket) and places the bytes into the client application cache. At the same time, the client application periodically grabs video frames from the client application cache, then decompresses and displays them on the

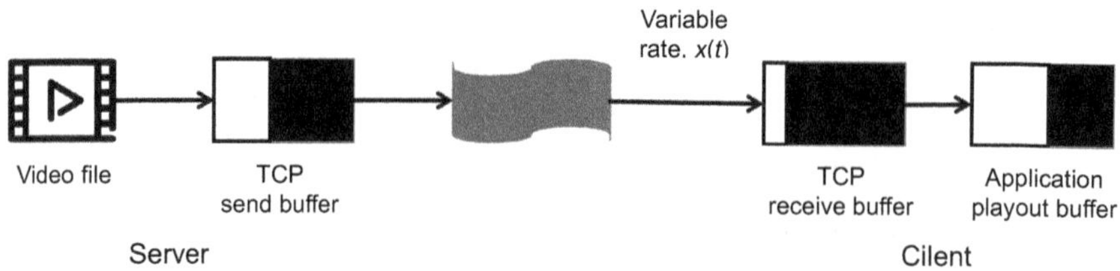

Figure 11.3 Video streaming with TCP buffers

user's screen. If the client application cache is larger than the video file, the transfer of data from the server memory to the client application cache can be likened to downloading a typical file through HTTP. This means that the client can directly fetch the video from the server at the fastest possible rate allowed by TCP.

When a client application requests data from a server, it caches the received data in its cache. However, if the client cache is finite and becomes full, it can cause "reverse pressure" on the server. This means that once the client cache is full, bytes are no longer removed from the client TCP receive cache, which also becomes full. When the client's TCP receive buffer is full, it indicates that the client cannot accept more data temporarily, so it does not acknowledge the received data. Consequently, the server's TCP send buffer fills up since it must wait for the client's acknowledgment before removing data that has been sent but not confirmed. When the server TCP send cache becomes full, it cannot send more data into the socket. Therefore, if the user pauses the video, the server may be forced to stop transmission, which is blocked until the user resumes the video.

Even during regular playback (i.e., without pauses), if a client application cache becomes full, the reverse pressure will cause a TCP cache to become full, forcing the server to reduce its rate. To determine the speed it generates, notice that when the client cache removes f bits, it generates f bits of space in the client application cache, allowing the server to send additional f bits. Therefore, the server cannot ship more than the client video consumption rate. Thus, when using HTTP streams, a full client application cache indirectly limits the server-to-client video rate that can be sent.

The subsequent conversation pertains to the premature termination and realignment of the video. In HTTP streaming systems, the HTTP byte-range header is frequently used in the HTTP GET request message. This header indicates the byte range that the client is attempting to retrieve from the desired video. This is particularly useful when the user wants to promptly reposition (i.e., jump) to a future point in the video. When the user relocates to a new location, the client sends a new HTTP request, using a byte range prefix to indicate the server on which bytes of file to send data. When the server receives that new HTTP request, it can forget about any earlier requests and instead send from the byte indicated in the byte range request.

When a particular user repositions to a future point in a video or terminates the video early, specific data sent by the server that has been pre-fetched but not yet viewed will not be considered, i.e., resulting in a waste of network bandwidth and server resources. For example, it is assumed that at a point t_0 in the video, the client cache is filled with B bits, r represents the speed at which the user watches the video, at which point the user relocates to an instant $t > t_0 + B/r$ in the video and then watches the video from that point until the end. In this case, all the B bits in the cache will not be protected. Additionally, the bandwidth and server resources used to transmit these B bits are entirely wasted. In the Internet, a significant amount of bandwidth is wasted due to early termination, and these costs can be pretty substantial, especially for wireless links. For this reason, many streaming systems either utilize client application caches of an appropriate length or restrict the amount of video pre-fetched in HTTP requests using byte range headers.

11.2.5 Emerging trends in streaming stored video

The field of Streaming Stored Video has been constantly evolving, reshaping the way people consume and transmit video content. Emerging trends are transforming how videos are watched and distributed, presenting both challenges and opportunities to the industry. Here, the following content will delve into some of the significant developments in Streaming Stored Video:

- **Efficient video encoding and decoding technologies:** With the continuous emergence of efficient video encoding and decoding technologies, the landscape of video transmission is undergoing a revolution. Two crucial encoding standards, H.265/HEVC (High-Efficiency Video Coding) and AV1, have increased video compression efficiency [21]. This enables smoother video streaming of high-quality videos, including HD and 4K, even with limited bandwidth. Users can now enjoy smooth video streaming without sacrificing quality, even with reduced bandwidth.
- **Next-generation streaming transport protocols:** Next-generation streaming transport protocols like HTTP/2 and QUIC (Quick UDP Internet Connections) are replacing traditional HTTP/1.1 to provide a faster and more efficient video streaming experience [22]. These protocols support multiplexing, transmitting multiple data streams simultaneously, thereby improving bandwidth utilization. Moreover, QUIC can rapidly establish connections, reducing video loading times. These improvements enable users to watch videos more quickly, reducing buffering times.
- **HD and 4K video streams:** The demand for high-quality videos has steadily increased, especially with the widespread adoption of HD and 4K televisions and displays. Streaming Stored Video platforms can meet this demand by offering high-resolution video content. Simultaneously, hardware manufacturers and content providers are continuously upgrading their hardware and content libraries to support higher resolutions in streamed content.
- **Mobile streaming:** The proliferation of mobile devices has transformed the way videos are transmitted [23]. Users now expect the ability to watch videos not only on traditional desktop computers or TVs, but also on smartphones and tablets. As a result, Streaming Stored Video must adapt to various types of networks, including 3G, 4G, and 5G networks. New streaming technologies and algorithms

have been designed to accommodate different network conditions, ensuring that users can seamlessly watch video content at home, in the office, or on the move.

- **Cloud storage and CDN (Content Delivery Networks):** Cloud storage and CDNs are crucial in the Streaming Stored Video domain [24]. Cloud storage provides highly available and scalable solutions, ensuring that video content is always accessible. Additionally, CDN allows content providers to store their content on distributed servers closer to end-users, reducing loading times and enhancing the smoothness of video streaming. These infrastructure improvements enable the rapid global transmission of streaming media content.

These emerging trends in Streaming Stored Video will continue to shape the future of video transmission. Users can expect higher quality and more efficient video streaming, while the video industry will see more opportunities for innovation and development. These trends reflect ever-changing consumer demands and technological advancements, opening up new possibilities in Streaming Stored Video.

11.3 Voice-over-IP

11.3.1 Basic concept

From the user's perspective, Internet voice conversations are referred to as Internet telephony, as they closely resemble traditional phone services. It is also widely referred to as VoIP [25]. This section describes the principles and protocols that underlie VoIP. Session-based video is similar to VoIP in many ways, except that it includes video of the participants and their voices. This section covers voice only, not voice and video combined, to maintain focus.

The network layer protocol of Internet, IP, provides the best effort service [26]. In other words, this service makes every effort to move each datagram from sources to destinations, but it does not guarantee a specific delay range or limit the packet loss percentage. The design of real-time session applications that are sensitive to packet delay, delay jitter, and packet loss is seriously challenged by the lack of guarantees.

This section will explore different methods to improve VoIP performance on best-effort networks [27]. Specifically, application layer technologies will be the focus, which does not require modifications to the network core or the transport layer of the end system. One must first outline the limitations of a best-effort approach to IP services in a specific VoIP environment. The sender generates bytes at a rate of 8000 bytes per second and aggregates those bytes into blocks every 20 ms. Each block and a memorable header are encapsulated in a UDP message segment (via a call to a socket interface). Thus, the number of bytes in a block is, and a UDP message segment is sent every 20 ms.

If each data packet arrives at the receiver with a constant end-to-end delay, the packages arrive at the receiver every 20 ms. In this ideal case, the receiver can play it directly after each block comes. Inevitably, packets can get lost and experience varying end-to-end delays, even with minimal Internet congestion. Therefore, the receiver must more carefully determine (i) when to play a block and (ii) how to handle a lost block.

11.3.2 VoIP principles and architecture

The VoIP technology allows the transmission of analog audio or video over an IP network. Simply, it involves a series of transcoding, encoding, compression, and packaging processes. These processes enable voice data to be transmitted over the IP network to the destination. Subsequently, the data is restored to the original voice signal for the receiver through the reverse process.

The first step is to encode the analog voice signal at the originating end, primarily using the ITU-T G.711 voice encoding standard [28]. The second process involves compressing the voice packets while adding address and control information, allowing the transmission of IP packets to find the message's destination in the vast IP network. At the destination end, the IP packets are decoded and converted into analog audio that speakers, handsets, or headphones can play.

In a basic VoIP architecture, there are four essential elements [29]:

- **Media Gateway:** It mainly plays the role of converting voice signals into IP packets.
- **Media Gateway Controller:** Also known as Gate Keeper or Call Server, it is primarily responsible for managing the transmission and conversion of signals.
- **Voice Server:** It mainly provides voice response service when the phone is not available, occupied, or busy.
- **Signaling Gateway:** The main job is to control the exchange process, decide whether to establish a call and provide value-added services for related applications.

The working principle of VoIP encompasses several key steps. First, the audio signal is digitized and segmented into small data packets, typically compressed using audio codes. Second, a media gateway is responsible for converting audio data packets into IP packets that can be transmitted over IP networks. It also addresses issues related to the audio stream, such as packet loss recovery and delay control. A media gateway controller manages and controls the operation of media gateway, including connection establishment, teardown, traffic management, and audio packet transport control. Additionally, a signaling gateway is crucial in translating signaling information from traditional telephone systems (such as SS7, ISDN, etc.) into signaling protocols used by IP networks (such as Session Initiation Protocol (SIP), H.323, etc.). This enables VoIP systems to communicate with traditional telephone networks. This series of steps allows voice to be transmitted over IP networks, enabling real-time voice communication.

11.3.3 VoIP: fixed playback delay

The variable queuing delay of a packet in network routers is a key factor in the end-to-end delay. This occurrence is referred to as delay jitter. To understand fixed playback delay in VoIP communication, it is essential to first grasp the concept of network latency and its significance in voice communication [30].

Transmission delay: This is the time it takes for data to travel from the sender to the receiver. It encompasses the time for electrical signals to travel and data to move through the transmission medium. Physical distances and the characteristics of transmission medium, such as cables or wireless signals, influence transmission delay.

Processing delay: This is when routers, switches, and other network devices process data. It includes tasks like routing, buffering, and inspection of data packets.

Queuing delay: Queuing delay occurs when data packets wait in a queue for processing within network devices. It is often associated with network congestion, where incoming data packets exceed the device's processing capacity, leading to delays.

Propagation delay: This is the time it takes for signals to propagate through the physical medium, typically determined by the speed of electromagnetic waves in the cable or through the air. The propagation delay increases with greater physical distances.

In the context of VoIP communication, these latency factors significantly impact call quality [31]. Voice communication requires real-time performance. Therefore, consistent and timely playback of audio packets is essential to avoid interruptions or audio artifacts. However, network latency jitter, which refers to fluctuations in latency, can cause the arrival time of voice packets to differ from their generated initial time. To address this issue, fixed playback delay is employed.

For VoIP applications, the receiver should aim to play back voice blocks despite network delay jitter. This is often achieved by combining two mechanisms: First, pre-plan a timestamp for each block. Second, during transmission, the sender adds a timestamp indicating the moment each data block was generated. They are delaying the playback of block at the receiver. The playback delay for the received audio chunks must be long enough to ensure that most packets are received before the scheduled playback time. This delay in playback can either be fixed for the whole session or change adaptively during the session.

Figure 11.4 shows the timing of packet generation and playback for a single speech burst period. Two different initial playback delays are considered. As shown in the ladder on the left, the sender generates a set of packets at regular intervals. The first packet in this speech burst period is received at the time reference. For the intermediate ladder, the arrival time interval of subsequent packets is uneven due to network delay jitter.

For the first play schedule time, the fixed initial play delay is set to $p - r$. With this scheme, the fifth packet does not arrive at its scheduled play time, and the receiver considers it lost. For the second scheduled time, the fixed initial play delay is set to $p' - r$, and p represents the scheduled playback time for the audio packets in the second play schedule. For this scheme, all packets arrive before their scheduled play time, so they are not lost.

In adaptive playback delay, let t_i be the timestamp of the ith packet, which is the time when the packet is generated at the sender, r_i be the time when packet i is received by the receiver p_i be the time when packet i is played at the receiver, the end-to-end network delay of the ith packet is $r_i - t_i$. Due to network delay jitter, this delay tends to vary between different packets. Let d_i represent the estimate of the average network delay when the design receives the ith packet. This estimate is constructed based on the following timestamp:

$$d_i = (1 - \mu)d(i - 1) + \mu(r_i - t_i) \tag{11.1}$$

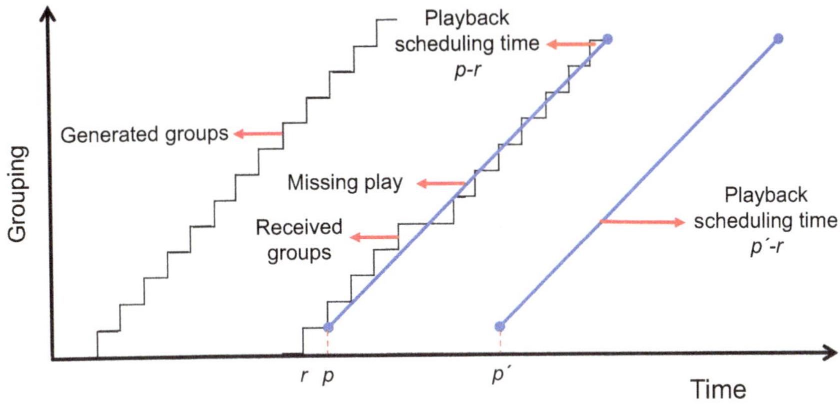

Figure 11.4 Fixed playback delay

where μ is a fixed constant. d_i is a smoothed mean of the observed network delay $r_1 - t_1, \ldots, r_i - t_i$.

This estimate emphasizes recent network delays over past delays. It also calculates the absolute deviation between the average and estimated mean delays. This estimate can also be constructed from these timestamps

$$v_i = (1 - \mu)v(i - 1) + \mu|r_i - t_i - d_i| \tag{11.2}$$

Here, the estimated values d_i and v_i are computed for each received packet, although they can only be used to determine the playback point for the first packet of any voice burst period.

Once these estimates have been calculated, the receiver applies the following algorithm for packet playback. If packet i is the first packet of a voice burst period, its playback time p_i is calculated as follows:

$$p_i = t_i + d_i + Kv_i \tag{11.3}$$

where K is a positive constant, the purpose of Kv_i term is to set a large enough playback time for the future, so that only a tiny fraction of the arriving packets in the voice burst period are lost due to lateness. The playback point of any subsequent packet in a burst is calculated as an offset to the playback point of the first packet in this burst. Let

$$q_i = p_i - t_i \tag{11.4}$$

denote the length of time from the first packet generated in the voice burst to the time it is played. If packet j also belongs to this burst period, the moment it is played is

$$p_j = t_j + q_i \tag{11.5}$$

The algorithm described above assumes the receiver can identify whether a packet is the first in a voice burst period. This can be done by examining the signal energy in each received packet.

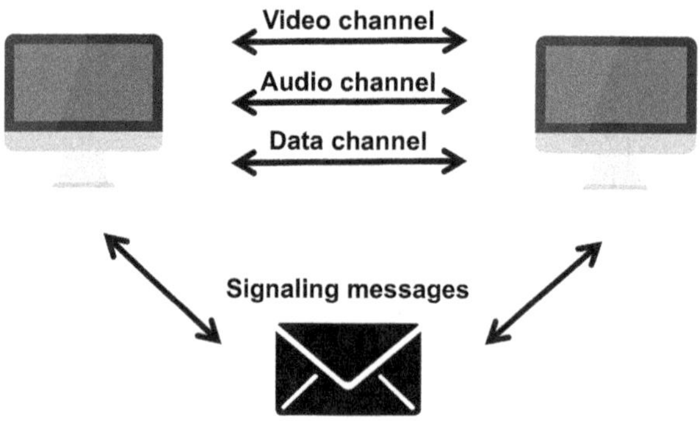

Figure 11.5 Core WebRTC architecture

11.3.4 VoIP evolution: WebRTC, 5G, and AI

When considering the latest trends in the VoIP domain, three key aspects stand out: the rise of WebRTC (Web Real-Time Communication), the influence of 5G networks, and the applications of Artificial Intelligence (AI) in VoIP.

The rise of WebRTC: As shown in Figure 11.5, the WebRTC is an open standard project designed to enable real-time audio and video communication directly in web browsers using simple JavaScript APIs, without the need for plugins or third-party applications. This trend has greatly impacted the VoIP industry, making real-time communication more convenient. Users can now engage in audio and video calls directly within web browsers. The WebRTC has become the foundation for applications such as online meetings, remote collaboration tools, and online customer support [32]. The WebRTC technology has several benefits, such as high-quality transmission of audio and video, low latency, and cross-platform support. Additionally, it is open-source, which simplifies the integration of real-time communication features into applications, leading to innovation in the VoIP field.

The WebRTC implementation principles encompass various aspects. First, it involves capturing audio and video data from devices. Next, the data is transmitted using the RTP. The connection establishment is coordinated through signaling protocols. Addressing network obstacles is achieved with Interactive Connectivity Establishment (ICE) technology. Additionally, WebRTC handles media processing and encoding/decoding. It also prioritizes ensuring network security. Lastly, it provides browser support for seamless integration. The WebRTC simplifies the development of real-time communication, enabling developers to easily create web applications with high-quality audio and video communication features. It is suitable for various applications such as online meetings, remote collaboration, customer support, and more, all while maintaining privacy and security in communication.

The impact of 5G networks on VoIP: The deployment of 5G networks significantly impacts VoIP communication due to their high-speed data transfer capabilities [33]. The low latency and high bandwidth of 5G networks result in clearer and more stable VoIP calls. Additionally, 5G networks have widespread coverage and significant capacity, which supports high-quality audio and video communication across multiple devices, which is beneficial for mobile and IoT devices. Furthermore, 5G networks provide improved mobility support, enabling users to maintain seamless VoIP communication, especially in high-speed trains, cars, and other mobile scenarios. This is vital for future remote and mobile working environments.

AI applications in VoIP: AI technologies are increasingly important in the VoIP domain [34]. Through Natural Language Processing and Speech Recognition technology, VoIP systems can implement voice assistants, Automatic Speech Recognition, and intelligent voice interactions. Users can initiate calls, find contacts, or configure communication parameters through voice commands. Furthermore, AI can enhance audio quality, including noise suppression and echo cancellation, improving call clarity. Some VoIP providers are implementing the use of facial expression recognition technology to detect emotions during calls. This advancement improves the user experience and allows for a deeper understanding of user needs in future remote and mobile working environments.

In conclusion, the rise of WebRTC, the impact of 5G networks, and the applications of AI are expected to continue driving the development of VoIP domain. Users can experience real-time communication, while businesses can innovate to meet increasing demands. As technology advances, VoIP will remain a crucial player on the global stage, shaping the future of communication.

11.4 Protocols for real-time conversational applications

11.4.1 RTP

RTP basics: The RTP is a real-time transmission protocol for transmitting real-time data, especially audio and video data, in computer networks [35]. The RTP is designed to meet the requirements of applications with high real-time demands, such as voice communication, video conferencing, and streaming media. The RTP usually runs on top of UDP: the sender prefixes each block of voice data with an RTP header, which includes the type, serial number, and timestamp of the audio encoding. The RTP header is typically 12 bytes long and is combined with the audio block to create the RTP packet. This packet is then sent to the UDP socket interface. On the receiving end, the application retrieves the RTP packet from its socket interface, extracts the audio block, and uses the initial field of the RTP packet to properly decode and play it.

The RTP does not provide any mechanism to ensure timely data delivery or other quality service guarantees. It cannot even guarantee packet delivery or prevent out-of-order delivery of packets. The RTP permits each source to be allocated a separate RTP packet stream. Additionally, RTP packets aren't exclusively utilized for unicast applications. They can also be disseminated over one-to-many and many-to-many multicast trees. During a many-to-many multicast session, all session senders and sources typically utilize the same multicast group to transmit their RTP streams.

Head structure: As shown in Figure 11.6, the length of payload type field in the RTP packet is 7 bits. For audio streams, the payload type field indicates the type of audio encoding. If the sender decides to change the encoding during the session, the sender

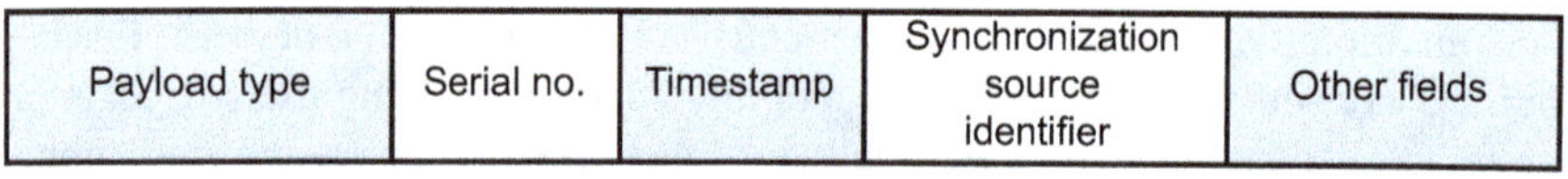

Figure 11.6 First fields

Table 11.1 Current types of audio payloads supported by RTP

Payload type No.	Audio format	Sampling rate	Rate
0	PCM μ	8 kHz	64 kbps
1	1016	8 kHz	4.5 kbps
3	GSM	8 kHz	13 kbps
7	LPC	8 kHz	2.4 kbps
9	G. 722	16 kHz	48–64 kbps
14	MPEG audio	90 kHz	–
15	G. 728	8 kHz	16 kbps

Table 11.2 Current types of video payloads supported by RTP

Payload type No.	Audio format	Payload type No.	Video format
26	Motion JPEG	32	MPEG1 video
31	H.261	33	MPEG2 video

can use the payload-type field to notify the receiver of this change. By changing this encoding, the sender may want to improve the voice quality or reduce the RTP stream bit rate. Table 11.1 lists some of the audio payload types currently supported by RTP.

For a video stream, the payload type indicates the video encoding type. The sender can also dynamically change the video encoding during the session. Table 11.2 lists some of the video payload types currently supported by RTP.

- **Serial number field.** The sequence number field is 16 bits long. With each RTP data packet sent, the sequence number increments by 1. The receiving party can use this sequence number to detect packet loss and recover the sequence of packets. This sequence number is incremented by 1 for each RTP packet sent and can be used by the receiver to detect packet loss and recover packet sequences.
- **Timestamp field.** The timestamp field is 32 bits long [36]. It reflects the moment when the first byte of the RTP data packet was sampled. The receiver can use the timestamp to synchronize playback and eliminate packet delay jitter caused by the network. The timestamp can be used by the receiver to eliminate packet delay jitter caused by the network, resulting in synchronized playback on the receiver end. The receiver can use the timestamp to remove packet delay jitter

introduced in the network and provide synchronous playback on the receiver side. The timestamp is obtained from the sender's sample clock of sender.

- **Synchronization Source Identifier (SSRC).** The SSRC field is 32 bits long. It identifies the source of the RTP stream. Typically, each stream within an RTP session is assigned a unique SSRC. Usually, each stream in an RTP session has a different SSRC. The SSRC is a random number assigned by the source at the beginning of a stream, not the IP address of sender. The SSRC is not the IP address of the sender, but a number randomly assigned by the source at the beginning of a new stream. The probability of two streams being assigned given the same SSRC is very small. If it happens, both sources should choose a new SSRC value.

RTP security:

- **Encryption:** The encryption in RTP communication is achieved through Secure Real-time Transport Protocol (SRTP) [37]. The SRTP uses robust encryption algorithms like Advanced Encryption Standard (AES) to encrypt media data. The encryption ensures that third parties cannot intercept or understand the media content during transmission. The SRTP also provides configurable encryption strength and key length options to meet various security requirements.
- **Authentication:** The RTP communication is implemented through SIP or other authentication mechanisms. Digest authentication is commonly utilized to authenticate User agents and allow only authorized users to participate in communication. This prevents unauthorized users or devices from accessing the communication.
- **Integrity:** The SRTP provides encryption and integrity protection to prevent data from being tampered with during transmission. The integrity protection uses Message Authentication Codes (MACs) to verify the integrity of data packets. If a data packet is tampered with, the receiving party will refuse to decrypt and play it.
- **Key Management:** The RTP security requires an effective key management mechanism. Secure key negotiation protocols like Multimedia Internet KEYing (MIKEY) or Datagram Transport Layer Security for SRTP (DTLS-SRTP) are commonly used to negotiate, exchange, and manage encryption keys securely. Effective RTP security requires proper key management to ensure that both parties possess the correct keys.
- **Preventing Denial of Service (DoS) attacks:** RTP communication is vulnerable to DoS attacks. Attackers can flood the communication with excessive network traffic or other means to make it unavailable. To mitigate such attacks, firewalls, intrusion detection systems, and anti-flooding measures can be employed.

RTP extensions:

- **RTP Control Protocol (RTCP) extensions:** The RTCP is used to control and monitor RTP streams. Extensions can offer improved RTCP reports for more details on media stream quality and performance. This aids in network management and troubleshooting.

- **RTP events:** The RTP event extensions allow the transmission of non-audio and non-video events within RTP streams, such as text messages, images, and control commands. These events can enhance interactivity and diversity in media streams.
- **Redundancy Encoding (RED) in RTP:** The RED is an RTP extension that allows the transmission of redundant data packets to improve error recovery in the case of packet loss. It achieves this by transmitting multiple copies of data packets over different network paths, reducing the impact of packet loss on media quality.
- **RTP roaming:** The RTP roaming extensions support RTP communication in mobile devices and wireless communication environments. They address device roaming and network switching issues to ensure communication continuity.
- **RTP and WebRTC:** The RTP is widely used for implementing WebRTC technology, which enables real-time communication within web browsers. Related extensions and APIs support the direct use of RTP protocol in web browsers, facilitating browser-to-browser real-time communication.

These extensions and security measures make RTP a powerful tool for real-time media transmission, adaptable to various communication needs and application scenarios while ensuring data security and quality. To design and manage real-time media communication systems effectively, it is crucial to have a clear understanding of RTP security along with its extensions.

11.4.2 Session Initiation Protocol (SIP)

The SIP is an open and lightweight protocol with three main features: it facilitates the establishment of calls between the caller and the callee over an IP network, allows the caller to notify the callee of the intent to start a call, and enables participants to negotiate media encoding as well as terminate the call [38]. In addition, it also provides a mechanism that allows the calling party to determine the current IP address of the called party. This capability is important because users may be dynamically assigned addresses (using DHCP) and may have multiple IP devices, each with a different IP address. Therefore, they do not have a single, fixed IP address.

Mechanisms for call management include adding new media streams during a call, changing encoding during a call, inviting new participants during a call, call transfer, and call hold. The SIP is a protocol that facilitates setting up, managing, and terminating communication sessions over IP networks. Its flexibility and support for various media types make it a fundamental component in VoIP and video conferencing systems.

- **SIP's characteristics and transport options**

Out-of-band protocol: The SIP is an out-of-band protocol, which means that control messages (SIP messages) are sent and received using a different channel than media data (voice or video). This separation allows for flexibility, independent routing, and handling of control, as well as media traffic.

Readable ASCII (American Standard Code for Information Interchange) Messages: The SIP messages are typically represented in plain text and are readable

ASCII, similar to how HTTP messages are structured. This human-readable format makes it easier for developers to understand and debug SIP interactions.

Message acknowledgment and transport: The SIP requires acknowledgment to ensure reliable communication [39]. However, it is worth noting that SIP can operate over both UDP and TCP. The SIP messages transmitted over UDP are lightweight, and suitable for real-time communication, but they lack message delivery guarantees. In contrast, SIP over TCP provides a reliable transport mechanism, ensuring that all messages are acknowledged and delivered in the correct order. The choice between TCP and UDP depends on the specific use case, with different trade-offs between reliability and efficiency.

- **Establishing a call to a known IP address**

Establishing network communication involves using available IP information to connect to a known IP address. It typically involves using VoIP or other real-time communication protocols to communicate with a specific device or user at a known IP address. As shown in Figure 11.7, this is a direct way to establish a connection with a specific target communication terminal, as opposed to using traditional phone numbers or other identifiers. This can be used for both one-on-one communication and multi-party communication, depending on the support of communication protocol and application.

1. INVITE: The calling party, Tesla, first initiates an INVITE message to the called party, Marconi. The INVITE message contains the session type and necessary

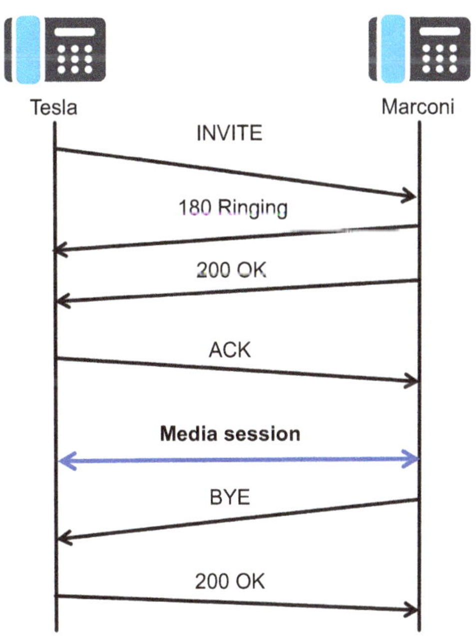

Figure 11.7 SIP example

parameters for the call. The session type may be a simple voice, a multimedia video used for web conferencing, or a game session.

2. 180 Ringing: When a called party receives an INVITE request message, they reply with a 180 Ringing message. This message indicates that the caller is connected and waiting for the called party to answer. The called party will also receive an INVITE message that will ring or otherwise indicate that there is an incoming call, as set by the called party. The 180 Ringing response is a provisional message indicating that the call is ringing at the called party's device.
3. 200 OK: If the called user Marconi picks up the call after it rings, a 200 OK response is issued. In addition to being a connection indication, this response specifies the allowed connection media format for the called party to confirm whether the media can be received.
4. ACK: The last step before the call is the caller's confirmation of the 200 OK response. This acknowledgment proves that the connection is allowed, and that another protocol is about to be used to start the media connection. Another protocol is the RTP format negotiated in the Session Description Protocol (SDP) message segment above.
5. BYE: After the call is completed, the called party, Marconi, hangs up first and sends the BYE request command.
6. 200 OK: After the BYE, the called party is required to send a 200 OK acknowledgment, which means that the caller knows that the called party has hung up. For example, after a call, one party asks to hang up, and the other must see that it has hung up.

The current call process is quite simple. It involves only two terminals communicating directly with each other using their respective IP addresses. This method's straightforwardness stems from the absence of any intermediate devices between the two endpoints. However, it is worth noting that this type of call is not very common in practice.

In SIP communications, SIP proxies, extensions, standards, security, and privacy are critical components beyond point-to-point connection. SIP proxies play a crucial role in SIP communication. SIP proxies can be divided into User Agent, Proxy Server, and Registrar Server. User agents, such as softphones or SIP client applications, are terminal devices used to initiate and receive SIP requests. Proxy Servers act as intermediary devices responsible for routing SIP requests, performing call routing, load balancing, and enforcing security policies. Registrar Servers handle user registration requests, maintaining user location information to ensure that future calls can be routed to their intended destinations correctly.

SIP is a flexible protocol that supports a range of extensions and standards to meet various communication needs. SIP standards, defined by IETF, ensure interoperability for SIP communication, while extensions offer adaptable functionality for specific scenarios. The format of SIP requests and responses, status codes, SIP header fields, and more are defined in Request for Comments (RFCs), such as RFC 3261 and RFC 6665.

The SIP security is crucial to ensure the safety of SIP communication and protect user privacy. Authentication in SIP communication is implemented through digest authentication, providing that only authorized users can use SIP services. Encryption can be achieved through Transport Layer Security (TLS) to safeguard the confidentiality of communication content. To enhance communication security, SIP also supports security extensions, such as SIP (Secure and SIP) over TLS. Additionally, privacy protection in SIP communication can be achieved by limiting the disclosure of personal information to safeguard user privacy. In summary, SIP proxies, SIP extensions, and standards, as well as SIP security and privacy, are fundamental components of SIP communication. Collectively, they ensure the effectiveness, flexibility, and security of the SIP protocol, making it a crucial foundation for real-time communication.

11.4.3 Dynamic Adaptive Streaming over HTTP (DASH)

The DASH is a technical standard introduced by the international standardization group MPEG (Moving Picture Experts Group) in 2014 [40]. Its primary goal is to establish a unified solution for streaming media over IP networks in a single format, providing efficient and high-quality services. It addresses challenges posed by the coexistence of multiple streaming protocols, such as HTTP Live Streaming (HLS), Microsoft Smooth Streaming (MSS), and HTTP Dynamic Streaming (HDS), including issues related to storage and service capacity wastage, high operational costs, and system interoperability weaknesses.

The DASH is based on HTTP and utilizes dynamic adaptive bit rate streaming technology. It employs the TCP transport protocol (although some older live client broadcasts may use the UDP protocol, e.g., YY Live Platform, etc.). Like HLS and HDS, it segments videos into small fragments and delivers them via the HTTP protocol for client-side playback. MPEG-DASH supports various formats, such as MPEG-2 TS and MP4, enabling video segmentation based on multiple encodings. Consequently, when clients load videos, they retrieve and play the corresponding video segments based on their current network speed and supported codecs, with the media format being either TS or MP4 files.

- **How DASH works**

On the server side, media files are divided into equal time length segments, each with different bit rates and resolutions. Typically, when assessing network bandwidth or buffer size, the client selects segments with other parameters. This selection is made through standard HTTP GET requests for the corresponding segment. Initially, the client requests to download the MPD (Media Presentation Description) file from the server. The client requests to download suitable media segments based on the MPD file and its conditions. Since the segments are time-aligned, seamless switching between different segments allows for uninterrupted playback.

- **DASH Standard**

The critical concept to understand is the MPD file. The MPD is an XML file representing media content with various qualities and segments using URL within HTTP [41]. It follows a layered data model, as shown in Figure 11.8.

- **Period**

It marks the duration information of video, which can also be considered the maximum duration for updating the MPD file. A Period typically represents a period of

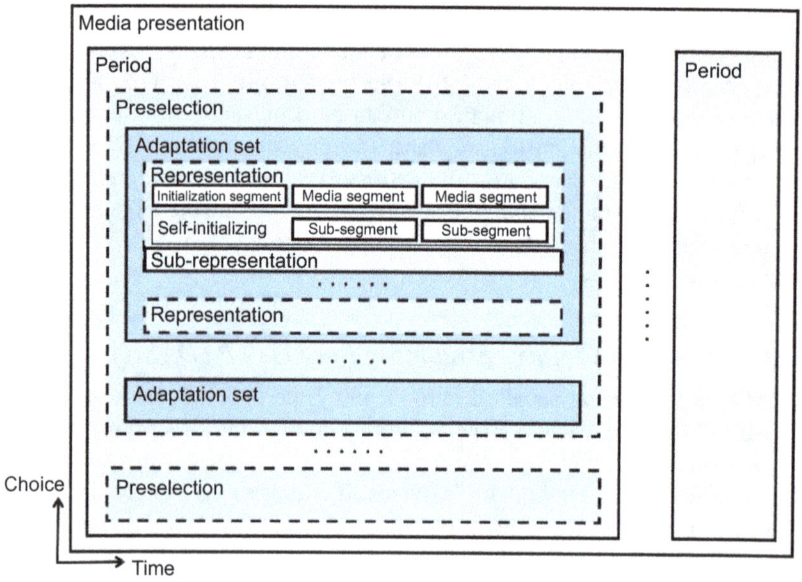

Figure 11.8 MPD file structure

media content containing a series of different encoded versions of media components, such as different views or different video codecs, different languages, audio tracks, subtitles, or captions with specific characteristics, like bit rates, frame rates, audio channels, etc. These characteristics remain unchanged within a Period. In live streaming scenarios, the MPD file updates the Period to remove old ones. Clients can adjust based on the available bit rates, resolutions, codecs, etc., within a Period. Periods can also segment content, such as inserting advertisements or changing camera angles during a soccer match.

- **Adaptation set**

It encompasses the form of media presentation (video/audio/subtitles). Adaptation sets represent a series of interchangeable encoded versions of logically identical media content components [42]. For example, elements with the same codec, language, resolution, audio channel format, etc., can be included in the same Adaptation Set. This mechanism allows clients to eliminate multimedia components that do not meet their needs. For instance, a client that can only decode HEVC streams would not want HEVC and Advanced Video Coding (AVC) streams to be packaged together in one Adaptation Set.

Additionally, a period can only contain a single Adaptation Set to fulfill the creator's intent. For example, the creator may only want users to view high-definition video content with 5.1-channel audio. If there are other media components like subtitles, they can also be grouped into a separate Adaptation Set.

- **Representation**

It includes different bit rates, encoding methods, frame rates, etc. A representation describes a deliverable encoded version of one or more media content components.

Representations may differ regarding the employed codec, decoding complexity, and the required CPU resources or rendering technologies. A representation contains one or more media streams (one for each media content component in multiplexing, where multiplexing refers to combining multiple signals into one). Any single representation is sufficient to render the included media content components. This means clients can dynamically switch between representations within an Adaptation Set.

- **Segment**

It represents each segment within a representation, enabling accessible and deliverable access. Each segment typically has the same duration and is arranged according to the media content's presentation timeline [43]. The MPEG-DASH does not restrict segment length or provide recommendations for optimal length. Longer segments imply more efficient compression, while shorter segments, like mobile networks, are used for real-time scenarios and highly variable bandwidth conditions. In live streaming scenarios, segments also have an attribute called "availability time," which indicates when they are accessible in a live context. To access a segment, the MPD provides a URL for each segment, and thus, a segment is the largest data unit retrieved through a single HTTP request. There are two subsegments for segmented representations: initialization segments and segments containing static media data. Segments include a segment index describing the subsegment's presentation time range and byte range. By leveraging this data, HTTP1.1 byte-range requests can be pre-fetched to generate appropriate subsegment requests. MPEG-DASH introduces Stream Access Point (SAP) to facilitate switching within representations. For example, each segment typically starts with an Intra-coded Picture, Decoded Reference (IDR) frame to enable switching to different representations after transmitting a segment.

11.5 Network support for multimedia

11.5.1 Three network layer approaches

Table 11.3 lists three broad approaches that can provide network layer support for multimedia applications:

- **Utilize best-effort services whenever possible**

This is a guiding principle in network design and management [44]. This principle recommends using best-effort services or protocols when service quality or guaranteed performance is not critical. It is worth underscoring that the suitability of best-effort services depends entirely on the unique requirements of application or use case. Critical services like financial transactions or medical data transmission typically require reliable, guaranteed delivery and should not utilize best-effort services. However, for applications where loss or delay is acceptable, and resource efficiency is critical, best-effort service is an effective option. The key is to make informed decisions based on the application's needs and the network's characteristics.

- **Differentiated services**

Using differentiation services, when two types of traffic are queued in a router, one kind of traffic can be given strict preference over the other. The Internet Diffserv architecture provides service differentiation, that is, the ability to handle

Table 11.3 Current types of audio payloads supported by RTP

Methods	Particle	Assurance	Mechanism	Complexity	Current deployment status
Utilize best-effort services whenever possible	Fair processing of all traffic	None of soft	Application-level support, CDN, overlay network, network-level resource provisioning	Min	Everywhere
Differentiated services	Different types of traffic are handled differently	None of soft	Group Identification, Supervision, Scheduling	Medium	Some
Perconnection QoS guarantees	Each source-to-destination flow differently or hard	Once the stream is prospective people, soft is handled	Group Identification, Supervision, Scheduling, Call Admission, and Signaling	Max	Rarely

different types of traffic scalable across the Internet [45]. The Differentiated Services architecture is composed of a collection of two functional elements:

- Boundary functions: Boundary functions include packet classification and traffic regulation. At the incoming edge of network, arriving packets are marked. More specifically, the Distinguished Service (DS) field in the IPv4 or IPv6 packet header is set to a specific value. The group gets a tag that identifies the type of traffic to which the group belongs. The different types of traffic will then be served differently in the core network.
- Core function: The core function is forwarding. When a packet with a DS tag reaches a Diffserv-enabled server, it is forwarded to the next hop based on the Per-Hop Behavior (PHB) linked with the packet type. A router's behavior in the Diffserv architecture is determined by the packet tag, which indicates the traffic type.

In summary, Differentiated Services is an approach to implementing Quality of Service (QoS) in IP networks by classifying, marking, and prioritizing network traffic based on Differentiated Services Code Point (DSCP) values. It is designed to manage network traffic with scalability and simplicity while providing different levels of service differentiation, to meet various application and user requirements.

- **Per-connection QoS guarantees**

Using per-connection QoS guarantees, each instance of an application explicitly reserves end-to-end bandwidth and has guaranteed end-to-end performance [46]. The hard guarantees mean the application will always receive the QoS it requests. The soft guarantees mean the application will receive the QoS it requests with a high probability.

- Resource reservation. Once a call has reserved resources, it needs to secure its resources [47].
- Call establishment signaling. The RSVP (Resource Reservation Protocol) is used to coordinate the reservation of resources and call admission.

The specific role of QoS consists of several aspects:

- Prioritization: The QoS allows prioritizing network traffic based on the particular needs of applications or services. For example, real-time applications like voice and video conferencing may be given higher priority to minimize latency and ensure smooth operation.
- Bandwidth management: The QoS enables allocating and managing available bandwidth to different traffic classes. This ensures critical applications receive the necessary bandwidth, preventing non-essential traffic from monopolizing network resources.
- Traffic shaping: The QoS mechanisms can shape traffic flows to match desired profiles. This helps conform to traffic contracts and avoid sudden data bursts that can cause congestion.
- Congestion control: The QoS includes mechanisms for identifying and managing network congestion [48]. When network resources become scarce, QoS

can prioritize significant traffic, delay less critical traffic, or even drop packets strategically to alleviate congestion.

- Packet classification: The QoS involves classifying packets into different categories based on specific criteria, such as source, destination, application type, or DSCP markings (in the case of Differentiated Services, as mentioned earlier). This classification is essential for applying QoS policies.
- Queue management: Network devices like routers and switches maintain multiple queues to handle traffic classes. The QoS determines how packets are placed into and dequeued from these queues, ensuring that high-priority traffic is served first.

To provide high-quality service for users on computer networks like the Internet, in addition to the methods mentioned above, the following issues must be addressed:

The classification and definition of QoS. Defining and classifying QoS is allocating network resources based on different types of QoS. For instance, real-time services may be given greater bandwidth and CPU processing time. The classification and definition of QoS also enables users to specify their QoS requirements for various applications.

Access control and negotiation. That is, according to the use of resources in the network, users can enter the network for multimedia information transmission and negotiate their QoS.

Resource reservation. To provide users with satisfactory QoS, the corresponding resources, such as end systems, routers, and transmission bandwidth, must be reserved to ensure that these resources are not forced to be used by other applications.

Resource scheduling and management. After the reservation of resources, the availability of these resources depends on the corresponding resource scheduling and management system.

The current Internet offers only the best possible transmission services and expedited business transactions. As a result, there is no specific guarantee of timing or reliability. With the rapid development of network multimedia technology, multimedia applications on the Internet are emerging, such as IP telephony, video conferencing, video-on-demand, distance education and other multimedia real-time services, e-commerce transmission on the Internet, etc. The Internet has gradually evolved from a single data transmission network to a comprehensive transmission network for data, voice, images, and other multimedia information. These different applications require different QoS requirements, and QoS is usually measured by bandwidth, delay, delay jitter, and packet loss rate. As various applications demand high-quality services, the importance of QoS continues to grow.

However, existing best-effort delivery services can no longer meet the different requirements of various applications for network transmission quality, and the Internet is needed to provide a variety of quality-of-service types of services. The best-effort service will still be provided to those applications that only need connectivity.

QoS refers to any combination of attributes used to represent the performance of a service. These attributes must be available, manageable, verifiable, billable, consistent, predictable, and sometimes decisive. Different quality service mechanisms are essential to build optimal networks for IP, which can meet the needs of various user applications.

11.5.2 Three important regulatory principles

The three regulatory principles are often associated with regulating network traffic and are critical for managing network data flow. These principles are especially relevant in QoS and traffic-shaping mechanisms.

- **Average rate**

The average rate refers to the average data transmission rate over a specified period [49]. It represents the sustained rate of data transfer that a network or device can handle over time. When regulating network traffic, setting an average rate helps ensure the network operates within its capacity and provides consistent performance. It prevents network congestion by limiting the average data rate allowed for a particular type of traffic.

- **Peak rate**

The peak rate is the highest data transmission rate a network or device can support for a brief period, often called a burst [50]. While the average rate represents sustained traffic, the peak rate accounts for short data bursts that can temporarily exceed the average rate. Networks and devices should be able to handle such peaks without dropping packets or degrading service quality. Limiting the peak rate helps effectively manage short-term traffic spikes, preventing a decline in service quality.

- **Burst length**

The Burst Length measures the duration a traffic flow can exceed the specified rate (average or peak) [51]. It indicates how long a data burst can last before it should be limited or smoothed out to comply with the rate limits. Burst lengths are essential for shaping traffic and ensuring bursts do not overwhelm the network or disrupt other traffic flows.

The leaky bucket mechanism is an abstraction that can be used to characterize these regulatory restrictions [52]. First, a leaky bucket is one capable of holding b tokens. Tokens are generated at a steady rate of r tokens per second. When a new token is generated, if the bucket is not already full with b tokens, the new one is added. Otherwise, it is ignored, and the bucket stays full.

Second, before sending a packet stream to the network, a token must be taken from the bucket. If the bucket is empty, the packet has to wait for a new token. The maximum number of tokens the bucket can hold is b, so the longest burst of packets a flow can send is b packets.

Finally, the token generation rate r is used to limit the average rate at which packets can enter the network over a longer period. In any time interval of length t, the maximum number of packets that can enter the network is determined by $rt + b$.

Thus, the token generation rate is used to limit the long-term average rate at which packets can enter the network.

In order to ensure effective and controlled data transmission in networks, especially when different types of traffic compete for limited resources, it is essential to define and control various network parameters, such as average rates, peak rates, and burst lengths. Network administrators and QoS mechanisms can prioritize and shape traffic based on specific requirements, thereby ensuring optimized performance and resource utilization.

11.5.3 Edge computing and multimedia networks

The combination of edge computing and multimedia networks has become crucial in the digital age, especially as demands for data transmission and real-time processing continue to rise. By processing data at the edge of the network, edge computing significantly reduces latency and enhances the efficiency of multimedia content transmission. Below, we explore several specific application scenarios and the technologies involved.

- **Real-time video surveillance**

Real-time video surveillance is a key application in smart cities and security systems. Traditional video monitoring requires uploading data to the cloud, leading to high bandwidth consumption and potential delays [53]. Edge computing allows for preliminary video analysis, such as facial recognition and behavior detection, at devices near the cameras. By sending only essential data (like facial features and alerts) to central servers, bandwidth requirements are greatly reduced, and response times are improved. Technologically, the H.265 video encoding standard is beneficial, as it offers efficient compression that enables high-quality video transmission in low-bandwidth environments [54]. Additionally, using streaming protocols like RTSP allows for low-latency video processing, ensuring the effectiveness and timeliness of surveillance systems.

- **Augmented Reality (AR) and Virtual Reality (VR)**

AR and VR technologies demand high levels of real-time data processing. Edge computing enables data handling near user devices, significantly lowering latency and enhancing user experience [55]. In AR games, real-time environmental recognition and content rendering are critical. Users' devices can utilize edge nodes to perform deep learning analyses of their surroundings, quickly identifying scenes and rendering corresponding virtual objects with the help of algorithms like convolutional neural networks. In this context, the WebRTC protocol is widely used for real-time media transmission due to its ability to minimize latency associated with traditional TCP protocols. WebRTC leverages UDP for data transfer, making it suitable for low-latency applications and allowing AR/VR experiences to be smooth and responsive.

- **Content delivery networks**

CDN plays a significant role in accelerating multimedia content distribution by storing content at edge nodes close to users. The integration of edge computing enhances

CDN's capability for real-time data analysis and user behavior predictions. Machine learning algorithms can be used to analyze viewing habits, enabling edge computing to automatically cache potentially popular content at edge nodes for rapid access when requested. Technically, various algorithms, such as collaborative filtering and association rule mining, improve content recommendation accuracy and enhance user personalization. Moreover, dynamic bandwidth control techniques allow CDNs to adaptively allocate bandwidth, addressing challenges during peak traffic periods.

In summary, the combination of edge computing and multimedia networks offers efficient solutions for diverse application scenarios. By reducing latency, improving bandwidth utilization, and enabling intelligent processing, these technologies significantly enhance user experiences and drive digital transformation across industries. They not only improve real-time capabilities but also establish a solid foundation for future multimedia applications.

11.5.4 Multi-cloud networking services and Web 3.0

As digital transformation accelerates, Multi-Cloud Networking Services (MCNS) and Web 3.0 are becoming pivotal in modern network architectures, especially in the context of multimedia applications [56]. These technologies not only enhance system reliability and flexibility but also facilitate the development of decentralized multimedia applications that prioritize user engagement and data sovereignty.

MCNS enhances multimedia networking by leveraging multiple Cloud Service Providers (CSPs) to create a highly redundant and flexible cloud environment. By distributing workloads such as video streaming and content delivery across various CSPs, MCNS ensures high availability and disaster recovery. This is particularly beneficial for multimedia networks that require low latency and high bandwidth for seamless experiences.

SDN is critical for optimizing multimedia traffic within MCNS. By decoupling network control from forwarding functions, SDN enables dynamic management of multimedia data streams, improving overall performance. Tools like OpenFlow can be used to prioritize traffic for applications like video conferencing and live streaming, ensuring minimal buffering and latency. In the realm of Web 3.0, decentralized multimedia applications take advantage of blockchain to provide secure content distribution and ownership [57]. Technologies such as InterPlanetary File System (IPFS) allow for decentralized storage of multimedia files, reducing reliance on centralized servers and enhancing accessibility. Smart contracts can automate licensing and payment processes for digital content, ensuring fair compensation for creators.

Moreover, the integration of Decentralized Identity (DID) systems allows users to have full control over their multimedia assets, enhancing privacy and eliminating the need for centralized platforms [58]. Users can share and control access to their content in a secure manner, promoting trust and transparency in multimedia interactions. High bandwidth and low latency remain essential for delivering rich multimedia experiences. Edge computing complements these technologies by processing data close to users, thereby reducing latency for real-time applications like live streaming and interactive gaming. Solutions such as AWS Greengrass and Azure IoT Edge can facilitate local processing of multimedia streams, improving responsiveness.

Finally, interoperability between multiple decentralized multimedia networks is crucial. Cross-chain solutions like Polkadot and Cosmos ensure that various multimedia applications can interact seamlessly, enabling a richer, more interconnected user experience. In summary, the convergence of MCNS and Web 3.0 with multimedia networks not only enhances the reliability and flexibility of current multimedia services but also sets the stage for innovative, decentralized applications that prioritize user ownership and engagement.

11.6 Conclusion

This chapter explores the core applications, principles, and challenges of multimedia networking technologies. Multimedia networks, which require high bandwidth and low latency, are widely applied in video conferencing, voice communication, and real-time streaming. The chapter details audio and video processing techniques, stored video streaming technologies, the evolution of VoIP, and multimedia-supporting protocols.

Advancements in network and compression technologies have greatly improved multimedia transmission efficiency. Encoding standards such as H.265/HEVC and AV1 enable seamless streaming of HD and 4K video even under bandwidth constraints. Adaptive streaming protocols such as DASH optimize user experience in variable network conditions through flexible bit rate adjustment. The key protocols discussed include RTP, SIP, and HTTP-based streaming, each addressing challenges such as real-time communication, session management, and secure data transmission. Optimization strategies, including edge computing, CDNs, and traffic control mechanisms such as QoS and Diffserv, further improve network efficiency and stability. However, challenges persist, including bandwidth constraints, latency, jitter control, and maintaining stable transmission in dynamic environments. The chapter outlines solutions such as improved buffering, advanced protocols, and distributed architectures, providing information for future multimedia networking development.

In summary, multimedia networking technologies are rapidly advancing, integrating innovative protocols and encoding standards to overcome technical limitations. These innovations support the widespread adoption of multimedia applications and provide essential foundations for fields such as intelligent transportation and telemedicine. As demand grows, the solutions and insights in this chapter will shape the future of multimedia networking.

References

[1] Stallings W. High-Speed Networking: A Systematic Approach to High-Performance Networking. 2nd ed. Prentice Hall; 2019.
[2] Kurose JF and Ross KW. Computer Networking: A Top-Down Approach. 8th ed. Pearson; 2018.
[3] Smith J. Digital Audio: Principles and Applications. Springer; 2021.
[4] Brown D. Understanding Bit Rates in Digital Audio. IEEE Transactions on Audio, Speech, and Language Processing. 2021;29:150–158.

[5] Williams S. Challenges in Analog to Digital Signal Conversion. International Journal of Digital Technology. 2019;15(2):90–98.

[6] Taylor M. Sampling Rate and Its Effect on Audio Fidelity. Audio Research Journal. 2022;45(1):45–52.

[7] Kumari A, Abhinav, and Jayaprakash B. An Overview of Applications of Data Compression & Source Coding in Wireless Networks. In: 2024 15th International Conference on Computing Communication and Networking Technologies (ICCCNT). IEEE; 2024. p. 1–6.

[8] Davis E and Brown L. Speech Codec Technologies: Efficiency and Quality. IEEE Transactions on Audio, Speech, and Language Processing. 2022;30(4):726–734.

[9] Li J and Wang T. Analyzing Bitrate Efficiency in Video Streaming. International Journal of Multimedia Tools and Applications. 2022;81(4):4763–4780.

[10] Patel A and Kumar R. Video Compression Techniques and Applications. IEEE Transactions on Circuits and Systems for Video Technology. 2021;31(12):4567–4581.

[11] Zhang Y and Li M. Throughput and Performance Measurement Techniques for Video Streaming. IEEE Transactions on Multimedia. 2021;23(4):789–802.

[12] Mondal A, Trestian I, Qin Z, *et al.* P2P as a CDN: A New Service Model for File Sharing. Computer Networks. 2012;56(14):3233–3246.

[13] Jones B and White H. VoIP Technologies: An Overview of Challenges and Solutions. International Journal of Communication Systems. 2022;35(2):e4871.

[14] Silvestre-Blanes J, Almeida L, Marau R, *et al.* Online QoS Management for Multimedia Real-Time Transmission in Industrial Networks. IEEE Transactions on Industrial Electronics. 2010;58(3):1061–1071.

[15] Patel S and Kumar J. Exploring Live Audio and Video Streaming Over the Internet: Technologies and Applications. Journal of Digital Media. 2022;15(1):67–80.

[16] Lee S and Kim J. Streaming Video Applications: Services and Challenges. International Journal of Multimedia Systems. 2022;19(1):45–58.

[17] Davis E and Brown T. Adaptive HTTP Streaming: Techniques and Implementation. IEEE Transactions on Multimedia. 2020;23:987–998.

[18] Kumar R and Sharma P. Content Delivery Networks: Architecture and Applications. Journal of Network and Computer Applications. 2023;210:103421.

[19] Thompson A and Clark T. Characteristics of UDP Streaming in Multimedia Applications. International Journal of Digital Multimedia. 2021;18(2):56–74.

[20] Nguyen T and Lee J. Passing Video through Firewalls: HTTP Streaming Protocols. Computer Networks. 2022;205:107516.

[21] Patel M and Gupta L. Efficient Video Coding Standards: H.265 and AV1. Journal of Visual Communication and Image Representation. 2023;90:102102.

[22] Zhang X and White H. Improving Video Streaming with HTTP/2 and QUIC. IEEE Access. 2022;10:30000–30012.

[23] Miller R and Brooks A. Mobile Streaming: Transformations and Trends. Journal of Mobile Multimedia. 2022;18(1):1–15.

[24] Garcia F and Hernandez N. The Impact of Cloud Storage and CDNs in Video Streaming. Global Journal of Computer Science and Technology. 2021;21(3):48–59.
[25] García F and López MJ. Understanding VoIP: Concepts and Challenges. International Journal of Communication Systems. 2018;31(4):e3594.
[26] Wang X and Zhang L. Analyzing VoIP Quality over Best-Effort Networks. IEEE Access. 2021;9:123456–123466.
[27] Kumar R and Rai A. VoIP Performance Enhancement Techniques. Journal of Network and Computer Applications. 2022;210:103391.
[28] Singh A and Agarwal P. Voice Coding Standards and Their Importance in VoIP. International Journal of Electronics and Communication. 2019;100: 56–62.
[29] Hussain A and Mahmood T. VoIP Architecture: An Overview. Journal of Computer Networks. 2020;176:107234.
[30] Li J and Xu K. Latency Jitter in VoIP Communications: An Analysis. IEEE Transactions on Wireless Communications. 2021;20(5):3456–3466.
[31] Nguyen T and Pham DN. Analyzing VoIP Call Quality Factors: A Comprehensive Review. Computers & Electrical Engineering. 2020;87:106708.
[32] Alaka A and Anton M. WebRTC and its Impact on VoIP: Current Trends and Future Directions. Journal of Internet Technology. 2022;23(1):35–45.
[33] Zhao Y and Chen F. The Impact of 5G Networks on VoIP Quality. International Journal of Mobile Communications. 2021;19(2):123–135.
[34] Chen R and Kumar S. The Role of AI in Enhancing VoIP Services. Artificial Intelligence Review. 2022;55:128–145.
[35] Schmidt T and Wu R. Real-Time Protocols for Multimedia Communication: An Overview. Journal of Communications and Networks. 2020;22(3): 203–215.
[36] Rizk H and Kim JM. RTP Profiles and Payload Types: An Analysis. IEEE Transactions on Multimedia. 2021;23:1300–1310.
[37] Zhou Y and Zhang L. SRTP: Secure Real-time Transport Protocol for RTP Streams. Computer Networks. 2022;192:108135.
[38] Khan S and Kumar A. Session Initiation Protocol: A Detailed Perspective. International Journal of Network Management. 2021;31(1):e2219.
[39] Patel N and Bhargava RB. SIP Protocols: Features and Transport Mechanisms. Journal of Internet Technology. 2019;20(2):291–304.
[40] Chen X and Wang A. MP3 Encoding: Technical Insights and Applications. International Journal of Multimedia Information Retrieval. 2020;9(3): 215–227.
[41] Oda H and Yamamoto Y. Understanding MPD in DASH: Media Presentation Description. IEEE Communications Surveys & Tutorials. 2021;23(1): 331–350.
[42] Morales E and Sanchez T. Adapting Media Presentations in Dynamic Adaptive Streaming: A Survey. Journal of Multimedia and Broadcasting Engineering. 2019;6(3):22–35.

[43] Yadav R and Singh S. Segmenting and Delivering Adaptive Media in DASH. Journal of Digital Media Technology. 2022;18(4):251–265.

[44] Orozco D and Smith J. Network Layer Support for Multimedia Applications. International Journal of Network Management. 2019;29(5):e2148.

[45] Clark C and Zhou LH. Differentiated Services: Enabling Quality of Service in IP Networks. IEEE Communications Magazine. 2018;56(12):74–80.

[46] Kumar R and Sharma P. End-to-End Quality of Service Guarantees in Multimedia Applications. Journal of Network and Computer Applications. 2019;126:135–144.

[47] Chung H and Lee S. Resource Reservation in Multimedia Systems. ACM Transactions on Multimedia Computing, Communications, and Applications. 2020;16(3):52–67.

[48] Choudhury S and Gupta A. Congestion Management Strategies in IP Networks. ACM Computing Surveys. 2019;51(7):131–145.

[49] Sharma N and Gupta A. Understanding Network Traffic and Average Rate Management. Journal of Internet Technology. 2020;21(2):251–259.

[50] Zhang Y and Liu B. Managing Peak Data Transmission Rates in Network Applications. International Journal of High Performance Computing Applications. 2019;33(4):747–758.

[51] Li S and Chen W. Burst Length Management in Network Traffic Flow. IEEE Transactions on Networking. 2018;26(7):1245–1257.

[52] Wang T and Yang M. Leaky Bucket Mechanism for Traffic Regulation. Journal of Computer Networks. 2020;178:107178.

[53] Alsayfi MS, Dahab MY, Eassa FE, Salama R, Haridi S, and Al-Ghamdi AS. Securing Real-Time Video Surveillance Data in Vehicular Cloud Computing: A Survey. IEEE Access. 2022;10:51525–51547.

[54] Bai Y, Chen H, and Xu C. Efficient Video Compression and Streaming with H.265. IEEE Transactions on Circuits and Systems for Video Technology. 2020;30(4):1184–1196.

[55] Kim S, Lee D, and Park J. Real-Time Data Processing for AR/VR in Edge Computing Environments. ACM Transactions on Multimedia Computing, Communications, and Applications. 2021;17(2):1–20.

[56] Zhao Y and Lin H. Web 3.0: The Future of the Internet. Journal of Internet Technology. 2020;21(1):5–11.

[57] Buterin V. Smart Contracts: The Future of Digital Transactions. International Journal of Blockchain and Cryptocurrency. 2018;2(1):15–21.

[58] Nakamoto S. Cross-Chain Interoperability Solutions in Blockchain Networks. Journal of Distributed Ledger Technologies. 2019;5:12–25.

Chapter 12

Open questions and future directions

Yue Cao[1], Hai Lin[1], Bo Zhao[1] and Yuan Zhuang[2]

Chapter 2 provides an overview of the technologies, including their architecture, advantages, applications, challenges, and future research directions. It highlights unresolved issues in Software-Defined Networking (SDN), Network Function Virtualization (NFV), Software-Defined Wide Area Network (SD-WAN), and Intent-Based Network (IBN). For SDN, key challenges include addressing security issues such as protecting controllers, securing OpenFlow protocols, and improving controller reliability through enhanced redundancy design, distributed architectures, and fault recovery capabilities. NFV faces challenges in ensuring the security of virtualized network functions and addressing compatibility issues between solutions from different vendors, which could be resolved by establishing standardized protocols. In SD-WAN, optimizing technology for dynamic networks and ensuring service stability and performance remain priorities. Strengthening encryption and authentication mechanisms is also critical to mitigate risks of data eavesdropping and tampering in WAN environments. IBN requires further efforts to define "intent" more clearly, improve intent translation accuracy, address dependencies and conflicts, and enhance training datasets for network assurance. Additionally, improving IBN's dynamic adaptability is crucial to handling unexpected events and traffic fluctuations, ensuring efficient intent execution in large-scale networks. Future research directions for SDN, NFV, SD-WAN, and IBN technologies are distinct. For SDN and NFV, research primarily targets enhanced security, including the design and development of more secure controllers and network operating systems, enabling cross-domain cooperative secure communication between controllers, establishing standardized security protocols for northbound interfaces, and developing advanced DoS/DDoS attack detection or prevention technologies. In the context of SD-WAN, future studies aim to improve adaptability and performance across diverse network environments, optimize traffic management, and achieve greater cost efficiency through the integration of advanced machine-learning techniques. For IBN, future research focus on advancing network automation and flexibility, enhancing network robustness via closed-loop and continuous learning, or addressing key challenges (such as improving the accuracy of intent translation, mitigating the impact of intent dependence on performance, and overcoming dataset limitations).

[1]School of Cyber Science and Engineering, Wuhan University, China
[2]The State Key Laboratory of Surveying, Mapping and Remote Sensing, Wuhan University, China

Chapter 3 introduces the protocol from perspectives of its origins, segment structure, functionalities, evolutions, security issues, and defense mechanisms. The chapter emphasizes the importance of Transmission Control Protocol (TCP) in reliable and orderly end-to-end communication. Although TCP has advanced significantly, several challenges still remain. In 5G networks, TCP congestion control faces difficulties due to blockages and handovers. The performance of TCP is degraded by high path losses in millimeter-wave (mmWave) frequencies and the need for beamforming further in high-mobility scenarios. Moreover, although there exists cross-layer design aiming to optimize performance by exploiting interdependencies between protocol layers, yet integrating this design into existing protocols proves complex in practice. Furthermore, optimizing TCP performance in data centers is also crucial. Data centers require efficient handling of high traffic volumes, low latency, and high throughput. Nevertheless, existing TCP algorithms are not fully suitable for the high-speed and low-latency environment of data centers. Consequently, there is a pressing need to develop TCP algorithms capable of adapting to rapidly changing network conditions, mitigating security threats, achieving cross-layer optimization, and supporting the performance requirements of data centers. The future of TCP, particularly in the realm of 5G networks and data centers, holds great promise and diversity in research directions. Key areas include leveraging machine learning for congestion control in 5G/6G Internet of Things (IoT) networks to predict and optimize network conditions, developing adaptive algorithms that switch between mechanisms based on real-time network status for more precise control, exploring TCP variants tailored for 5G networks to address specific challenges. Other focus areas involve further refining cross-layer designs to enhance performance while preserving layered architecture integrity and innovating TCP in data centers to tackle issues like distorted congestion signals and suboptimal buffer management.

Chapter 4 explores dynamic routing algorithms and examines Internet protocols like Routing Information Protocol (RIP), Open Shortest Path First (OSPF), and Border Gateway Protocol (BGP). It also explores Mobile Ad hoc Network (MANET) routing algorithms [geographic, Artificial Intelligence (AI)-based, secure-aware, Blockchain-based, etc.] and provides an overview of Access Control List (ACLs), including their principles and applications. While significant progress has been made in routing algorithms and access control techniques, several open questions remain. The trade-off between routing security, performance, and complexity remains a key challenge, as battery-powered devices have limited computational resources. MANETs vulnerability to security threats, as they consist of self-organizing mobile nodes without centralized administration or infrastructure, and most routing protocols assume the absence of malicious nodes. Ensuring the effectiveness of ACLs in highly dynamic environments, such as IoT and edge computing, is also a challenge, as adaptive, real-time access control must be achieved without compromising network performance. The future research in dynamic routing and ACLs will likely focus on the convergence of intelligent algorithms and emerging technologies. AI-driven routing protocols are expected to play a central role, leveraging predictive analytics and reinforcement learning to achieve optimal performance in dynamic, large-scale networks. Blockchain technology will continue to enhance security, particularly in decentralized and ad hoc environments. Additionally, research will explore energy-efficient routing algorithms for battery-constrained devices in IoT networks and hybrid approaches that combine proactive, reactive, and geographic routing. For ACLs, future developments will involve dynamic and context-aware policies that adapt to changing network conditions, ensuring secure and efficient access control in modern networking paradigms, including edge and cloud-based systems.

Chapter 5 introduces deterministic networks and their applications in automotive, IoT, and industrial systems. It covers key components such as time synchronization hardware, real-time systems, flow management strategies, and machine learning-based data control. Additionally, it highlights advancements in switch technology and explores future frontiers in deterministic networking. Despite significant advancements, several questions remain in deterministic networking. Improving time synchronization to maintain nanosecond-level accuracy across large-scale, heterogeneous networks is a critical area of focus. Developing new flow scheduling algorithms that can adapt in real time to dynamic traffic patterns while minimizing computational overhead is another pressing need. Optimizing machine learning models for packet filtering and classification in real-time environments must address issues of energy efficiency and data privacy. Additionally, innovative approaches are required to ensure scalability and interoperability across both legacy and emerging systems. Finally, effectively integrating deterministic networks with emerging paradigms like quantum communication and 6G networks remains a key research direction. The future of deterministic networking spans advancements across Industrial Automation and Control Systems (IACS), the automotive industry, smart grids, and IoT/IIoT applications. In IACS, research should focus on ultra-reliable, low-latency communication to support real-time decision-making in complex industrial processes. For the automotive industry, deterministic networks are key to enabling autonomous driving and vehicle-to-everything communications, requiring further innovations in time-sensitive networking and safety-critical protocols. Smart grid systems demand resilient and scalable deterministic networks for real-time monitoring, control, and optimization of energy distribution. In IoT and IIoT, integrating deterministic principles can enhance the reliability and efficiency of connected devices in dynamic and resource-constrained environments. Future research should also address challenges in interoperability, security, and energy efficiency while exploring synergies with emerging technologies like 6G, edge computing, and AI-driven automation.

Chapter 6 introduces several aspects of Delay-Tolerant Network (DTN), including background, representative characteristics, architecture, advantages and disadvantages, technologies, security, and applications. Specifically, several traditional problems (e.g., energy constraint, limited bandwidth, and insufficient buffer) in DTN are addressed by optimizing the energy consumption of on-board units, improving data transmission rate with the constraint of low bandwidth, organizing the data and storage buffers, and designing dynamic routings. With advancements in communication, optimization, and security technologies, DTN has emerged as a supplemental framework to the core Internet, serving numerous innovative applications like disaster rescue, ad-hoc networking, and in-vehicle entertainment. However, although previous efforts have been made to enhance the reliability of DTN (e.g., data transmission, routing, and resource management), DTN fails to establish a trust system for improving the security of data services. Several new challenges arise, e.g., unclear DTN boundaries, untrusted network entities, and cross-domain untrustworthiness. Specifically, several open questions of the above challenges are shed light on, such as the ambiguity of system boundary, the robustness of trust system, the data privacy protection during data sharing, and the effective trust management in dynamic environments. Based on the above consideration, several research directions can be deeply explored, including security routing, cross-domain trust management, and dynamic networking.

Chapter 7 describes the evolution of mobile networks from 1G to 6G, emphasizing the central role of wireless communication technologies in shaping modern society. Despite significant advancements, several unresolved issues persist in the domain of mobile and wireless networks. First, at the physical layer, frequency planning and interference mitigation strategies need to be developed for base stations and access points in order to satisfy user demand while improving spectrum utilization. Second, at the data link layer, it is necessary to consider cellular network channel management schemes for different traffic categories, so that low call blocking and switching failure probabilities can be achieved. Finally, at the network layer, integrated and intelligent routing protocols need to be designed, so as to support all communication options in heterogeneous environments. Here, adaptive machine learning techniques, such as federated learning and distributed learning, offer promising solutions to meet the dynamic demands of 6G wireless network applications. Future research could explore methods for efficiently training models to adapt to rapidly evolving demands. Second, an important research direction is the design of zero-energy communication systems powered by renewable energy sources, such as radio frequency energy harvesting, to tackle the energy challenges of mobile networks. Finally, terahertz and millimeter wave communication models can be designed. Optimization frameworks adapted to mobile nodes need to be developed in the future in order to meet high throughput and low latency requirements.

Chapter 8 introduces the existing edge computing development and architecture in detail. Then, a brief overview of the existing optimization problems, optimization goals, and corresponding solutions for edge computing scenarios is given. In addition, various application scenarios of edge computing in reality are analyzed. Finally, the technical challenges that edge computing may face are analyzed and studied. Although edge computing has been well studied, there are still some problems that need to be solved. First, how to protect the data privacy and security of edge nodes is one of the problems that need to be solved. In addition, in the process of computing offloading, the data transmission rate is a key issue that needs to be solved in communication resource scheduling. Finally, mobility is an important challenging feature of edge computing. Therefore, in order to enable participants to access edge servers uninterruptedly, designing a mobility management strategy to improve service stability is also a problem that needs to be solved. It can be seen that various technologies have shown the potential to be combined with edge computing to solve current problems. With the development of emerging technologies such as Metaverse and generative AI, more possibilities have been brought to the development of edge computing. First, edge computing provides lower latency and more efficient reasoning capabilities for generative AI. This makes it possible to deploy generative AI applications on edge nodes such as mobile devices and smart cameras. In addition, by combining Metaverse with edge computing, edge devices can perceive, understand, and respond to the virtual world more intelligently. Second, security can be improved by designing an authentication mechanism for users covered by a specific edge node. Here, edge data centers can also improve the credibility of edge servers by adding privacy modules. Finally, in order to improve data transmission rates, it is necessary to explore more flexible computing models and design more targeted communication models based on real-life scenarios. In order to address the impact of mobility, trajectory prediction can be performed and targeted deployment decisions can be made in advance to improve its service quality.

Chapter 9 introduces the basic architecture of the IoT, analyzes common security issues in each layer, points out solutions, and finally introduces some application cases of IoT. There are still many remaining open questions unresolved, posing challenges to the widespread application and security of the IoT. The IoT encompasses a wide variety of devices that are distributed extensively. However, the lack of unified management mechanisms often makes it difficult to implement effective security management. Due to incomplete legal regulations regarding IoT management, the responsibility allocation among manufacturers, service providers, and users regarding the security of IoT devices is not entirely clear. In the event of a cyberattack, the delineation of responsibility and accountability may lead to conflicts. The future perspectives and research directions for IoT primarily focus on several key areas. First, the widespread deployment of 5G networks will provide IoT with unprecedented high-speed, low-latency communication capabilities, significantly enhancing data transmission efficiency and system response speed. Furthermore, in response to the challenges posed by global climate change, green IoT has become an important aspect of IoT's future development. It focuses on energy management, environmental monitoring, and other fields. Finally, integrating digital twins with IoT devices enables real-time monitoring and tracking of physical entities, improving the accuracy of their digital representations.

Chapter 10 introduces the development of Intelligent Transportation System (ITS), presentative characteristics, architecture, advantages and disadvantages, technologies, security, and applications. Specifically, untimely data sharing, non-uniform industry standards, inadequate infrastructures, poor data quality, privacy leakage risk, and cross-domain cooperation are shed light on in ITS. To address the above problems, the status data of dynamic environments is reconstructed by perceiving, collecting, processing, and aggregating data. Then, communication, networking, and decision-making technologies underpin the development of ITS. With the continuous development of communication, networking, optimization, and security technologies, the evolution of ITS faces various challenges, including the integration and compatibility of technologies, data privacy protection in dynamic environments, traffic behavior modeling, as well as sustainable development and environmental adaptability. First, the integration and compatibility of technologies are focused on underpinning the holistic system of ITS for self-organization, cross-layer data sharing, and cross-domain cooperation. For example, numerous heterogeneous devices are established with each other in different physical and network domains. Second, how to strike a balance between data sharing and privacy in dynamic environments has become a significant topic for improving the security of ITS. Third, to satisfy the requirements of dynamic network management (e.g., adaptive network topology), the accurate trusted modeling of traffic behaviors is considered based on real-time traffic data and network entity behaviors. Fourth, due to the limited physical and network resources (e.g., frequency spectrum and energy), balancing energy consumption and environmental synergy becomes an interesting topic for green ITS. Considering the aforementioned factors, several research directions can be deeply explored, including sensor-computer-integrated vehicle-circuit coordination, cross-domain network organization and reconfiguration, and dynamic environmental adaptive trust management.

Chapter 11 explores various aspects of multimedia networking technologies, including edge computing, Quality of Service mechanisms, and the integration of Web 3.0 for decentralized applications. It also raises several open questions. One key issue is how to ensure interoperability between decentralized multimedia networks, especially as technologies like Web 3.0 and blockchain evolve. Another question is how to effectively balance bandwidth allocation and network resources in dynamic multimedia environments with varying traffic loads. Additionally, the long-term impact of edge computing on multimedia data privacy and security remains uncertain. Lastly, there is ongoing research into how to handle the increased complexity and scalability demands of next-generation multimedia applications. Future research will focus on optimizing multimedia transmission in Multi-Cloud Networking Services. Specifically, the research direction will explore dynamic bandwidth allocation based on network slicing to optimize traffic priority scheduling. Quantum computing can potentially play a significant role in accelerating data processing and encryption algorithms. Additionally, further exploration is needed on the collaboration between low-power networks and edge computing devices to improve the responsiveness of real-time multimedia services. Moreover, the integration of cross-chain technology and decentralized storage is expected to enhance the interoperability of multimedia applications and promote broader digital asset management and sharing.

Index

access control 22, 129–30, 245, 259, 265
access control lists (ACLs) 12, 101, 130, 338
  applications 104
  operating principle 103
  overview 101–2
  usage 102–3
access/devices layer 189
ACK (ACKnowledgment) bit 56
  flood attack defense 67–9
  flood attack methods 67
acknowledgement number mechanism 59
action field 25
adaptive algorithms 76
additive increase/multiplicative decrease (AIMD) 61
ad hoc network 88
  Artificial Intelligence (AI)-based routing protocols 94–6
  blockchain-based routing protocols 100–1
  geographic routing 92–4
  hybrid routing 91–2
  proactive routing 89–90
  reactive routing 90–1
  secured ad hoc routing protocols 96–100
Ad hoc On-demand Distance Vector (ADOV) 90–1, 145
  blockchain-based authentication for 101
Ad hoc On-demand Distance Vector and Cuckoo Search (AODVCS) 95
advanced encryption standard (AES) 319
Advanced Message Queuing Protocol (AMQP) 252
Advanced Mobile Phone System (AMPS) 179
Advanced Research Projects Agency Network (ARPANET) 17–18
Advanced Video Coding (AVC) 324
Agent Discovery 198
agriculture 193
AIoT 257–8
Ant Colony Optimization (ACO) 94
application layer 20, 52–3, 61, 67, 155, 190, 261
Application Programming Interface (API) 22
Application-Specific Integrated Circuit (ASIC) chips 116
approximation algorithms 225–6
Artificial Intelligence (AI) 10, 40, 226, 258, 275, 316–17
  based routing protocols 94
    biologically inspired algorithms 94–5
    Machine Learning (ML) algorithms 95–6
asynchronous message 25
auction theory 228–9
Augmented Reality (AR) 209, 330–31
Authenticated Routing for Ad hoc Networks (ARAN) 98
authentication 153, 170
  handover authentication 204
  mutual authentication 204
  three-factor authentication 204
Automatic Repeatre-Quest (ARQ) 154
Autonomous Systems (ASes) 81
autonomous vehicles 192–3

autonomy 156
availability 178–9, 203
availability time 325

Backlog parameter 65
bandwidth 77
bandwidth management 327
Base Station (BS) 181–2
Base Station Controller (BSC) 186
Bellman–Ford algorithm 80, 89
Berkeley Software Distribution (BSD) 83
big data 20
binary offloading 218–19
Binary Spray and Wait (BSaW) 157
black hole attack 97
Blockchain AODV Routing Protocol (BAODV) 101
blockchain-based routing protocols 100–1
Blockchain Radio Access Network (B-RAN) 100
blockchain technology 338
Bluetooth 244
Border Gateway Protocol (BGP) 86, 338
  path vector routing 88
border router 81
boundary functions 327
buffer management 157–8
Building Baseband Unit (BBU) 31
bundle layer 153–4
bundle layer security 170
burst 329
bus topology 111

Call Session Control Function (CSCF) 189
CDMA2000 188
cell sites 185
cellular base station virtualization 31
Cellular Networks (CN) 145, 181, 249–51
  analog-to-digital communications 187–8
  components of 185
  evolution and architectural mastery 190–1
  first-generation mobile networks (IG) 186–7
  fundamentals of 181–2
  handover processes in 184–5
  industrial revolution with high-speed connectivity 191–3
  infrastructure components 185–6
  limitation of 199–200
  Mobile IP and mobility in 196–9
  mobility in 199
  next frontier of connectivity 193–5
  security defense in 202
    authentication 204
    availability 203
    confidentiality 202–3
    integrity 203
  spectrum management methodologies 182–4
  voice-centric to data-centric services 188–90
Central Processing Unit (CPU) 30, 75
Certificate Authority (CA) 98
chaotic time series 69–70
checksum field 56
Circuit-Switched (CS) voice network 190
Cisco Kinetic 230
Class-Based Weighted Fair Queuing (CBWFQ) 122–3
clock synchronization management 126
clock synchronization mechanism 118
clock synchronization technology 133–4
cloud computing (CC) 18–20, 27, 39, 40, 256
cloud data center network function virtualization 31
cloud layer 212–13

Cloudlet computing 211
Cloud Operating System (Cloud OS) 27
cloud RAN 31
cloud security 294
Cloud Service Providers (CSPs) 331
Code Division Multiple Access (CDMA) 249
coding-based routing protocols 163–4
Common Application Service Element (CASE) 155
communication security 293–4
communication void problem 93
Community-Partition Aware replica Allocation method (ComPAS) 164
computation offloading 216
computing and communication model 235
computing paradigm 211
  Cloudlet computing 211
  fog computing 211
  MEC 211–12
confidentiality 170, 202–3
congestion control 61, 151, 327
  additive increase/multiplicative decrease 61
  TCP NewReno 62–3
  TCP Reno 62–4
  TCP Tahoe 61–2
  TCP Vegas 63–4
  TCP with SACK 63
congestion management 135
  Explicit Congestion Notification 136–7
  flow control 137
  load balancing 137
  priority-based queuing 135–6
  QoS 136
  traffic policing and shaping 136
Connected Domaining Set (CDS) 163
connection management 58–9
connectivity for everything 194
Constrained Application Protocol (CoAP) 252–4
content delivery networks (CDN) 32, 312, 330–1
Contention-based Geographic Routing (CGR) 92–4
control layer 189–90
convex optimization method 224–5
Convolutional Neural Networks (CNNs) 258
cookie 66, 71
copy-based routing protocols 159–61
core function 327
counter field 25
Credit-Based Shaper (CBS) 126
cross-domain technology 286–7
cryptography 39–40
Cuckoo Search Algorithm (CSA) 95
Cumulative Coded ACKnowledgment (CCACK) routing protocol 163
Customer Premises Equipment (CPE) 32, 41
Customer Relationship Management (CRM) 246
Cyber-Physical Systems (CPS) 15, 261
  use cases of 261
    intelligent manufacturing 266–7
    smart agriculture 262–3
    smart city 263–5
    smart grid 267–9
    smart home 265–6
CYCLADES networks 51

data checksum 59
Data Distribution Service (DDS) 252
data encryption 203, 245
Datagram Transport Layer Security for SRTP (DTLS-SRTP) 319
data link layer 149–50
data link layer security 168
  link collision risk 168
  non-fair competition risk 168
  resource depletion risk 168
data offset 55

data organization 158
data privacy 232–3
data processing 258, 288
  data cleaning 288–9
  identification and extraction 288
  reconstruction and integration 289–91
data security 232–3
data services 188
Dedicated Road Infrastructure for Vehicle Safety in Europe (DRIVE) 276
Dedicated Short Range Communication (DSRC) 277
deep learning 226
Deep Packet Inspection (DPI) 128
deep reinforcement learning 227
Deficit Round Robin (DRR) 123–4
delay-tolerant network (DTN) 13, 145, 339
  advantages 155–6
  applications in 171
  architecture of 148
    overall architecture 148
    protocol stack 148–55
  challenges 157–8
  disadvantages 156–7
  presentative characteristics of 146
    connectivities 147
    networks 147–8
    nodes 146–7
  security 166
    bundle layer security 170
    data link layer security 168
    network layer security 168–9
    physical layer security 166–8
    security requirements 170
    transport layer security 169
  technologies in 158
    routing category 158–66
    store-carry-forward mechanism 158
Denial of Service (DoS) attacks 97, 129, 234, 259
Destination Sequenced Distance Vector (DSDV) 89
deterministic communication protocols 118
deterministic networks
  bandwidth allocation and flow control method 125
    Credit-Based Shaper 126
    Frame Preemption 126
    QoS classes 126
    Time-Division Multiple Access 125
    token bucket 125–6
  basic concept of 109
  classification of flow scheduling algorithms 120
    Class-Based Weighted Fair Queuing 122–3
    Deficit Round Robin 123–4
    First Come, First Served 121
    Round Robin 121
    Shortest Remaining Processing Time 124
    token bucket algorithm 124
    Weighted Fair Queuing 122
    Weighted Round Robin 121–2
  classification of network topology 110
    bus topology 111
    ring topology 110–11
    star topology 110
  common network protocols and communication modes 111–12
  data and control 126
    clock synchronization management 126–7
    packet filtering and classification 127–9
  equipment of 115
    design of hard real-time system 116–20
    time synchronization hardware 115–16
  evolution and applications of 112

aerospace and defense 115
automotive industry 114
healthcare 115
industrial automation and control systems 113–14
IoT and Industrial IoT 115
smart grids and energy systems 114
telecommunications 114
related standards of 139
IEC 61508 and ISO 26262 139
IEEE 802.1 standards series 139
IEEE 802.3 standards series 139
security measures 129, 260
access control 129–30
encryption 130
firewalls 130
Intrusion Detection and Prevention Systems 130–1
network segmentation 131
patch management 132
physical security 132
security policies and compliance 131–2
technology of switch 132
clock synchronization technology 133–4
congestion management 135–7
switch equipment 132–3
time-sensitive scheduling 134–5
DetNet 112–3
device interoperability 245–6
digital signatures 203
digital twins (DT) 232–3
Dijkstra algorithm 78–9, 84
Direct Memory Access (DMA) 119
direct transmission model 289
distance vector routing algorithm 79–80
distributed Bellman–Ford routing algorithm 80
distributed cloud computing 257
Distributed-Denial-of-Service (DDoS) attacks 64, 168
Domain Name System (DNS) 155
double intelligence 277
Dynamic Adaptive Streaming over HTTP (DASH) 323–5
dynamical routing 158
Dynamic Host Configuration Protocol (DHCP) 32
dynamic routing 12, 75–6
data transmission by 76
dynamic source routing (DSR) 91

earth gate station 252
East-West API 41–2
eavesdropping attack 97
ECE bit 55
edge caching 220–2
edge computing 14, 209, 257, 330–1, 342
application of 229
digital twins 232–3
healthcare 230–1
intelligent transportation 231, 263
retail industry 231–2
smart city 230, 263
smart IoT 230
smart manufacturing 232
basic model overview 215
computing paradigm 211
Cloudlet computing 211
fog computing 211
MEC 211–12
multi-cloud networking 214
optimization methods in 224
incentive mechanism methods 228–9
machine learning methods 226–8
mathematical optimization methods 224–6
optimization objectives in 222
cost 223
energy consumption 223
latency 222–3
multi-objective trade-off 224
profits 223–4
resource utilization 224
utility 223

optimization problems in 215
computation offloading 216–19
edge caching 220–2
resource allocation 219–20
origin of 209–10
overview of 210
technology challenges of 233
development opportunity 236–7
dynamic 236
model and architecture 235–6
security and privacy 233–5
three-tier network architecture 212–14
edge layer 212
Edge Servers (ES) 210
Electronic Toll Collection (ETC) 276
emergency wireless communication 171
encryption protocols 70
encryption techniques 10, 130, 260
end layer 212
End-to-End communication 51–2
End-to-End (E2E) latency 146
energy constraints 157
energy consumption 223
Energy Efficient Greedy Forwarding (EEGF) routing protocol 162
energy management 268
Enterprise Resource Planning (ERP) 246
error detection and correction 151
error handling mechanisms 120
European Telecommunications Standards Institute (ESTI) 26
Evolved Packet Core (EPC) 186
Explicit Congestion Notification (ECN) 136–7
Extensible Messaging and Presence Protocol (XMPP) 252
External Gateway Protocol (EGP) 81

fault-tolerance technology 10, 120
federated learning 227–8
Field-Programmable Gate Array (FPGA) 116
5G networks 191–3, 265, 316–17
drivers 202
new trust models 202
radio network security 202
security for new service delivery models 202
user identity and confidentiality 202
5G NGC 292–3
File Transfer Protocol (FTP) 155
FIN (FINish) bit 56
firewall filtering 68
firewalls 66–7, 130
First Come, First Served (FCFS) 121
First-In-First-Out (FIFO) 158
flag field 55–6
flooding 89
Flooding attack 97, 169
flow control mechanism 60, 137
Floyd-Warshall algorithm 101
fog computing 211
Foreign Agent (FA) 196
forwarding-based routing protocols 161–2
forwarding layer 20
4G networks 190–1
physical layer issues 201
Wi-Fi security issues 202
WiMAX MAC layer issues 201
Frame Preemption (FP) 126
Frequency Division Multiple Access (FDMA) 186, 249
frequent transmission interruption 147
Fungi algorithms 95

game theory 228
Gate Keeper or Call Server 313
Gaussian similarity function 164
generative AI 237
Generic Routing Encapsulation (GRE) 198
geographic-based routing protocols 165–6
Geographic-based Spray-and-Relay (GSaR) routing protocol 166

Geographic Information System (GIS) 263
geographic routing 92
  Contention-based Geographic Routing 92–4
  Greedy Perimeter Stateless Routing 92–3
Geostationary Earth Orbit (GEO) 251
Global Navigation Satellite System (GNSS) 246–7, 249
Global Positioning System (GPS) receivers 115–16, 127
Global System for Mobile Communications(GSM) 250
Greedy Perimeter Stateless Routing (GPSR) 92–3
green energy 235

handoff 184
Hardware Abstraction Layer (HAL) 119
healthcare 193, 230–1
heterogeneity 260
heterogeneous architecture 235
heuristic algorithm 226
hierarchical routing 81–2
high queuing latency 147
holographic communications 194
home network 197
Home Subscriber Server (HSS) 189
hybrid routing 91
  Zone-Based Hierarchical Link State 91–2
  Zone Routing Protocol 91–2
Hyper Text Transfer Protocol (HTTP) 155, 254–5
HyphaNet algorithm 95

IEC 61508 and ISO 26262 139
IEEE 802.1AS Precision Time Protocol (PTP) 127
IEEE 802.1 standards series 139
IEEE 802.3 standards series 139
IEEE 1588 Precision Time Protocol (PTP) 116, 127
IEEE 1588 PTP network switches 116
implicit “deny any” statement 103
incentive mechanism methods 228–9
  auction theory 228–9
  game theory 228
indirect delivery 75
Industrial Automation and Control Systems (IACS) 339
Industrial Internet of Things (IIoT) 234
Information Technology (IT) 27
infrastructure layer 20, 36–8
Initial Sequence Number (ISN) 66
  prediction attack defense 70
  prediction attack process 69
  prediction methods 69–70
integrity 170, 203
intelligent manufacturing 266
  production process control 266–7
  quality control 267
  supply chain optimization 267
intelligent transportation system (ITS) 15–16, 231, 234, 275, 341
  advantages 283
    easy management 284
    high efficiency 284
    high security 284
    low cost 284
    precise visibility 283–4
  application in 295
    road digital perceiving 295
    road smart maintenance 295
    smart bus 295
    smart hub 295
    smart parking 295
    vehicle supervision 295
  architecture of 282
    command center 283
    comprehensive strategy 283
    networking and communication 283
    operation center 283
    overall architecture 282
    perceiving system 282

autonomous transportation 278
challenges 285
cross-domain technology 286–7
inadequate financial 286
inadequate infrastructures 286
non-uniform industry standards 285–6
poor data quality 286
privacy leakage risk 286
untimely data sharing 285
digital transportation 278
disadvantages 284
deployment and replenishment of sensors 284–5
user privacy and security 285
green transportation 278
holographic transportation 278
information security in 293
cloud security 294
communication security 293–4
terminal security 294
presentative characteristics of ITS development stages 278
digital intelligence and automation 280–2
electronation and informatization 279
networking and cooperation 279–80
robustness transportation 278
technologies in 287
data processing 288–91
networking and communication 283, 291–3
operation and management 293
perceiving with sensors 287–8
intent-based networking (IBN) 11, 337
architecture of 43
challenges of 44–5
introduction of 42–4
intents 43–5
interfaces 75
Interior Gateway Protocol (IGP) 81
Intermodal Surface Transportation Efficiency Act (ISTEA) 275
International Organization for Standardization (ISO) 17
Internet Engineering Task Force (IETF) 44
Internet of Things (IoTs) 13, 18, 152, 177, 209, 277
architecture of 244–6
basic concept of 243–4
enabling technologies of 246
data processing and intelligent analysis 256–8
IoT protocols 252–5
network communication technology 249–52
perception layer technology 246–9
security issues and defense 258–61
use cases of 261–9
Internet Protocol (IP) 17, 189
Internet Protocol Television (IPTV) 32
Internet Service Providers (ISPs) 81
InterPlanetary File System (IPFS) 331
Interplanetary Networks (IPNs) 145
interrupt handling mechanism 117–18
interstellar network communication 171
intra-domain routing protocol 81
Intrusion Detection and Prevention Systems (IDPS) 130–1
Intrusion Detection System (IDS) 259
Intrusion Prevention Systems (IPS) 64
in-vehicle security 294
IPv6 over Low-Power Wireless Personal Area Networks (6LoWPAN) 260
ITS-1.0 279
ITS-2.0 279

John Deere's precision agriculture solutions 230

Kalman filter mechanism 289
KEEPALIVE packet 88
K-Nearest Neighbor (KNN) algorithm 259

Large Deviations Theory (LDT) 162
latency 178, 222
Layered Network Model 17
Layer Two Tunneling Protocol (L2TP) 198
Learning Automata (LA) 96
Learning Automata-based Fault-Tolerant Routing Algorithm (LAFTRA) 96
least-cost path algorithm 78
Licklider Transmission Protocol (LTP) 154
Lightweight Machine-to-Machine (LwM2M) 252
limited bandwidth 157
linear analysis 69
linear regression 69–70
link layer 52
Link State Database (LSDB) 84
link state routing algorithm 78–9
load balancing 137
Local Area Network (LAN) 168
Long Range Wide Area Network (LoRa/LoRaWAN) 252
Long-Term Evolution (LTE) technology 250
lose-step attacks 169
Low Earth Orbit (LEO), 251
low transmission speed and high latency 147

Machine Learning (ML) algorithms 45, 95, 226, 259
  deep learning 226
  deep reinforcement learning 227
  federated learning 227–8
  Learning Automata (LA) 96
  Q-learning 96
  reinforcement learning 95–6, 226–7
Man-in-the-Middle (MITM) attacks 259
manipulation attack 97
match field 25
mathematical optimization methods 224–6
  approximation algorithms 225–6
  convex optimization method 224–5
  heuristic algorithm 226
maximum segment size (MSS) 57
Maximum Transmission Unit (MTU) 57
Media Access Control (MAC) 24
Media Resource Function (MRF) 190
Medium Access Control (MAC) 164
Medium Earth Orbit (MEO) 251
Memory Management Unit (MMU) 119
Message Authentication Codes (MACs) 203
Message Queuing Telemetry Transport (MQTT) 252–4
Metropolitan Area Network (MAN) 168
Military Network (MILNET) 18
Mobile Ad hoc Network (MANET) 89, 338
  blockchain based multi-hop routing protocol for non-cooperative 100–1
Mobile Ad-hoc Networks (MANETs) 145
Mobile Edge Computing (MEC) 210–12, 291
Mobile IP 196
  Agent Discovery 198
  concept 196–7
  example 196
  indirect routing 197–8
mobile networks 177
  future security trends in 204
  key performance indicators 178–9

overview of mobile network generations 178–181
security in 199–204
Mobile Switching Center (MSC) 186
mobile vehicle communication 171
mobility 179
Mobility Management Entity (MME) 199
Moore's law 19
MP3 encoders 302
multicast OSPF (MOSPF) 84
Multi-Cloud Networking Services (MCNS) 214, 331
multi-hop transmission model 289–91
Multilevel-scenario-oriented Greedy Opportunity Routing protocol (M-GOR) 166
Multimedia Internet KEYing (MIKEY) 319
Multimedia Message Service (MMS) 250
multimedia networks 301
audio and video nature 301–3
multimedia networking applications 301
multimedia networking application types 303–5
network support for multimedia 325
edge computing and 330–2
multi-cloud networking services and Web 3.0 331–2
three important regulatory principles 329–30
three network layer approaches 325–9
problems faced in application development 305
protocols for real-time conversational applications 317
Dynamic Adaptive Streaming over HTTP 323–5
RTP 317–20
Session Initiation Protocol 320–3
streaming stored video 306
emerging trends in 311–12
HTTP 309–11
need for streaming storage video 307–8
overview 306
UDP 308–9
voice-over-IP 312
Artificial Intelligence (AI) 316–17
basic concept 312
5G 316–17
fixed playback delay 313–16
principles and architecture 313
WebRTC 316–17
multi-objective trade-off 224
Multi-Protocol Label Switching (MPLS) 24, 198

Nash Equilibrium (NE) 228
National Science Foundation Network (NSFNET) 18
Neighbor Information Query (NIQ) packet 93–4
Network Address Translation (NAT) routers 23
network communication technology 249
cellular network 249–51
satellite network 251–2
Network Control Protocol (NCP) 17
Network Domain Security (NDS) 201
Network Function Virtualization (NFV) 11, 27, 31, 292, 337
advantage of 28–9
application of 30
cellular base station virtualization 31
cloud data center network function virtualization 31
home network virtualization 32
mobile core network virtualization 31–2

virtualization of content delivery network 32–3
architecture of 29
concept of 27–8
framework 29–30
security issues 38
in NFV outsourcing scenario 39–40
in traditional NFV architecture 39
Network Function Virtualization Infrastructure (NFVI) 29
Network Function Virtualization Management and Orchestration (NFV M&O) 29
Network Function Virtualization Orchestrator (NFVO) 30
network interconnection 151
network layer 52, 150–1, 244, 260
network link multiplexing 151
network management 151
network mode 291–2
networks
interoperability 147–8
security 148
network segmentation 131
network slicing 293
Network Time Protocol (NTP) 118, 127
network traffic analysis 67–8
NewReno algorithm 62–3
nodes 146
limited lifespan 146
limited resource 146
low occupancy ratio 147
non-adaptive algorithms 76
NO-Operation (NOP) 57
Nordic Mobile Telephone (NMT) 186
Northbound API 41–2
northbound interface 20, 38
NOTIFICATION packet 88
offloading
cloud-to-edge 218
device-to-device 218
device-to-edge 217
edge-to-cloud 218
edge-to-edge 218
offload ratio 219
Open Daylight 23
OpenFlow 20, 331
network architecture of 24
protocols 337
security issues of 35
table diagram 24
Open Networking Foundation (ONF) 20
Open Network Operating System (ONOS) 23
OPEN packet 88
Open Shortest Path First (OSPF) 82, 84, 145, 338
hierarchical OSPF networks 86–7
packet format 87
working process of 85
Open System Interconnection (OSI) model 17, 75
open wireless access medium 199
operating principle 103
opportunities and challenges 10–16
Optimized Link State Routing (OLSR) 89–90
options field 56–7
Orthogonal Frequency Division Multiple Access (OFDMA) 190, 288
Orthogonal Frequency-Division Multiplexing (OFDM) 191, 249
overlay 40–1

packet classification 328
Packet Data Serving Node (PDSN) 188
packet filtering and classification 127
application layer proxies and gateways 129

- Deep Packet Inspection 128
- load balancing and traffic scheduling 128
- machine learning-based packet filtering and classification 128
- port and protocol-based classification 128–9
- rule-based packet filtering 128
- traffic marking and tag-based classification 128

packet switching 150
partial acknowledgement 63
partial offloading 219
Particle Swarm Optimization (PSO) 94–5
patch management 132
pathfinder 75
path vector routing 88
pattern recognition 258
perception layer technology 246
- GNSS 249
- RFID 248
- WSNs 247

per-connection QoS guarantees 327–8
Philips Emergency Intensive Care Unit program 231
physical layer 149
physical layer security 166
- message stealing and tampering 167–8
- node capture and simulation 167
- physical damage 167
- signal interference 167

physical security 132
PLS 203
Positive Orthogonal Coding (POC) method 164
prediction and decision-making 258
priority-based queuing 135–6
privacy protection technology 203
proactive routing 89
Probability Routing Protocol using History of Encounters and Transitivity (PROPHET) 161
Protection Against Wrapped Sequence (PAWS) numbers 57
protocol stack 148
- application layer 155
- bundle layer 153–4
- data link layer 149–50
- network layer 150–1
- physical layer 149
- transport layer 151–3

Pseudo Random Number Generator (PRNG) 69–70
PSH (PuSH) bit 56
PSO-based Bandwidth and Link Availability Prediction algorithm (PSOBLAP) 95
PTP Grandmaster Clocks 116
Public Switched Telephone Network (PSTN) 186

Q-learning 96, 165, 227
quality control 267
Quality of Experience (QoE) 212, 277
Quality of Service (QoS) 126, 136, 146, 210
quantization 302
quantum computing 342
quantum edge computing 236
queue-based time scheduling 135
queue management 328
Q-value 227

Radar 288
Radio Access Network (RAN) 31, 186
Radio-Frequency Identification (RFID) 248
Random Access Memory (RAM) 75
Random and Encounter Time (RET) 161
Rate Monotonic Scheduling (RMS) 117
reactive routing 90
- Ad Hoc On-Demand Distance Vector 90–1

dynamic source routing 91
real-time data acquisition 232
Real-time Differential GPS (RTDGPS) techniques 249
Real-Time Kinematic (RTK) measurement 249
real-time monitoring 268
real-time task scheduler (RTOS) 116–17
real-time video surveillance 330
Receive WiNDow (RWND) 60
recovery acknowledgement 63
Recurrent Neural Networks (RNNs) 258
reinforcement learning 226–7
Reinforcement Learning Routing Packet Protocol (RLRP) 96
reliability 170, 179
reliable transmission protocol 59–60
remote area communication 171
renewable energy integration 268–9
Reno algorithm 62
replay attack 97, 259–60
replication-based routing protocols 162–3
Representational State Transfer Application Programming Interface (RestAPI) 41
reserved field 55
Residential Gateways (RGs) 32
resource allocation 219–20
resource management 260
resource utilization 224
retail industry 231–2
retransmission mechanism 59
Retransmission Time Out (RTO) 60
ring topology 110–11
Roadside Units (RSUs) 148
Road Weight Evaluation (RWE) routing protocol 166
robustness 156
Round Robin (RR) 121
Round Trip Time (RTT) 69
Round Trip Time VARiation (RTTVAR) 60
routers 21–3, 75
routing 75, 150–1
  based on cryptography 97
    asymmetric cryptography solutions 98
    symmetric cryptography solutions 97–8
  based on one-way hash chain 98–9
  hybrid solutions 99–100
routing algorithm 76–7
  in ad hoc network 88
    Artificial Intelligence (AI)-based routing protocols 94–6
    blockchain-based routing protocols 100–1
    geographic routing 92–4
    hybrid routing 91–2
    proactive routing 89–90
    reactive routing 90–1
    secured ad hoc routing protocols 96–100
  distance vector routing algorithm 79–81
  hierarchical routing 81–2
  in the Internet 82
    BGP 87–8
    OSPF 84–7
    Routing Information Protocol 82–3
  link state routing algorithm 78–9
routing category 158
  coding-based routing protocols 163–4
  copy-based routing protocols 159–61
  forwarding-based routing protocols 161–2
  geographic-based routing protocols 165–6
  replication-based routing protocols 162–3
  social-based routing protocols 164–5

Routing Information Protocol (RIP) 82–3, 145, 338
RQ_SEC_GURANTEE 98
RST (ReSeT) bit 56
RSU security 294
RTP 317–20
rushing attack 97

Saratoga 154
satellite network 251–2
scalability 12, 15, 245
SDN controller 22–3
SD-WAN 40
 advantage of 42
 architecture of 41
 control plane 41
 data plane 40–1
 orchestration plane 41
2G networks 187–8
Secure Access Service Edge (SASE) 234
Secure Efficient Ad hoc Distance vector (SEAD) 98–9
Secure Real-time Transport Protocol (SRTP) 319
Secure Sockets Layer (SSL) 130
Securing Nodes in Perception Layer (SNPL) scheme 259
Security-aware Ad hoc Routing (SAR) protocol 97
security protection 258
seed 99
Selective ACKnowledgements (SACK) 57, 63
selective forwarding attack 169
sequence number and acknowledgment number fields 55
sequence number mechanism 59
serial number field 318
service selection 151
Session Description Protocol (SDP) 322
session hijacking 169
Session Initiation Protocol (SIP) 320–3
Set-Top-Boxes (STBs) 32
Shannon's theorem 235
Shortest Remaining Processing Time (SRPT) 124
Short Message Service (SMS) 250
Signaling Gateway/Media Gateway Control Function (SGW/MGCF) 190
signature extension 99
Single-Copy Replication (SCR) 159
sink hole attack 169
sixth-generation (6G) networks 177, 193–5
smart agriculture 262
 environmental monitoring 262
 intelligent early warning 263
 remote control 262–3
smart bus 295
smart city 194, 230, 263
 intelligent environmental protection 264
 smart community 264–5
smart grid 267–9
smart home 235, 265
 family member care 266
 home safety and security 265–6
 home service intelligence 265
smart hub 295
smart IoT 230
smart manufacturing 192, 232
smart parking 295
Smoothed Round Trip Time (SRTT) 60
social-based routing protocols 164–5
software-defined networking (SDN) 11, 337
 basic concepts and architecture of 20
  centralized network control function 22
  flow-based forwarding 21
  forwarding plane separated from control plane 21
  programmable network 22
 development of network 17
 motivation of 19–20

OpenFlow 23–6
security of 34
comparison of SDN safety models and traditional cyber security models 34–5
security issues of OpenFlow 35
typical security problems in 35–8
structure of 21
software-defined wide area network (SD-WAN) 11, 337
Software Guard eXtension (SGX) technology 40
source port and destination port fields 54
Southbound API 41–2
southbound interface 20–1, 23, 25, 38
Space-Air-Ground Integrated Network (SAGIN) 235
Special Application Service Element (SASE) 155
Spray and Focus (SaF) routing protocol 161
Spray and Wait (SaW) 157
spread spectrum technology 188
Stackelberg equilibrium 228
star topology 110
static routing 76
Store-Carry-Forward (SCF) mechanism 13, 146
Subscriber Identity Module (SIM) 188
Successive Convex Approximation (SCA) method 224
Supervisory Control and Data Acquisition (SCADA) 246
supply chain optimization 267
Sybil attack 97, 169
symmetric message 25
SYN (SYNchronization) bit 56
Synchronization Source Identifier (SSRC) 319
SYN flood attack 64
Backlog parameter 65
defense 65–7
incomplete connection queue 64–5
normal TCP connection establishment 64–6
SYN flood connection 65
SYN queue 64–6

table-driven routing 89
Tahoe algorithm 61–2
congestion avoidance 62–4
fast retransmission 61–2
slow start algorithm 62
terminal security 294
terminologies 1–10
3G networks 188–90
insufficient confidentiality of user identity 200–1
limitations of traditional network security technologies 201
network domain security issues 201
three-tier network architecture 212–14
throughput 178
Time-Aware Scheduler (TAS) 135
time-aware traffic shaping 135
Time Division Multiple Access (TDMA) 118, 125, 249
timestamp field 318–19
timestamps 57
time synchronization modules 116
Time-To-Live (TTL) 154
timing analysis 119–20
token bucket algorithm 124–5
traffic control function 53
traffic policing and shaping 136
transit ASes 81
transmission control protocol (TCP) 11, 17, 51, 255, 338
end-to-end communication 51–2
functionality and implementation principles 57
congestion control 61–4
connection management 58–9
flow control 57, 60–1
reliable transmission 59–60

IP protocol stack 52
paradigm of 152
security problems 64
ACK flood attack 67, 71
ACK flood attack defense 67–8
ISN prediction attack 69–70
ISN prediction attack defense 70
SYN flood attack 64–7
SYN flood attack defense 65
structure of TCP segment 51, 54
checksum field 56
data offset 55
flag field 55–6
options field 56–7
reserved field 55
sequence number and acknowledgment number fields 55
source port and destination port fields 54
urgent pointer field 56
window size field 56
TCP/IP protocol stack 52
three-way handshake 64–5
transport layer 52–4
transport layer 21, 23, 25, 46, 52, 53–4, 151–3, 189
Transport Layer Security (TLS) 26, 42, 130, 169, 323
tunnelling/wormhole attack 97
two-way authentication 261

underlay 40
Uniform Resource Identifier (URI) 254
United States Department of Transportation (USDT) 275–6
Universal Traffic Management System (UTMS) 188, 276
University of California, Los Angeles (UCLA) 17
University of California, Santa Barbara (UCSB) 17
UPDATE packet 88
upward offloading 216
URG (URGent) bit 55
urgent pointer field 55–6
User Datagram Protocol (UDP) 25, 53, 152, 254
user layer 212

Vegas algorithm 61, 63–4
Vehicle Information and Communication System (VICS) 276
vehicle supervision 295
Vehicle-to-Everything (V2X) technologies 204, 278
Vehicle-to-Infrastructure (V2I) communications 277
Vehicle-to-Vehicle (V2V) communications 277
Vehicular Ad-hoc Networks (VANETs) 145, 288
verification tools 119–20
Virtualization Network Function Managers (VNFM) 30
virtualization technology 10, 18
Virtualized Infrastructure Manager(s) (VIM) 30
Virtual Local Area Networks (VLANs) 131
Virtual Machines (VMs) 27
Virtual Private Network Gateway (VPN Gateway) 32
Virtual-range-Forwarding-Based Opportunistic Routing (VFBOR) method 162
Virtual Reality (VR) 209, 330
Visitor Location Register (VLR) 200
Voice over Internet Protocol (VoIP) call 198
Voice over LTE (VoLTE) 190
void node 93

Web 3.0 331
WebRTC 316–17
WebSocket 254–5
Weighted Fair Queuing (WFQ) 122

Weighted Round Robin (WRR) 121–2
White Gaussian Noise (WGN) 201
White Rabbit (WR) 127
Wide Area Network (WAN) 168
Wideband Code Division Multiple Access (W-CDMA) 188
Wi-Fi 244
wildlife tracking 171
WiMAX networks 201
window scaling option 57
window size field 56
wireless communications 10
Wireless Local Area Networks (WLAN) 145, 248
Wireless Mesh Network (WMN) 146
wireless networks 177
Wireless Sensor Networks (WSNs) 246–7
wormhole attack 169
Worst-Case Execution Time analysis 120

Xerox Network System (XNS) architecture 83

0-1 offloading 218
Zero Trust Architecture (ZTA) 130
ZigBee 244
Zone-Based Hierarchical Link State (ZHLS) 91–2
Zone Routing Protocol (ZRP) 91–2

www.ingramcontent.com/pod-product-compliance
Lightning Source LLC
LaVergne TN
LVHW011838200926
848484LV00002B/370